D0998807

High Quality Low Cost Software Inspections

Other books by Ronald A. Radice

Software Engineering: An Industrial Approach
With Richard W. Phillips

ISO 9001: Interpreted for Software Organizations

High Quality Low Cost Software Inspections

By

Ronald A. Radice

Principal Partner
Software Technology Transition

and

Visiting Scientist
Software Engineering Institute
Carnegie Mellon University

Paradoxicon Publishing, PO Box 1095, Andover, MA 01810 USA

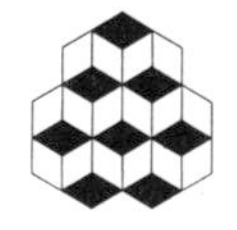

A division of Software Technology Transition
PO Box 1095
60 Elm Street
Andover, MA 01810
USA

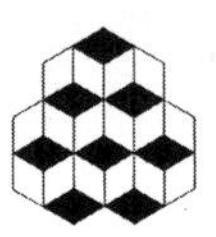

Production supervision: Claire Legrand Radice
Editor: John Abbott
Cover design: Software Art

Library of Congress Cataloging in Publication Data

Radice, Ronald A.
High quality low cost software inspections / by Ronald A. Radice
p. cm.
Includes bibliographical references and index.
ISBN 0-9645913-1-6 (perm. paper)
1. Computer software--Quality control. I. Title.
QA76.76.Q35 R32 2002
005.1'068'5--dc21
2001004926

Printed in the United States
10 9 8 7 6 5 4 3 2 1

DEDICATION

This book is dedicated in the memory of O. Robert (Bob) Kohli.
Without Bob's work the Software Inspection process would not have been a success.
All of us in the software community have benefited from his work and dedication
to the Software Inspection process

FOREWORD

In the 1960's and 1970's Ron Radice and I both worked at IBM, although on different sides of the country. Ron was one of the early pioneers of software inspections, and I worked in Software Quality Assurance at the IBM San Jose Programming Laboratory. As soon as data from inspections became available, I started to follow the work of Ron, Mike Fagan, and other inspection researchers. It is of interest to consider how and why inspections were developed.

During the pioneering era of business computers in the 1950's and early 1960's IBM became the world's largest and most successful computer manufacturer. But computers are driven by software, so without really intending to do so, IBM also became the world's largest software producer.

The software that was built for early IBM computers such as the IBM 650, IBM 1401, IBM 7090, and several others was comparatively small and comparatively simple by today's standards. Not only that, but software was almost a disposable asset since applications only worked on one kind of computer, and when that computer was replaced the software had to be rewritten for the newer model.

When the IBM System/360 was put on the market, software began to grow in both size and importance. The operating system for the IBM 360 computer was OS/360. This operating system changed the economics of computing and made software a product of immense economic importance.

IBM's OS/360 operating system was intended to remain stable from generation to generation. That meant that software developed for OS/360 circa 1968 might have a life expectancy of more than 10 years. Software was no longer a disposable asset, but one that proved to have unexpectedly long life times.

The OS/360 operating system was very large by the standards of the day. Indeed, this was the first piece of software to push beyond 1,000,000 lines of source code. As IBM discovered with some dismay, building large systems is a very hazardous undertaking. The initial development of IBM's OS/360 operating system was discussed in Dr. Fred Brooks' classic book *The Mythical Man-Month*, which remains a popular book after more than 30 years of publication.

Although IBM had long had world-class quality assurance departments for hardware and engineered products, software was a new kind of product. IBM responded by establishing a number of Software Quality Assurance (SQA) departments in all of its major laboratories throughout the world.

These SQA groups were research-oriented, and actively explored ways of improving the quality of large and complex software applications. IBM had discovered through trial and error that testing by itself was not sufficient to guarantee high-quality for large software applications. In fact, most forms of testing only removed about 30% of the software errors, and even a whole series of test stages such as unit test, component test, stress test, regression test, system test, and external Beta test might remove less than 80% of the defects actually present.

Ron Radice, Mike Fagan, and their colleagues began to study the effectiveness of formal inspections using teams of trained personnel who knew what kinds of problems to look for. The results of formal inspections were extremely good. Inspections were more than twice as efficient as most forms of testing and averaged about 65% in defect removal efficiency.

Further, inspections also benefited testing because materials such as specifications that had been inspected could be used to create better test cases than uninspected materials. Also, inspections served as an excellent method of defect prevention, because participants in formal inspections began to make fewer errors in their own work as a result of seeing the kinds of problems that were found in other people's work.

What finally developed within IBM was a very synergistic approach that coupled formal design and code inspections with multiple stages of formal testing. The pre-test inspections could top 85% in defect removal efficiency, and the test stages could also top 80%. The combined results of both inspections and tests could approach 99% in cumulative defect removal efficiency.

Since the U.S. industry average for removing software defects has only been about 85%, projects that approach 99% stand out as having much better user satisfaction and much lower maintenance costs than average projects.

There was one other surprising economic benefit from formal inspections noted in the 1970's. Software projects that used formal inspections had higher productivity rates and shorter development schedules than similar projects that used only testing! The reason for this quickly became known. Although the front-end of the development cycle with inspections was longer than average projects, the testing stages were dramatically reduced. Since testing occupied more than 50% of the time and effort of conventional software projects, the use of formal inspections was proven to benefit every aspect of software development at the same time: costs, schedules, quality, and user satisfaction.

In this book Ron Radice is presenting more than 25 years worth of his observations and data on the use of formal inspections. My own company, Software Productivity Research, Inc., has been collecting similar data on inspections since 1984. Our conclusions are congruent with Ron's. Inspections are among the most effective software technologies yet developed.

Capers Jones, Chief Scientist Emeritus
Software Productivity Research, Inc.
Burlington, Massachusetts
September 2001

ACKNOWLEDGEMENTS

Its reviewers often make a book better. I have been more than fortunate to have reviewers who are well known in the software field on an international level. I give my thanks to each of them for their time and excellent input to me. I list the countries represented when outside the United States.

Reviewers:

John Abbott, Gale Group
Jim Boulton, Thales (UK)
Bill Brykczynski, Software Productivity Consortium
Tom Gilb, independent consultant (Norway)
Jack Harding, Software Technology Transition
Jean-Claude Heliard, Thales (France)
Tony Hutchings, JP Morgan Chase
Seshadri Iyer, MitoKen
Jean-Yves Le Goïc, Bull (France)
Ed Maher, Stratus Technologies
Don O'Neill, independent consultant
Mark Paulk, Software Engineering Institute
Louis Poulin, GRafP Technologies, Inc. (Canada)
Claire Radice, Getronics
Raj Shekar, Mastek (India)
Radhika Sokhi, Tata Consultancy Services (India)
Toru Takeshita, Chubu University (Japan)
Ed Weller, Softwrae Technology Transition
Dave Zubrow, Software Engineering Institute

For my wife Claire for always being there, despite what she calls my moods when I'm writing.

☆

CMM is registered in the U.S. Patent Trademark Office by Carnegie Mellon University and should be suffixed with an ®. CMMI, is serviced marked by Carnegie Mellon University and should be suffixed with ^{SM}. But as I use these acronyms so often I will quote the rights here once rather than befuddle the book for the reader with these registered marks.

TABLE OF CONTENTS

PREFACE

"If you believe you can or if you believe you can't, you will be right."
Henry Ford

INTRODUCTION

I have never found a manager or programmer who purposely wanted to deliver a product late, over cost, or of poor quality. Yet projects continue to ship late, with less function than committed, at higher costs, and with questionable quality. There are a number of factors that lead to these undesirable project results, but a major contributor is the lack of control of defects. Defects are created or injected into work products throughout the project life cycle. This seems to be an unfortunate fact of software development. It can be difficult and expensive to remove the defects in test, and when customers find defects the costs can increase by a factor of 100 or more.

These costs to remove defects are part of the Cost of Quality, or more significantly the lack of quality, and can represent as much as 65% of total project costs. Clearly there is economic opportunity to improve both the quality and consequently the return on investment (ROI) for software projects.

In this book I will address both subjects using two primary processes:

1. Inspections to find defects earlier and at a lower cost
2. Defect Prevention to reduce the volume of defects injected

The software community has used Inspections for almost twenty-eight years. During this timeframe Inspections have consistently added value for many software organizations. Yet for others, Inspections never succeeded as well as expected, primarily because these organizations did not learn how to make Inspection both effective and low cost. We will see that in fact the cost of Inspections is very often paid back with a handsome return during the first project's use.

The original Software Inspection method served the purposes of proving to the software community that there was a better way to achieve quality while delivering products earlier and at a lower cost.

Throughout the book I will always focus first on the effectiveness of Inspections; i.e., how to find the most defects as early as possible at controlled and low cost, since without effective removal of defects the ROI will be less than its potential. Then I will focus on efficiency; i.e., finding the most defects at an increasingly lower cost to further improve the ROI.

So what is an Inspection? The IEEE defines Inspections as "A visual examination of a software product to detect and identify software anomalies, including errors and deviations from standards and specifications. Inspections are peer examinations led by impartial facilitators who are trained in inspection techniques. Determination of remedial or investigative action for an anomaly is a mandatory element of a software inspection, although the solution should not be determined in the inspection meetings." [IEE98]

I will explore, extend, and tailor this definition from a number of perspectives. I will restate what I have learned to be best practices using Inspections, where *best practices* mean those that lead to highly effective removal of defects at efficient costs. We have repeating evidence that as an organization improves its capability with Inspections that it becomes both more effective and more efficient in removing injected defects. I will show how Inspection practice should start from the proven basics and then should purposefully change as the organization's software development capability increases.

As a result, we will learn that there is more than one way to perform effective Inspections.

WHO SHOULD READ THIS BOOK

Writing for one audience would not serve the many needs that exist to understand and practice Inspections. Managers and Project Leads may only want to know the economics of Inspections, programmers may only want to learn the method for effective and efficient use, and Software Engineering Process Group members, Inspection Champions, and teachers/trainers may want it all. This book is written for all these needs.

If you are not yet using Inspections, I hope that this book convinces you that an opportunity awaits you. If you have tried Inspections and abandoned them for whatever reason, I anticipate that you will give them another chance based on what has been learned about successful Inspections and best practices. If you are already using Inspections successfully, this book should serve to reestablish their significance, to give you some new tips for improvement in effectiveness and efficiency, and to extend your thinking about future possibilities with Inspections.

Inspections have been used successfully with all types of software design and coding languages, document types, and development life cycles.

Join me now to see how you can more successfully apply Inspections effectively and efficiently in your organization.

PROGRAMMERS

The people who build the software work products will be actively involved in the Inspection process when their organization makes the decision that Inspections will help to deliver products at a lower cost, in a shorter time, and with higher quality. The decision to use Inspections is a business decision. The successful use of Inspections requires that the programmers be enabled for effective performance and success.

For the programmers I provide the basics of Inspections, including best practices, including insights into tailoring Inspections to focus on further effectiveness and efficiency.

SEPG

The Software Engineering Process Group (SEPG) is usually the group that coordinates process improvement in an organization. Since Inspections are a primary factor affecting improvement, the SEPG will be active in initiating, coordinating, and supporting successful use of Inspections.

The SEPG, as Inspection Coordinator, needs to know the mechanics and purpose of all aspects of Inspections, including the practices, cultural requirements, costs, and economic returns. This book will provide them that knowledge.

INSPECTION CHAMPIONS

History has demonstrated that when organizations starting with Inspections have an Inspections Champion, they make quick strides for success. A champion is someone who understands Inspections and believes with a passion that Inspections can help the organization achieve rapid improvement and reduce the costs to develop software.

This book is for all the Inspection Champions who want to know the history of effective use, present best capability, and future possibilities using Inspections.

PROJECT LEADS AND MANAGERS

This group includes all levels of management from the project lead to the senior management in the organization. While I often will deliberately focus on the Project Lead, since they are the most actively involved of the management for successful adoption of Inspections, this book is for all levels of management.

This book is written with management's very question in mind;
i.e., how much do Inspections pay off?
Additionally management will learn how to get the most value
from Inspections while controlling costs for investment in Inspections.
The answers will astound some managers and confirm for others what
they already know: Inspections pay off big.

The management group are often the most difficult to win over, because they appear to be challenging Inspections when asking questions about return on investment. These are the right questions to ask, the answers need to be given to them, and this book provides those answers. In their asking, however, management often present themselves as anti-Inspections. But I have rarely seen a manager at any level who did not agree to give Inspections a fair try when they see the possibilities for ROI. Once they understand the possibilities and see them in their own projects and organization, they can become the most ardent supporters.

TEACHERS

Anyone who teaches or trains others in Inspections will find that this book serves their purpose with pragmatic examples and anecdotes that help prove the point of Inspections. I taught the first Inspection course in IBM and have since from time to time continued to train, so I know that teachers will sometimes encounter participant resistance to Inspections. I sincerely hope I have made the challenge easier for all Inspection teachers in the future.

THEMES

The following themes will be seen throughout the book:

- How to remove defects effectively
- How to improve efficiencies without reducing effectiveness
- How to prevent defects being injected into work products

WHY THIS BOOK WAS WRITTEN

I have seen Inspections work successfully time and time again to the surprise of some of its staunchest opponents. At the same time I have seen Inspections abused, misused, and aborted for some of the most shortsighted and irrational of reasons.

The lesson to be learned from these experiences is that methods and tools can be misapplied, treated as a failure, and then dismissed as a bad experience by users who were not enabled for success.

As the reader will learn, if they are not already aware, the Inspection method itself is simple and straightforward, but it does require a belief in its capabilities, application of necessary preconditions, and good management support to make it work to a software organization's best advantage. If management does not support the principles of good quality, then overworked programmers and managers will find innumerable excuses to cause Inspections to fail. If the software managers and software engineers in the organization do not believe that the process will work, then there is a good chance that they will fulfill their expectations.

On the other side, given a fair chance, support by management, a commitment of some early time investment in the project, proper training by example, and practice of proven principles, the Inspection process will take root and work effectively and efficiently. When practicing

Inspections one should always work to achieve effectiveness first, then, while maintaining high effectiveness, work to improve the efficiency. Throughout the book we will learn that this is the desired two-step with Inspections: first effectiveness, then efficiency.

Another reason for this book is to celebrate the twenty-eight years of value brought to the software community by Inspections. I started to write this book fifteen years ago, then suspended it, then restarted it, and now I am happy to be completing it. I hope that this book adds some value even to those readers who are well versed in Inspections. And for all readers I wish that Software Inspections would serve you as well as they have served me.

In this book I speak from my experiences in:

- Helping to develop the Inspection method
- Refining the Inspection method with over twenty-eight years in practice worldwide
- Observing its use in numerous projects ranging from small applications to large operating systems
- Staying current with the experiences of countless other believers and practitioners
- Teaching Inspection workshops
- Seeing data that repeatedly demonstrates the value of Inspections across an ever increasing number of companies and organizations

I have been fortunate enough to be on the receiving end of many other people's experiences throughout the global software community. I write this book as my contribution to the software community from what I have learned from others.

I moderated the very first applied Inspection in December 1972 under conditions that should almost have guaranteed its failure. I will discuss more about this first Inspection in Chapter 1. Despite the obstacles, it was a success both in the first instance and as part of the study we were commissioned to perform. The success permitted us to continue with further Inspections and gather sufficient data to prove that Inspections were superior to other approaches for defect removal. Since that time Inspections have consistently proven to be more effective than walkthroughs and other types of less rigorous defect removal reviews.

CHAPTER SYNOPSES

Chapter One introduces the cost of defect removal as seen in test and with users. These costs are compared to data for removal of defects using Inspections. I then briefly discuss the history of Inspections. I provide some previously undocumented experiences from the first study of Inspections in 1972 at IBM. I demonstrate why Inspections are the most essential process improvement action an organization can take. Then when coupled with Defect Prevention I show how Inspections become a strong management tool to reduce cost and shorten schedules while improving quality for users in any software project. I discuss a number of common issues people have expressed regarding Inspections, some of which are valid and some not.

In Chapter Two, a definition of Inspections is given to set a foundation for the rest of the book. Here I take the highest-level view of Inspections from both practical and business perspectives. I discuss the primary as well as the ancillary benefits organizations achieve when using Inspections. The basic model for viewing the Inspection process activities will be introduced. The ETVX structure for this model will be described to serve as a basis for understanding preconditions for establishing a stable and capable Inspection process. Effectiveness and efficiency are defined to ensure common use of terms.

In Chapter Three, I define the Inspection process and related activities in detail. This chapter is expressly written as a set of procedures with the intent to provide sufficient detail for the readers to:

- Implement an Inspection process in their organization
- Assess their presently applied Inspection processes against the evolved model in this book
- Improve their presently practiced Inspections where the evolved model in this book has advantages over their current practice.

In this chapter each activity in the Inspection process is written as a procedure that can be immediately applied as is or tailored, as appropriate. This tailoring, we will see can culminate in Solo:Inspections where only one participant is involved.

In Chapter Four, I define the role of the Moderator. A separate chapter is provided for this role since it is so significant to the successful application of Inspections. 1:1 Inspections, a major improvement step for Inspections without compromising effectiveness, where there are only two participants during an Inspection is discussed.

In Chapter Five, I define and discuss the other roles and related responsibilities of each participant in the Inspection process. I will explore the psychology of Inspections, the types of personalities that might be encountered in Inspections, and possible adverse behaviors some participants might demonstrate. The roles of the Inspection Coordinator and Software Quality Assurance are discussed, as well as that of the Inspection Champion.

In Chapter Six, I explore the use of data, including statistical process control (SPC) with Inspections. While I would have preferred to give more examples and details, this chapter would have become a book by itself. I believe the discussion and examples I provide are enough to enable the reader to use data to achieve improved effectiveness and to consider applying SPC to their Software Inspections.

In Chapter Seven, I discuss Defect Causal Analysis and Defect Prevention as major extensions to the original Inspection method, wherein these activities become important for further reducing the costs of defect removal.

Chapter Eight introduces and defines the criteria for Re-Inspections to achieve higher effectiveness in defect removal when Inspection data signals suggest such possibilities.

Chapter Nine tackles the important issue of the economics of Inspections. There is a cost for Inspections.

More importantly, there is a return on the investment in Inspections and this return is significant.

Human nature seems to resist spending more money up front in a process or project, especially when there is limited experience in previously doing so. Spending money later on a project seems to be more easily accepted than doing it the right way early in the project. Examples are provided demonstrating how the ROI can be calculated.

Chapter Ten builds upon the return on investment from Inspections to explore the necessary role of management in enabling and facilitating successful Inspections.

Chapter Eleven builds from the previous chapters to guide the reader on some practical issues, gives rules of thumb for successful Inspections, and discusses the little things that make an Inspection more effective, efficient, and sometimes fun.

In Chapter Twelve, I discuss other approaches to defect removal that have been practiced. Some of these are close to the Inspection process recommended in this book, while some are similar only in name. The key is not the name applied to the process but the results of the process; i.e., is the process effective in removing injected defects?

Chapter Thirteen explores other areas where Inspections have been and may be applied. This book is written with a focus on inspecting software production work products such as requirements specifications, designs, and code, but the process applies to all types of work products, including those in Systems Engineering. I note key differences to consider when inspecting other work products.

Chapter Fourteen looks toward the future and addresses:

- Work in progress that can change the effectiveness of Inspections
- Work in progress that can change the volume of injected defects through prevention practices
- Practices that improve efficiency to further reduce the costs of Inspections

Lastly, I will explore the possibility of software development without Inspections. The possibilities of achieving 100% effectiveness are discussed. Solo:Inspections, where only one participant is active during the Inspection, are introduced, as a further improvement to efficiency. This chapter concludes with a discussion on aspects of a best practice Inspection process.

A number of appendices are provided to help the readers apply Inspections in their organizations. These include:

- Checklists
- Materials needed for successful Inspections of work products
- Inspection and Data forms

A Bibliography is provided to give the reader other places to look for added information.

BY WAY OF APOLOGY

An author should never intentionally or even by accident slight someone who has contributed to the field. Many people have contributed to making Inspections what today is a far superior process to what existed in 1972. It is my intent to give credit to all those who have defined, redefined, and evolved this very important method that we have in software engineering. Thus I refer to sources that I believe are the first recorded instances of an aspect regarding Inspections, as primary sources. I will also quote individuals who, while not always the primary source, gave a particular noteworthy statement about some aspect of Inspections.

This is not to say others did not have similar thoughts or even experiences. We live at a time where information is transferred so quickly and permuted into new thoughts while still in the process of being transmitted, and this makes giving credit a more difficult task. So if I've missed someone who has contributed, I apologize in advance.

INVITATION TO THE READER

I invite the reader to send comments, ask questions, or simply chat about Inspections past, present and future. Please contact me at rradice@stt.com or via www.stt.com.

Ron Radice
June 2001

CHAPTER 1

INSPECTIONS: BACKGROUND

"Works are always followed by their defects just as the fire is enveloped with smokes."
From the Bhagavad Gita, Ch. XVIII, 48

1.1 Why Inspections?

So what's the problem? Why do we need Inspections? We need Inspections to remove software defects at reduced cost. Inspections enable us to remove defects early in the software life cycle, and it is always cheaper to remove defects earlier than later in the software life cycle. It's important to note that Inspections are a way to remove defects at a lower cost, not a way to prevent defects from occurring.

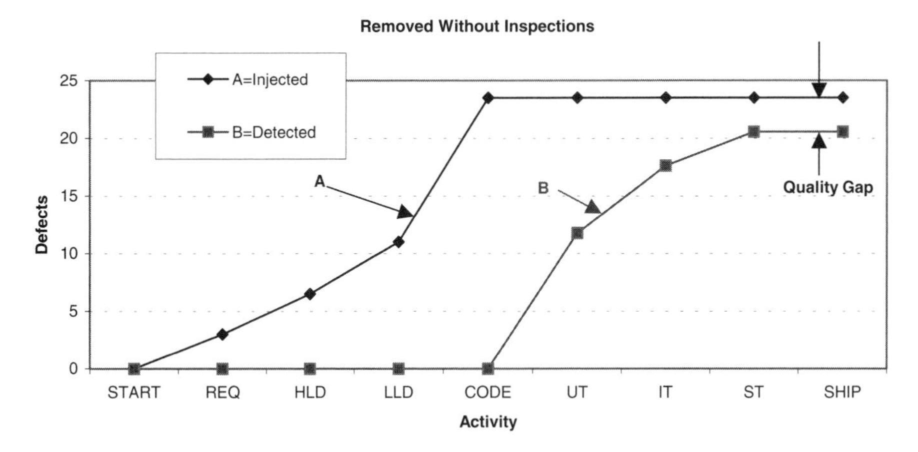

Example of Defect Injection and Defect Removal Curve
Figure 1.1

In Figure 1.1 the curve A from START to CODE represents the numbers of defects that were created or entered into the production processes during requirements analysis (REQ), High-level design (HLD), Low-level design (LLD), and Code in a software project. Curve A shows no pre-test defect removal activities. Consequently each test activity; e.g., (Unit Test (UT), Integration Test (IT), and System Test (ST)), as shown in curve B, finds and removes varying volumes of the generated or injected defects.

In this example let's assume that each test removes 50% of the defects present at entry to the test; e.g., UT, IT, ST. In a well-defined, well-behaved series of tests, we would expect that the number of defects removed would decline in each subsequent test activity. While this is a simplistic view, evidence to the contrary would suggest a quality problem for the product under test. In this example we will make the assumption that the tests are well behaved. The gap that remains at the end of system test (ST) represents latent defects that have the potential to be found by the users. Latent defects are defects remaining in the software product delivered to the customer at SHIP.

So far in this example we can see that:

- Defects are generated in each life cycle production activity
- Injected defects are removed in testing activities after code is completed
- Not all defects are removed at SHIP

Had we tried to deliver the product at the conclusion of coding, we would most probably not have had a working product due to the volume of defects. There is a cost to remove defects found during test, and as we'll soon see, the cost to remove defects during test is always higher than in pre-test. Users of software products all too frequently encounter problems and we can assume that these defects will usually require resolution and repair and therefore these are an added cost to the software project or organization. Both of these costs will vary for a number of reasons, such as the number of defects entering from each production activity, the types and severities of defects, and the quality policy in the organization. The sum of these costs increases the Cost of Quality for the project, where the Cost of Quality is money spent due to poor quality in the product.

Our objective with Inspections is to reduce the Cost of Quality by finding and removing defects earlier and at a lower cost.

While some testing will always be necessary, we can reduce the costs of test by reducing the volume of defects propagated to test. We want to use test to verify and validate functional correctness, not for defect removal and associated rework costs. We want to use test to prove the correctness of the product without the high cost of defect removal normally seen in test. Additionally we want to use test to avoid impacting the users with defective products.

So the problems we must address are:

- Defects are injected when software solutions are produced
- Removal of defects in test is costly
- Users are impacted by too many software defects in delivered products

With Inspections we can manage and reduce the effect of these problems. In Figure 1.2 the same curve (A-Injected) is shown as in Figure 1.1. An additional curve (C-Detected with Inspections) represents defects remaining after removal by Inspections for the volume of defects injected and remaining during each production activity as shown in curve A. In this example the assumption is 50% defect removal effectiveness for each Inspection and test activity. Effectiveness is the percentage of defects removed from the base of all the defects entering the defect removal activity. As is seen in Figure 1.2, the number of latent defects in the final product is reduced with Inspections.

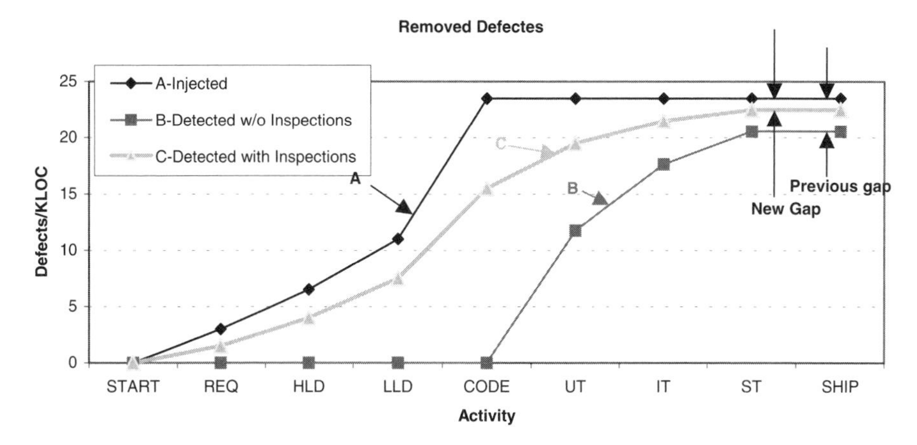

Example of Defect Removal With Inspections
Figure 1.2

After Inspections, residual defects are removed during testing, but typically not all injected defects are removed. There is still a gap of latent defects that the users could potentially find. In the scenario, with Inspections, the gap is smaller, due to the defects removed by Inspections. This reduced gap represents a quality improvement in the product delivered to the users.

Ok, so we have removed defects earlier, but why is it cheaper you may ask. It is cheaper primarily due to the following:

- Defects are not discovered all at once during test or by the users. There are likely to be a number of cycles of finding defects, fixing them, and integrating the fixes into each delivery to test. There is a recurring set of costs for discovery, problem determination, problem solution, re-integration, re-test, re-baselining, etc. Whereas in Inspections all identified defects are noted in the same proximate time period and the recurring costs are consequently reduced. Furthermore, when a defect is found during Inspections, we know where the defect is and often know how to fix it. Inspections find the defect and often the fix is apparent, but in test and with users often only the symptom is found.
- The increased labor hours required for fixing defects after the product is shipped is often due to loss of project team knowledge. Often another team will maintain the product and may need more time to discover what the defect is and what may have caused it before fixing it. Even when it is the same team, time has often reduced their ability to quickly determine the cause of a defect.
- When fewer defects enter test, the productivity of test improves; i.e., the costs of test are lower and the time to complete test is reduced.

Several studies have confirmed the reduction in project costs when defects are removed earlier. The relationship of costs to remove defects in production, test, and post-test was first shown in 1976 in Mike Fagan's article based on the study we performed in IBM during the first release of the telecommunications subsystem VTAM. [FAG76] Subsequent studies have continued to reconfirm these results with the same nominal cost relationship. [BOE81] [KIT86] [ACK89] [REV91] [DOO92] Figure 1.3 shows this relationship as increasing costs over time. Thus, if it costs on average $100 to remove a defect in Inspections, it will cost $1000 in test, and over $10,000 when a user finds a defect.

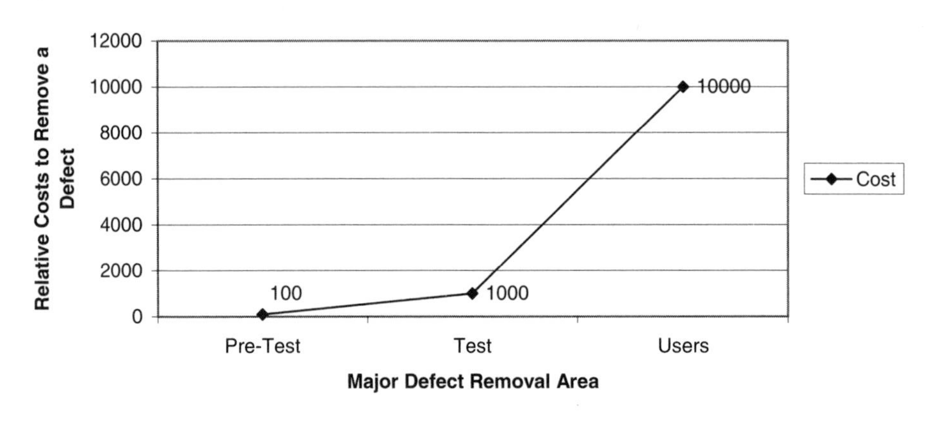

Defect Cost Relationship
Figure 1.3

The relationship is not always so orderly as 1:10:100, but the pattern is reasonably consistent as shown in Figure 1.3. The relationship has remained consistent since the first Inspections were performed.

Besides the costs to the project, we should also note that there is a cost to the customer for downtime, lost opportunity, etc. These costs while often transparent to the project can have a negative effect on future sales or contracts with the customer.

Table 1.1 shows some examples from published sources reflecting the pattern of significantly higher costs for defect removal in test or with customers compared to Inspections. Unfortunately they use different dimensions and units such as $/defect, hours/defect, hours invested, and not all have provided cost factors for all three areas. Nonetheless, the pattern repeats.

There are other aspects that make doing Inspections compelling, but even if it were only for cost reduction, the Inspection process is well worthy of consideration. Ancillary benefits, which are discussed in Chapter 2, include:

- Improvement in productivity
- Education and increased knowledge sharing

- Developing backup/replacement capability
- Process improvement
- Early product quality visibility
- Product re-development
- Building team spirit

COMPANY	COST IN INSPECTIONS	COST IN TEST	COST WITH CUSTOMER DISCOVERY	SOURCE
IBM	$48/defect	$61- $1030/defect	$1770/defect	[NOR78]
AT&T	1 unit	20 units	—	[EIS85]
ICL	1.2-1.6 hours/defect	8.47 hours/defect	—	[KIT86]
AT&T	1.4 hours	8.5 hours	—	[ACK89]
JPL	$105/defect	$1700/defect	—	[BUS90]
IBM	1 unit	9 times more	117 times more	[LIN91]
Shell	1 unit	30 units	—	[DOO92]
Thorn EMI	1 unit	6.8 - 26 units	96	[GIL93]
Applicon, Inc	1 hour	—	30 hours	[SPE94]
Infosys	1 unit	3 - 6 units	—	[JAL00]

Cost Relationship References in Public Documents
Table 1.1

We will return to defect injection and detection curves as shown in Figure 1.2 later in Chapter 9 to discuss:

- The results of increasing effectiveness
- The results of practicing Defect Prevention to reduce the volume of defects entering the work products
- Fixed and variable costs of test
- How the effectiveness of test might be refocused based on knowledge obtained during Inspections

Some projects seem to never come out of final test. Oh, of course they do come out, because test must end sometime. After all there is a delivery requirement, but the test seems to take longer than planned, test costs more than planned, function is deferred, and too often not all the tests planned are completed successfully. Because the time to deliver has arrived and cannot be delayed any longer, a product gets shipped to a customer and no one is pleased. The supplier and the customer make concessions. Programmers feel they could have done a better job, management is glad its done but know they should have controlled the project better. Sounds sad, and it is at least less than professional, but still far too typical in software. Inspections can change this undesirable situation, and has for those who have used Inspections well.

Inspections offer significant return on investment even in their initial use.

O'Neill initiated The National Software Quality Experiment in 1991 to gather and analyze data on defects and Inspection practices across dozens of companies. He found that the companies that used Inspections reaped a return on investment (ROI) ranging from four to eight dollars for every dollar spent. [ONE96] I'd put my money in that bank any day, even if they were only half right.

1.2 Inspection Preconditions

There are some necessary preconditions that repeatedly enable successful Inspections and we should ensure that these preconditions are satisfied when performing Inspections. These preconditions include:

- Clear and visible management support
- Defined policy
- Good training for all
- Effective procedures
- Proper planning
- Adequate resources

When these preconditions are satisfied, it has been repeatedly demonstrated that Inspections have a higher probability of success. There is also a correlation between organizations that know how to satisfy the preconditions and the maturity of the organization using reference models such as the Software Capability Maturity Model (SW-CMM) from the Software Engineering Institute (SEI). [CMM93]

Inspections will drive other process improvements in an organization. For example, if processes are not defined or procedures do not exist or decisions have not been made on how to do design or how to represent the design, these shortcomings will become clear during an Inspection, and process improvements will need to be addressed if Inspections are to become more successful. There is a risk, however, that an organization may fail with Inspections, when it tries Inspections before it is ready, before the culture is enabled, and before management and personnel are ready to improve such processes.

Figure 1.4 shows the SW-CMM from a high-level view. Here we see that there are five levels of capability and maturity that are determined by satisfying criteria defined in each of the related Key Process Areas (KPA) for each level as defined in the model. Each KPA has a dominant area of influence or process category such as management, organizational, or engineering. The reader is referred to the SEI's web page for additional detail about the SW-CMM as noted in the Bibliography.

Inspections in the SW-CMM are addressed in the Peer Reviews KPA. While the SEI defines Inspections at Level 3, there is good evidence that Inspections can be successfully performed in organizations that may not yet have developed a mature software production process. For example, Inspections can and have been successfully applied in Level 1 organizations. In the original IBM study on the VTAM project the organization was not a Level 2. I will discuss this study later in this chapter. In Bull Inspections were started while the organizations were Level 1 as described in Weller. [WEL93]

	PROCESS CATEGORIES		
CMM Levels	**Management**	**Organizational**	**Engineering**
5 Optimizing		▸ Technology Change Management ▸ Process Change Management	▸ Defect Prevention
4 Managed	▸ Quantitative Process Management		▸Software Quality Management
3 Defined	▸ Integrated Software Management ▸ Intergroup Coordination	▸ Organization Process Focus ▸ Organization Process Definition ▸ Training Program	▸ Software Product Engineering ▸ Peer Reviews
2 Repeatable	▸ Requirements Management ▸ Software Project Planning ▸ Software Project Tracking & Oversight ▸ Software Subcontract Management ▸ Software Quality Assurance ▸ Software Configuration Management		

The key Process Areas Assigned to Process categories [CMM93]
Figure 1.4

In ISO 9000, Inspections or *in-process inspections* are defined as one of the 20 elements required to be addressed to achieve certification, and Inspections can and have been used successfully in organizations not certified and perhaps not even certifiable to the standard. One does not need a formal quality system or SW-CMM maturity level to perform successful Inspections.

Inspections have clear value independent of any model or standard for software development.

When I am asked which KPA in the SW-CMM I think gives the most value or which should be the highest priority, I always respond with Inspections (Peer Reviews in the SW-CMM). I believed this to be true in the 1980's and I still believe it today. With an honest effort given to Inspections, we can open the eyes of management for more rapid process improvement. Inspections never fail to deliver as promised, or prove to be too difficult, when the preconditions are satisfied. We know how to make Inspections successful.

1.3 So Why Isn't Everyone Using Inspections?

If Inspections provide significant benefit, why has adoption been so slow? Why is not all of the software community using the method? The publicly published data twenty-four years ago clearly demonstrated their effectiveness, and recent reports continue to demonstrate their effectiveness. Why have Inspections not taken a firmer root and achieved wider use?

The reasons for this vary. I believe this is partially due to views that Inspections can only be done one way. This book will eliminate at least some of this misunderstanding. Another reason for the resistance to Inspections is the view that they are not easy to do well. There are factors, including social and psychological, that we must consider. Management often views Inspections as an added cost, when in fact Inspections will reduce costs during a project. We will see throughout this book how Inspections save both cost and time.

Since the inception of Inspections, with the advent of each new development tool or language, the providers and users seem to believe that Inspections do not add value or are less necessary. This is clearly not true, since programmers still make defects with these tools and languages. However there often is little documentation as to how well Inspections work in these new environments, so a false belief that Inspections do not apply may be propagated by myth. We will see later in the book that Inspections do apply in these development environments also.

Because of these and other factors, shortcuts in the Inspection process have been taken without any proof that the change is an improvement. Some of these homegrown changes cause the Inspection process to be less effective. In turn the value of what was defined as the Inspection process is diminished. Thus failure becomes a self-proving "fact."

Inspections may not be the most enjoyable engineering task compared to designing and coding. Also, programmers are very possessive about artifacts they create. Inspections are labor intensive and low tech, but they do work.

Since 1972 there has been continuing growth in application and success with software Inspections. Wheeler et al. showed an example of increased interest by tracking the number of publications regarding Inspections. [WHE96] See Figure 1.5. While the tracking has not been updated since 1996, many articles continue to appear yearly in various technical and professional journals and at conferences worldwide.

Since they do work, they should be used until the software community has truly evolved to a position where the software process and environment permit fewer defects to be generated when software products are created. Until the day when the economics show that Inspections are no longer the most effective or efficient way to remove defects one should continue to use them. That day has not yet come, and may not be fulfilled for some time, but it may be within reach. I will address the possibilities in Chapter 14: Inspections Future, as the change has already begun.

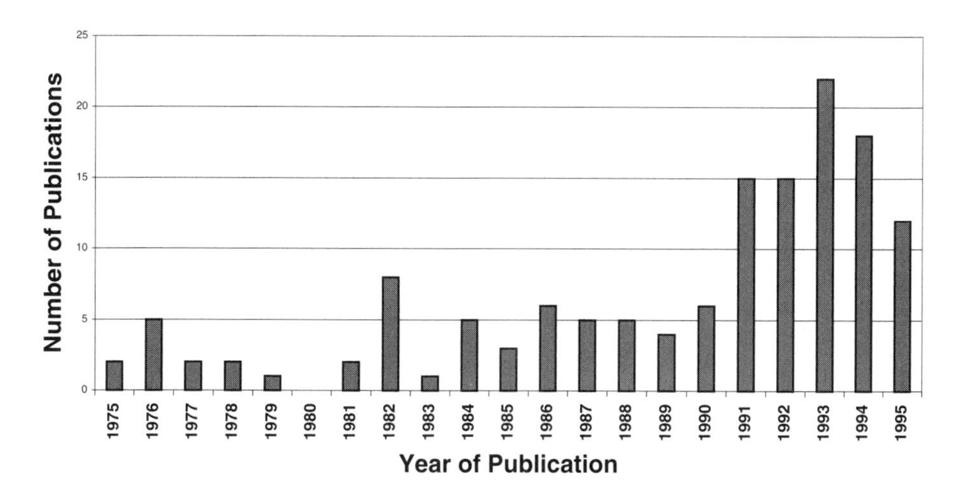

Increasing Published Articles on Inspections [WHE96]
Figure 1.5

One of the reasons I am writing this book is because during the last twenty-eight years various people have evolved the Inspection process from its original definition. Many have done so with little or no data, proof, or evidence that the "evolution" was indeed an improvement and not just a change. Often it seems they just had a "better idea", but it was not always better.

Since we do not always have empirical information to know if a change is a better way than what was defined in the original method, I will first go back to the original method. I will build upon what has worked and evolve the definition based on data and results made available to the software community from changes successfully applied over the years. The end result in this book will be a defined process for Inspections that represents current best practice.

If there is a major element we still lack in the software community today, it is data. I am speaking about process data. We often have access to product data, but almost universally there is still a lack of process data.

This situation is improving since the SW-CMM has been applied, but the number of organizations with substantive process data is still in the minority. Figure 1.6 shows the number of organizations at the different SW-CMM levels at the time of the writing of this book. As may be inferred, the number of software organizations reporting use of the SW-CMM is not large compared to the many who develop or maintain software. Therefore these organizations are a subset of the many more that exist worldwide. The reader is referred to the Software Engineering Institute's web page (www.sei.cmu.edu) to get the latest data on organizations using the SW-CMM. This data is updated twice a year.

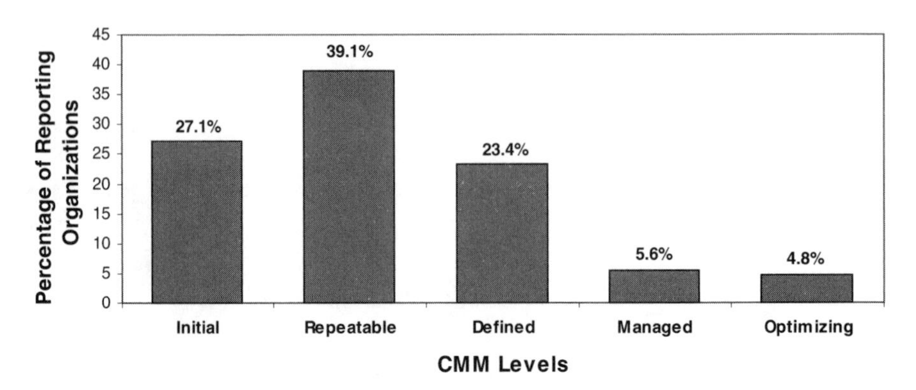

Maturity Profile: Recent assessments, since 1997, of 1018 organizations. [SEI01]
Figure 1.6

Given that only 1018 organizations have reported assessment data to the SEI [SEI01] since 1996 and there are clearly many more software organizations worldwide, we know the software community has a long way to go yet with mature processes such as Inspections. The data from the SEI, while it shows improvement in process maturity over the last ten years, is hardly reflective of worldwide software organization maturity. But we can look at it as a best case and view it for possibilities for improvement, as the pool of SEI assessed organizations is probably skewed toward higher maturities.

1.3 Do Good Programmers Make Defects?

How many times have you been convinced, absolutely convinced, that you had either written a defect-free program or had "tested out" all of the defects only to sadly discover that there was yet another "bug"? One has to wonder how we as programmers have been able to repeatedly survive this cruel onslaught to our egos. I am not talking about the slovenly programmer who in some instances seems to develop as many defects as lines of code (LOC) in a program or paragraphs in a document, or about the programmers who have found themselves in a schedule crunch and don't have enough time to develop their best work. Rather, I am talking about that qualified programmer (you and I are probably good examples; well, at least you), who does have sufficient time to produce a defect-free piece of work. Yet, after the program is delivered to test or to the user, defect fixes have to be applied to the work product. I am not going to try to come to terms here with why this may happen, for there can be many systemic reasons. Let it be known for now that good programmers do indeed make defects, and if this is true for good programmers then it must follow for all others in the population of programmers. All programmers can and do want to learn from their injected defects. We will see later in the book how both Inspections and Defect Prevention are natural combined processes for programmers to use, when they are adapted for effective success.

ANECDOTE

IF ONLY WE COULD SEE

When I joined IBM earlier in my career, we were provided with six months of programming induction training. We received training in a variety of subjects such as IBM programming languages, operating systems, programming practices, etc. We were required to write, as exercises, components of operating sub-systems. I was coding the Dispatcher and encountered a bug during program execution. As hard as I tried, I could not find the bug that was causing the system to fail. We had been asked to not work as teams on this exercise, but as individuals without aid from others in the section. I tried and tried, but for the life of me could not find the bug.

Finally, with my tail between my legs I approached the instructor and explained my situation. He asked to see the code. He looked at it briefly and announced that he could see where the bug was. Wow, I thought, that was fast. Why didn't I see it? He refused to show me the defect and asked that I continue to look for it. Was he a good or masochistic instructor? I eventually did find it, but learned many times in later years, that a defect may not be readily seen even when it is right there in front of us. As it turned out, this particular error was a simple transposition of two similar variable names. It was there all the time; I just couldn't see it, because I was too close to it. I was looking through my biased eyes.

Inspections help bring those other eyes that are not biased to help us see the defect. Unfortunately we did not have the Inspection process while I was in induction training.

Anecdote 1.1

Every organization or company hires the best people. At least that is what we hear. One has to wonder where the worst people go. Some of them exist in every organization. Most cultures will not easily accept the reality of a natural distribution of capability and talent. It seems to be almost a taboo subject. Nonetheless it exists in every organization. What we should want to do, and what the SW-CMM enables, is to achieve a higher maturity and improved capability in software processes for all people in an organization.

People and processes become more capable as an organization moves up the SW-CMM levels. An example is shown in Figure 1.7 for the Inspection process from organizations I have come across over the past twenty-eight years. This figure represents by example that as an organization moves up the SW-CMM ladder, the effectiveness; i.e., the percentage of defects removed with Inspections increases with each level attained. Improved effectiveness should also be seen in other processes as an organization's maturity grows, but for Inspections it is easier and faster to see.

SW-CMM LEVEL	EFFECTIVENESS
1	<50%
2	50-65%
3	65-75%
4	75-90%
5	90-100%

Inspection Effectiveness and Maturity Levels
Figure 1.7

Acknowledging that even good programmers produce defects is often difficult to do. One software company in the course of training their programmers in quality has tried to attack this fear by admitting to it and making it visible in their training for new hires. They state that, "Human beings are animals who make mistakes continuously; i.e., the essence of man is to make mistakes." While this may appear harsh to some, it is a natural truth to others. I am not sure I would like people to simply default into making defects as a fact of nature. The fact that programmers make mistakes makes it easier to focus on improving once the admission can be made and accepted. Inspections and Defect Prevention can help us do better.

We all make mistakes and we may even make them more than once. To answer why, is not in the scope of this book, but we all do make mistakes. In fact we sometimes make mistakes and then cannot even see them, even when we finally admit to ourselves that there must be one.

1.4 Do Good Managers Foster Defects?

Yes, they do! However, managers do not intend to foster defect injection. Nonetheless, as a part of the organization, software managers seem to directly and indirectly permit or enable defects. Deming suggests that 94% of the causes of defects "belong to the system (responsibility of management)." [DEM86] These sound like harsh words, and suggest that managers are the "bad guys." This bad guy view of management seems to be why so many Dilbert cartoons make direct hits on management.

This anecdote is an example of why Inspection data (defects) must never be used by management to appraise, reward, promote, or in any way judge the capability of an individual. The defect data only tells us part of the story and data must have integrity when it is used. We should use it very carefully. This value should be communicated to all in the organization via a policy statement. I will discuss Inspection policy in Chapter 10 and provide an example.

People in a software production system or environment can be handicapped by the system itself. Yes, people make mistakes and cause defects, but if given a reasonable chance to produce good quality, they can and will. The 94% of the defects injected can be addressed by looking at the causes within the organization's system, which includes management.

ANECDOTE

WHO MADE THE DEFECTS?

A programmer is asked to give his best estimate for a critical enhancement required by a key client. The programmer tells his manager that he could complete the enhancement in two months if he is not tasked with other work, training, or meetings.

This estimate is based on the programmer's experience, domain knowledge, and understanding that this enhancement must be done as quickly as possible. The manager, however, now tells the programmer that he can only have one month for the enhancement work.

When this enhancement goes to test, it is most likely that the one-month scenario will have more defects found during test than the two-month scenario.

Question: Who made the defects? The programmer or the manager?

If one month were critically necessary for the client, what could have the manager and programmer derived as a best-case approach working together?

Anecdote 1.2

1.5 Is There Any Way To Control Defect Injection?

The short answer is yes, and we'll explore this in Chapter 7: Causal Analysis and in Chapter 14: Inspections Future. In the meantime, it should be accepted that defects do get injected and we must first determine the best way to remove them, then how to prevent them.

Not all organizations yet practice Inspections, for many reasons; e.g., they are not willing to step up to the cultural shift that is required, they do not sufficiently believe defects are an issue with their customers or for their organization, they do not believe Inspections will help, they do not believe there is business value, or they are just stubborn.

Defect Prevention will build upon successful Inspection practice to further reduce the Cost of Quality by enabling prevention of defects, and further reducing the costs of both test and Inspections.

Doing an Inspection is not intellectually exciting for most people, but doing an Inspection well is not a difficult task. People, and especially management, within an organization must believe that Inspections are the best alternative before they try to practice them. If people including management do not believe Inspections will work, then they will prove themselves to be right.

This does not mean proper Inspections are a religious experience, but it does mean that Inspections must be given a fair chance to succeed.

For those who are learning how to engineer better software with fewer defects, the volume of Inspections can and should be reduced. We will discuss this possibility in Chapter 14: Inspections Future, where we will see that for some organizations who have matured their software processes, the possibility of 100% defect removal prior to test is within reach, and that for some even 100% prevention of defects before Inspections is within the realm of possibility.

1.6 Common Questions

In this section we will review some of the common questions that people have expressed in training and when beginning to use Inspections.

Is There a Better Business Answer?

Not for the vast majority of software organizations, so I strongly suggest that they employ Inspections within their business until they can consistently demonstrate a better alternative. As long as the economics demonstrate that it is cheaper to find defects with Inspections than in test and with users, then Inspections should be used. Should the reverse become true, then Inspections will no longer be needed or they can be modified in application.

In the meantime we will assume that Inspections are a good business answer for all software organizations. There is just too much evidence to say otherwise. Will it ever be cheaper to remove defects in test? Perhaps, but I think we can safely say Inspections will be a better answer for a long time, yet. Will it ever be cheaper to have customers find the defects? Perhaps! Some users today seem to want function delivered earlier, even if it is buggy.

I have seen Inspections work successfully for twenty-eight years. I have also seen them fail when people and management are not supportive or prepared to make them successful.

If you have already decided that Inspections do not work or will not work in your environment, then keep reading this book.

What Is Practical?

This question is usually asked with the implication that Inspections are not practical or that there is some minimal subset that can be used and still call it an Inspection. The question itself is impractical as it starts by looking for a short cut.

For example, with the current increase in visual coding and modeling tools, a belief exists that injection of defects is radically reduced, since the tools generate code, but in fact defects are still injected with the use of these tools. They have not eliminated defects. The defects are simply injected at a different point; i.e., pre-code generation. They still must be removed.

Practical means business sense in use. Don't take short cuts at the expense of quality and cost reduction. There are none!

What Is Most Necessary for Success?

First, it starts with the management. They must support, sponsor, monitor use, and believe that Inspections are necessary in all projects. This sponsorship needs to be expressed to all in the organization. If support is not visibly shown to the people in the organization, too many failure points can become manifest.

Second, all people will need good training. Without effective training, the organization is off to a risky start. Good training is a necessary precondition to success.

Third, effective procedures are needed. Too often procedures are not useful to, or usable by, the practitioners. It is a difficult skill to make procedures that are both complete and useful. It is easier to make procedures overbearing in their definitions. Keep them as simple as possible. Examples of procedures are included in this book.

In every case where I have seen Inspections take root quickly and show a quick return on investment, there has been an Inspection champion in the organization. The champion can be one of the technical leads or a manager. It has worked both ways, but they must be believers who have the respect of others in the organization.

Finally, proper planning for Inspections is needed. If Inspections are not sufficiently included in initial project plans, they probably will not be scheduled, and if not scheduled, they will not happen. People are often overloaded with work and adding Inspections when they are not planned becomes an easy rationalization for not doing them.

These are some of the necessary preconditions for successful change of any type, and introducing an Inspection culture is a significant change that must be set up for success.

How Did Others Implement Inspections Successfully?

Successful organizations had good management support and sponsorship, and they:

- Kept to the basics
- Trained teams rather than individuals
- Established a policy that Inspections are safe
- Followed the proven method, before adapting or tailoring it
- Gave proper time for Inspections to take root
- Analyzed and used the data resulting from Inspections
- Built on their own successes
- Learned what was not necessary to inspect
- Rewarded the performance of Inspections
- Shared the success
- Allocated budget and time for Inspections

ANECDOTE

SHOW THE PROJECT IMPACT

In one organization the senior manager was a strong believer that Inspections would help the programmers become more like engineers. However, his management team did not yet see the value. He required that all projects move to Inspections by a set date. Each month he had an all-managers meeting to discuss Inspections and process. Each meeting he would ask the managers their status and if they had any issues. He knew he had to keep constant and win the skeptics over one by one.

One month he asked very specifically if any manager had any issues that would prevent them from using Inspections on all of their project's work products. As he started with the first manager and moved to the next they began testing him. First there were no issues. Then as one manager would put a small issue on the table and the senior manager did not challenge it, the next was likely to agree and add one more issue on the pile.

Eventually we came to a manager who stated quite bluntly that Inspections were going to cause his project to ship later. After all the managers had their say, the senior manager, who to this point had not challenged or debated any issues, said simply, "I expect all projects to use Inspections by the date we previously set. However, any manager who can show me in my office that Inspections will impact their committed ship date will be relieved from using them in *this* release."

He gave them all the option to use or not use Inspections, but they had to prove their case if they chose not to use Inspections

No one, to my knowledge, came to see him. All projects used Inspections, and none shipped late.

Senior management must listen, provide options, but be forceful in their view of how they want the option interpreted.

Anecdote 1.3

How Do We Pick What to Inspect?

Any work product can be inspected. When first starting I suggest that requirements specifications, design, code, and user documents be inspected, in that order. Under situations where the software is not safety or life critical, I also suggest that you try to choose what not to inspect in the code. This choice should be based on data, but can be initially based on the group experience within the project team. There must be selection criteria based on experience, not on opinion. We will discuss this subject in more detail in Chapter 9.

As you become more successful using Inspections, then you should consider extending them to other work products; e.g., plans, processes, procedures. I suggest the approach of stepwise use and application of Inspections. If you really believe that you are ready to start, and will be successful, with all work products, go for it! But be advised that there is added risk of acceptance by the organization members and high potential for failure. I have seen too many organizations try to do too much too fast only to struggle more than is necessary and sometimes abandon Inspections. Learn to walk first.

Convince Me That They Work!

If you can accept documented results from twenty-eight years of practice with Inspections, then the references in the bibliography will help you reach full conviction. I would also hope that this book would complete or reinforce your convictions.

There are no documented results showing that Inspections increase the overall cost and time of a project.

How To Deal with Egos?

Egos can become more pronounced and visible using Inspections. This is a primary reason that Moderators, who are discussed in detail throughout the book, have such an important responsibility for the successful performance of Inspections. Training for all participants is required and during the training the subject of egos and personality types should be addressed. Just teaching technique does not bring about successful Inspections.

Inspections are an objective method and require that people behave objectively and professionally. Often we need only to ask them to do so. But if we don't ask or don't require proper behavior, people may resort to behaviors they have previously used. Sometimes these behaviors are less than professional. In software, some people seem to believe that creativity is a key to good programming solutions and that we should tolerate unacceptable behavior in creative programmers. Who says creative people need not be professional or civil? Go figure!

We probably can never prevent some super-egos from making negative statements about Inspections or anything for that matter, but we can include checks and balances within the Inspection process to help them be more successful despite adverse personalities. Inspections will not change personalities but when managed, Inspections can contain them. See Chapter 5, where we discuss personality types.

When Does It Make Sense To Start an Inspection?

Basically you can do an Inspection when any work product is completed or is determined to be ready for propagation within the life cycle of the project. This assumes inspectors have been trained and the other preconditions for a good Inspection have been satisfied.

You do not have to wait until a new project begins to implement successful Inspections. When we performed the first study of Inspections in 1972 in IBM, they were started when most of the product had already been coded.

**You do not have to wait until a work product is fully complete.
You can inspect a partially completed work product,
just know and accept that you are doing so.**

What's The Comparison to What We Already Do?

This presumes that you are doing some type of review of your work products. See the comparisons of Inspections to other types of reviews in Chapter 13: Other Approaches.

I have learned that in most cases when this question is raised, an organization is doing some type of informal reviews, which may or may not be consistently applied and that there is no (or limited) data analysis from their reviews. Of course informal reviews are better than no reviews, but Inspections will yield an even better advantage. The question is not what method you are using, but how effective (first) and efficient (second) is the method and its application. Experience and studies show that Inspections are *the price performer* for organizations that are starting to bring control to software development. I define price performance as something that has a low cost entry and a good return on investment.

What Are the Pitfalls?

Well, the biggest pitfall is not to do Inspections.

When Inspections are chosen to be a defect removal method, then the organization should work from what has been proven to be effective and efficient, rather than evolving the method because there is a "better" opinion on how Inspections should be performed. As we will see later in the book, a better method has evolved from the original, but the evolution was through analysis of data and evidence of improvement. While the method has evolved, the essentials remain similar to the original definition. We will explore these evolutions and improvements throughout this book.

If we sum up these learning experiences of the software community, we have learned to make Inspections more effective and efficient and have evolved from the original method definition in a stepwise fashion, but we did not throw away the basics. Rather we built upon them. So you too, when you evolve the method in your own organization, should proceed in a stepwise learning approach building upon the proven basics.

Taking shortcuts under pressure of time is another pitfall. Transition of the whole organization's population will not occur overnight and time pressures may persist for some projects. The temptation will be to skip "just this one Inspection", but that one skip is often the first of many in what becomes an erosion of objectives. If you accept that test will remove defects, why skip an Inspection, which is known to be less costly? The problem is that management is under time pressures and tends to postpone the crisis to a later time or another management team.

Not making Inspections safe and especially not making the resultant data safe is a major cause of failure. If people know or believe management will use the data in some adverse, or potentially adverse way, Inspections will be performed in name only.

Not training the project members as a team is also a pitfall. If team members work as a team, do not train people as individuals or subsets of projects. After these individuals go back to their project and try to apply what they have learned, no one else may know or accept the value of Inspections. The result often is resistance and eventual decay. Train them as a team

How Does Management Rate Performance on Inspections?

They shouldn't! If they do, Inspections will never be successful in the organization.
People do make mistakes, but as we've seen management is part of the cause for most of these mistakes, so trying to rate the programmer's performance from Inspection data can lead to distortions in the Inspection process; e.g., the data may look good when in fact it isn't reflecting the actual Inspection results. Numbers are entered into the Inspection database, but they are not data. They are just numbers that are treated as data. With poor data, analysis may reflect that Inspections are not paying off, so management may try to remove the cost of Inspections, and the organization can spiral into a black hole.

Given this important caution, managers have a responsibility to monitor the use of Inspections; e.g., are they occurring according to plan, are Re-Inspections being held sufficiently, is the process working. Allow for learning. Acknowledge that mistakes will be made in the work products and in the early use of the Inspection process itself. Don't use the data in any adverse way. Constantly ask what can be done to improve Inspections in your environment.

Where Do Inspections Apply in the Software Lifecycle?

Inspections are not limited to any one life cycle type.

Inspections can be used for any work product resulting from any activity in any part of the life cycle. This includes all activities from requirements management and analysis through completion of a product after delivery and maintenance.

Is There Only One Way To Do Inspections?

The answer is Yes and No.

Yes, there is one way that consistently results in a good return on investment, but this way has acceptable variations that should be considered across different organizations.

No, because the method is not the primary concern, but effectiveness of the method is. So if your data and results show that you have evolved a better way, then use it. Until then, begin with the basic method and evolve from there.

Are All Reviews Inspections?

There are many, perhaps too many, types of reviews. All are less rigorous than Inspections and consequently are less effective in removing defects. Despite the lower payback, many of these are popular throughout the software community. As we will see later in the book, it is not a question of what the review type is called, be it Inspection, walkthrough, or review.

Rather the question that must be asked is how effective is the review process. We will see later that Inspections have been the most effective approach and that there are now increasing occurrences of 90% or more removal of defects when using Inspections.

There is, however, a review type that has a different purpose and serves a software project well, when appropriately used. These reviews are usually called Technical Reviews and are best employed early in the project "by a team of qualified personnel that examines the suitability of the software product for its intended use and identifies discrepancies from specifications and standards. Technical Reviews may also provide recommendations of alternatives and examination of various alternatives." [IEE98] Technical Reviews, of this type, best serve to understand if the requirements or a technical approach are well stated, understandable, doable, and whether there are better alternatives to satisfy the customer need.

1.7 When To Start Inspections

The answer is simple; start now. There is no reason to wait to employ Inspections only on new projects. Begin as soon as you can on your project. Even if you are half way through your testing stage you can begin to use Inspections on fixes to defects found during test. If you are in the code stage, begin to inspect the code. There is no need to wait for the right time, because there never is a right time except now.

The payoff is immediate. No sooner will you begin Inspections than you will begin to remove defects, which would only have been found later at a higher cost and more than likely at a critical time with critical effect on you or the user. Training is easy. Training is also key. Training is another pitfall that people encounter when they begin to use Inspections. The usual argument given is that the programmers can learn all they need by reading a manual on Inspections rather than spending two to three days in a training session. The principles are simple and the ideas are easy. Why train for two or three days? The answer is that if you do not train you will not have good Inspections and worse, you will not have people who are convinced that Inspections work, so they will, without forethought or maliciousness, cause erosion in the Inspection effectiveness.

Clearly the best time to start is at the beginning of the project, but this situation does not always present itself unless the organization has many projects. In the VTAM case study performed in

1972, this project was well over 50% completed with design and code when Inspections were begun. We had wanted to begin earlier, but the organization was not ready.

In 1990 at Groupe Bull we made an edict that all projects must begin to apply Inspections by a set date. We expected push back and knew that in some cases the project could be right to push back, so we let them show objective reasons why they should not begin to apply Inspections on any project; e.g., would a committed date be missed as a result of Inspections. As I recall all projects applied Inspections by the set year-end target, and we were successful in applying Inspections at Bull in all locations. This is partially discussed in Weller's paper on the success of Inspections in Bull. [WEL93]

So the decision to start Inspections should be made in light of the project's situation, but I believe that in almost every case it can be started successfully as long as it is before 75% of the project is completed in coding. Above 75% it is a toss up, as there could be impact to commitments. Above all we do not want Inspections being used as the reason why a committed date was missed to a customer. The non-believers could use this "ammunition" to further defer use of Inspections in the organization.

We know that Inspections have an upfront cost. This cost seems to vary between 8-20% of budget for the project in organizations that are 65% or more effective in removing defects with Inspections. This cost would include Inspections for all work products; e.g., requirement specifications, designs, code, test plans, test cases.

"Ok," you say, "I accept that we will see a quality improvement, but how can 8-20% be added to a project and result in a productivity improvement?" With this range it almost seems that a cost must be added to get the quality, but it is quite the contrary. Spending for Inspections early in the project leads to savings in the overall project costs.

This shift in thinking makes Inspections an investment rather than a cost. The 8-2% cost is spent up front in the project and recovered with a profit during the project. The Inspection cost is not added to the project costs. The project will spend more up front to get even more in return later. "How can this be?" you might ask. Refer back to Figure 1.3 where it is shown that there is a pattern of cost for defect removal and that the cost to remove defects during Inspections is significantly less than when a defect is found in test or by the user. We will work the numbers later in the book, but at this time you can do a quick exercise showing the savings that accrue when Inspections find only 50% of the defects.

Is it possible to deliver a defect-free product? Yes. Has it been done? Yes, but not often enough. The real issue is not how we can create defect-free products, but why it is not done more often. Another way to view this concern is to ask, why are software products as defective as they are? Why are they not better? All software products can be made less defective. It becomes a question of choice by both the supplier and the customer.

1.8 An Historical Perspective

Most people cite 1976 as the reference point for the start of Inspections, since that's the date of Mike Fagan's seminal article. However, the actual definition and pilot work began in 1972 and the study itself was begun in late 1972 in the referenced project VTAM (Virtual Telecommunications Access Method). There were a number of internal IBM technical reports written prior to the article. [KOH73] [FAG74] [KOH75] [KOH76]

Since we are discussing Inspections of software work products, we should begin with IBM in 1972, as this is where the story on software Inspections starts. There were other defect removal activities discussed, written about, and used before 1972. The Inspection method evolved from these prior experiences, so perhaps we should briefly look at these.

First, even where no method such as Inspections was defined, good engineers did do something to remove defects prior to the start of test. Their actions could have been anything from showing the work product to another pair of eyes all the way to the equivalent of a repeatable type of informal review by peers. Many engineers unfortunately let the compiler or assembler and test activities find the defects they injected.

In any case there typically was no management requirement to do anything more. If time permitted, fine. If the engineer was inclined, fine. Thus there was a wide variation in the effectiveness of these types of defect removal actions. Unfortunately data was not kept on these occurrences, so we simply cannot know for sure if any of these were reasonably effective. Most probably were not. We do know, however, that different types of reviews were performed. It just made sense to do something. Norman L. Chase defined the earliest documented review process I found in IBM. Its objective was "to provide an early independent design evaluation of planned programming support." [CHA68] It was not defect focused, but was a view of how to control design to contain cost, schedule, and maintenance problems that were becoming more of a concern as more and more software was being produced.

Second, management was not blind to the effect of defects being found in test and by users. Thus we hear of various versions of what were called reviews or walkthroughs being performed prior to 1972 in some quality or cost directed organizations. Papers and organization technical reports had been written from some of these experiences and pre-date or co-date the VTAM study. [WEI71] [JON73] [KOM74] [WAL74] [JON75]

Third, Weinberg's book, "The Psychology of Computer Programming" [WEI71] captured the attention and imagination of many readers regarding why software development seemed to be so defect prone. This book, more than any other publication, opened up the eyes of the software community that there could be another approach to developing software. It introduced to many people the idea of egoless programming using a code review; i.e., "one person reading the program of someone else," and it set the foundation and some of the tone for Inspections in software.

In 1972, Lew Priven, the senior software manager for telecommunications products in Kingston, N.Y. asked Mike Fagan to join his group as a process manager to explore possibilities for improving quality and productivity working with the development managers and programmers in the VTAM project. Mike had been in a hardware area previously and Lew believed someone with hardware and manufacturing experience might be able to apply some other disciplined engineering practices to the software work we were doing in VTAM.

Lew had sponsored a number of other quality and productivity experiments. He was clearly open to improvement and change in the existent VTAM situation. Some ideas did not prove to be practical, such as re-training personnel in manufacturing to write code from Low-level design. Some experiments succeeded, such as Inspections. In March 1972, Priven documented the ideas of "a management system, which views the Programming Development Cycle as a complex set of inter-related elements." [PRI72] This system definition included "points of management control" using *process monitors* that then became Inspections, though the term Inspections was not used in this report. The genesis of the life cycle definition in this report was from the TSS operating system development experiences, and included the then innovative concept of continuous and staged integration of an evolving product while there were multiple and dynamic inputs for change during the release.

Historically it is interesting to note that TSS was one of two operating system solutions that IBM was pursuing during the 1960's. OS/360 was the decision that IBM took, not because of best product or best process for development, but because of where the marketplace was with existing applications and programming languages. TSS was more process focused than OS/360, so had TSS been the decision, it would be interesting to project how much further the software community might be with process discipline.

In 1972 I had the good fortune to attend three months of training roughly equivalent to post-graduate studies in selected software domains at the IBM Systems Research Institute (SRI). I had elected to focus on telecommunications and my advisor at the SRI was James Martin, so I was learning from the best. I was planning to return to the IBM Kingston facility and work on the VTAM project that had been located there. Other people who were influential on my thinking about software methods included Larry Constantine who was also on the SRI staff at that time. These people and the time away from project work certainly opened my eyes and left me feeling that there must be a better way to build software than what I had just recently left when coming to the SRI, although I was not clear what it all would become.

When I returned to IBM Kingston in late July 1972, I was to be assigned to the VTAM project, a new technology for a software telecommunications access method within IBM's System 360 solution set. Since I had prepared myself in telecommunications while at the SRI, it was expected by all that I would be on that project. However, when I looked at the project, it was in almost total chaos. It was behind schedule, multiple times; people were exhausted, working vast amounts of overtime; inter-group dependencies were falling apart, etc. You know the story.

Basically this was the equivalent of a SW-CMM Level 1 software organization, although that concept did not exist at that time. The project did have an excellent software configuration management (SCM) system and probably satisfied the requirements for software configuration control boards (SCCB), although there were high volumes of changes every week due to an unstable requirements baseline. The software quality assurance (SQA) group was funded at about 8% of the project budget. The project team had in various ways been involved during the project proposal stages, but constant changes, together with a new telecommunications technology, kept the baseline in flux. Plans included size (using KLOC), effort, costs, and schedules by task and phase. Performance characteristics were defined and tracked (even during the design work), risks were identified and discussed at status meetings, which were held every Tuesday morning for all who needed to be in attendance. There was no sub-contracting of note, although there were significant inter-group dependencies in other IBM locations for parts of the solution in IBM operating systems. These dependencies were fraught with political and turf issues. So while VTAM was probably a Level 1 organization, it was not a low Level 1. Mostly what was missing were agreement on, and control of, requirements of the VTAM product.

It was into this environment that Lew Priven had asked Mike Fagan to come and help. Lew had taken over the senior management of this VTAM project about four months earlier. I had not known Mike; he had joined the VTAM organization during my three-month tour at the SRI. When I was asked to join VTAM and I declined, for obvious reasons, I was told that I would either have to join VTAM or work with Mike Fagan. “Who is Mike Fagan?” I asked. When I was informed of what he was tasked to do, I asked for the interview. His work sounded like an opportunity to do something that could improve the way software was being developed. There might be hope after all, I thought.

I met with Mike and understood more deeply what he was being asked to do; i.e., extend the concepts of walkthroughs to be a more rigorous method for removing defects before test. He added that we would also be working in other areas of software quality, productivity, methods, etc. This was the light at the end of the tunnel I was beginning to sense was possible while I was at SRI. Mike had at that time two other people working with him, Bob Kohli and Ted Brooks. I would be the third. While I worked with Mike, our group never grew to more than five people, as I remember. We were a rough equivalent to a software engineering process group (SEPG), although we did not use that terminology. We did call ourselves a process group. I continued to work with Mike until March of 1974 when I finally accepted an offer to join the ranks of first line management on the very project I previously avoided, VTAM, in its next release. It was now under substantially more stable operation and definition.

After this introduction to the possibilities of software process, I continued to work in process regardless of the management position I held. Mike left VTAM to join another new technology area, DPPX, an operating system for the 8100 series, I believe in 1975. His assignment was to repeat and extend what had worked so well in VTAM, which, to say the least, had been a difficult environment in which to introduce a new method such as Inspections

1.9 Early Experiences

As mentioned, the VTAM project was in a chaotic state when Inspections were posed as a method that would help. You can imagine the response of most of the management and programmers to this offer of help. While they might have been sympathetic to the idea, they just never seemed to find the right opportunity for us to try the method in a live environment. I should restate that we had excellent support from senior management. The sponsorship was in obvious evidence. The difficulty was overloaded middle management, project management, and project teams.

The first live product Inspection was for Low-level Design (LLD) and was held in December 1972. I moderated that Inspection. We had practiced many times on other work products, but this was the first "live" demonstration. The team of Mike Fagan, Bob Kohli and myself worked on Mike's proposed idea between July and December 1972. Ted Brooks had left the group shortly after I joined and resumed his primary work in the technical publications department. We prepared the method by running mock and trial Inspections on materials available to us within our group and from VTAM. We improved and iterated the method with each trial. We were always prepared and ready to try the method in a live situation.

Mike was the constant visionary to keep us focused, but it was the team working together that made the significant differences in the final definition and details of the Inspection method. We assumed that we could take a reasonable slice of the project and have "controlled" rigorous Inspections. We could then compare this slice with a comparable slice of the project where Inspections were not used. Much of the project was already completed with design, code, and unit and integration tests. The project was designed to have incremental builds of successive functions being added in each build prior to field release.

The project plans reflected multiple drivers of incremental working function that could be designed, coded, and tested concurrently, so we had some opportunities while the project was in flight. We had gone to the VTAM management a number of times before with a slice that we thought would permit reasonable approximations to a "controlled" study. It was our view at that time that we should inspect module work products three times; i.e., after Low-level design, code, and unit test were completed. This would allow us to follow the module through a reasonable portion of its life cycle of defect removal with Inspections, all tests after unit test, and eventually customer use.

We called these three Inspections I_1, I_2, and I_3, respectively. High-level design was already completed on this VTAM project, but frankly we had not considered it during this period. Later in the next VTAM release an Inspection type was added for High-level design and took the awkward tag of an I_0. In fact, it was later understood that Inspections could be applied to any life cycle artifact or work product including requirements, test plans, and test cases, and these types were subsequently added. During 1973, Larson began work to define the Inspection process for test work products, which were called IT_1 and IT_2. [LAR75] Roughly about the same time McCloskey wrote a process definition for technical publications, which became known as PI_0, PI_1, and PI_2 as noted in Fagan's article. [MCC75]

We had been turned down by VTAM middle management on a number of occasions for reasons that probably seemed right to them; e.g., "this was not the best time, given everything else that was happening", the right programmers would not be available, etc. It began to appear that we might never get an opportunity to try the Inspection study. But each time we approached management, we were ready and prepared. All we needed was the go ahead.

I still vividly remember the day that Phil Kolko, the 2nd level design manager, gave us that go ahead. It was late Friday afternoon. I was talking with Mike in an aisle near some outside facing windows. I was explaining to Mike that Bob Kohli and I had identified another slice of the product that would be a good candidate since it had sufficient Low-level design, code, and unit test scheduled for the next build and seemed to be a representative sample of the VTAM project. It would make a good comparison to the remainder of the VTAM product. We were trying to be careful to get 1) a size of reasonable significance and 2) a mixed cross section of new and changed modules, since some modules had already been in test from earlier drivers or staged product builds.

As Phil approached us we stopped him and informed him that we had identified another slice that we believed would work. Previously Phil and his managers had always found a reason to say the slice was not good, they were late, this was a key delivery for test and could not be delayed, the slice was not representative of the project or its members, etc. At first Phil just looked at us without saying a word. His countenance and body language as he walked toward us suggested a man who had come from one more difficult meeting, which in fact he had. He paused to gather his thoughts, and then said, "You guys never give up, do you?" He made some humorous analogies that I won't repeat here, but catch me over a drink sometime. He said, "Go ahead, you're probably right." He left us and we moved into action immediately. The training sessions started and the schedules for all the I_1, I_2, and I_3 Inspections within the study were determined with the VTAM team.

There are a number of lessons that can be drawn from this incident, but the paramount one for me was that success in process improvement is driven by persistence backed up with readiness and management support. Since that time in 1972, I have seen and heard of numerous process improvement efforts, which all had the right ideas, but that just didn't make it to fulfillment due to lack of persistence, readiness, or both.

In some respects process groups should understand that to work hard might not be enough. They must be persistent. They will often be told," No!" Or they will be strung along. The keys to success are to have a well-defined plan and never give up. We had the plan and the determination with the VTAM project. Process groups must respond to changes, as they will continue to happen even in high maturity organizations. On VTAM we had no choice. It was either to remain persistent in our goals or to go away. If you know Mike, you'll know that he is persistent with a determined and driven focus. I learned these from him.

Phil Kolko by the way became a good friend in years after and remained a strong believer in process value.

1.10 First Inspections

We trained each of the programmers who were involved in this slice of VTAM and who would be participants in one or more of the planned Inspections. Bob Kohli and I were the Moderators during the study. The method was very similar to that written up in Mike's 1976 article in the IBM Systems Journal. [FAG76] After we knew the study was successful, Bob and I wrote an IBM Technical Report detailing the method entitled "Design and Code

Inspection Specification". [KOH73] This Technical Report was specifically available only to IBM employees, but it served as the first defined basis for the Inspection method. We provided this as an early documented source for Inspections, since we believed that IBM at large could benefit from the experiences. And they did. There were multiple Technical Reports for early Inspections in IBM showing the same basic pattern of ROI resulting from use of Inspections. [KRE75] [MAH75] [NOR78] Mike was more cautious and wanted to see the results from customer reported defects before he published his paper, although he also published an internal Technical Report in December 1974 entitled "Design and Code Inspection and Process Control in the Development of Programs." [FAG74]

The first Low-level design Inspection held in December 1972 was with a reasonably motivated team, but we did have one unexpected barrier, which fortunately did not become a major distracter. IBM at that time of year would play Christmas carols over all loud speakers starting around 2:00 pm the day before the designated start of the holidays. Our first VTAM product Inspection was scheduled to start at 2:00 pm, and we did so to the sounds of Jingle Bells and other music for almost two hours. Despite this joyous, celebratory sound interference, this first Inspection worked.

Since this first study, the focus on Inspections has grown as a result of the increasing interest in delivering higher quality software products. In all cases, as seen in the examples in this book, when viewed from the global perspective that includes the test and maintenance stages, Inspections have proven time and time again to be the least costly way we have today to remove defects from the work products we create for software.

1.11 Another Approach to Success

I have always felt fortunate to be involved in the IBM Inspection study during 1972-74 and to moderate the first Inspection. Since that time I have seen a continuous, though not constant, acceptance and application of Inspections within the software community. There now are instances where 100% effectiveness has been accomplished. I await the day when we in the software community can say we do not need Inspections, at least in some projects. I know that day will come. We are closer than many may admit. The ability that some projects have today to achieve 100% effectiveness is one step in that direction. Will all projects be able to achieve 100% effectiveness? No. Should all projects try? I believe yes, but the customer will drive the decision taken, and that's the way of business.

In this book we will explore some ways where you too can move in the direction of 100% effectiveness and possibly reduce and eliminate the need for Inspections. The path is not always the same, but the possibilities are.

While the VTAM environment had clear senior management sponsorship, we had many obstacles to overcome and we needed to continuously sell the potential value of Inspections. There was no benchmark to point to; we were about to become that benchmark.

When I was at Groupe Bull, where I held a corporate position for software process improvement, we issued an edict that all locations practice Inspections on all work products.

Again we had senior management sponsorship, and again we needed to sell, but now we were selling into an organization that had previously tried and abandoned Inspections. Not only had they abandoned Inspections, but each location had tried Inspections in different ways and some continued with some form of review. We had to build upon bad experiences and inconsistent reviews, but we wanted one consistent approach to be practiced.

I do not normally like edicts for process change, but they can work, and it did work in Groupe Bull with Inspections.

We issued the edict, because:

- We wanted to move as fast as possible
- We believed that Inspections would save project costs
- We were prepared and able to help the locations with available
  - Training materials
  - Corporate procedure definitions
  - Hands on consulting and coaching

ANECDOTE

INSPECTIONS! WHY INSPECTIONS?

With the vast amount of Inspections occurring at all levels within the organization, a question frequently asked is, " Is all this time well spent?" It's easy to gather metrics on how many problems are found inspecting specific lines of code, and how much time and effort this saves. But do these really reflect the true savings, or are there some hidden savings or savings that are too difficult to measure?

Recently during an Inspection of File System code for HVS V2.30, the inspectors queried the author about some existing code that interfaced with the code being inspected. After a little more investigation on this point it was determined that this problem, dealing with the flushing of Indices during a Cleanpoint operation, was a problem that had existed since HVS 2.10. This particular problem had caused four defect problem reports to be written from four different accounts in the U.S. and Europe. Since the problem resulted in an index that had not been updated, the responses to the problem were more of a recovery (i.e., how to fix the index) than a solution to this elusive, sporadic problem. How much would this have saved Bull and our customers no one knows, and it won't be factored in to the value of this Inspection.

How many such hidden savings do we have with each Inspection? Each ten Inspections? Successes like this lead us to believe that the "hidden savings " could be substantial. And they were.

Anecdote 1.4

An insightful result documented by a new Inspection advocate from the Bull Billerica, Massachusetts's location is noted in Anecdote 1.4. The defect that was found one day during an Inspection of changes was to in old module and had eluded the best of the programmers in that location for three years!

Weller's article on experiences in the Bull's Phoenix location shows results achieved before and after the edict for Inspections in maintenance projects. [WEL93]

While Weller gives a good analysis with data for the experiences in Phoenix, there were successes in other Bull locations. Le Goïc at Les Clayes-sous-Bois in Bull stated, "The return on investment is always impressive and often above 6." [LOG98]

End Quote:

**"Inspections find the defect,
while testing – which usually occurs one or more development phases after the opportunity to inspect has passed – finds only the symptom."
Priscilla J. Fowler**

CHAPTER 2

INSPECTIONS – AN INTRODUCTION

**"When I use a word, it means exactly what I want it to mean,
nothing more and nothing less."
Humpty Dumpty to Alice in Through the Looking Glass**

2.1 What Is an Inspection?

An Inspection is a rigorous team review of a work product by peers of the Producer. The size of the team will vary with the characteristics of the work product being inspected; e.g., size, type. An independent Moderator usually leads the Inspection. The primary purpose is to find defects, recording them as a basis for analysis on the current project and for historical reference and improvement for future projects, analyzing them, and initiating rework to correct the defects. Inspections are most effective when performed immediately after the work product is completed, but they can be held any time the work product is deemed ready for Inspection.

Finding defects earlier not only has a direct bearing on the quality of the product going into test and on delivery to the customer, but also improves the productivity of the project. Quality and the related Cost of Quality have been remarkably improved in products using Inspections. Data analysis has repeatedly shown that removing defects later in the production process is more expensive for the project, organization, and customers in cost and time. There are numerous testimonies to the advantages achieved from Inspections.

An Inspection is most successful when:

- All team members treat it as a cooperative effort to find and remove defects as early as possible during production activities
- Inspectors with good domain knowledge of the material are available for the Inspection
- Inspectors are trained in the Inspection process

It should be noted that Inspections succeed to varying degrees even when these three conditions are not met. Effectiveness may not be as good, but this still beats propagating all defects into test.

It must always be remembered that Inspection data must not be used to evaluate the performance or capability of the work product Producer. All levels of management must accept this value, practice it, and communicate the commitment to all personnel.

The Inspection team uses a checklist to prepare for the Inspection and to verify the work product against historical, repetitive, and critical defect types within the domain of the project. The Inspection is used to determine the suitability of the work product to continue into the next life cycle stage by either "passing" or "failing" the work product, based on predefined exit criteria. If the work product fails, it should be repaired and potentially re-inspected. If it passes, any defects found need to be repaired before the work product passes to the next project stage. Specific data items are captured during the Inspection process to facilitate repair, improvement, and learning.

A software work product is not only code, but includes work product types such as requirements specifications, design specifications, user documentation, plans, maintenance repairs, incident and problem reports, trouble log fixes, and test cases, among others. The particular life cycle, project plan, and related software processes used by the project define the complete set of applicable work products. See Appendix B for details on the different types of Inspections.

The original Inspection method defined by Fagan followed a predefined set of five activities, not all of which are required for each Inspection; e.g., the Overview. Each of these activities is fully defined in chapter 3:

- **Overview** to provide the Inspection participants a background and understanding, when warranted, of the scheduled Inspection material
- **Preparation** to allow time for the Inspection participants to sufficiently prepare for the Inspection Meeting and list potential defects
- **Inspection Meeting** to identify defects before the work product is passed into the next project stage
- **Rework** to fix identified defects and resolve any Open Issues noted during the Inspection
- **Follow-up** to verify that all defects and Open Issues have been adequately fixed, resolved, or closed out

Since Fagan's definition in the 1970's, it has been found that other process activities are key to repeated success, and these include:

- **Planning and Scheduling** to ensure adequate time and resources are allocated for Inspections and to establish schedules in the project for work products to be inspected, to designate the Inspection team, and to ensure the entry criteria are satisfied
- **Data Recording** to record the data about the defects and conduct of the Inspection
- **Analysis Meeting**, which is held after the Inspection Meeting, to begin Defect Prevention activities
- **Prevention Meeting**, which is held periodically after sets of Inspections have been performed to determine probable causes for selected defect types, instances, or patterns

Throughout the use of Inspections, there is an activity of **Monitoring** to ensure effective and efficient practice and to improve the Inspection process performance.

An Inspection exists in one of three states:

- **Planned**, which includes any time during the project's life cycle where the schedule has been defined for a required Inspection; this state concludes with the start of the Inspection Meeting; this state includes Planning, the Overview, and Preparation activities
- **Performed**, which includes all activities from the start of the Inspection Meeting up to Follow-up closure
- **Closed**, which is after Follow-up when closure has been achieved and signed-off and the data from the full Inspection process has been captured

2.2 Definitions

The idea of Inspections itself is not new. Yet, there still exists a large degree of either misunderstanding or re-interpretation regarding the meaning and purpose of Software Inspections. It is not clear to me if this comes from the inherent nature of programmers to try to re-invent or "improve" everything they are asked to use, or if it comes from the lack of good repeatable training for Inspections. I suppose to some degree it is both. But in any event, today we ramble about in another Babel when we in the software community speak about Inspections or Peer Reviews. In either case it may not be clear what is really meant or intended by each term.

The term *inspection* does not always mean the same thing. The issue has been further complicated by the use of numerous other names for the same concept of removing defects from work products. Later I will discuss the differences between these terms and their meanings: Inspections, Walkthroughs, Reviews, Self-check, etc. (See Chapter 13: Other Approaches to Defect Removal.)

Inspections are a static technique in that the code or document is not executed. Each inspected document during the project life cycle is examined and compared to a previous state to see if the transformed state has been correctly transformed and is itself correct. For example, code is examined and compared to design and High-level design is examined and compared to the requirements specification. See Figure 2.1 for an example of this relationship for Inspections.

There are other review methods that have specific purposes and can be useful, but they are not Inspections. These alternatives include Management Reviews and Technical Reviews. The IEEE STD 1028-1997 also includes walkthroughs and audits as two other review types. I will discuss all of these in Chapter 13.

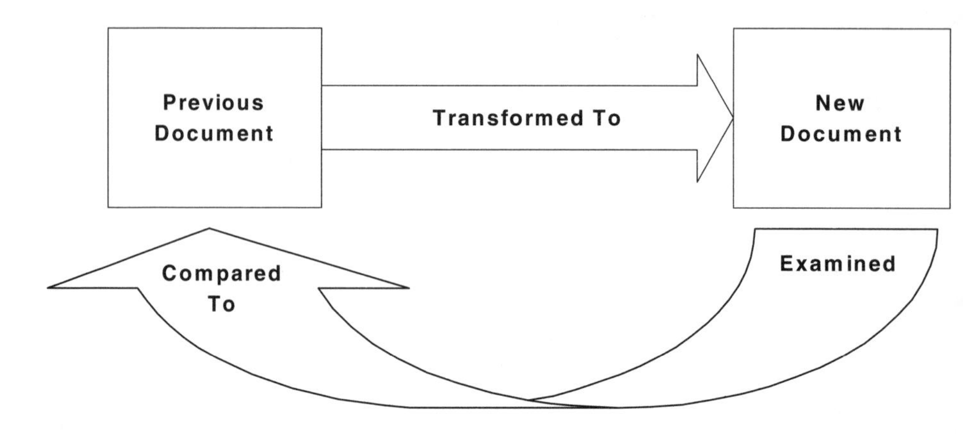

Relationships of Documents For An Inspection
Figure 2.1

I quoted the IEEE definition for Inspections in the Preface. Definitions given by IEEE for other review approaches are:

- "**Management Review** A systematic evaluation of a software acquisition, supply, development, operation, or maintenance process performed by or on behalf of management that monitors progress, determines the status of plans and schedules, confirms requirements and their system allocation, or evaluates the effectiveness of management approaches used to achieve fitness for purpose.
- **Technical Review**: A systematic evaluation of a software product by a team of qualified personnel that examines the suitability of the software product for its intended use and identifies discrepancies from specifications and standards. Technical reviews may also provide recommendations of alternatives and examination of various alternatives.
- **Walkthrough**: A static analysis technique in which a designer or programmer leads members of the development team and other interested parties through a software product, and the participants ask questions and make comments about possible errors, violation of development standards, and other problems.
- **Audit**: An independent examination of a software product, software process, or set of software processes to assess compliance with specifications, standards, contractual agreements, or other criteria." [IEE98]

These definitions attempt to differentiate the approaches, but they have overlaps and therein lies some of the confusion for the new user. These approaches sound alike in many ways, but they actually serve different purposes and their rigor is different. Therefore, the results will be different.

There are so many misinterpretations, and worse, misstatements about what Inspections are, that there is confusion throughout the software community. "Terms for review approaches are not universally agreed upon, and this causes a great deal of confusion. An organization might, for example, conduct a review that it calls an Inspection but which would also fit under the category of an IEEE STD 1028-1988 technical review, or walkthrough, or some other category. Freedman and Weinberg [Freedman 1982] define a review process that they call an Inspection that is very different from the Inspection process defined in IEEE STD 1028-1988." [WHE96]

When people say they are performing Inspections, we must ask other questions before we can conclude that they are actually performing Inspections as intended.

See Chapter 3: The Inspection Process, where a set of attributes of an Inspection are listed.

But even with the term walkthrough there are too many definitions and confusion; e.g., "Walking through the product, a lot of detail can be skipped – which is good if you are just trying to verify an overall approach or bad if your object is to find errors of detail." [WEI84] So let the user beware when hearing the terms Inspection and walkthrough! I'll come back to this subject in Section 2.9.

In this book I will build upon the definition of Inspection noted in Mike Fagan's 1976 article and the latest IEEE definition, STD 1028-1997. [IEE98] Later in the book, I will note where extensions such as the optional Analysis Meeting and other tailoring of the traditional method have been successfully applied. I will write from the point of view of my experiences over the last twenty-eight years with Software Inspections. While the total view I will present will be somewhat different than the Fagan and IEEE definitions, it will build upon them and evolve them.

2.3 The Process Model Used in this Book

All processes, including the Inspection process, have a rules set that determines the definition of the process. In this book I define the Inspection process using the Entry-Task-Validation/Verification-eXit (ETVX) structure. [RAD85a]

ETVX, shown in Figure 2.2, represents the notion that, for any process, there must be entry (E) and exit (X) criteria, that there are tasks to be performed (T), and what is performed needs to be validated/verified (V) before exiting the process. Without these four simple and easy to use basic building blocks a process definition is incomplete and there is no assurance of the product or its subparts being developed as required. Note that the original definition of ETVX the V was only stated as validation, although both validation and verification were intended.

In addition to using the ETVX structure, each Inspection activity defined in Chapter 3 for the Inspection process will identify related roles within each defined Inspection process activity.

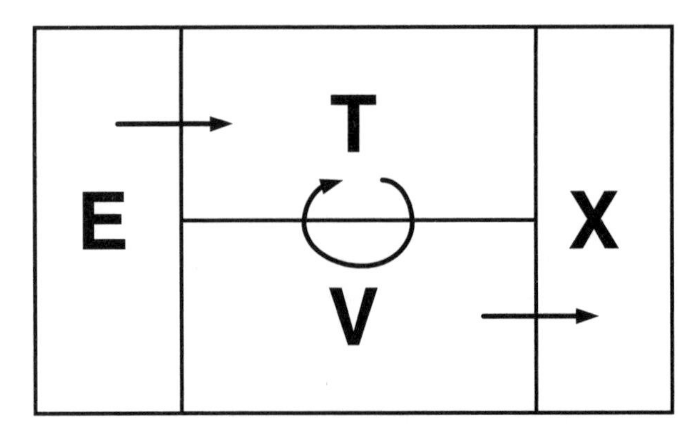

The ETVX Process Definition Paradigm [RAD85a]
Figure 2.2

Observe in Figure 2.3 that the Inspection process has input; i.e., the work product to be inspected. Entry criteria that should be satisfied prior to beginning an Inspection are provided. There are exit criteria as specific predetermined objectives that should be satisfied before an Inspection can be considered completed. Outputs include the Inspection reports, the data basing of relevant data and information, and the reworked work product, among others. This figure is only shown as an example. The details of the process activities and practices are defined in Chapter 3: The Inspection Process.

The full set of activities proceeds from Planning and Scheduling through the Prevention Meeting. Each of these process activities has a predefined list of entry and exit criteria. There is a flow that binds all these activities into the fully defined Inspection process. This process is imparted to the participants through training and documented procedures. The process consists in a way of thinking about how best to find defects and includes a self-reflective way of improving the Inspection process steps or activities themselves.

Finally the Inspection process includes a set of checklists for each type of work product that may be developed. These checklists will vary based on the product environment, domain, and work product. For example, a checklist for code Inspections where C++ is used would be different than one where Visual Basic is used. We would also see that there are similarities in these two checklists because we would be working with a code work product in both cases. A checklist for a requirements specification would be different than one for Low-level design. Sample checklists are included in Appendix A. Organization and project checklists should be managed and controlled by the Inspection Coordinator or Software Engineering Process Group (SEPG), but individuals can and should have their own checklists to help themselves improve.

We will see in Chapter 3 that some of the preconditions for successful Inspections are a reasonably well-defined process and standards for the work products themselves. Without these the work products will be too variable in definition/solution and can lead to unnecessary debates during the Inspections.

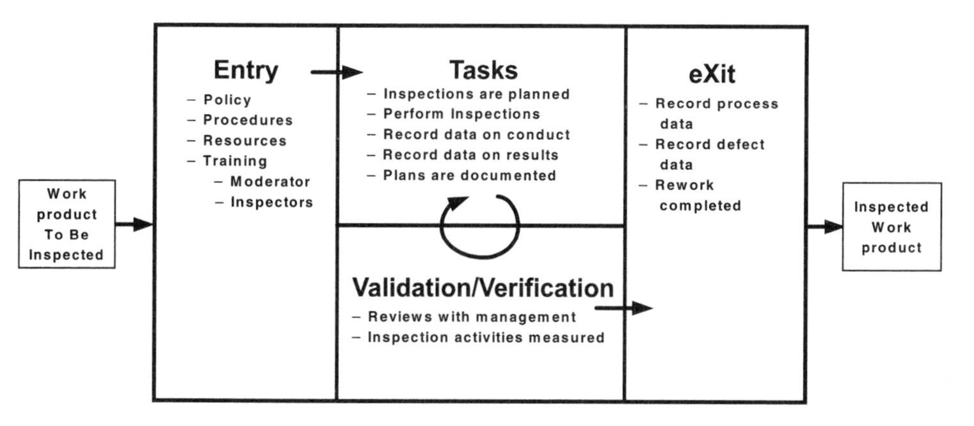

Example Practices In the Inspection Process
Figure 2.3

Although Fagan defined exit criteria requirements for Inspections, he did not fully define entry criteria for Inspections. [FAG76] [FAG86] It was suggested that the code should compile or the Low-level design should be in a 1:5-10 ratio of design statements to code lines. The ETVX paradigm extends his intent.

To define Entry and Exit criteria is a necessary step for any process, but if they are not enforced, the performance of related tasks in the process is fraught with risk. While taking risk may be acceptable, not identifying the risk while taking it may lead to decline in quality. ETVX provides visibility of risks when the Entry and Exit criteria are used.

2.4 Primary Purpose

As mentioned earlier, the primary purpose of an Inspection is to find defects, inconsistencies, and ambiguities as early in the development life cycle process as is possible. Ideally this would occur immediately after the point of defect injection in a work product. For example, all defects injected during High-level design would be found immediately after each part of the High-level design is ready for Inspection and before the next level of design is begun for that part.

Performing an Inspection immediately after the completion of a work product, or a part, and analyzing the resultant data of the detected defects will provide an early quality indicator to the management and technical team.

Prior to the Inspection method, software errors had been scheduled to be removed beginning with unit test; i.e., the first machine-assisted test after a clean module compilation. While this is less true today, it still exists as a way of life in many software projects.

Where test is used as the primary defect removal activity, if there is poor quality in the product, then it is not determinable until unit test and in most cases not until later. This means that over 50% of the project resources may have been spent without giving management a good understanding about the product quality. Furthermore, if the quality is bad in test, there is little that can be done except to spend more resources trying to regain a satisfactory level of quality. However, in many cases this proves frustrating, if not futile. Once the pathology of poor quality has been permitted, and practically unchecked in the product, it is very difficult to set it right even with good testing. The result is late delivery, with reduced or diluted function, and unacceptable quality at a higher product cost. Often trying to test out the defects causes more defects to be injected in the fixes, especially when there is a schedule crunch.

Fagan demonstrated the significance of Inspections on quality and on schedule reduction as indicated in the example shown in Figure 2.4, where he showed that with Inspections the point of management control over quality is moved up in the schedule, the project ships earlier, and that rework on defects is less costly earlier in the project cycle. [FAG76]

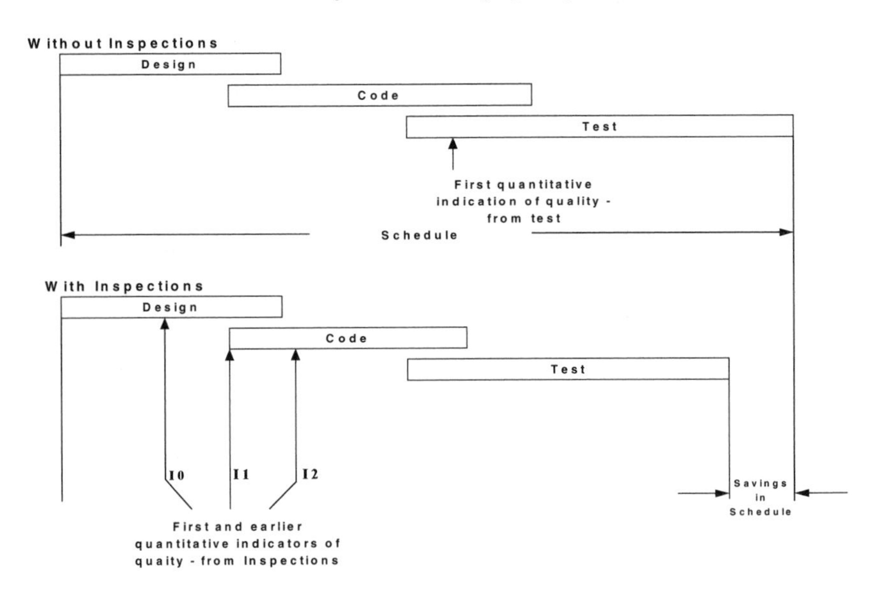

Earlier Quality Indicators With Inspections [FAG76]
Figure 2.4

This example shows that we can get quality indicators earlier in the project when using Inspections. In fact, if we were to perform Inspections on the first work product; i.e., requirements specifications, we could get a quality indicator after less than 10% of the project resources may have been used.

Projects start with a business need or an idea that a customer has. After the customer's "idea" of what they want is understood, we typically transform that idea or customer requirement into some internal project representation. While these representations go under many different names; e.g., requirements specifications, they do represent a transformation and extension of the customer's idea toward the delivered solution. During the project, we continue reviewing the quality indicators after work products are refined through each transformation and into code by using Inspections.

Inspecting after each transformation enables earlier defect detection. Earlier defect detection gives us a measure of the project's progress. See Figure 2.5. After each transformation there is an Inspection, represented by the triangle.

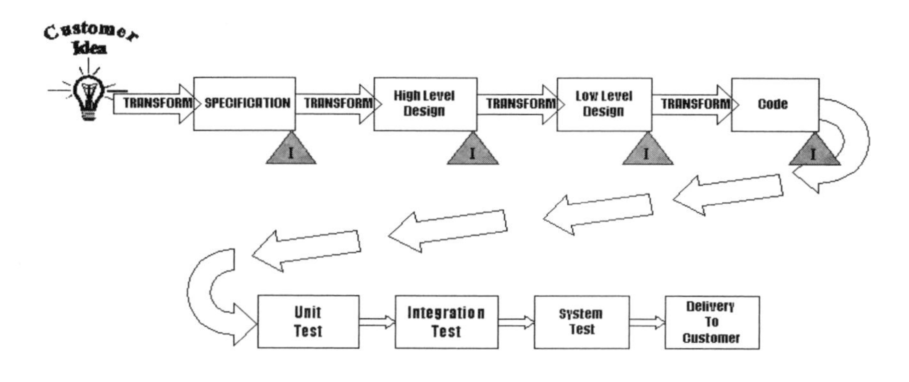

Transformations of The Customer's Idea to a Delivered Product
Figure 2.5

Most defects will be found during two Inspection activities; i.e., Preparation and Inspection Meeting. As we will see later, defects can also be found during the Overview of the work product, during Rework, and when analyzing the causes of discovered defects. The method as defined by Fagan did not note that the Preparation activity could be a key activity for finding defects, but did note that defects should be identified if found. While the original method defined during the VTAM study focused on defects found during the Inspection Meeting, we actually found many defects during Preparation. We just did not discretely count them as found in that activity. Later we learned that Preparation would be a major contributor to finding defects. Later I will discuss situations where Preparation could find in excess of 90% of the defects.

While finding defects is the primary objective there may be disagreements on what is a defect. I'll discuss this difficult subject in Chapter 6: Inspection Data, but for now let's agree that the intent is to find major defects that would prevent a product from working the way it is intended and required by the customer; it is something that would cause the product to malfunction in use and in an undesirable way. These are what are often called major defects. Only secondarily will we be concerned with minor defects in the form and format of the work product. These defects will provide some value in early discovery, but they are not the defects that are the primary target of Inspections or of concern to customers. One can find many minor defects, but if the major latent defects are not found, then the Inspection did not focus on the defects with the highest business value.

2.5 Ancillary Purposes

There are ancillary purposes or positive side effects from Inspections. These ancillary purposes have been addressed either directly or indirectly by many Inspection practitioners, and include:

- Improvement in productivity
- Education and increased knowledge sharing
- Developing backup/replacement capability
- Process improvement
- Early product quality visibility
- Product re-development
- Building team spirit

PRODUCTIVITY IMPROVEMENT

Fagan calculated a 23% productivity improvement during the VTAM study. He showed that one programmer month would be saved during development for each one thousand lines of code (KLOC) in the product. This result, once proven, was quickly seen to be another advantage in addition to the reduction in defects delivered to test and users.

Later Fagan rightly stated that productivity improvement was key to selling the value of Inspections, "An improvement in productivity is the most immediate effect of purging errors from the product." [FAG76]

Norris, in another early IBM study, concluded "Inspection reduces the development cost during test by 50%." [NOR78] And later he noted, "While not proven here, there is an implication that shorter development cycles can be planned when inspections are used."

EDUCATION AND INCREASED KNOWLEDGE SHARING

Inspections were never originally intended to address education or knowledge sharing as a direct outcome for the participants. Nonetheless, even when used solely for its primary purpose to find defects, Inspections will provide education or learning as a by-product. The participants will learn how the work product under Inspection functions as a part by itself and in relation to other work products. Even experienced programmers will learn different techniques for writing documents, designing, or coding.

The education and knowledge sharing are accomplished through five activities of the Inspection process:

- The Overview activity, in which the Producer of the material presents the perspective of the work product to the participants. The Overview can be held immediately before an Inspection Meeting, such as with code, when warranted. It can be held as much as a few days prior to a scheduled Inspection Meeting; for example, when requirement specifications are being inspected or when a large volume of the High-level design is being inspected. The purpose is to enable sufficient understanding by the participants for the Preparation and the Inspection Meeting. This understanding is education about the work product.
- The Preparation activity is an education source. A participant typically does this work alone using the work product and related materials. The intent is to identify defects or to raise questions or issues about the work product and how it satisfies its intended need. While preparing, the participants are not only finding defects but are also learning about the work product. This type of learning can be especially helpful to team members who are dependent on the work product, for example testers or the coder for a design work product.
- During the Inspection Meeting learning is accomplished for the Producer and participants. Feedback, another form of learning, is given to the Producer about defects detected and therefore learning can begin immediately.
- During the Analysis Meeting the participants will discuss the causes of defects and these discussions are another form of interactive learning for the participants. This analysis will later help identify areas for improvement.
- During the Prevention Meeting learning will occur about the probable causes of defects and potential ways to prevent them in future work.

These forms of education or learning are all by-products of the Inspection process. However, Inspections could be used primarily for education. When this choice is taken there are some results we should consider. For example, the apparent costs for Inspections will increase. While the results of the added costs may be beneficial, we should acknowledge the additional cost and corresponding benefit and track them separately, especially when measuring return on investment or costs for defect removal. This tracking might be nothing more than noting that education was a key intent with Inspections and then approximating a fixed percentage of the recorded costs as education and leaving the remainder as the costs of Inspections to find defects.

Why bother, you may ask? If you are introducing Inspections into your organization, there may be skeptics and if the costs are inflated due to education, you may find that the higher costs might be used as an argument to challenge the value of Inspections. Additionally, it might be of interest to understand the costs from both perspectives: early defect removal and education. If you do not have skeptics or you think it adds little value to track separate costs, then simply track Inspections as one cost factor. I'd be the first to agree that one should not make extra work in tracking process data. In both cases, however, you should always note the value of the education that comes from Inspections.

Organizations that have used Inspections primarily for education are often those in a rapid growth pattern. For example, in India the common growth rate of software companies has been 50-100% per year as of this writing. I saw a similar growth in the industry at the time I joined IBM. This type of growth results in a high volume of new people who need to be integrated into the process and given responsibility for work products. Inspections then become a reasonable way for training and educating the new talent. One might conclude that these Inspections have an increased cost in hours per defect due to the training focus, but since this new talent is at the lower end of the pay scale, the real costs in $/defects found may be lower assuming a reasonable effectiveness of defect removal.

I have encountered more than a few times the suggestion that people can learn by simply viewing an Inspection. This is called the *surgical arena approach* where groups of programmers "observe" an Inspection with the intent of trying to receive some knowledge by viewing the product under Inspection. While some organizations have used this approach, I believe that in most cases it might lead to negative results for those being observed. Inspections are not a spectator sport. There are far better ways to get new programmers educated. I have found that this approach leads to more questions than can be answered productively at the Inspection Meeting and the costs tend to be higher. I have not seen good effective detection rates; i.e., >50%, when organizations have taken this approach.

BACK-UP/REPLACEMENT CAPABILITY

Sometimes an organization finds that its knowledge base is too thin. Only a few programmers or perhaps only one will have the required knowledge of a product or key part of the product. In Indian software organizations today it is not unheard of that, in addition to high volume of new hires entering a company, turnover can be as high as 30%. With this amount of movement, the people who were up to speed on work products now must be replaced with others who do not know the work product. Turnover is not limited to India. In Silicon Valley I saw one organization with a 67% turnover in one year.

Where turnover is high, knowledge can be literally walking out the door. To mitigate this risk, some organizations have elected to inspect 100% of all work products. Basically they are providing backup, but the difference is that it is dynamic backup rather than appointing someone to be a new work product owner. In these situations Inspections are used to spread the knowledge as fast and far as possible, just in case someone is needed to help on a work product if a primary knowledgeable person leaves. This education also provides a flexibility to react quicker when there are customer needs.

In other situations, maintenance of a product may be transferred to a new organization or a sub-contractor. Yet in others, such as some sub-contractor shops, the staff may be in high turnover, flux, downsizing, or replacement. These situations require that new people become knowledgeable as backups or replacement owners for the work product. Inspection is one way to create backup/replacement capability. And who knows, defects may be found as a by-product during these Inspections.

The choice for when to consider these types of Inspections is determined by:

- Defect backlogs
- Change request backlogs
- Possibilities for re-engineering
- Risk mitigation for volatile product sections
- Turnover rates
- Recruitment rates

The work products for these Inspections may not always need to be chunked into smaller units since the rates during the meeting may be faster. This should be true for at least some work products, as the primary purpose is quick assimilation of work product understanding versus defect identification. Indeed, it is possible that the work product is stable and defect free when the need for this type of education arises.

The new people will obviously gain the most when an expert is made available for this type of Inspection to help the learning. I question the ability of an Inspection to develop backup capability when an expert or author is not available. However, we may be constrained and can only hope for the best.

We could intentionally use these Inspections to focus on developing backup/replacement capability rather than finding defects, or we can accept the propagated knowledge as a by-product, for example Norris found "Inspections broaden the knowledge base of the project in the group, create potential backup programmers for each module, and better inform the testers of the functions they are to test." [NOR78]

In this use of Inspections, any latent defects found would be an added benefit. It is better when we do both under the eyes of some guiding person with knowledge of the work product being inspected. Regardless, the time costs should reflect the purpose of this type of Inspection; i.e., to train backups.

PROCESS IMPROVEMENT

Another ancillary purpose is process improvement of the Inspection process itself.

While no one probably performs an Inspection solely for the purpose of improving Inspections or other production processes, the data from Inspections can serve improvement in all processes.

Data is gathered during the Inspection and later analyzed to understand the process of doing the Inspection. This data covers all of the activities in the Inspection process from Planning through Rework. The types of data that need to be collected are what is sometimes called "data about the conduct" of an Inspection and includes time spent in Preparation, time spent in the Inspection Meeting, size of the work product, and numbers of defects found by specific classifications. These data can then be analyzed with other product and process life cycle data to determine the effectiveness and efficiency of the Inspection process against organization goals and targets. I will address this topic more fully in Chapter 6: Inspection Data and Chapter 9: Economics of Inspections.

We can determine what we think should be modified in the Inspection process with the use of Inspection data; e.g., is there anything about the Preparation that can be handled differently? We can turn this process and product data over to people who are most knowledgeable about the Inspection process; i.e., the programmers, and ask them how the process should be improved. Thus, we can assess the Inspection process dynamically and modify it dynamically and incrementally to achieve our primary purpose to find more defects faster and cheaper.

Improvement to the Inspection process is one benefit and we should be looking for opportunities to improve. We can also learn how to improve other software processes using the Inspection data, since there are inter-relationships between all life cycle processes and the resultant quality and costs of the product. For example, we may determine that Inspections are not effective because the checklists are not well written or that the previous work product was not well done, such as the Low-level design for the code.

It may seem obvious or assumed that life cycle process improvement was an objective of the original method, but it was not completely stated. It did not take long for others to begin to study and explore improvements in the Inspection process itself and the overall project process; e.g., Frank Buck and Carole Jones, both of whom I will reference in later sections. Fagan later admits to these extensions of purpose in his 1986 paper when he states, "Because of the clear structure the inspection process has brought to the development process, it has enabled study of both itself and the conduct of development." [FAG86]

Fagan does note that defect data can provide information on how to improve quality, but he did not develop the idea of process improvement sufficiently. He notes only that:

- "To increase their error detection in the inspections, the inspection team should first study the ranked distributions of error types found by recent inspections." and
- "Obtain a suitable quantity of errors, and analyze them by type and origin, cause, and salient indicative clues. With this information, an inspection specification may be construed. This specification can be amended and improved in light of new experience and serve as an on-going directive to focus the attention and conduct of inspection teams."

I often see that when Inspections are practiced in safe and supportive environments that people quickly begin to see the shortcomings in other parts of the organization's and project's processes. In so doing, they begin to suggest improvements in these related processes. When this occurs we see the full potential of Inspections and process improvement.

The first publicly published use of Inspections for process improvement is Carole Jones' article [JON85] in the IBM Systems Journal where she discusses the relationships between Defect Prevention and Inspections. While others, like Buck [BUC81a], may have also been using Inspections for process improvement, we have no earlier public documentation. Shortly afterward Gilb publicly took up the Defect Prevention theme in his practice and training for Inspections, and he documented his views in his book on Inspections. [GIL93] I will discuss more on this subject in Chapter 6: Causal Analysis.

EARLY PRODUCT QUALITY VISIBILITY

There is clearly a relationship between defect removal by Inspections and the latent defects that reflect the product quality. Specifically, we can look at the articles of Fagan [FAG86], Barnard [BAR94], Buck [BUC81a], Christenson [CHR90] among others for indications of final product quality being determined from the results of Inspections. More will be discussed on this topic in Chapter 9.

Fagan stated that Inspections would provide an early progress indicator of milestone achievement. This was quite an accomplishment in the 1972-76 timeframe. Also, as we learned in the VTAM study, the time required in later life cycle stages could be reduced as a result of Inspections. "Since individually trackable modules of reasonably well-known size can be counted as they pass through each of these checkpoints, the percentage completion of the project against schedule can be continuously and easily tracked." [FAG76] Thus we see an early use of earned value tracking using Inspection results.

PRODUCT RE-DEVELOPMENT

Products with multiple releases can have high volumes of change in some areas. Additionally some code units can have high defect rates when the product is in customer use. These two forms of change or volatility may suggest units that should be re-engineered. Each new change can increase the complexity of a unit that may already be too complex. Thus the probability of new defects can be high in these volatile units.

Management tends not to like to re-engineer a work product, since this appears as additional cost and the return on investment cannot often be seen. We can help management see the opportunity for re-engineering using Inspection results as one input to consider. For example, Doolan found that, for older products under maintenance and upgrade, Inspections are "a very good mechanism for highlighting and prioritizing candidate areas for enhancement." [DOO92] Whether the suggestion to re-engineer is accepted, even with good data and analysis, is a different issue, but Inspections definitely can provide knowledge about work products that should be considered for re-engineering.

BUILDING TEAM SPIRIT

During the VTAM study in 1972 we saw that Inspections facilitated team spirit. This by-product tends to repeat in projects where Inspections are practiced in a supported and safe environment. Almost 10 years later I saw the Guidelines for Technical reviews of Software Products from the Hartford Engineering Development Laboratory where it was stated "The review process also promotes team building. It becomes one of the first steps toward establishing a good development team, by substituting an environment where programmers work alone throughout their career, for a programming team environment in which each individual feels free to discuss and critique everyone else's program. Implicit in the concept of a team is the notion of working closely together, reading each other's work, sharing responsibilities, learning each other's idiosyncrasies both on a technical and personal level, and accepting altogether as a group shared responsibility for the product where each member can expect similar rewards if the project is a success and similar penalties if the project fails." [WIL82] I thought Wilburn captured this well.

I do not know anyone who comes to work with the intent of making defects or having made a defect, passes it on without correction. People take pride in doing good work, but the system sometimes gets in their way. One result of Inspections will be that the programmers will see themselves as more professional in their work. They will see Inspections as a way to improve their work, increasing their sense of competence and control.

Inspections bring people together and when the behavior is collaborative, team members get to know each other quickly. They learn each other's strengths and weaknesses. They can learn to support each other in the interest of delivering a better product to the customer.

When the team is empowered to make improvements to the process based on Inspection results, their pride in doing it right begins to visibly grow. Everyone seems to win: the team members, management, the customer, and even the shareholders.

2.6 Where Do Inspections Fit in the Software Development Process?

There are typically between two to six classic stages in the production phase of software projects. Each of these stages may produce work products, including subsets, delivered at the completion of the stage as a result of activities within the stage. Work product subsets are typically completed concurrently during a project stage.

The question as to where Inspections fit into these stages is answered simply by saying that any work product, which has reached a milestone of completion or readiness, can be inspected. By doing so we gather data and ensure that it is an effectively verified work product, or portion of a work product, that represents a stable base for the next stage in the process. Defects that may have gotten into a work product are not allowed to leak and percolate across the subsequent stages in the process. They are removed with Inspections.

What this means, for example, is that at the end of the requirements stage we can inspect the requirements specifications before we begin to design using those requirements; and that we can inspect each design document after it is completed and before we refine the design into its next physical transformation; e.g., the code. We can inspect each code unit at the point of its completion. We can inspect each test case before beginning the test activities. We can inspect each external user publication related to the delivered product. Refer again to Figure 2.5 for the transformations of the product across the life cycle with the noted Inspection activities. While there are advantages to inspecting a fully completed work product, we do not always need to wait for a work product to be fully completed before we do an Inspection.

In essence we can and should give consideration to inspecting any work product produced by a group or an individual. We can stabilize the product quality by not allowing defects to proceed down through the life cycle and potentially to the user. We basically establish the applicability of the work product for the next stage in the life cycle before moving it into that stage.

Use of Inspections does not necessarily mean all defects will have been removed. It does mean there will be fewer defects remaining and that, if we performed a capable Inspection, we have reasonably removed all we are capable of removing under the system conditions that exist in the organization at that time.

During Inspections we are able to determine which parts of the work product should be reworked before going into the next stage of development. Additionally we may choose to re-inspect these reworked work products to ensure their quality after rework. Two Inspection activities (Rework and Follow-up) allow us to literally pull a work product "off the development line", rework it at the most appropriate point in the life cycle, and ensure that a final product with a higher level of quality is shipped to the testers and ultimately to the users.

2.7 The Costs of Inspections

There is a cost for every activity during a project life cycle. The cost is determined by many factors; e.g., capability of the programmers performing the activity, the defined process for the activity, the stability of the input. Inspections also have a cost. So the obvious question will be, "Why spend more when we don't have enough time as it is?" The answer lies in a shift in thinking.

Time spent on Inspections is an investment.
You inspect now, you invest now,
and then you reap the benefits down the line.

As noted, all who give Inspections a fair try are seeing the benefits.

This cost will also vary by the stage in which the Inspection is held. For example, during code, an Inspection may cost 50-80 programmer-hours for every 1000 LOC or Function Point equivalent. In the design stage we might see as much as 50 hours being required for every equivalent 1000 LOC of estimated function. For documents, we can see a cost of one hour for every 2-10 pages depending on how the documents are written.

When we perform Inspections we are spending resources earlier in the development process than we were before. The payback comes later in the project life cycle in improved testing, a shorter time period for the project, and lower maintenance costs. Thus Inspections are a form of investment, and as always with investments, the time or money may not be available when we most need or should apply them. There may be resistance to spending time and money earlier, especially when the organization management and members may not yet have fully bought into the value of Inspections.

This concern of early expenditure should only occur when Inspections are used for the first time and when a product has a committed delivery date that is too close to the introduction of Inspections in an organization. What we need to do in this latter case is reevaluate the project schedules to understand if there might be any impact to delivery dates due to training and startup costs. If there is schedule impact, we might choose to defer the introduction to another project and inspect this product in the next release. If we can show that schedules will not be impacted, then we can proceed with full force.

Schedules are very rarely impacted when Inspections are introduced, but there can be cases when Inspections are introduced too late in the project's life cycle. Obviously the best point to introduce Inspections is at project startup, but we may not always have this choice.

We should note that the tradeoff of the cost to find the defects early with Inspections or to find them later in test and with the user should almost always be a compelling argument for management. When a defect is found in test or by a user, the costs typically increase roughly 10 times and 100 times respectively. Figure 1.3 shows these cost relationships.

The management and technical team should also learn to view the cost to produce a product from the global perspective, which includes the cost of test and maintenance, and as they do so they will learn to accept the cost of Inspections at the appropriate time in the development cycle. For example, there will be added costs during the design stage for an Inspection and if design is not allocated sufficient time to include the Inspections, they will not happen. The need to inspect for design defects will be pushed off to code and test where more time will be required than if the design Inspections had been held. After management understands the payback potentials with Inspections, they are quick to accept and support them.

Once the cost question is removed from management's thinking, the time needed up front in a project is no longer a concern.

Later in Chapter 9, we will see that the cost can be controlled and that once the Inspection process becomes capable the costs can be further reduced while maintaining effectiveness. Always we first work toward effectiveness and then efficiency. We will be constantly tuning our Inspection process as we gather data about the process itself. This data will lead us to continuing improvement in both effectiveness and costs.

A question often asked is how many defects will be found for each hour invested. The numbers will vary for many reasons, but they are always less than the cost of finding the defects in test or later. See Table 2.1 for some publicly documented sources.

Do defects multiply if they are not removed in early work products? That is, if a defect in the requirements specification is allowed to propagate, will more defects be made in design and code? We do not have empirical evidence of this phenomenon, but it seems logical that a defect in requirements will amplify misinterpretation during design. Likewise a defective design statement will probably amplify misinterpretations during coding. Hence defects can multiply.

Numerous publications document the effectiveness and cost reductions resulting from Inspections starting with Fagan in 1976. [FAG76] [BUC81a] [DOB81] [MCC81] [PEL82] [KIT83] [ACK89] [GRA97] [MCC01]

COMPANY	HOURS/DEFECT	REFERENCE
AT&T	.67 – 1.4	[ACK89]
ICL	1.2 - 1.6	[KIT86]
JPL	1.5 - 2.1	[BUS90]
Bell-Northern	Les than .4	[RUS91]
HP	.2	[BLA91]
Bull	1.43	[WEL93]
ITT Industries	~1	[TAC99]

Examples of Cost in Hours/Defect During Code Inspections
Table 2.1

Let's look at some of the early studies pro and con.

FAGAN'S STUDY

Fagan's article was the first that publicly shared data showing that Inspections provided a cost and also a productivity advantage. Fagan makes two points in his paper that show there is a productivity advantage.
In the quotes below it is key to note that:

- "I_1 and I_2" in Fagan's article are Low-level design and code Inspections respectively
- Fagan uses the term efficiency where effectiveness is the actual measure as I discussed earlier.

"Because errors were identified and corrected in groups at I_1 and I_2, rather than found one-by-one during subsequent work and handled at the higher cost incumbent in later rework, the overall amount of error rework was minimized, even within the coding operation. Expressed differently, considering the inclusion of *all* I_1 time, I_2 time, and resulting error rework time (with the usual coding and unit test time in the total time to complete the operation), a net saving resulted when this figure was compared to the no-Inspection case. This net saving translated into a 23 percent increase in the productivity of the coding operation alone. Productivity in later levels was also increased because there was less error rework in these levels due to the effect of Inspections, but the increase was not measured directly." [FAG76]

This is a key finding, as it shows that we may not need to wait until test begins to see productivity increases and cost reductions. While the coding activity is only one segment of overall project costs, a 23% reduction in the cost of coding is significant, as Fagan notes.

Later in the article Fagan recounts an example of Inspections performed at Aetna Life and Casualty on application code versus the systems code in the VTAM case study.

"An automated estimating program which is used to produce the normal program development time estimates for all the Corporate Data Processing department's projects predicted that designing, coding, and unit testing this project would require 62 programmer days. In fact, the time actually taken was 46.5 programmer days including inspection meeting time. The resulting saving in programmer resources was 25 percent. The Inspections were obviously very thorough when judged by the inspection error detection efficiency of 82 percent."

This may not be fully conclusive evidence for all readers, but it was a finding consistent with what we found in the VTAM study and significant in its own right.

MYER'S STUDY

Myers is one of the few documented less than fully positive views about the cost effectiveness of Inspections. In his "controlled" study in 1978 he compared three approaches:

1. Computer-based testing where the tester has access to only the program's specification
2. Computer-based testing where the tester has access to the program's specification and source language listing
3. Non-computer based testing by teams of programmers employing the walkthrough/inspection method

While he never defines what he means by Inspection or how the inspectors were trained, etc., he concluded "One result of the experiment is that the three original methods are equal in terms of error-detection capability, although the walkthrough method was not as cost-effective as the computer-based methods in a 'unit testing' environment under the condition that the person doing the testing was not the programmer of the program. To repeat an earlier warning, this does not imply that the walkthrough technique, in and of itself, is not cost-effective; experience has shown the opposite to be the case." [MYE78]

I could argue that he did not really use Inspections, since he keeps using the term walkthrough. But he does not clearly state what he used as a walkthrough process either. Nonetheless, his study stands as another view. To my knowledge, it has never been duplicated, and 1978 is a long time ago.

FREEDMAN'S ANALYSIS

In the Freedman and Weinberg book on Inspections they note that "In larger systems, where accurate records have been kept, projects with a full system of reviews report a ten times reduction in the number of errors reaching each stage of testing. The concomitant cost reduction for testing runs between 50 and 80 percent, even when the cost of reviewing is added to test costs." [FRE90] "Reviews also have a very favorable effect on *maintenance* costs. A typical program that has been thoroughly reviewed during development and for which maintenance changes are also reviewed shows a five to one reduction in maintenance costs." Now this would be appreciable on most projects!

2.8 Differences from Manufacturing Inspections

Software Inspections have their genesis in the inspections performed in manufacturing. Inspections in manufacturing have been used for a much longer period. Harmer E. Davis et al., in their book on the *"Testing Of Engineering Materials"* draw the distinction between testing and Inspections by stating that "testing refers to the physical performance of operations, the tests, to determine the quantitative measure of certain properties. Inspections have to do with the observations of the processes and products of manufacture or construction for the purpose of ensuring the presence of desired qualities." [DAV55]

This is an important distinction and consequently requires that we perform both Inspections and Test for three reasons:

1. It may be difficult for some products to inspect for all quantitative measures; e.g., performance, usability. This may be more easily done in test.
2. The Inspection process may not yet be at a high enough effectiveness. Too many defects may leak into test, and test can find some of these defects before delivery to users.
3. Test effectiveness will probably never be 100% except for trivial solutions. This makes defect removal in test increasingly costly to remove each remaining defect, especially when few latent defects remain. The cost for incremental defect removal increases with each defect found in test.

Given the distinction between Inspections and test in manufacturing, we see that we have a different but similar situation in software. Software testing organizations do indeed try to determine quantitative measures of certain properties; e.g., response time, storage utilization, recovery procedures, functional capability, etc. However, for too many software organizations today, testing is still used to ensure the presence of a level of quality by "testing the defects out."

As noted earlier, Inspections help to control work product quality by the application of certain criteria, which have been pre-established via checklists. Inspections also involve, as Davis says, the rejection of substandard material. In the case of software, however, it is not so much the rejection; i.e., discarding of substandard material, but it is the reworking of substandard elements before allowing them to continue on through the project life cycle.

Testing is concerned with determining the existence of quality versus trying to control quality. The control of quality should occur at the time of development with good methods and processes, then followed by Inspections where necessary. During test we should determine the quality level of the available product regardless of the implication of the results. In some cases these results will tell us to not deliver the product as it exists, but to rework it and then to retest before delivery to the customers. Unfortunately, project management does not often enough take this choice.

ANECDOTE

SOFTWARE IS NOT LIKE MANUFACTURING

We were once commissioned to teach Inspections to a software organization, but literally one day before the training was to begin we received a call from the software process lead who informed us that the senior manager did not want to proceed with the training. When we asked why, we were told the senior management was not convinced that this would be a good use of money or time.

We asked if we could talk with the senior manager. After a bit of negotiations we reminded them that there was a penalty clause for such a late cancellation. We were told we could meet with the senior manager at 7:00 AM the next day. Fortunately they were near to our office and the next day was the original planned first day of training. So hoping for the best, we had the meeting.

The senior manager's issue was straightforward — his site was a manufacturing site and he had stopped doing Inspections on his assembly line 3 years ago, so why should he pay to have college graduates learn to remove defects with Inspections when his people in manufacturing already knew how to build it right the first time, and many of them had not graduated from high school.

After I explained that we in the software community were not yet that capable with our production processes and that we had a way to go and a lot to learn, he accepted and we held the training and the organization was successful in using Inspections.

Anecdote 2.1

We see then that Software Inspections are not really so different from manufacturing Inspections in concept. It is interesting to see that some manufacturing organizations have been able to remove the need for Inspections, since they are focused on building the product right the first time using good production processes. Perhaps some day we too can remove the need for full Inspections in the software process. More will be discussed on this subject in Chapter 14: Inspections Future.

2.9 Inspections Compared to Walkthroughs and Reviews

Mike Fagan in his article in the 1976 IBM System Journal showed two charts comparing walkthroughs and Inspections. [FAG76] See Figures 2.6 and 2.7. Others have also documented similar conclusions. [ACK89]

We see in this evaluation that walkthroughs are a less disciplined method and the suggestion is that they will be a less effective process for defect removal. This evaluation could also be applied to reviews, as defined in Yourdan's book [YOR79] and by Freedman and Weinberg [FRE90].

Inspections		**Walkthroughs**	
Process Operations	Objectives	Process Operations	Objectives
1. Overview	Education (Group)		
2. Preparation	Education (Individual)	1. Preparation	Education (Individual)
3. Inspection	Find errors (Group)	2. Walkthrough	Education (Group) Discuss design alternatives Find errors
4. Rework	Fix problems		
5. Follow-up	Ensure all fixes correctly installed		

Inspections Process Activities Compared to Walkthroughs [FAG76]
Figure 2.6

There are many other methods for defect removal used across the software community: walkthroughs, reviews, peer groupings, etc. All of these have a process that is less repeatable than that of Inspections.

This is due to factors like:

- Lack of a defined process
- Not requiring formal training for the participants
- Lack of consistent checklists to evaluate the process and product
- Not requiring the capture of relevant data and information for later analysis
- Lack of causal analysis
- Lack of dynamically re-evaluating the process itself to determine if it can be made more effective
- Lack of feedback about the defects and the conduct of the defect removal activity, etc.

Inspection is a term that has many meanings, as I noted earlier. The same problem is true of walkthroughs. To generalize, however, walkthroughs are a process of "walking through" the work product. This can be done in a cursory manner or by "playing computer" in which the participants walk through the work product step by step. If it is code, the team emulates what a computer does from start to finish with a program. This can actually be amusing when reviewers play the parts of computer registers and one reviewer acts as the central processor by executing each instruction and asking others what their state changes are. See Citron for an example of walking through a work product while playing computer. [CIT84]

In the original studies, when Inspections were compared to walkthroughs, it was found that aside from the differences in methods of performing Inspections and walkthroughs, Inspections were indeed more effective in finding defects. Much of this effectiveness can be attributed to the added formalities of Inspections as seen in Fagan's comparison shown in Figure 2.7. [FAG76] Compared to walkthroughs Fagan calculated Inspections found 38% more defects.

Properties	Inspection	Walkthrough
1. Formal moderator training	Yes	No
2. Definite participant roles	Yes	No
3. Who "drives" the inspection or walkthrough	Moderator	Owner of material (Designer or coder)
4. Use "How To Find Errors" checklists	Yes	No
5. Use distribution of error types to look for	Yes	No
6. Follow-up to reduce bad fixes	Yes	No
7. Less future errors because of detailed error feedback to individual programmer	Yes	Incidental
8. Improve inspection efficiency from analysis of results	Yes	No
9. Analysis of data → process problems → improvements	Yes	No

Inspections Process Properties Compared to Walkthroughs [FAG76]
Figure 2.7

2.10 Effectiveness and Efficiency

Let us now take a look at the distinction between effectiveness and efficiency. They are different and both have business; i.e., economic, value to organizations practicing Inspections.

EFFECTIVENESS

Simply stated, effectiveness of Inspections is the percentage of defects removed by Inspections compared to the total sum of defects eventually found by Inspections, test, and in use by the customers. Data on the customer-found defects may require a longer period of time to acquire and may never be complete. In some cases the best we may be able to do is to extrapolate from a shorter period of customer use and assume a ratio for the entire set of defects that remain latent in the product.

For example, taking the first 3-6 months of customer use and resultant defect data and applying a model of distribution based on history in the company or organization for similar projects, then extrapolations of the total shipped defects can be made. It can never be precise, but it can be a reasonable calculation. The goodness of the extrapolations is dependent on the history available from comparable products and use of the products by customers.

Regarding the true volume of latent defects shipped with a product to users, in most cases this can never really be determined. We do not yet have the ability to decisively determine the real number of defects shipped with a product. We can project total defects based on other characteristics in the process or we can assume zero defects based on other process data and patterns, but we cannot prove it. For example, we can analyze error depletion curves prior to delivery to make a prediction of latent defects after delivery. I will discuss more on effectiveness in Chapter 9.

EFFICIENCY

Efficiency of Inspections is represented by various cost relationships; e.g.,

- $ spent / defect found in Inspections
- $ for Inspections / total project costs; this is a subset of Cost of Quality (COQ) measures
- $ ratio of cost of finding defects in Inspection to cost of defects found in test and by the customers
- hours spent / defect found in Inspections

The use of the terms *effectiveness* and *efficiency* of Inspections including the relationship between them is not consistently applied in the software community. Some of this misinterpretation derives from Fagan's article where he refers to effectiveness as *efficiency*. This was because a focus at the time was on costs.

If we go back to first principles; i.e., use Inspections to find defects earlier because the costs for defect removal are reduced, then this is a measure of the efficiency. Defects are a cost driver to a project; i.e., the more defects the higher the cost to remove them. Therefore, the lower the cost to remove defects the more efficient we are.

Effectiveness has a relationship to efficiency in the project; i.e., if Inspections find more defects as a percentage of the total found and the cost to remove defects with Inspections is lower, then a higher Inspection effectiveness should be desirable since it drives the costs lower for defect removal on a project and hence also improves efficiency of the project.

While Inspections have historically proven to be more efficient, the technology of producing software is changing, so too may the understanding of where and how to best remove defects. Some defects may not only be cheaper to find in a test environment, but some may not even be able to be reasonably found with Inspections.

For example, the use of visual modeling tools and code generators; e.g., Visual Basic, PowerBuilder, JBuilder causes us to re-think what is the best way to remove defects. We need to revisit whether we should still read the code as in traditional Inspections or to map the code while reading the screen while executing the code. Mapping is a technique of keeping two documents in synch while reading the primary document during the Inspection.

2.11 Defect Detection and Defect Prevention

It is the nature of Inspections that they remove defects that have already been injected. Inspections do not prevent defects from coming into a work product. Inspections are a post facto action. This is to say that if the process of transformation to a work product; e.g., from design to code, is flawed and defects are injected, then an Inspection after the transformation can serve us best by early defect removal. But this is detection, not prevention.

Inspections detect defects, and at the same time prevent defects from moving into later project cycles. Over time the Inspection process will be preventing defects from going to the users, but this is a result of corrective actions taken due to the defects injected during transformation and detected during the Inspection. Transferring the knowledge of how and which types of defects are injected into other process artifacts such as templates could help prevent defects.

Additionally we would expect that Inspection checklists, if refined through data analysis, will begin to incorporate some preventive knowledge into the future development of products and consequently we should see fewer errors getting through the production process. This then will be a defect prevention consequence of the Inspection process over time, even though Inspections are clearly focusing, at least initially, on defect detection. But we should take steps to integrate this knowledge into the checklists to improve the programmer's expertise. I will explore Defect Prevention in relationship to Inspections in Chapter 7: Causal Analysis.

2.12 Feedback, Feed-forward, and Control

Feedback occurs immediately during the Inspection for the Producer who can quickly integrate this knowledge to avoid similar defects on the next work the Producer is assigned. Feedback will effect the same process that was just performed and analyzed, but in the future. After the Inspection, each defect can be analyzed in the Analysis Meeting, an extension to the Inspection process, to provide feedback that can be used by the organization to learn and improve.

Feed-forward occurs when analysis is provided to re-inspect, to re-engineer, or to focus testing on error prone areas. Feed-forward is usually directed to management, as the information may result in a plan change; e.g., Re-Inspection, changes to test plans. Feed-forward should also be directed to the project team members. Feed-forward will effect a different process on the same project and can be the immediate next process; e.g., unit test after a code Inspection.

Feed-forward, when used with defect injection/detection analysis, can help predict the volume of defects that might be shipped to the users. I will discuss more on defect prediction in Chapter 9. Feedback, feed-forward, and control will be derived from the analysis of the data captured at the Inspection. See Figure 2.8.

Feedback includes:

- Fixing the defect (product problem)
- Fixing the process
- Learning by inspectors
- Modifying selection criteria for work products to be inspected

Feed-forward includes:

- Analysis of data to re-engineer

- Test changes
- Re-Inspection recommendations
- Changes to test processes after Inspections; e.g., removal of unit test based on Inspection results

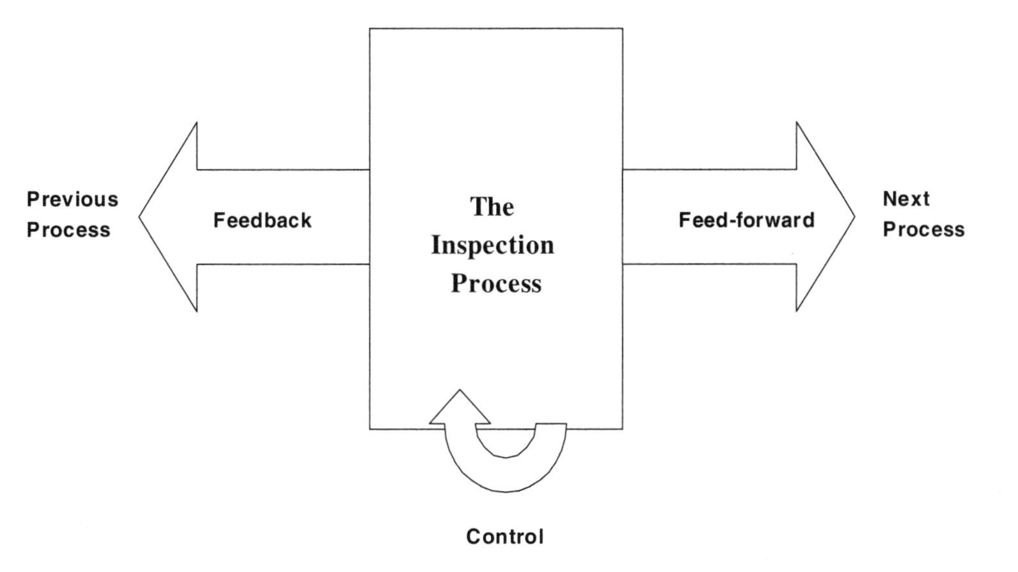

Feedback, Feed-forward, and Control on Processes
Figure 2.8

Control occurs when real-time actions are taken based on the analysis, which affect the very process we are presently performing or about to perform; e.g., is Preparation sufficient, is the reading rate appropriate, was the Inspection Meeting rate within bounds of expectation?

Control includes:

- Changing the pace of the Inspection Meeting
- Postponing the Inspection Meeting based on Preparation input

2.13 Characteristics That Make Inspections Easier to Deploy

Not all organizations are the same, for sure. For some it will be much easier to deploy Inspections successfully and for others it will be more difficult. The following characteristics in an organization facilitate success for deployment:

- A quality and process culture exists
- Open yet directive leadership

- Minimal organization politics
- No fear of Inspections
- Homogeneous projects
  - Size
  - Complexity
  - Technology
  - Domain
- An Inspection champion
- Reasonable time constraints
- Effective planning
- Budget allocation and resources assigned
- Sponsorship
- A team work culture
- Learning culture

It will help if organizations understand the risks they have for deploying Inspections and then take risk mitigation and management actions to manage Inspections to success despite the risks.

2.14 What Inspections Are Not

I've discussed what Inspections are and some benefits that accrue with their use. While practices that differentiate an Inspection from other review methods can help us know why we should use Inspections, it is important sometimes to look at Inspections from the other side.

So briefly, Inspections are not:

- A review of the style of a work product
- A review of the Producer, and especially not a means to evaluate the Producer by management
- An impromptu meeting; it is a scheduled meeting with resource considerations to enable effectiveness
- A casual or informal meeting; there is structure and rigor for a purpose
- Typically the time or place to fix defects or discuss possible solutions
- Free! But they do yield a high return on investment
- A vehicle for shifting responsibility to inspectors for quality of the work product
- Quality Assurance performed at the end of development

2.15 Characteristics of Inspections

Regardless of what one calls them, if they look like a duck, walk like a duck, and quack like a duck, then there is a very high probability that they are a duck.

The following are the Duck Characteristics of Inspections:

- Budget is allocated to perform Inspections

- A defined process is followed
- Use of peers who have sufficient domain knowledge of the product
- Use of peers who have sufficient knowledge of the development environment and related tools, processes, and methods
- Entry criteria are defined
- Work product Inspections are planned as a vital part in the project plan
- Adequate time is provided for all inspectors
- Checklists are used to focus defect identification and detection
- Producer is a participant during the Inspection Meeting
  - NOTE: In Solo:Inspections, the Producer is available to the inspector for any questions, but is not at the Inspection Meeting
- Roles are defined and assigned to other participants, as appropriate
- A Moderator coordinates
- Primary purpose is to find defects
- Data is gathered about defects and the conduct of the Inspection
- Exit criteria are defined
- Defects are analyzed and the analysis is used
- Defects are repaired

2.16 Summary of Benefits from Inspections

The following benefits will be seen as a result of good Inspection practice:

- Early removal of defects
- Improved schedule predictability
- Improved quality delivered to the users
- Cost reduction in test and maintenance
- Earlier delivery of committed products
- More satisfied customers
- More satisfied employees
- Education and spreading of knowledge
- Improved processes
- More business

These benefits in Figure 2.9 by example reflect the Deming cycle.

Deming's Chain Reaction

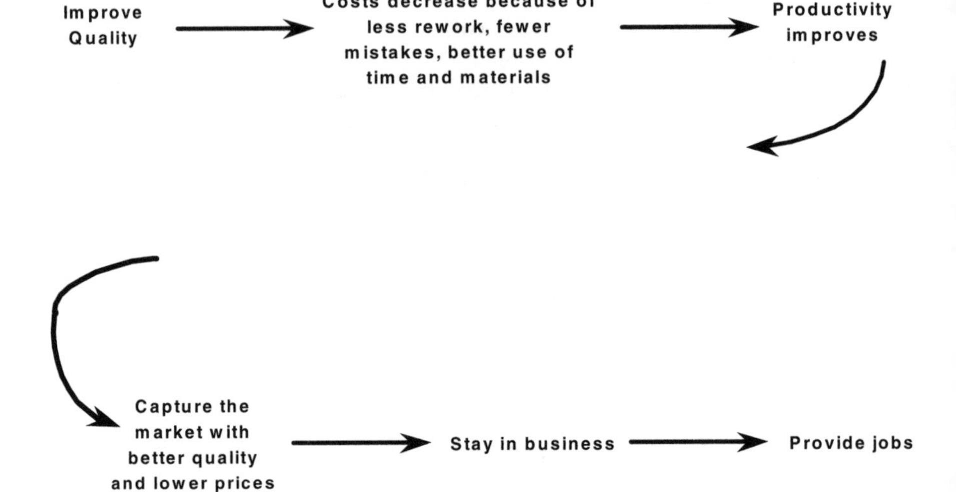

Deming's Chain Reaction [DEM92]
Figure 2.9

End Quote:

"We can conclude from experience that inspections increase productivity and improve final program quality. Furthermore, improvements in process control and project management are enabled by inspections."
M.E. Fagan, 1976

CHAPTER 3

THE INSPECTION PROCESS

"It's not the products but the processes that create products that bring companies long-term success."
Michael Hammer and James Champy

3.1 Introduction

This chapter is written in the format of procedures, because:

- The Inspection process is best performed when guided by clear procedures
- Reading the procedures will enable understanding of the Inspection process
- The procedures can be directly reused or modified for application by the reader

The procedures that follow in this chapter are written as a complete package for all Inspection activities. While the procedures are in alignment with IEEE STD 1028-1998, they are different.

The intent is to keep the procedures useable and complete in reference to the original method, IEEE definition, and proven evolutions. Therefore, there may be more in this set than some readers require. A scissors icon will show suggested tailoring options.

Readers can further tailor or modify the procedures, as they deem appropriate for their organization. I recommend that the procedures be put on a web facility; hyperlinks will make navigation easier for the users.

More is provided in this chapter than you will need in your procedures, for this chapter is written to also provide explanation and notes to assist in understanding the intent of each procedure.

I suggest that the reader first read the Introduction sections to each Inspection activity and then follow up with a complete reading of the procedures. This two-step approach will facilitate integrating the material for use in the reader's organization.

The procedures are written for teams of participants during an Inspection. While these procedures are consistent with Fagan and IEEE, they are extensions to both these definitions for Software Inspections.

Not discussed directly in this chapter, but introduced later in the book as evolutions of traditional Inspections are:

- 1:1 Inspections where there is only one inspector with the Producer
- Solo:Inspections where the Producer does not participate directly in Inspection activities and there is only one inspector

Each procedure is written in the following format:

INTRODUCTION

This section gives a brief explanation of the corresponding Inspection activity and its related procedure. This section is always optional for an organization to include or not in its tailored procedures. In this book the Introduction sections are for expository reasons.

Responsible Individual:

This section identifies who is the primary responsible person for performing this activity.

Other Roles:

This section identifies other individuals or roles involved in the Inspection activity.

Entry Criteria:

This section lists and defines the relevant entry criteria for the Inspection activity. If the entry criteria are not satisfied, then the activity's tasks will be executed at risk and may fail to perform to the full desired intent for the defined tasks or may perform ineffectively.

Tasks to be performed:

This section lists each of the key tasks to be performed within the Inspection activity.

Validation/Verification

This section lists the relevant validation/verification tasks to be performed to assure control of the tasks to be performed.

Exit Criteria:

This section lists and defines the relevant exit criteria, which must be satisfied before the activity is considered completely performed. If an exit criterion is not satisfied, then the work product may be at risk for remaining latent defects and the next activity may be at risk in how well it can be performed.

For all Activities the Exit Criteria will include *measurements* that should be considered.

NOTES: When a NOTE is provided it is information for the reader. It can be deleted from the organization procedures.

3.2 Flow of the Inspection process

The flow in Figure 3.1 shows all the activities in the evolved Inspection process, including the Defect Prevention additions.

In addition to these Inspection process activities there are two others that do not occur as discrete process steps but rather as continuous activities within each process step, as appropriate. These are:

- Data recording and reports
- Inspection process monitoring

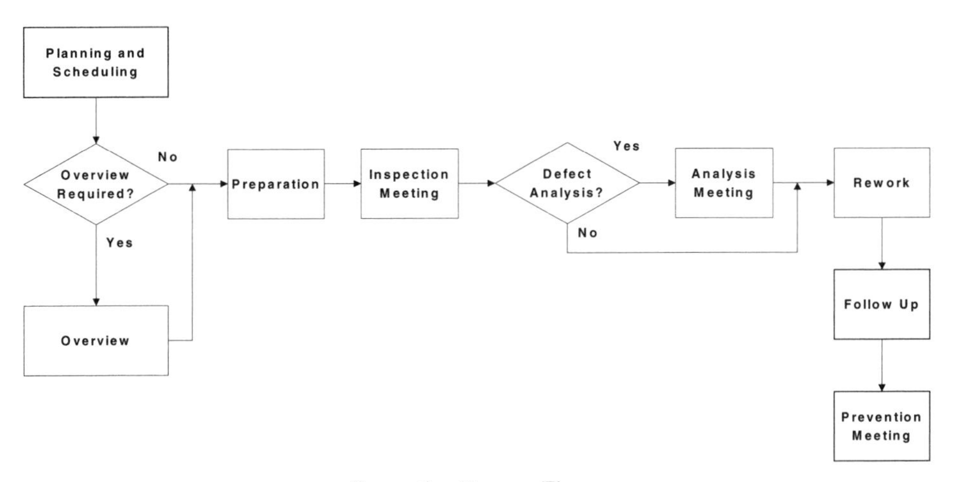

Inspection Process Flow
Figure 3.1

It should be noted that the Inspection process flow now has ten activities compared to the five in the original method as noted in Chapter 2. Planning and Scheduling, Analysis Meeting, and Prevention Meeting have been added. Additionally there are two activities that are performed throughout the Inspection Process for Inspection Monitoring and for Data Recording and Reports.

While the process at large includes Re-inspection of work products based on the results of the Inspection Meeting, this activity is not shown in this flow, since it results in a recursion of the Inspection Process Flow. Re-inspections are fully discussed in Chapter 8 as a separate topic.

3.3 Planning and Scheduling

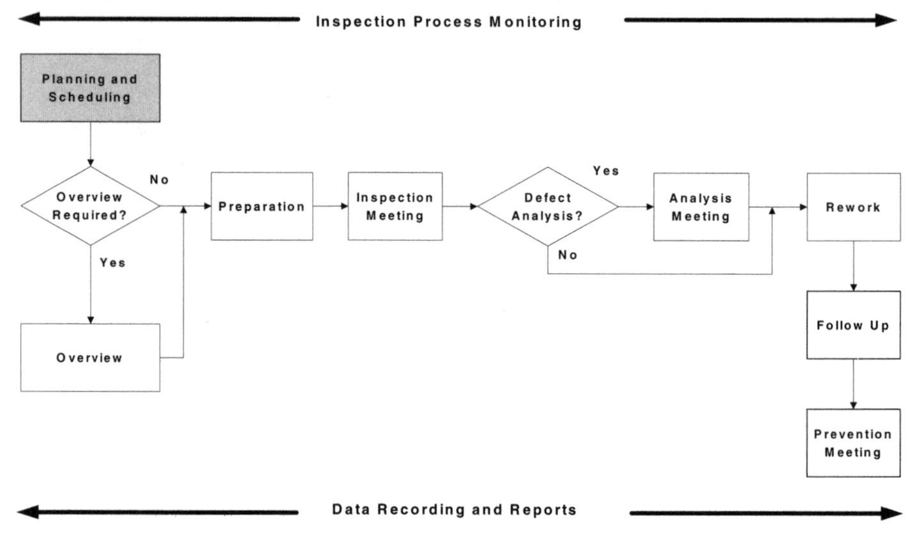

Activity 1: Planning and Scheduling
Figure 3.2

INTRODUCTION

All project plans exist at three levels of knowledge as the project progresses:

- Those things that are unknown
- Those things that are becoming known
- Those things that are known

This concept is attributed to Jack Nevison. [NEV98] The view is that plan details reveal themselves to the planner as a rolling wave. In the beginning not all can be known, seen, or understood in sufficient detail for the project. The details of the plan and revised knowledge come with time. Therefore, some decisions and details should naturally be deferred to a later date in the project. As the project proceeds the waves continue and more becomes known with each wave.

The Project Lead must plan which Inspections are to be performed at the initial stages of the project.

With respect to this plan we can say the following for Inspections later in the project:

- What are unknown are the actual dates when particular Inspections will occur. The actual dates will become known as we approach the completion of various planned work products.
- What is becoming known is the amount of time we should allocate for Inspections.
- By the conclusion of the project all will be known; e.g., specific dates and volumes inspected.

Therefore during the project one will always be moving from the becoming known and unknown states to the known state. This implies that Inspections that are known should be both planned and scheduled. With planning we can identify what we know and what is becoming known, and with scheduling we will eventually address what was unknown during planning. We can plan for the Inspections that will be needed and for the boundaries of time that may be needed to perform the Inspections. Later we can schedule the specific Inspections when the probable dates are more clearly in sight; i.e., when the work product will be complete and sufficiently stable.

The complete planning and scheduling for Inspections occurs in two stages:

- When the Project Lead defines the initial project plan
- When specific work products approach Inspection readiness

The first type is called **Inspection Planning** and the second **Inspection Scheduling**. Both are required, but they occur at different times during the software project.

Responsible Individual:

Inspection Planning:

The Project Lead or whoever is responsible for managing the work for a specified software project is responsible for performing the activities for Inspection Planning.

Inspection Scheduling:

The Project Lead is responsible for requesting, selecting, or assigning Moderators when a work product approaches Inspection readiness, for ensuring the work product will be ready for Inspection, for ensuring that the participants are made available, and for making known to a qualified Moderator that an Inspection is to be scheduled.

Other Roles:

The Moderator is responsible with the Project Lead for completing Inspection Scheduling. This includes agreeing to a specific date for the Inspection Meeting, assuring entry criteria are satisfied, completing all logistics requirements for the Inspection, and scheduling the participants and Inspection activities.

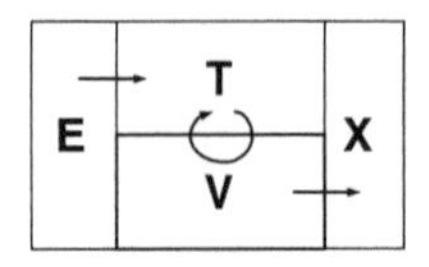

Entry Criteria:

Inspection Planning:

1. A policy exists for Inspections in the project's organization.
2. Planning procedures, including planning for Inspections exist.
3. A project begins and includes the requirement to plan for Inspections.
4. Work product types to be inspected are identified in the project plan.
5. Well-defined work product completion or readiness criteria are available.
6. Initial estimates are provided for the size of the work products to be inspected.
7. Expected project participants have been trained or a training plan is defined.
8. Goals and targets have been established for the volume or percentage of work products to be inspected.

Inspection Scheduling:

1. A work product is approaching Inspection readiness.
2. Resources are available.
3. The Project Lead makes a request to a Moderator for an Inspection or set of Inspections.

Tasks to be performed:

Inspection Planning:

1. Determine what will be inspected:

In the early stages of the project, the Project Lead identifies the work products that will be inspected. If this does not include all work, the selection criteria must be defined. Later, during Inspection Scheduling, this will enable consistent decisions on each work product to be inspected as it becomes ready. See the list of work products defined in Appendix B: Materials for work products to consider. As the project plan is revised, so must the Inspection planning be re-planned or reconfirmed.

2. Estimate resources for Inspections and allocate budget:

The numbers in Table 3.1 are a reasonable set to use when first starting Inspections. They are nominal rates established through experience and from Software Inspections literature. They are not sacrosanct. They are only guidelines to get started. The rates will change as your software organization collects its own data over a period of

Inspection performance and analysis for effectiveness. Table 3.1 indicates that the rates for working through a particular work product type are the same for the Inspection Meeting activity as they are for the Preparation activity. For organizations starting to do Inspections, these rates can be considered approximately the same. As you collect your own data, they should become different.

These rates reflect an estimate for the total number of pages or lines of code (LOC) scheduled for an Inspection. When inspecting just changes to a work product, rather than a complete work product, the total should include relevant surrounding material. If a document is changed, it may be useful to inspect not only the changed lines or paragraphs, but also some of the lines or paragraphs that surround these changes. For example, for code changes, approximately 2 to 5 times the number of changed lines of code should be inspected. The Producer provides the estimate for the total number of LOC to be inspected, accounting for changes and code surrounding the changes as appropriate.

Work Product Type	Preparation	Inspection Meeting
Architecture Documents	2 - 3 pages/hour	2 – 3 pages/hour
Requirements Documents	2 - 3 pages/hour	2 – 3 pages/hour
High-level design	3 - 4 pages/hour	3 – 4 pages/hour
Low-level design	3 - 4 pages/hour	3 – 4 pages/hour
Code Units	100 - 150 LOC/hour	100 - 150 LOC/hour
Unit Test Plan	4 - 5 pages/hour	4 – 5 pages/hour
Unit Test Cases	100 - 150 LOC/hour	100 - 150 LOC/hour
All Test Plans	5 - 7 pages/hour	5 – 7 pages/hour
All Test Cases	100 - 150 LOC/hour	100 - 150 LOC/hour
User Documentation	8 - 12 pages/hour	8 - 12 pages/hour
Fixes and Changes	50 - 75 LOC/hour	50 - 75 LOC/hour

Preparation and Inspection Meeting Rates
Table 3.1

Initial planning should take into account the work product types (see Appendix B) that will be inspected during the project. Calculations for resources needed should be based on your own data or the starting rates shown in Table 3.1. This table provides input to estimate the resources needed for Inspections.

The rates in Table 3.1 should be updated periodically with actual results of effective Inspections as the organization proceeds to practice Inspections. The data should be recorded in the organization's Process Database.

After the required resources are estimated, a budget must be allocated. This allocation will lock in the commitment of management.

3. Set milestones for the Inspections:

The Project Lead should set target dates for work products that will be inspected early in the project; e.g., requirements specifications, architectures, and High-level designs. These milestones, as they are earlier in the schedule, should be set with a conviction that the work products will be ready on those dates.

The Project Lead should set boundaries for the dates for work products that will be inspected later in the project; e.g., Low-level design, code, test plans, test cases, external documentation. These milestones should include trigger dates by which the chosen target dates for the Inspection schedules are revised or committed. These milestones are for work products later in the project schedule and are more vulnerable to change. Additionally, it cannot be known with conviction early in the project what date a specific Low-level design, or code module, or test case will be ready for Inspection. Therefore, boundary dates by which the sets of Low-level designs, code units, and test cases need to be complete should be known, even early in the project. The trigger dates are put into the plan to allow the Project Lead to begin the process of setting the specific dates for these types of work products. See Figure 10.2 for an example.

4. Identify dependencies on other groups:

If there are dependencies on other groups to participate in any Inspections for any project work product, these should be made known to those groups, so they can plan and commit to provide the inspectors when needed.

5. Identify risks to any Inspections in the project plan, as appropriate.

Inspection Scheduling:

1. Send a notification that an Inspection will be needed:

When the Project Lead knows that a specific work product is approaching Inspection readiness, a Moderator should be designated to complete the scheduling with the Project Lead. The Project Lead should notify a Moderator or have a Moderator selected.

2. Determine the Inspection Meeting date:

The Moderator based on availability and readiness of the work product determines the specific date for an Inspection and ensures that the following will be available:

- Inspection materials
- Necessary inspectors
- Inspection room and other logistic needs

3. Ensure that the work product to be inspected meets Entry Criteria:

The Moderator should ensure that the material for the work product to be inspected meets the required Entry Criteria. If the Entry Criteria cannot be satisfied, the Inspection should be considered for postponement or rescheduling. Otherwise, the Inspection will be at risk during its performance. If the Project Lead still takes the risk, it should be noted and managed.

4. Schedule the Inspection Meeting:

The Moderator can proceed to schedule the Inspection Meeting after ensuring that:

- Inspectors are available
- If warranted, an Overview is scheduled and held
- Sufficient time for Preparation is provided
- There is availability of a meeting room and other logistics for the duration of the Inspection Meeting
- A data recording/tracking system, including a template, is available to capture data and action items, and the Moderator knows how to use the system and template

Validation/Verification:

The following are examples of verification/validation:

Inspection Planning:

The Software Quality Assurance (SQA) function in the organization should assures that the project plan has been documented and includes planned Inspections as required by the organization policy and procedures.

Measurements: Data should be gathered during this activity; e.g.,

- Which work products are planned for Inspection
- The estimated size of work products to be inspected
- Risks
- The number of planned Inspections
- Planned effort to be spent on Inspections

Inspection Scheduling:

1. The Moderator remains actively involved during the Inspection Scheduling period. There should be a reasonable time lag between the time the Project Lead notifies that an Inspection is required and the actual Meeting is held. The Moderator is responsible for assuring that all tasks up to the completion of the Inspection Meeting are performed.

2. The SQA function in the organization ensures, once notification is sent, that a Moderator has been assigned and is performing the necessary Scheduling tasks. This can be done via audits of the process records or sampling of Inspections.

Measurements: Data should be gathered during this activity; e.g.,

- How much in advance the Project Lead is sending notification to the Moderator
- How long is the period between notification and the Inspection Meeting
- How many Inspections required postponement
- Actual versus planned Inspections

NOTE: With adequate planning and scheduling there should be minimal delay between the scheduled Inspection and its occurrence. Track the delay to help improve the process in the future.

Exit Criteria:

Inspection Planning:

1. There is a project plan showing the Inspections to be held, including resources and milestones that may be known in the early stages of the project.

2. Where milestones may not be known a boundary of probable dates should be noted in the plan for the Inspections. It should also be noted as another milestone when these boundary dates should be reviewed for refinement and commitment. Triggers for revisiting the planned boundary dates are defined in the project plan.

3. Adequate resources are allocated in the project plan for Inspections.

Inspection Scheduling:

The Inspection activities have been recorded as Performed on the scheduled dates and Closed within the dates determined at the Inspection Meeting for Rework.

3.4 Overview

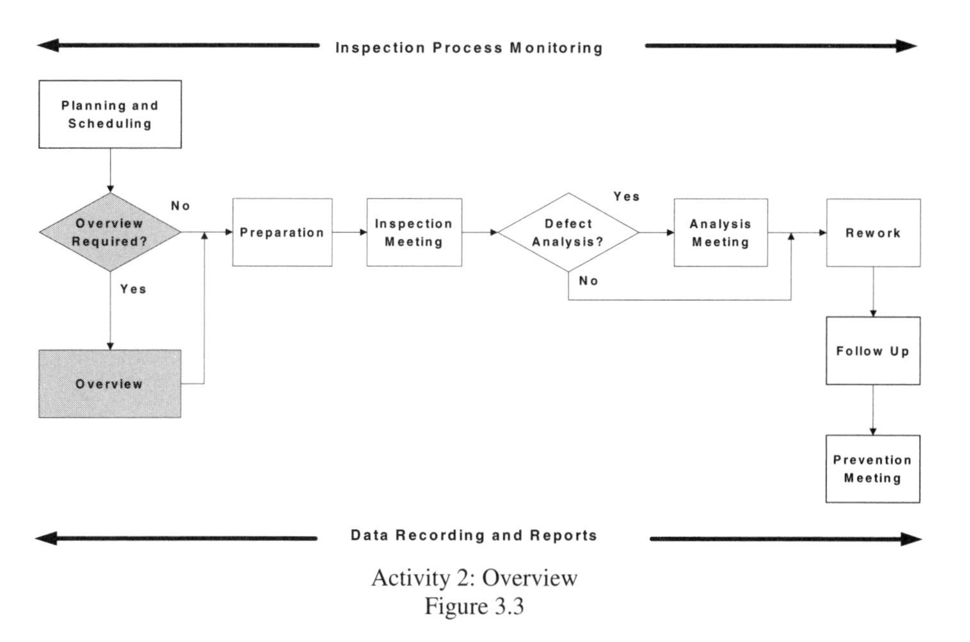

Activity 2: Overview
Figure 3.3

INTRODUCTION

The Overview Meeting is scheduled based on a need as determined by the Moderator with the Project Lead and Producer. This need includes education and transfer of information necessary for the participants to perform an effective and efficient Inspection. If an Inspection is being used to provide education or backup capability an Overview is usually warranted.

The Producer presents the Overview material to the Inspection team members to enable their better understanding during the Preparation and the Inspection Meeting by supplying background information about the product and work product. An alternative is to give a tutorial on areas of special interest in the work product. The Producer can use any format for presentation that enables the understanding. The amount of time needed is determined by the Producer with the Moderator and Project Lead, but needs to be verified at the conclusion of the Overview to ensure that the Inspection team had a sufficient Overview.

If deemed not sufficient, the Overview can be extended or a follow-up session can be scheduled. A follow-up may affect the schedule for the Inspection Meeting. The Overview optionally addresses the complete set of material or only portions that are judged to be necessary for understanding the work product to be inspected. The Overview can be used to ensure that the participants know what is expected of them and what the business rationale is for the work. The Producer should also explain any historical problem areas if the work is a modification or enhancement of an existing product.

Overview Meeting Decision Checklist:

1. An Overview should be strongly considered under the following conditions:

    - Participants are not sufficiently familiar with the material to be inspected, it is new technology, or it is infrequently used
    - Inspections are in early use in the organization
    - The material is critical to the success of the project; e.g.,
        - Innovative
        - Safety critical
        - Defining/changing a significant algorithm
        - Performance critical
        - Large in volume
    - Education of the participants is a desired objective
    - The work product is large or complex

2. An Overview should always be required when creating or making changes to significant product baselines, for example:

    - Requirements Specifications
    - Software Development Plans
    - Architectures
    - High-level designs
    - Significant changes to baselines

3. An Overview is optional for all other work product Inspections, which include:
    - Low-level designs
    - Code
    - All other plans
    - Test suites and test cases
    - Fixes
    - Less significant changes

4. An Overview may address not just one work product but also a set of work products to be inspected, especially when they are small.

5. If the inspectors are already familiar with the work product, the Overview can be skipped.

✂ Defects found at the Overview should be treated and tracked as defects for the subject Inspection if the material has already been provided to the inspectors and the Inspection Meeting follows shortly afterward. Alternately, the material that will be inspected can be updated by the Producer to include resolution of the defects discovered during the Overview and these defects not counted. I suggest it will be beneficial for the project to track and log the defects found at the Overview Meeting to learn whether this meeting is substantially finding defects and what this may suggest about Inspection readiness.

NOTE 1: The Overview is not an Inspection Meeting, although defects may be identified during the presentation.

NOTE 2: The Overview Meeting is not a meeting to rework the material into an alternative solution.

NOTE 3: Another reason for an Overview, even if brief or done electronically, is to identify any Open Issues in the work product. An Open Issue is an acknowledgement of the fact that a subpart of the work product is not complete for some reason. The Producer may also want to focus the inspectors on subparts that are problematic or of some concern.

While it is the intent that there are no Open Issues when an Inspection begins, it sometimes is necessary to move the work product along a parallel path of production. It might be unproductive to hold back an Inspection until all Open Issues are completed, but it would also be unproductive to inspect incomplete material. Or would it?

As long as we know the boundaries of completion, we can inspect an incomplete work product, if it serves the purpose of parallel production. We must require, however, that the Open Issues defining what is not complete be specified at the start of an Inspection. Admittedly, this option could be misused, so the Moderator along with the Project Lead and Producer must make a decision to proceed or not when Open Issues are identified. When Open Issues are accepted, there must also be a planned Re-Inspection of the work product when the Open Issues are resolved. If the Open Issues are too many, this may suggest a postponement is warranted.

Responsible Individual:

The Producer's primary responsibility for the success of the Overview Meeting is to deliver the presentation. If Overview material is provided, it is the Producer's responsibility to make sufficient copies for the meeting either directly or via the Moderator.

Other Roles:

The Moderator determines with the Producer or Project Lead whether an Overview is necessary, schedules the Overview Meeting, obtains the meeting room, and records the time for the meeting, the number of participants, and the results of the meeting.

Inspectors participate during the Overview meeting and must concur that the Overview met the exit criteria.

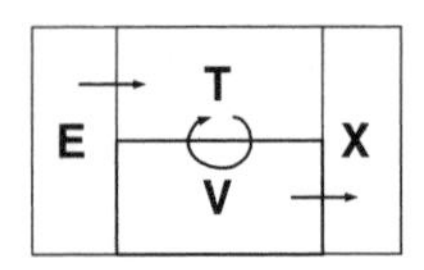

Entry Criteria:

1. A Project Lead has sent notification for an Inspection.
2. The Inspection requires a mandatory Overview, or criteria for an optional Overview have been satisfied; e.g.,

   - Complexity of the work product solution
   - Volume of material in the work product
   - Criticality of the work product
   - Customer requirements

3. The Producer is ready to present the Overview.
4. Open Issues and any potential problem areas are highlighted.

Tasks to be performed:

1. Producer prepares for the Overview using a format and style that will best convey the information to the participants.
2. Moderator invites the participants to the Overview meeting.
3. Producer presents the Overview.
4. Inspection team members concur that the Overview satisfies the needs for Preparation and the Inspection Meeting.
5. Any Open Issues are documented in the Inspection Report. See Appendix C.
6. If the Overview is used to familiarize the participants with their roles, the Inspection process, or some other aspect key to this Inspection, the Moderator will provide this briefing.
7. Defects, if any, are documented.

NOTE 1: The Producer may come to the Overview with known Open Issues. These issues may be resolved or restated by the time of the Inspection Meeting and then tracked to resolution. If there are too many or too important a set of Open Issues, the Moderator must make a decision to either postpone or continue with the Inspection Meeting. Any risks taken should be managed.

NOTE 2: The Producer should either resolve these Open Issues before the Preparation materials are distributed or note them as known Open Issues with the materials provided to the inspectors for Preparation. All Open Issues are to be noted and tracked to resolution.

Validation/Verification:

The following are examples of verification/validation:

1. The Moderator uses the work product Overview Meeting entry criteria and procedure to determine if a meeting is necessary.
2. The Inspection team is in concurrence with the decision taken to have an Overview or not.
3. The inspectors have the responsibility to state that the Overview, when held, is satisfactory for their Preparation and subsequent Inspection Meeting.
4. The SQA function in the organization ensures that the Moderator has used the Overview Meeting criteria and ensures that an appropriate decision was made to have an Overview or not. This can be done via audits of the process records or sampling of Inspections.

Measurements: Data should be gathered during this activity; e.g.,

- How much participant time was spent in the Overview
- The clock time for the Overview
- Time between notification and the Overview meeting
- How many Overviews required rescheduling
- How many defects were identified at the Overview

Exit Criteria:

1. The Overview meeting was determined to be satisfactory by the inspectors and SQA.
2. Open Issues are documented.
3. Potential problem areas are noted to the participants for Preparation and for the Reader for the Inspection Meeting.
4. Defects, if any, are documented.

3.5 Preparation

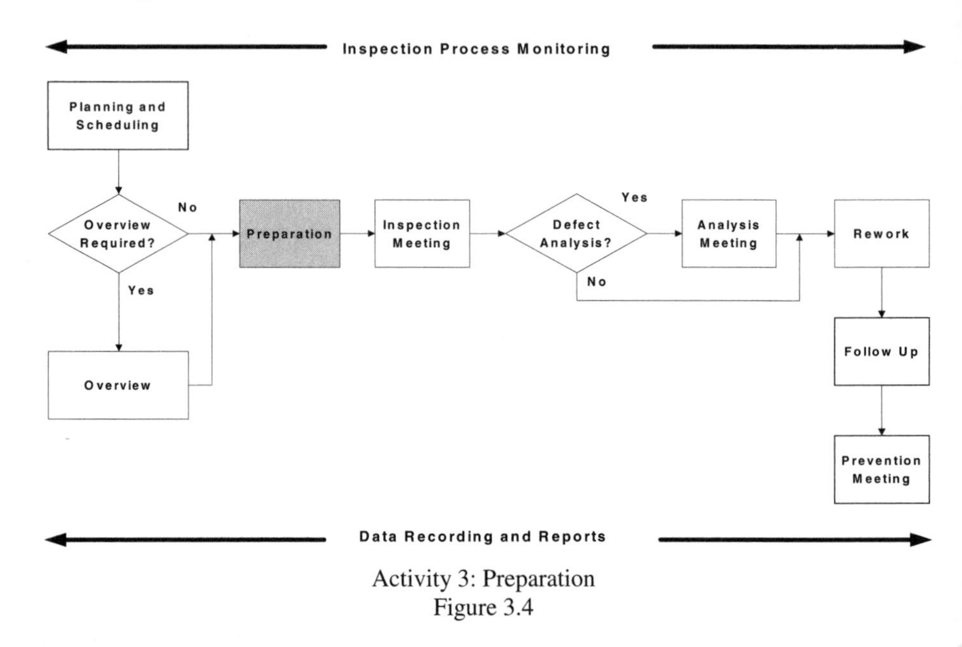

Activity 3: Preparation
Figure 3.4

INTRODUCTION:

Preparation precedes the Inspection Meeting. The time allocated should be sufficient to allow each Inspection participant to prepare for an effective and efficient Inspection Meeting. Calendar time between scheduling Preparation, performing Preparation, and the Inspection Meeting will vary based on the needs of the Inspection and availability of the Inspection team participants. It is usually an individual activity, but can be performed as teams of two or more. When groups meet for Preparation, they should not treat these as Inspection Meetings.

Preparation is required for each Inspection Meeting. All members of the Inspection team should prepare, including the Moderator, who is also another inspector. Also the Producer should prepare, but very likely will require less time. All inspectors should prepare.

The materials to be inspected should be provided in advance to allow proper Preparation for the inspectors to understand the work product and note apparent defects or questions. See Table 3.1 for suggested rates at which Preparation should proceed. The Moderator must confirm that sufficient time has been allocated for Preparation and that the inspectors have the time available. Required additional materials, as appropriate, should also be provided or made available online; e.g., baseline material to map the inspected material against, checklists, previous versions of the work product, templates for logging defects. See Appendix B for materials by Inspection type. The inspectors should mark the material to be inspected with questions and possible defects as they proceed through their Preparation. The Preparation material is for the inspectors to use as best suits their needs.

During Preparation the inspectors should:

- Increase their understanding of the material
- Inspect the work product using the checklist appropriate to the work product
- Identify possible defects that will be discussed at the Inspection Meeting
- For minor defects:
  - Either provide the marked work product material to the Producer at the end of the Inspection Meeting for correction during Rework, or
  - Create a list on a separate sheet of paper; this list will be collected at the start of the Inspection Meeting
- Note the amount of time spent during Preparation

✂ Although some Inspection advocates state that the Moderator should only moderate, I have found that they can effectively serve as an inspector and sometimes are among the best inspectors. Since some organizations prefer that the Moderator not inspect, this is an option they can choose. If the Moderator is not an inspector this may require another inspector at the Inspection Meeting. Having the Moderator be an inspector also tends to guard against assigning the Moderator role to less technically qualified organization members.

✂ Some organizations may choose not to create the minor defect lists, but rather to provide the marked up work product with noted minor defects and discuss each minor defect after the Inspection Meeting. Some teams prefer to discuss the minor defects at the Inspection Meeting. This will require more time at the meeting. I have found that minor defects often take more time than warranted at the Inspection Meeting with little payback. If the rule is to trust that the Producer will fix all relevant minor defects, the Inspection Meeting can then be used for the more important defects identified. Minor defect lists, however, can provide some indication of how well the preparation was performed. For example, the numbers of minor defects found and whether they have been found throughout the work product can give an indication of coverage during Preparation. Additionally, the data can be used to analyze the effectiveness and efficiency of Preparation and the Inspection Meeting. During Follow-up, the Moderator or designee verifies that all valid defects, including the minors, were repaired.

✂ The original method did not require classification of defects during Preparation. This was done at the Inspection Meeting. I suggest that the inspectors can classify fairly quickly during Preparation and that this will save time at the Inspection Meeting. The classification should include where found, probable type of defect, and consideration for cause. The classification is the same as used during the Inspection Meeting.

✂ The Recorder should identify which, or at least what volume of, defects were identified during the Preparation activity versus the Inspection Meeting and should also record time spent for actual preparation made by each inspector. The defects found recorded should be both the major and minor. These data and subsequent analysis will facilitate improvements in Preparation tasks and in individual personal processes for work product production.

Responsible Individual:

Primary responsibility is with the inspectors to ensure they have properly prepared for the Inspection Meeting. If any inspector cannot prepare sufficiently, the Moderator must be notified immediately and a backup inspector selected. If a backup cannot be selected in time, then based on who is not prepared the Moderator must decide whether the Inspection can still be effective with a smaller team or if it should be rescheduled. In both cases the decision should be recorded to learn from analysis of the results.

Other Roles:

The Moderator should first estimate the Preparation time needed for the Inspection based on the material to be inspected. These estimates should be verified with the Inspection team participants. At the same time, the Moderator needs to get a commitment from each participant that enough time is allocated and that it will be sufficient for him or her to prepare.

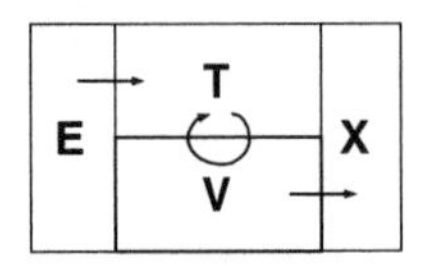

Entry Criteria:

1. The Overview, if needed, has been satisfactorily completed.
2. Any Open Issues identified for the Overview have been closed and addressed in the work product or are documented as Open Issues and provided as ancillary material for the Preparation.
3. Open Issues not closed are documented for tracking within the change control system used by the project.
4. The Producer determines that the work product is ready for Inspection.
5. The work product has achieved closure; e.g., the code compiles, any tools if available have been used (syntax checkers, static analyzers, or dynamic analyzers), and the code complies with defined standards, style guides, and templates for format.
6. All necessary ancillary materials have been made available well in advance. See Appendix B for ancillary materials by Inspection type.
7. The work product includes all baselined function and approved changes for this planned work product completion date.
8. The amount of time needed for Preparation has been confirmed with the inspectors and is available to them.
9. Predecessor and dependent work products are available, have been inspected, and meet exit criteria.
10. The Moderator and Producer have defined the coverage of material to be inspected.

11. The work products allow easy identification of defects by location in the material; e.g., documents including requirements and design are written to show section numbering or some other form of chunking of material, numbered lines in the code.
12. The Moderator agrees that the work product is inspectable.

NOTE 1: It is possible to perform an Inspection Meeting with a modified work product and without predecessor and dependent work products having been inspected, but this is a risk to a stable and effective Inspection process. This risk should be noted if the Inspection proceeds. This is a typical situation in maintenance type projects, where predecessor work products are just not always available.

NOTE 2: In projects where the organization intranet is used to house and distribute documents, there is a clear advantage for making required documents and work products available. One caution that must be addressed is to assure that documents are under configuration controls facilitating same version distribution and preventing inadvertent changes that will cause confusion between inspectors with different documents. Definitely move to the intranet capability as soon as possible, but ensure document control.

Tasks to be performed:

1. Each inspector uses the scheduled time to complete the Preparation in a style and format they are comfortable with.
2. The material to be inspected is marked with questions, concerns, and possible defects, both major and minor, found during the Preparation.
3. The minor defects are either recorded on a separate sheet that will be delivered to the Moderator at the start of the Inspection Meeting or they are clearly noted in the marked material that will be delivered to the Moderator at the end of the Inspection Meeting. Each minor defect should be noted by location in the work product when using a minor list.

Validation/Verification:

The following are examples of verification/validation:

1. The Moderator uses the Preparation entry criteria and procedure.
2. The Moderator uses the minor defect information to determine if all inspectors have properly performed preparation.
3. The inspectors have confirmed that they have prepared. If an inspector cannot properly prepare they notify the Moderator and Project Lead as soon as possible.
4. The SQA function in the organization ensures that the Moderator has used the Preparation procedure and that the inspectors performed sufficient preparation. This can be done via audits of the process records or sampling of Inspections.

Measurements: Data should be gathered during this activity; e.g.,

- How much time was spent in Preparation
- How long a period between notification of the Inspection and the Preparation
- How many Inspection Meetings required rescheduling due to insufficient preparation
- The number of major and minor defects found during Preparation

Exit Criteria:

1. Each inspector has completed sufficient Preparation based on organization and project preparation time criteria. See Table 3.1 for example rates.
2. Minor defect inputs are completed.
3. Preparation notes are recorded on the work product materials or defect lists.

3.6 Inspection Meeting

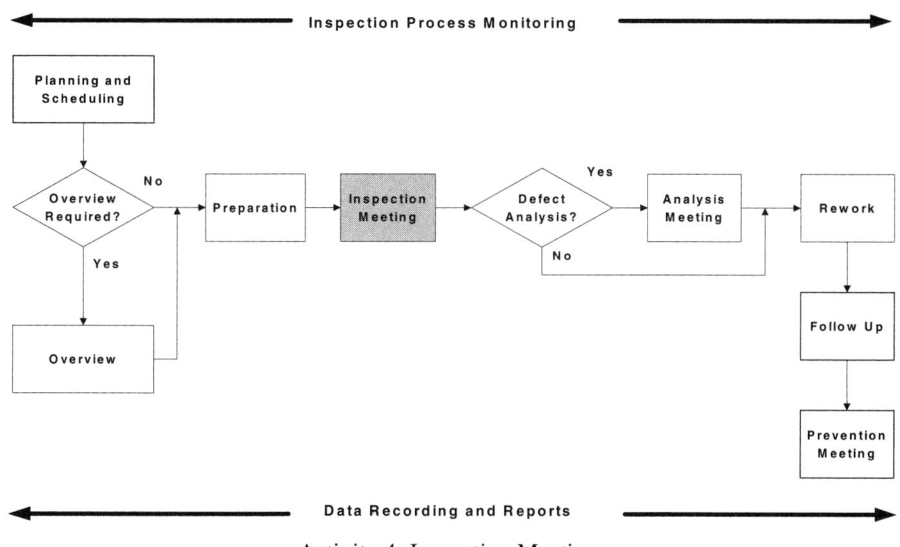

Activity 4: Inspection Meeting
Figure 3.5

INTRODUCTION

In the original method the Inspection Meeting was the heart of Inspections. Its primary purpose was to find as many defects as possible during the meeting. Guidelines were followed for courteous behavior and the focus was always intended to remain businesslike and objective during the process of inspecting and identifying defects.

Defects are identified either during the Preparation and captured in inspector notes or through the synergy of discussion between inspectors at the meeting. While some discussion at the meeting is necessary, it should be determined for each defect item discussion that:

- The discussion is within the scope of the Inspection (see NOTEs below)
- The identified defect is agreed to be a defect, or at least a potential defect, by the Inspection team, including the Producer
- If a discussion item cannot be agreed to be a defect, it should be noted as an Open Issue to be resolved after the meeting
- The defect can be classified by class, severity, and type
- The defect can be described crisply but sufficiently

The Inspection Meeting has schedule and entry requirements. If inspectors are not prompt for the meeting; e.g., in the meeting room within ten minutes of scheduled start, postponement should be considered. If the right inspectors or a sufficient number are not available for an Inspection, it should be postponed. The critical inspectors include the Moderator, Producer, and Reader. If other inspectors are late, the Moderator will need to make a decision about postponement, based on the probability of a successful Inspection Meeting.

NOTE 1: The team should avoid trying to fix defects at this meeting, unless the fix is readily evident, in which case, if the Producer agrees, it could be briefly noted in the meeting records. A fix discussion with the full team simply will take more time and effort compared to leaving the fix to the Producer during the Rework activity. The Moderator should remind the inspectors that they could meet with the Producer after the meeting for further discussion as warranted. The discussion item must either be captured as a defect or as an Open Issue when it is not accepted at the meeting as a defect.

✂ Some organizations may not accept not trying to identify a fix to a defect. If they choose to try to identify fixes, there will be an added cost for the meeting, but it may be the only reasonable way to get Inspections started on the path to becoming effective in these organizations. See Chapter 5: Other Inspector Roles where different organization personality types are discussed.

NOTE 2: The meeting is not to be used to discuss or define alternative ways of defining or implementing the contents of the work product. The Producer was authorized to make choices, and while there may be other ways to define or implement a solution, the Inspection Meeting is focused on whether the material is correct in its refinement or solution, not its style. Admittedly this can be a gray area, so the test should be whether the question of style is defined as a valid defect type for the work material; e.g., performance. If so, then it should be discussed and identified.

✂ There is some evidence that the Inspection Meeting can be avoided with minimal loss in effectiveness (~5%), but this has only been demonstrated for code Inspections. [VOT93] In my opinion, not using the Inspection Meeting should be considered as a valid option only when effectiveness consistently is greater than 90%.

Responsible Individual:

The Moderator is responsible for managing an effective and efficient meeting.

Other Roles:

The Producer is responsible for the inspected work product, answering questions, and concurring on identified defects or adequately explaining to the Inspection team's agreement why the identified possible defect is not a defect.

The Reader is responsible for focusing and pacing the Inspection Meeting by leading the team through the material.

The Recorder is responsible for correctly recording all identified defects and Open Issues.

All inspectors, including the Producer, are responsible for sharing their questions and identified defects found during Preparation. They should also actively follow the Inspection to try to find other defects through the synergy of group interaction with the material.

✂ Not all Inspections require that each role be assigned to separate participants. Highly effective Inspection can be performed with only one participant in addition to the Producer. In this case the inspector will serve in the roles of Moderator, Inspector, Reader, and Recorder. See Section 4.6, Moderating in 1:1 Inspections, for further discussion.

It is even possible to hold a highly effective Inspection when the Producer does not attend any Inspection activities, including the Inspection Meeting. These Inspections are called Solo:Inspections and are discussed in Chapter 14.

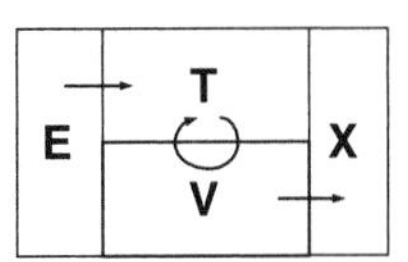

Entry Criteria:

1. The Inspection team members are sufficiently present in number and role assignments.
2. Inspection materials were available for Preparation with sufficient time for study and review before the Inspection Meeting, including any necessary reference materials.
3. Inspectors have adequately prepared.
4. Inspectors have submitted their minor defects list at the start of the meeting or have marked the work products that will be provided at the end of the meeting.
5. Scope of the Inspection Meeting has been defined.
6. Recorder and a data recording system are available.
7. Other roles; e.g., Reader have been assigned.
8. The Producer has identified any new potential problem areas.

Tasks to be performed:

After it is agreed that the Inspection Meeting activity has sufficiently satisfied entry criteria, the following tasks are addressed:

1. Brief introduction, where the Moderator:

    - Ensures all participants know each other's background, as appropriate, and roles for this Inspection

- Restates the rules of the Inspection process, if necessary, based on the experience of the inspectors

2. Preparedness check, where the Moderator:

   - Asks how much time each participant gave to Preparation
   - Collects the minor defect log each participant created during Preparation or confirms that marked work product materials will be provided at the end of the meeting
   - Confirms that the inspectors feel they are prepared
   - Decides if the meeting should proceed based on the amount of Preparation noted

3. Read the work product, where the Reader:

   - Explains how the sections of the material will be read and the order in which the reading will proceed
   - Gets consensus on the reading styles to be used and the order of reading if this has not been previously agreed to
   - Reads the material in accordance with the reading styles selected

4. Identify defects, where all inspectors:

   - Identify questions and possible defects from their Preparation materials as the material is read by the Reader
   - Discuss and come to agreement on the identified defects, or agree to have a new Open Issue noted for later resolution and follow-up

5. Record defects, where the Recorder:

   - Notes each agreed to defect and Open Issue with a location in the inspected work product
   - Classifies each defect by class, severity, type, where found; i.e., Overview, Preparation, or Inspection Meeting, and where caused; i.e., in the work product under Inspection or a previous document
   - Reviews recorded defects dynamically during the meeting or at the close of the Inspection Meeting to verify team acceptance of the defect write-up
   - Records time for the meeting, size of the work product, etc.
   - Ensures participants are in agreement with the recorded defects

6. Determine disposition of material, where the Inspection team decides from four possibilities:
   - Accept the material, as is when verification of defect repair is not required during Follow-up. This is usually only when minor defects have been found

or in cases where no defects have been found and the Inspection Meeting satisfied process performance criteria.

- Accept the material after verification of defect repair by the assigned Follow-up inspector, which can be the Moderator or another inspector.
- Request the work product to be repaired and a Re-inspection scheduled.
- Recommend re-engineering of the work product followed by a new Inspection.

NOTE 1: During Rework and Follow-up it must be determined if any newly identified Open Issues are defects or not. They must be resolved and classified as defects or any remaining Open Issues must be tracked via the organization's change control process.

NOTE 2: It is key that the Producer agrees to the identified defects. Sometimes agreement will be almost immediate. Other identified defects may require some discussion before acceptance; still others may not be accepted at the Inspection Meeting. In this latter case, the Moderator must make a judgment to continue discussion or note the item as an Open Issue to be resolved later.

NOTE 3: Discussion should be minimal and used to come to agreement, not to detail the solutions.

NOTE 4: See Chapter 8 for Re-Inspection criteria.

NOTE 5: While the team will be asked to make a consensus decision on disposition, the Moderator may override when the team is novice or the decision is in error and the Moderator cannot influence the team's thinking about the error. This overriding decision should only be taken in rare circumstances.

Validation/Verification:

The following are examples of verification/validation:

1. The Moderator, using the Inspection Meeting entry criteria and procedure, determines if the team has properly performed the Inspection.
2. The inspectors participated in an effective meeting; i.e., the process was performed within expected measures. If inspectors have not properly prepared, the question must be asked at meeting close how much the insufficient preparation impacted the effectiveness of the meeting.
3. The SQA function in the organization ensures that the Moderator has used the Inspection Meeting procedure and that the inspectors made a sufficient Inspection by reviewing the Recorder's report. This can be done via audits of the process records or sampling of Inspections.

Measurements: Data should be gathered during this activity; e.g.,

- How much time was spent in the Inspection Meeting
- How long a period between the Preparation and the Inspection Meeting
- How many Inspection Meetings required rescheduling due to insufficient preparation
- How many Inspections required Re-inspection
- How many defects were found
- How long the meeting took
- How many inspectors were in attendance

Exit Criteria:

1. The Inspection materials have been inspected and coverage of the work product is completed as planned.
2. The Inspection results fall within expected tolerance of performance for:

    - Time spent during preparation
    - Time spent at the Inspection Meeting
    - Defect density

    NOTE: See Chapter 6: Inspection Data for further discussion on these metrics.

3. The defects and conduct of the Inspection have been recorded and the team concurs with the contents.
4. Open Issues have been recorded for follow-up during Rework.
5. The Moderator or a designee has been appointed to perform follow-up with the Producer.
6. Data is available to update the Process Database.
7. Any associated deviations and risks are noted.
8. Decisions to re-inspect or not have been reviewed against criteria. Re-inspection criteria are discussed in Chapter 8.
9. Decision on re-engineering has been addressed.
10. Process defects have been recorded, as appropriate, as well as product defects.
11. The locations of defects in the inspected work product are clearly noted to facilitate repair.
12. A decision is taken on the timeframe by which defect repairs and Open Issues will be resolved.
13. The Inspection satisfies criteria to be indicated as Performed.

NOTE: Performed versus Closed Inspections:

1. The following criteria must be satisfied before an Inspection can be considered Performed.
    - Sufficient time was spent during the Inspection Meeting
    - Defects and other Inspection Meeting data have been captured
    - Someone has been selected to verify the rework and Open Issues
    - All Inspection Meeting exit criteria have been satisfied
2. An Inspection cannot usually be denoted as Closed until Follow-up has been completed. The following criteria must be satisfied before an Inspection can be considered Closed.

    - All Open Issues have been resolved
    - All defects identified have been corrected or have a change request written to allow addressing the defect later
    - The Moderator has completed the Inspection Report

3.7 Analysis Meeting

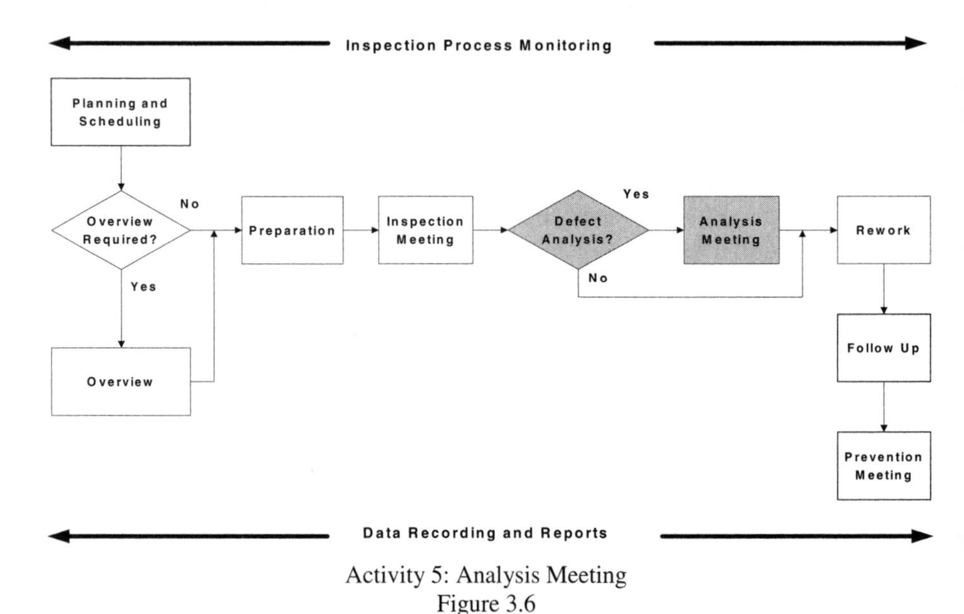

Activity 5: Analysis Meeting
Figure 3.6

INTRODUCTION

This activity was not included with the original method defined by Fagan. Carole Jones in Raleigh, IBM, had identified it as adding value and improvement when built upon the traditional Inspection method. [JON85] Gilb evolved this approach calling it the Analysis Meeting of Inspections. [GIL93] The intent is to provide the inspectors a time period to discuss the defects and what the causes are.

✂ This activity is viewed as optional by many Inspection proponents, but is highly recommended. If included, there is some added cost for Inspections. But as we will learn, there will be a return on investment seen in defects prevented in future work. See Chapter 7: Causal Analysis. Organizations starting with Inspections may choose to defer use of this Inspection activity until after they have gotten Inspections into practice.

✂ This activity can be performed immediately after the Inspection Meeting, which is my preference, or it can be scheduled for a later time and date. If scheduled for a later date, it should be reasonably close to the conclusion of the Inspection Meeting.

Responsible Individual:

The Moderator with the Project Lead determines whether this activity will be performed.

Other Roles:

The Producer should be willing to accept open input from the Inspection Team regarding the potential causes of the identified defects.

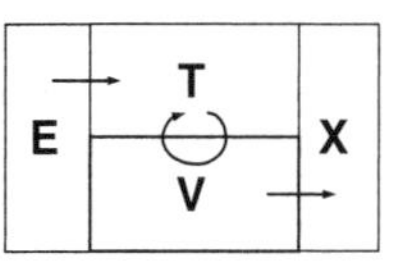

Entry Criteria:

1. The Project Lead and Moderator have chosen this activity to be performed.
2. The Inspection team has been trained in causal analysis techniques. Training in team dynamics and group behavior can be helpful.
3. Major defects have been found during the Inspection.
4. A defect taxonomy or set of cause categories has been defined.

Tasks to be performed:

1. Select the defects to discuss.
2. Determine the potential causes of the defects discussed.
3. The Recorder will record the Analysis Meeting results and provide them to the Inspection Coordinator or SEPG as input for process improvement consideration within the organization at the Prevention Meeting.

NOTE 1: The Analysis Meeting should not take long. It is sometimes called the Third Hour, since it occurs after the two hour Inspection, but rarely have I seen it take this long. Of course, the amount of time required is somewhat driven by the number of defects to discuss. However, in all cases, the meeting is not the Prevention Meeting where actions will be discussed for ways to prevent the defect types. My view is that one to two minutes per major defect is a reasonable planning rate for this meeting to classify defect causes since in many cases the cause is obvious at the time of discovery of the defect.

NOTE 2: Where the organization is reasonably under quality control for building work products correctly and few defects are injected, then all major defects can be analyzed. This is likely to be in higher maturity organizations on the SW-CMM scale. If there is a very high volume of defects, the team may choose a subset based on their view of the most critical or frequently occurring defects.

NOTE 3: The Analysis Meeting is used to gather immediate input for later processing and analysis at the Prevention Meeting where defects from multiple Inspections and other sources are discussed and actions proposed for prevention. If the cause classifications are not taken immediately after the Inspection Meeting, time may work against memory of probable causes.

Validation/Verification:

The following are examples of verification/validation:

1. The Moderator uses the Analysis Meeting entry criteria and procedure to determine if all inspectors have properly participated and the meeting was effective.
2. The inspectors have participated. If they cannot or choose not to properly participate, they must notify the Moderator at the start of the Inspection Meeting.
3. The SQA function in the organization ensures that the Moderator has used the Analysis Meeting checklist and reviews the Recorder's report for sufficiency. This can be done via audits of the process records or sampling of Inspections.

Measurements: Data should be gathered during this activity; e.g.,

- How much time was spent in the Analysis Meeting
- How many defects were discussed
- How many defects were assigned causes

Exit Criteria:

1. The Analysis Meeting records have been completed.
2. Data is provided to the SEPG or Inspection Coordinator.

3.8 Rework

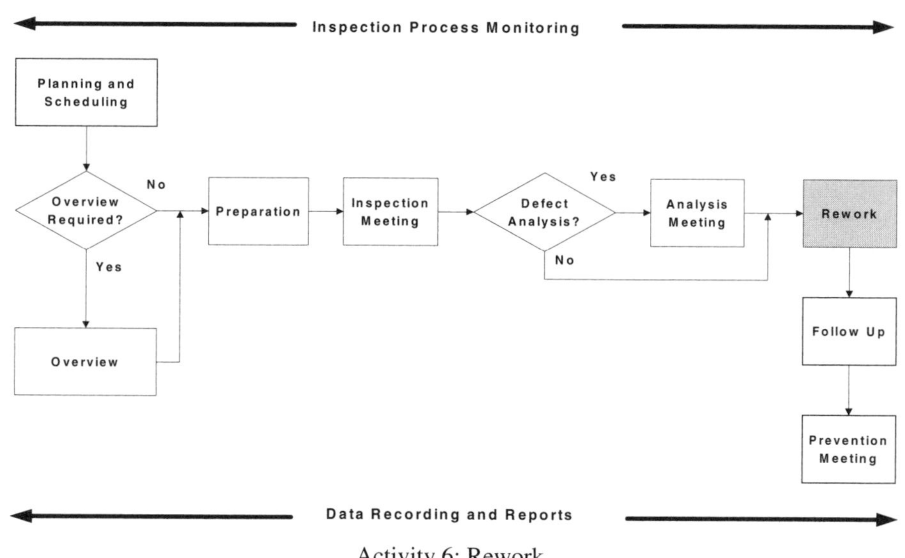

Activity 6: Rework
Figure 3.7

INTRODUCTION

All major defects must be fixed or, if not fixed, justified on the basis of business objectives. Defects elected to not be repaired must be noted as such for future analysis on the decisions taken and for improving the process of deciding which defects to repair. Defects can in most cases be fixed during the Rework activity.

In some cases, the repair may require a Change Request to be written because of the nature or impact of the defect; e.g., the repair affects the requirements or is not solely resolvable within the inspected work product. Open Issues not closed as defects must have a written Change Request allowing for the inspected work product to continue on to the next life cycle steps without unnecessarily holding up the work product or the project. The Change Request action will eventually be decided through the review and approval process; e.g., with the Software Configuration Control Board (SCCB).

Any changes that result from SCCB decisions should then be inspected as a separate work product item, which in this case would be a change to a previously inspected work product. The Change Request may result in a temporary constraint on function to be used but basically closes the defect as an Inspection defect to be tracked. These constraints should be made known to any affected individuals or groups.

Any Open Issues given as input to or identified during the Inspection process must be resolved during the Rework activity. Resolution can be:

- The Open Issue is accepted as a defect and repaired
- The Open Issue becomes a Change Request for further investigation
- The Open issue was incorrectly identified as a potential defect and is closed as a non-defect

Resolution of Open Issues must be verified and accepted by the Moderator. In some situations, the Moderator may require other Inspection team members to assist and agree to the resolution. In exception cases, the Moderator may need to escalate the Open Issue if closure or agreement cannot be achieved with the Producer.

Once the Change Requests are written and accepted defects repaired, the Inspection can be considered Closed.

Responsible Individual:

The Producer is responsible for resolving all Open Issues, fixing all defects, and writing any Change Requests.

Other Roles:

The Moderator or designee is assigned to discuss Open Issues with the Producer during Rework and to come to concurrence with the Producer.

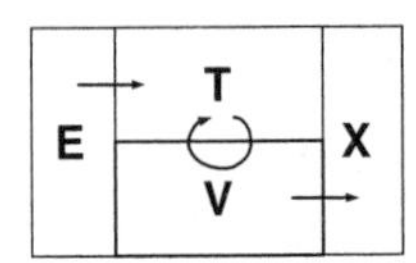

Entry Criteria:

1. The list of defects and Open Issues is provided to the Producer for resolution.
2. The Moderator or someone assigned meets with the Producer to review rework and Open Issues.
3. The Inspection Report is completed, is on file, and available.

Tasks to be performed:

1. The Producer repairs accepted defects identified during the Inspection Meeting.
2. The Producer resolves any Open Issues.
3. The Moderator meets with the Producer to discuss resolutions of Open Issues.
4. Change Requests are written for any Open Issues or defects not resolved during the Rework activity.

5. Either the minor defect list or marked work products with minor defects noted are used to repair the minor defects.

NOTE 1: Resolution of Open Issues may require agreement with the Project Lead and other stakeholders, as some of these may have compounding effects on requirements, resources, and schedule commitments.

✂**:** If only minor defects have been found, the Producer may elect to not repair any and therefore not open the work product for change and potential defects while making changes. When this option is selected, the Producer must ensure the minor defect information is controlled for use when the work product is opened for change in the future.

Validation/Verification:

The following are examples of verification/validation:

1. The Follow-up activity is scheduled; where the Rework will be verified by the Moderator or assigned designee.
2. SQA has reviewed sample results of this activity in the project.

Measurements: Data should be gathered during this activity; e.g.,

- How much time was spent in Rework
- How many Open Issues were resolved and accepted as defects
- How many Open Issues became submitted Change Requests

Exit Criteria:

1. The Producer resolves all defects and Open Issues.
2. Inspected work product materials are updated to account for repairs.

3.9 Follow-up

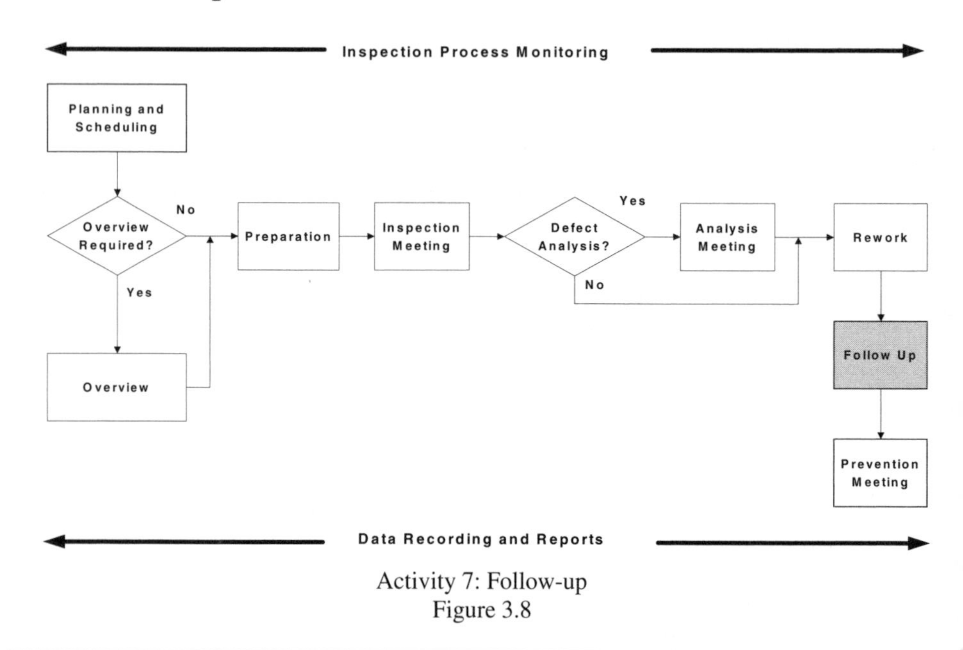

Activity 7: Follow-up
Figure 3.8

INTRODUCTION

This is the final activity of the traditional Inspection process and is a verification of the Rework activity. The Moderator or the person selected to represent the Moderator will review each fix made by the Producer and proposed closures on Open Issues.

Responsible Individual:

The Moderator is the individual primarily responsible for reviewing repairs. The Moderator will also review the Producer's decisions on repairs and Change Requests. The Moderator may delegate some or all of this responsibility.

Other Roles:

The Producer is to provide an explanation of the repairs and closures made.

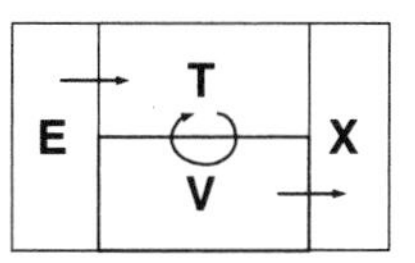

Entry Criteria:

1. Rework of defects has been completed; i.e., fixed or identified with a decision to not fix.
2. The Producer has completed the rework for defects and Open Issues resolved to be defects.
3. Change Requests are written for any defects or Open Issues not resolved.
4. The Moderator concurs with the Producer's decisions on defects, Open Issues, and Change Requests (CRs).

Tasks to be performed:

1. The Moderator meets with the Producer after the Producer has notified the Moderator that rework is completed. Optionally, the Moderator and Producer may meet during the Rework activity to discuss defects and Open Issues and try to reach consensus on the solutions proposed by the Producer, but they still must be verified for correct repair and closure.
2. If the Moderator or the delegated representative of the Moderator disagrees with any proposed repair or non-repair and the Producer accepts, then the material will require another upgrade and Follow-up. If there are disagreements between the Moderator and the Producer, the issue should be resolved by the Project Lead.
3. The Producer updates the work product to reflect the fixes to defects found and Open Issues accepted as defects.
4. The Producer writes any Change Requests that may be required.
5. The Moderator completes the Inspection Report and marks the Inspection as Closed.

Validation/Verification:

The following are examples of verification/validation:

1. The Moderator concurs with the defect repairs and Open Issue closures.
2. The Producer reviews the final Inspection Report.
3. SQA reviews the final Inspection Report.

Measurements: Data should be gathered during this activity; e.g.,

- How much time was spent in Follow-up
- How many Open Issues were disputed by the Moderator

Exit Criteria:

1. Any Change Requests resulting from unresolved Open Issues have been submitted to the change approval process for handling.
2. The Inspection Report is completed and the Producer agrees.
3. If necessary, a Re-Inspection is scheduled.
4. If necessary, issues are escalated to the Project Lead for resolution.
5. The Inspection is noted as Closed.

3.10 Prevention Meeting

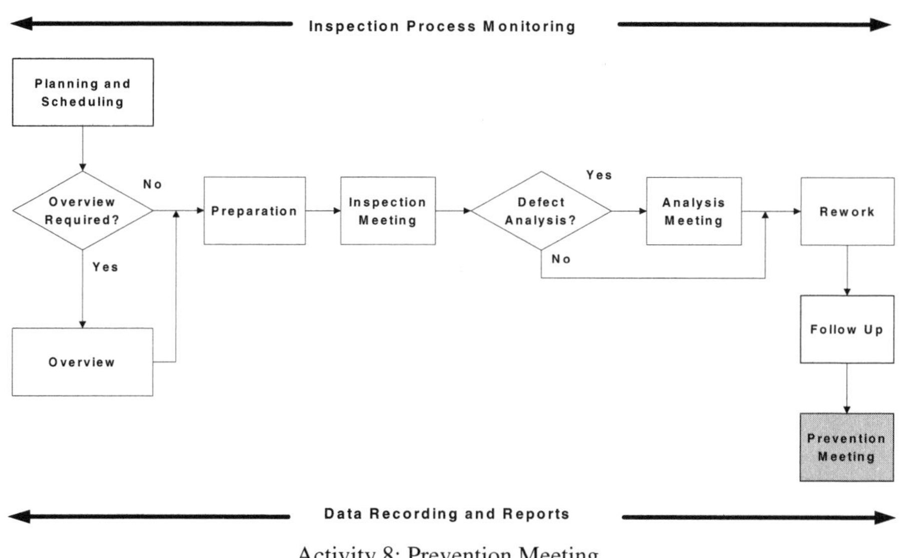

Activity 8: Prevention Meeting
Figure 3.9

INTRODUCTION

The Prevention Meeting as part of the Inspection process is considered optional and is dependent on the Analysis Meeting. This activity is held periodically after a series of Inspections have been completed. Typically they should be held monthly. This is the final activity in the evolved Inspection process.

The Prevention Meeting requires data about the defects found during a period of practice in the organization. These data include each defect instance, where found and where caused information, type of defect, and probable cause. Inspection data, although a primary source, is only one source of defect data for this meeting.

With this data, the members of the Prevention Meeting can come to consensus using various team meeting and Defect Prevention techniques to decide on proposed actions that could be taken to prevent types of defects from occurring in the future. See Chapter7: Causal Analysis for more details on Defect Prevention.

Responsible Individual:

The Prevention Team Leader for the Prevention Meeting will record the results of the meeting and deliver proposals for actions to the organization management.

Other Roles:

The members of the Prevention Meeting team will participate to determine actions for probable causes of selected defect types.

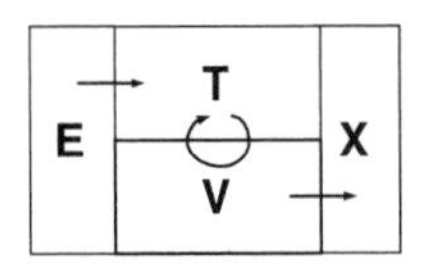

Entry Criteria:

1. An Inspection Meeting was held
2. The Analysis Meeting was held.
3. Defect data including causes are available to the Prevention Meeting team.

Tasks to be performed:

1. Record data from the Prevention Meeting.
2. Record proposed actions to be taken for Defect Prevention.
3. Initial preparation for the proposals to be presented to management for decision.

Validation/Verification:

The following are examples of verification/validation:

1. The Prevention Team has met based on defined cycles for the meetings.
2. SQA reviews sampled reports.
3. The SEPG reviews proposed actions and resultant actions taken.

Measurements: Data should be gathered during this activity; e.g.,

- Time in the Prevention Meeting
- Effort invested at the meeting
- Number of proposals brought forward to management
- Number of actions taken from the proposals

Exit Criteria:

The data is complete and agreed to by the Prevention Meeting participants.

3.11 Data Recording and Reports

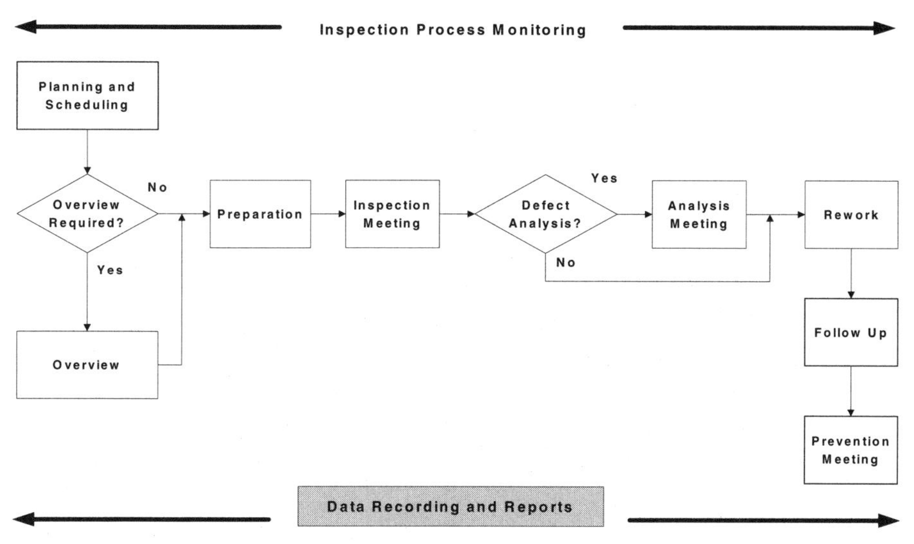

Activity 9: Data Recording and Reports
Figure 3.10

INTRODUCTION

This activity is held concurrently with other activities, including at the end of the Inspection process.

Data recording for defects found and the conduct of the Inspection process is completed using the organization's templates, database, etc. See Chapter 6: Inspection Data for specifics on the types of data to be recorded for the Inspection.

Data should also be recorded for the Overview, when held.

Responsible Individual:

The Recorder during the Overview, Inspection Meeting, and optional Analysis Meeting records data about the defects and the conduct of the Inspection. Alternately the Moderator can enter the data.

Other Roles:

The Moderator after the Overview and during the Follow-up activity ensures that the data has been entered correctly and completely.

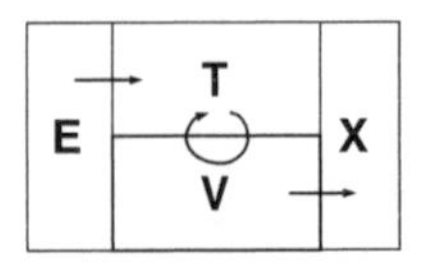

Entry Criteria:

1. The optional Overview Meeting was held.
2. An Inspection Meeting was held.
3. The optional Analysis Meeting was held.

NOTE: Even when an Inspection Meeting is postponed, an Inspection Meeting Report (See Appendix C: Forms) should be filed. It is helpful for the organization to learn how many and why Inspection Meetings are postponed so performance can be improved.

Tasks to be performed:

1. Record data from an Overview, if held.
2. Record data at the Inspection Meeting, including Preparation data.
3. Record data at the optional Analysis Meeting.
4. Record data during the Follow-up activity, including sign off to close the Inspection.

Validation/Verification:

The following are examples of verification/validation:

1. The Inspection team verifies the data at the end of the Inspection Meeting and optional Analysis Meeting.
2. SQA reviews sampled reports.
3. The Producer reviews the report completed by the Moderator.

Measurements: Data should be considered for this activity; e.g., how much effort is used for recording and reporting.

Exit Criteria:

1. The data are complete and agreed to by the Inspection Meeting and Analysis Meeting participants.
2. The data gathered during the Follow-up activity are complete and agreed to by the Producer and Moderator.

3.12 Inspection Process Monitoring

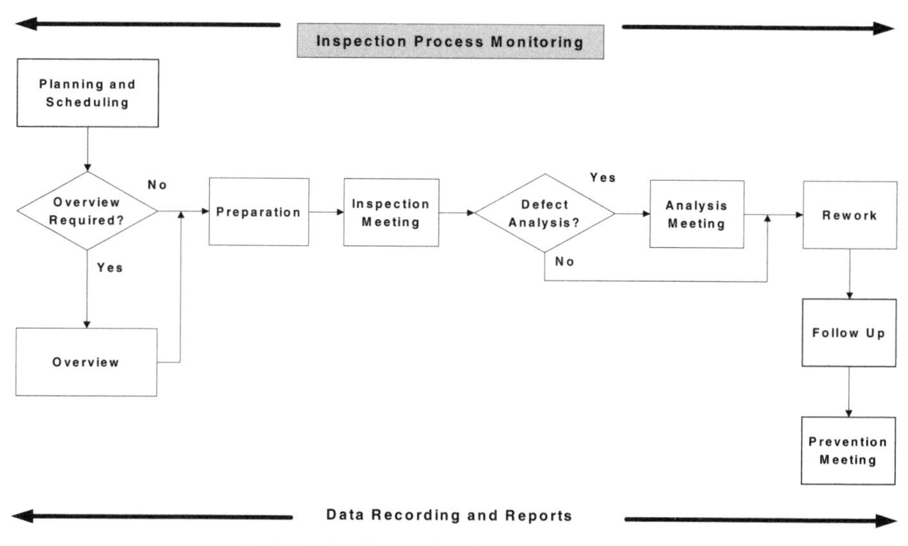

Activity 10: Inspection Process Monitoring
Figure 3.11

INTRODUCTION

This activity is held concurrently with other activities and after Inspections.

The purpose is to evaluate the results of the Inspection process as performed in the organization and to propose suggestions for improvement.

Responsible Individual:

The Inspection Process Coordinator or SEPG is responsible for monitoring and suggesting improvements.

Other Roles:

Management ensures that Inspection Process monitoring is integrated into the Inspection process.

The Inspection Process Improvement Team proposes actions for Inspection process improvements based on the monitoring and analysis of the Inspection Coordinator.

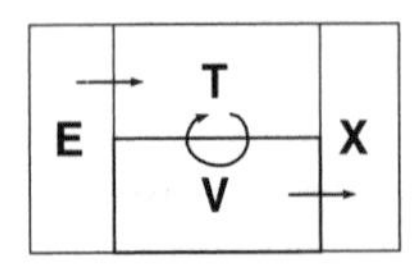

Entry Criteria:

1. Reports and results from Inspections over a period of performance are available.
2. A coordinator is assigned.
3. Resources are allocated for Inspection Process Improvement Team.

Tasks to be performed:

1. Gather the Inspection process data provided since the last Monitoring Report.
2. Review Inspection reports and related data for trends and results against objectives.
3. Interview Inspection participants to ensure understanding of results and to gather other inputs.
4. Perform analysis using the data from the Inspection reports, interviews, and surveys.
5. Provide the analysis to the Inspection Process Improvement Team for review and proposal to management for Inspection process improvements.

Validation/Verification:

The following are examples of verification/validation:

1. The Inspection Coordinator performs monitoring actions per agreed periods for analysis.
2. The Inspection Process Action Improvement Team meets per agreed periods for recommendations.
3. SQA reviews the Monitoring activity on a random basis to ensure it is being performed.

Measurements: Data should be considered during this activity; e.g.,

- How much effort is expended
- How many proposals for improvement are made
- How many improvements are put into action

Exit Criteria:

1. Reports of analysis are developed.
2. Actions for improvements are proposed.
3. Actions are implemented for Inspection process improvements.

End Quote:

"More software organizations today regularly use some from of technical review as a standard part of the process. But not all – not by any means."
Gerald M. Weinberg

CHAPTER 4
THE MODERATOR

"Leaders are like pilots on a plane: they are guiding the flight of which they are a part, using their charts, instruments, and coworkers to reach their destination successfully. First-time quality leaders, like first-time pilots, often feel overwhelmed at even beginning such a journey."
Steven George

4.1 Introduction

This chapter is written under the assumption that an Inspection will require a Moderator; i.e., there will be more than one inspector. When there is only one inspector, there is not a need for a separate Moderator, as the assigned inspector will perform all roles. The recommended approach for these situations is noted in Section 4.6 where 1:1 Inspections are discussed.

The Moderator is a key role in successful Inspections. The Moderator ensures that the Inspection procedures are followed, that the inspectors fulfill their responsibilities within their defined roles, and that the Inspection is performed successfully. Good Moderators enable the participants to see and learn the value of Inspections and, thus, are key agents in establishing buy-in and success for organizations starting Inspections.

A Moderator must have been trained in the process, principles, and practices of Software Inspections. A trained or qualified Moderator must be available to the Project Lead in sufficient advance of the Inspection activities to be performed.

Not everyone will be a good Moderator, but everyone should be required to moderate at least one Inspection. Some will find they like to moderate and some will learn that they can serve the team well when they do moderate, especially in areas where they are the knowledge experts. All will learn how to make Inspections more successful.

The Moderator is not a full-time job, but a part-time assignment, mostly given to senior and experienced programmers, designers, analysts, and writers who have active roles in a project. Moderators should be recognized for the extra time it takes to moderate, whether on their own project or other projects. The Moderator's role begins when the Moderator is selected and is completed when the Inspection is recorded as Closed. See Section 2.1 for definition of Closed and other status indicators of Inspections.

The Moderator is the Inspection team coordinator, facilitator, coach, mediator, and manager. The Moderator, while a manager of the scheduled Inspection, does not typically come from the management team. When the Moderator is also a manager, the organization must take care that this will not work against Inspection objectives, especially in keeping defect data safe and not using it to appraise or judge a Producer. My recommendation is not to have managers serve as Moderators when first starting use of Inspections, even though it has been known to work. After Inspections have been institutionalized in an organization, managers should be considered, as would any other team member who can best contribute.

Moderators best serve when they are objective and do not have a vested interest in the work product. If this is unavoidable, then the risk should be noted, analyzed, and reviewed. A Moderator with a vested interest in the work product should be an exception if it does occur. Over time most Moderators, even when involved in the inspected work product, can achieve distance as Moderators. During start up with Inspections, independence seems to lead to more successes from my experiences. Moderators best serve when they have technical or domain knowledge of the work product under Inspection.

The Moderator should pace the Inspection Meeting to ensure the participants are not overtaxed, working too long without breaks. Meetings should not be scheduled for more than two hours, but even then, if the work is intensive, it may be warranted to call a break midway.

ANECDOTE

MAJOR DON

In one organization we learned that one Moderator whose first name was Don was no longer being selected from the Moderator Pool. When we explored the reason, we learned that he was called Major Don by the developers. It seemed that he believed that if more major defects were found when he was the Moderator this would reflect well on him. So he would argue for converting too many minors into majors. As often happens, they coined a name for him that defined his behavior.

Needless to say he missed the point of his role.

Anecdote 4.1

All Moderators can serve, but some can serve better when properly deployed for key work products. For example, "The best moderators must be used for requirements inspections, because the inspectors are checking against undocumented information sources." [FOW86] While we can question the point of "undocumented sources", the point is that some Inspections are more difficult and have some have a higher impact on the success of the project. Therefore, these should have the best Moderators assigned to them.

Finally, Moderators are included in Inspections to serve the Inspection team and the objectives of the organization; i.e., to find defects effectively and efficiently. They are not in Inspections to serve themselves.

4.2 Qualities of Good Moderators

The best moderators seem to have repeatable characteristics:

- Independent and objective: the Moderator should not be a part of the team that worked on the work product under Inspection. Sometimes this cannot be avoided, especially on small projects.
- Leader: while the Moderator is not a manager, they serve best when they have management and leadership abilities. They will manage the Inspection once it has been scheduled. Some organizations have viewed how well a Moderator leads as an indication of management ability on future projects.
- Coach: good managers/leaders are often good coaches also.
- Technically astute: the Moderator does not have to be an expert in the domain of the work product, but the Moderator should be able to understand the technical aspects. When the Moderator is not technically knowledgeable, the team may discount them and they are less able to control technical discussions.
- Communication skills: the Moderator must listen and hear; the Moderator must give directions and explain so the participants understand the value of Inspections.
- Sense of humor: not a requirement, but it sure helps when the meetings get sticky. Besides, we all like someone with a sense of humor.
- Trained: the Moderator must be trained. Never, never have someone serve as a Moderator who has not been trained in Inspections and the requirements of a Moderator!

Not getting the best Moderators because the best are not available will occur more than one may want. We cannot always get the best people as Moderators, but we must especially ensure that we have the best when they are required at critical Inspections; e.g., requirements specifications.

Good behavior is important for Moderators, since they will tend to set the tone of Inspections, especially during early use. The Moderator must remain professional at all times. Yes, I know they are people too and subject to problems that we all must sort through during a business day, but the objective first and foremost must be professionalism from the Moderators. Not all writers hold the same view. Freedman and Weinberg state, "Results are more important than mannerisms. If a leader gets a good review by shouting at everybody, then why worry about shouting." [FRE90] I don't know about you, but I disagree.

Possible Problems with Moderators

Is aggressive: If Moderators are too aggressive in trying to find defects or run a tight Inspection, they may put some inspectors in an uncomfortable position.

Cannot control the meeting: If the meeting runs out of control, takes too long, or is not effective, it is usually because the inspectors get off track and do not follow the process. This will happen, but the Moderator is responsible to bring the team back on track or to call the meeting off, when it gets too far out of control.

Moderator is treated as a secretary: This seems to occur when the Moderator assigned is not technically strong or accepted as a team leader by some participants.

Biased Moderator: If the Moderator shows any biases, the team should call him on this. Typically it will not happen, but even the Moderator can work against a successful Inspection.

The Moderator should be sensitive that the inspectors are people and when their behavior is exceptionally different from normal, expected, or required, the Moderator must try to understand the reason. A little sympathy can go a long way when an inspector, and especially the Producer, is having a difficult personal situation and the team knows it. Just act in an Inspection the way you would in other work activities when this occurs.

Other behaviors such as doodling, window gazing, daydreaming, etc. should be called out or questioned by the Moderator. Again these should be done with delicacy or in an indirect manner, and may be even ignored at a meeting if there are other indicators that suggest the meeting is proceeding reasonably well.

4.3 Activities To Be Performed by the Moderator

Once the Project Lead has identified the Moderator for an Inspection, the Moderator is responsible to perform the following tasks:

1. INSPECTION SCHEDULING

The Moderator is dependent on the Project Lead to begin the Inspection Scheduling activities for any specific Inspection. The information for any specific Inspection should be contained in the project's plan, including the detailed schedule, which will evolve as the project progresses. The Project Lead is responsible for planning the Inspection, evolving the project plan, and keeping it up-to-date and relevant for Inspection activities.

The Project Lead should make known the need for any specific Inspection to be performed as the project progresses and as the probable date comes within view. The Project Lead makes the selection of the Moderator, unless the organization uses a pool of Moderators that are chosen by the Inspection Coordinator. In this latter case, the specific Inspection and the work product type to be inspected should be made known to the Software Engineering Process Group (SEPG) or Inspection Coordinator sufficiently in advance to allow selecting the Moderator from the pool of Moderators and providing sufficient time for Moderator preparation.

Once the Moderator has been selected, the following steps can be performed for the Specific Inspection Scheduling activity:

1.1 Determine the need for an Overview

Based on the type of work product to be inspected the Moderator works with the Project Lead and Producer to determine if an Overview is needed. The need for an optional Overview includes education and information necessary or deemed to be required for the Inspection participants to perform an effective and efficient Inspection. See Chapter 3, for determining when an Overview is required and for guidance on deciding when an optional Overview should be considered. Not all Inspections require an Overview. They should be performed only when needed. Once it is known that an Overview is required or desired, it must be included in the work product Inspection schedule.

1.2 Determine the Inspection team

The Moderator works with the Project Lead or the Producer of the material to select the Inspection team. The number of participating inspectors will vary with the type of work product and the needs to be met for the project. The number of inspectors should be the minimum number necessary for an effective Inspection. Every extra inspector adds to the cost of the Inspection, but may not add a sufficient return for the investment; i.e., extra inspectors may reduce efficiency without an increase in effectiveness. For some Inspections only one inspector may be sufficient. See Section 4.6 for further discussion of 1:1 Inspections.

The Moderator assigns the inspector roles to the participants (see Chapter 5: Other Inspector Roles). Also see Section 5.4 for considerations on choosing the participants on an Inspection team.

NOTE: There may be multiple roles separately assigned when the team is large enough. There may be concurrent roles when the team has only two or three participants. See Table 4.1 for suggested designated roles based on team size. A "Yes" indicates that this role is separately assigned to the indicated participant.

The Inspection team should be balanced as much as possible to provide various relevant viewpoints on the work product. If the materials are being handed off to someone else for completion, refinement, or transformation, this person should be on the Inspection team. If someone has a dependency on the materials; e.g., system test, user documentation, they should be considered for the team. If one programmer performs all the activities of analysis, design, code, and test, then one inspector may be sufficient.

Read this table as follow:

- First determine what the necessary team size is
- Then assign a role to each team member
    - In teams of 2, the Moderator serves in all the other roles

- In teams of 3, if there is a Receiver; i.e., the person next in the project's process to work with the work product under Inspection; e.g., an independent tester, they should serve as Reader
- If there is no Receiver, another inspector can serve as Reader

Team Size	Producer	Moderator	Reader	Recorder
2	Yes	Yes	Moderator	Moderator
3	Yes	Yes	Receiver	Moderator
4+	Yes	Yes	Receiver	Yes

Suggested Designated Roles
Table 4.1

Remember that the primary purpose of an Inspection is to find the maximum number of defects that may exist in the work product, so pick team members who have the best knowledge and skill to help find defects.

Clearly this is not always possible, but it should remain the objective.

If the Inspection is being used to provide training, then understand that effectiveness may be reduced during the meeting. If for any Inspection the most knowledgeable inspectors cannot be made available, the Inspection can still be held rather than delaying it or canceling it. Pick the next best available inspector. It may be useful to track the effectiveness and efficiency of these Inspections to learn if the process can be improved and what the effectiveness or efficiency differences may be in these situations. Downstream defect data analysis for inspected work products can be used to help inspectors learn why some defects were not found during the Inspection. This learning will enable Defect Prevention, which is discussed in Chapter 7.

1.3 Ensuring availability of materials

The material that is required is determined by the work product type to be inspected (see Appendix B). In all cases the material should meet the Entry Criteria for the type of Inspection. If the Moderator determines that the Inspection material is not ready, the Inspection should be postponed until the material is ready for Inspection. The materials include the work product, ancillary items, and reference materials, as appropriate. Lack of material; i.e., material needed for the inspectors to find any inherent defects, is a risk to an effective and efficient Inspection.

The Inspection materials may be delivered or made available before, during, or after the Overview. Where possible avoid paper copies, which require copying and distribution. With web-based facilities, the materials can be made available via controlled online libraries to all participants, but ensure everyone is working with the correct version. Since some inspectors may prefer paper copies, the Moderator should ensure that the online copy is in a printer friendly format.

1.4 Assigning roles

The Moderator assigns the roles to the inspectors and gets their concurrence on the assignments. This should be done building upon their domain knowledge, strengths, skills, and desires to accept assigned roles. For example, if someone will make a poor Reader, they should not be assigned that role, or if someone outright refuses to be a Recorder, then don't force them to do it.

Certain roles can be grouped for some Inspections. However, there are role groupings that should typically be avoided; e.g., Producer who is Reader, Producer who is Recorder, and Reader who is also Recorder. These relationships are discussed in Chapter 5.

1.5 Chunking the materials

Not all work products will fit into a two-hour Inspections Meeting. In these cases the Moderator must make some decisions. If the material will take more than two hours, but it is a containable overrun, then one meeting can be scheduled. The Moderator in these cases should give consideration to a logical break during the meeting. This should be discussed at the meeting start and agreed to by the participants. A break is not always required, but the option should be provided.

In situations where multiple meetings are required, split the work product to be inspected into reasonable chunks. This can be done in two ways: by form and by function. Function chunking, when it is obvious, is easier to do; e.g., subroutines within code modules, chapters or sections within documents. Chunking can be done almost anytime before the Inspection is scheduled.

As Freedman states, "Breaking down by form is not always so obvious. In essence, we seek *different points of view* on the same material." For instance:

1. Standards
2. Code versus other documentation
3. Efficiency
4. User interfaces
5. Maintainability
6. Operating convenience [FRE90]

Chunking by form will cause redundant coverage, but it is an option and when used it can ensure coverage with assigned viewpoints.

Chunking can also be used to assign the chunks to concurrent teams and perform concurrent Inspections of a large work product.

1.6 Defining the Inspection activities schedule

The dates for the Overview, when one is required, and for the Inspection Meeting should be determined with the Producer and Project Lead. Usually this will be straightforward, but in some cases may require negotiating and moving other commitments for the selected inspectors and Producer. Once the dates are determined, they should be posted to all participants. A friendly reminder a day or so before is often useful.

Notifications should be sent to all participants once the Moderator has determined that the Inspection can be scheduled. See Appendix B for a suggested Inspection Meeting Notice format.

Items that must be addressed in the schedules:

- Overview, when required
- Preparation time
- Inspection Meeting time
- Analysis Meeting time
- Logistics

1.6.1 Overview, when required

The Overview is held prior to the Inspection meeting. The amount of time required will vary with the scope of the material to be inspected and should be calculated to address the time needed for the participants to pre-review any Overview material that may be provided prior to the Overview and the time allocated for the Overview itself. The required amount of time should be determined with the Producer and the Project Lead.

There are no rules of thumb to guide the amount of time needed, since the Overview is affected by too many variables; e.g., complexity of the material, newness to the software solution, experience of the team members, collocation of team members, media used, density of the material. The objective is communication of understanding to the inspectors so they can perform an effective Inspection; it is not a forum to discuss details. While at times details may be needed to achieve understanding, the objective is to present at a higher level of abstraction.

Materials provided prior to the Overview, while optional, should be allocated sufficient time for the participants to read them. These distributed materials should be read for understanding, not for defect discovery. For both the preparation for the Overview and the Overview itself the Moderator should get concurrence from the participants regarding adequate time needed. It is not always necessary to distribute Overview materials beforehand, but when judged to be useful it should be done.

In some situations an Overview may be held at the time the Inspection Meeting materials are delivered to the participants for that meeting's Preparation. In this situation the schedule for the Overview is coordinated with the beginning of the Preparation activity.

In yet other situations the Overview may be quite brief due to the nature of the work being inspected; e.g., fixes or maintenance, and may be coordinated with a combined Preparation/Inspection Meeting. A combined Preparation/Inspection Meeting can be used with Inspection of fixes that need to be turned around very quickly or which are very small. Therefore, rather than not having an Inspection, it may be decided that a combined set of Overview/Preparation/Inspection Meeting may be held with participants.

Solo:Inspections, where the Producer is not in attendance during the Inspection, is another approach of a combined Preparation/Inspection Meeting. Solo:Inspections are discussed in Chapter 14. These types of Inspections should be understood as different, the results analyzed to ensure the Inspection process is executing under stable conditions, and tracked afterwards to see if any defects are leaked into subsequent product life cycle stages. We want to permit improvements to the Inspection process, but we want to make sure they really are improvements.

1.6.2 Preparation effort

The Moderator must first estimate the Preparation effort needed based on the material to be inspected. These estimates should be validated with the Inspection team participants. At that time, the Moderator needs to get commitment from each participant that enough time is allocated and that it will be sufficient for Preparation. See Table 3.1 for recommended Preparation rates.

It is important to understand that inspectors may have other commitments causing the elapsed time during the Preparation to appear longer than actually needed. For example, the time required for actual Preparation may only be 4 hours, but one or more inspectors cannot complete the Preparation for 3 days due to other commitments. This may not be desirable and when it cannot be changed, it will cause a lag in starting the Inspection Meeting. Earlier advanced notice from the Project Lead may help avoid this type of lag. As noted earlier, the Moderator should ensure that inspectors are given sufficient time for Preparation.

1.6.3 Inspection Meeting duration

The Moderator must estimate the Inspection Meeting time needed based on the material to be inspected. These estimates should be based on history within the organization, but Table 3.1 will serve as a reasonable start. It should be decided whether one meeting or a series of meetings will be required based on the volume of work product to be inspected.

In the original Inspection study it was found that 2 hours was a reasonable duration for an Inspection Meeting. If the material requires significantly more than 2 hours, the Inspection Meeting may need to be staged. The Moderator needs to validate that the inspectors will be available for the staged meeting times.

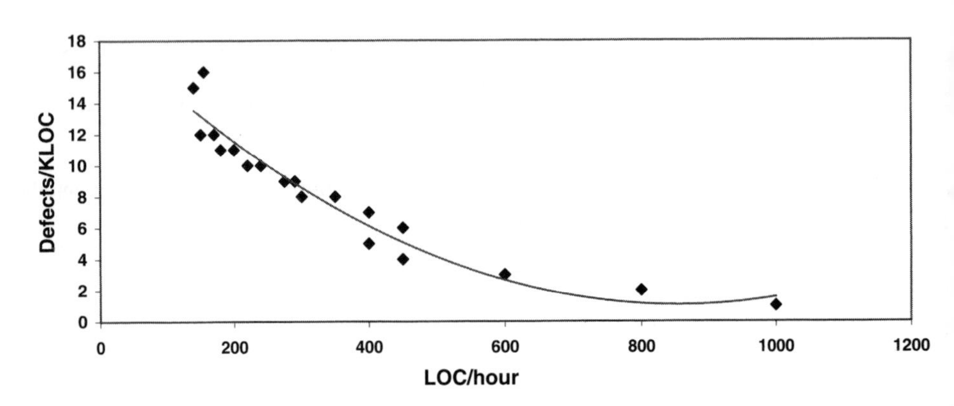

Relationship Between The Rate of an Inspection Meeting and Defect Find Rates
Figure 4.1

Figure 4.1 shows an example where the relationship between Inspection rate (LOC/hour) and defect removal rate (defects/KLOC) are correlated. We see that the defect find rate decreases as the speed of the Inspection increases. While this is only an example in one client project, this is a pattern that has recurred with Inspections since their first use.

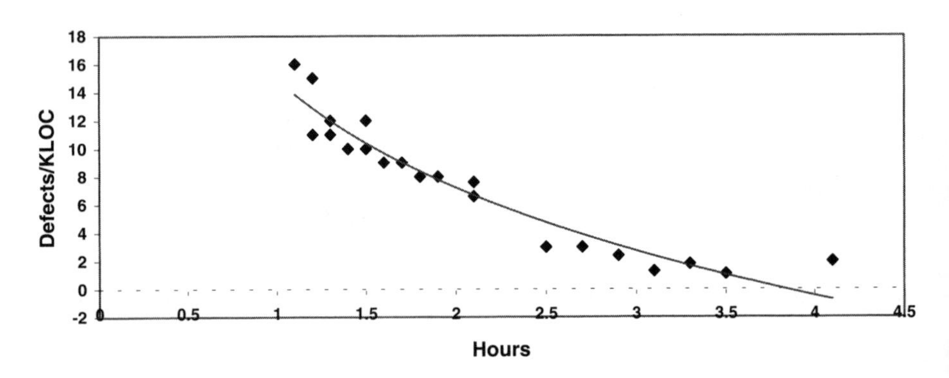

Relationship Between Time In Inspection Meeting and Defect Find Rate
Figure 4.2

There also appears to be a correlation after 2-3 hours where the defect find rate decreases. See Figure 4.2 as an example from a client project. In this example we see a clustering under 2.5 hours and another clustering after 2.5 hours. This pattern is not always so explicit, but does recur frequently. The decline in the defect find rate is due to long hours that wear on the inspectors' ability to maintain energy needed to concentrate and find defects. When a work product is large, rather than scheduling long Inspection Meetings the material should be chunked into smaller pieces that can be separately inspected.

1.6.4 Analysis Meeting

A decision should be taken prior to the Inspection Meeting to hold an Analysis Meeting or not, including whether it should immediately follow the Inspection Meeting. These meetings can be very brief, especially when few defects are found. Since the objective in the Analysis Meeting is to gather data that will enable Defect Prevention, some causal analysis performed right after the Inspection Meeting can save time and probably get better data about probable causes. In some Inspection Meetings the team members can determine the cause at the time the defect is identified and accepted.

1.6.5 Logistics

The Moderator will reserve an Inspection Meeting room or area for the duration of the meetings. If the Inspection is staged into multiple sessions, more than one room may be needed.

The room should be large enough for the size of the Inspection team. Preferably it is a room with a door that allows private meetings, especially in organizations that do not yet share an open culture. A round table would allow all members to see each other easily, but is rarely achievable. A table of some type is necessary for the inspectors to comfortably use the Inspection materials and for the Recorder to record the Inspection data.

When an appropriate room is not available for an Inspection Meeting, make use of what is available; e.g. a manager's office, the library, the cafeteria. There may be risk with some of these choices, but they also can serve quite nicely. Don't default into room unavailability as an excuse to postpone or cancel an Inspection. Teams have actually used stairwells effectively, though these should hardly be a steady practice.

When the materials are made available online, each inspector will require online access during Preparation, at least. During the Inspection Meeting, inspectors should bring annotated printouts unless the meeting room has sufficient online facilities. See Section 4.7 for discussion regarding online Inspections.

If materials are not available online, then all materials required for the Inspection should be duplicated and made available to all inspectors with enough time for them to prepare.

If the Reader requires visual aids, these should be made available.

If the Recorder requires a flip chart or a PC to record the data, these need to be available.

2. OVERVIEW

When the Overview has been scheduled and the Producer and other participants are at the Overview meeting, the Moderator begins the meeting and facilitates by:

- Introducing the Producer and material for the Overview
- Guiding, facilitating, and managing the meeting
- Ensure identified defects that were discovered at the Overview are recorded
- Ensure any Open Issues are recorded
- Concluding the meeting and asking the participants if the meeting met the objectives
  - If it is determined that the meeting was not sufficient to meet the objectives, another Overview may be required before proceeding to Preparation

The Overview is left to the Producer to execute, but the Moderator should facilitate and ensure a successful meeting.

3. PREPARATION

The Moderator as inspector prepares for the Inspection Meeting just as any other Inspection participant.

NOTE: This is a preferred role for the Moderator from my experience. Both Bob Kohli and I served as Moderators and inspectors during the VTAM study. These combined roles are not practiced by all organizations and I am not entirely sure why this drifting away has occurred. I suspect it is because some believe that the Moderator is active moderating and that participating, as an inspector, will deter from effective moderating. If the Moderator also serves as an inspector, the Inspection Meeting is more efficient especially when the Moderator has domain knowledge. Serving as an inspector also enables the Moderator to learn through active participation. In this book, I will always write under the assumption that the Moderator serves as an inspector, but it's a choice for how you implement this.

3. INSPECTION MEETING

The Moderator has two roles during all Inspection Meetings:

- Moderator
- Inspector

An active Moderator can maintain objectivity. It is, however, possible that these two roles will interfere with each other. For example, it would be a problem if the Moderator believes or demonstrates a belief that their opinion carries more weight than that of other inspectors. The Moderator does not have more say as an inspector than any other inspector! They may be right and they may have more experience, but they have a combined role when serving as Moderator. They should be helping the other inspectors to learn, not forcefully making others accept their views. Some organizations believe that the Moderator serving two roles is an overload to the Moderator. I have consistently found otherwise, but do not deny that others may have experienced problems. They could analyze why these problems occur and consider changing the process to accommodate a more efficient approach.

As the Moderator they manage, coach, and facilitate. As an inspector they identify, discuss, and come to agreement on defects with the Inspection team. (See Chapter 5: Other Roles.) When the team size is only two as in 1:1 Inspections, the Moderator will serve in all other roles. See Table 4.1 and Table 4.2 for activity assignments.

The Moderator must always maintain objectivity when serving as an inspector, and there is ample evidence that this can be done.

I recommend that the Moderator hold a mini lessons-learned session at the end of the Inspection Meeting asking:

- What worked well
- What could have been improved

This should only take a few minutes and is especially helpful when first introducing Inspections into an organization.

5. DATA RECORDING

The Moderator must review the defect report created by the Recorder and then complete this report during the Follow-up activity for the required contents of the Inspection Report. If the recording medium is visible throughout the meeting, all inspectors can review and verify the defect report as it progresses. The Moderator can also enter the data.

6. ANALYSIS MEETING

This meeting, while originally not in the defined method and while many consider it optional, is recommended for successful and more effective practice of Inspections and Defect Prevention. It should also be considered for organizations starting Inspections where there is clear management support and a defined policy that makes Inspection data safe. Other organizations may choose to wait until they have more evidence that Inspections are working well for them, but all organizations should have the objective of putting Analysis Meetings into practice as part of the Inspection process.

The Analysis Meeting is not a Prevention Meeting where probable causes are analyzed for preventive actions that should be considered, but is a brief analysis drawing on the Inspection team's knowledge to quickly identify probable causes of the found defects. Causal analysis can be made for most of the defects identified at the Inspection Meeting. Some cause identification may need to be determined by the Producer during the Rework activity, but these are a minority. The Moderator is both a facilitator and participant at this meeting. The output of this meeting will feed the organization's Prevention Meetings that I discuss in Chapter 7.

7. REWORK

The Moderator may work with the Producer during the Rework activity to address any Open Issues that may have come from the Inspection Meeting or to help defect classification and resolution. If there are no Open Issues, the Moderator will meet with the Producer at the agreed-to date by which the Rework is to be completed and can be verified.

8. FOLLOW-UP

The Moderator or a designee will verify that the Rework resolves the recorded defects and any identified Open Issues. Resolved Open Issues originating at the Inspection Meeting should not have changed the work product in any substantive way. If so, the Moderator should schedule the rework for a Re-Inspection.

Open Issues coming into the Inspection Meeting are not subject for resolution during Rework, as these were predetermined to be outside of the scope of the work product under Inspection. These Open Issues are to be completed later and inspected when completed. The Moderator must assure that these Open Issues are not included in the Rework. If they have been, then a Re-Inspection is needed.

Open Issues can be of two types:

- Identified by the Producer coming into an Inspection
- Identified during the Inspection by the team

Any Open Issues that are not resolved must be identified as such and assigned to the management tracking system for resolution using Change Requests.

During Follow-up the moderator will:

- Complete the defect report as provided by the Recorder to show that the Inspection is Closed
- Verify all rework
- Schedule a Re-Inspection, if warranted

Follow-up can optionally be assigned to another inspector on the Inspection team or someone else where expert opinion is needed. The Moderator or someone who is designated at the Inspection Meeting must meet with the Producer to verify that the rework is complete and correct. Once the verification is completed the Moderator must close the subject Inspection by completing and filing the Inspection report.

4.4 Code of Conduct for Moderators

The Moderator is essential to successful Inspections. Moderators, like other professionals, should work by a code of conduct to facilitate repeated success with Inspections.

To facilitate the best Inspections the following Code of Conduct is suggested:

1. Always remain professional and objective
2. Prepare well in advance for all meetings
3. Enable the team members for a successful Inspection
4. Keep each meeting focused to its specific objectives; e.g.,

    - Learning at the Overview
    - Finding and agreeing to defects at the Inspection Meeting
    - Performing causal analysis at the Analysis Meeting

5. Ensure all data is captured and recorded
6. Always maintain confidentiality
7. Use effective meeting practices: e.g.,

    - Properly notify all participants well enough in advance
    - Restate the purpose of the meeting, especially for first time participants
    - Monitor time and keep the meeting moving forward
    - Allow discussion, but table discussions that are taking too much time without making progress that helps the objectives
    - At the end of the meeting solicit input, including recommendations for improvements to the Inspection process

8. Be a team player; participate as another inspector
9. Remember that the Moderator, while not accountable for the quality of the work product, is accountable for the quality of the Inspection
10. Ensure appropriate behavior by all attendees
11. Enforce and adhere to Inspection activity entry and exit criteria
12. If it is clear that the Inspection meeting will run over the scheduled time, stop the meeting and ask if the team is Ok with this, and if not, discuss how to schedule the completion of the Inspection

4.5 Moderator Pools

Moderators can be assigned by the Project Lead, by the Inspection Coordinator or by Software Quality Assurance (SQA), depending on where the organization decision is assigned. This assignment will vary by organization type. All of these approaches have worked. Often when SQA assigns the Moderator, the Inspection is viewed as an SQA process and may become more of an assurance process rather than a control process for work product quality. I prefer that SQA serve to ensure the quality of Inspections rather than being responsible for them.

Moderators must be assigned in sufficient time for them to facilitate a successful Inspection. Finding one who is available may be difficult.

There are a number of approaches that have worked, including:

- Independent full time assignments
- Rotational assignments from a pool

Let's discuss the pros and cons of each approach.

Independent Full-Time Assignments

A few organizations have designated the Moderator to be a full time assignment. Another version is where moderating may be a primary assignment in addition to other quality assurance work. In both cases these Moderators tend to be drawn from the Software Quality Assurance part of the organization. This seems to be especially true when the Moderator does not serve as an inspector during the meeting. While this approach has been successful, I personally think it limits both the individuals assigned as Moderators and the organization. I do not recommend full time assignments for Moderators.

Rotational Pools

A more widely practiced approach is to use pools. Here a group of individuals who have been qualified as Moderators are subject to being called during a designated period of time to perform a defined volume of Inspections. This approach provides flexibility, since if any one Moderator is not available, another very likely is.

Each Moderator has an agreed amount of time that they will give to moderating. Their remaining and much larger portion of time is available for other software activities. This approach provides the maximum flexibility provided there is a sufficient number in the pool. Occasionally it can be misused. For example, a Moderator, when called, may always have a "reason" for not being available. This is a management problem. The Moderator's manager must ensure availability over the prescribed time period. The Inspection Coordinator should canvas the pool of Moderators for availability on a monthly basis to avoid surprises. We will discuss the role of the Inspection Coordinator in Chapter 10.

Regardless of how much time any person is assigned to do moderating, this activity should be in their performance objectives and time allocated to perform as a Moderator. I have seen too often where it was not, and the assigned individual feels compromised by the management for not getting credit for good moderating. You can surmise where this will lead!

Moderators, especially those used more frequently, should have group meetings with other Moderators and the SEPG or Inspection Coordinator to share ideas and experiences. I recommend quarterly meetings, but during start up these should be held more frequently, even

4.6 Moderating in 1:1 Inspections

1:1 Inspections occur when there are only two participants in an Inspection, the Producer and the Inspector/Moderator. In Table 4.1 I briefly noted how an Inspection could proceed with only two participants. Here I expand a bit further the role assignments for the 1:1 Inspection. I will discuss more about 1:1 Inspections in Chapter 14. Table 4.2 shows how the responsibilities for process activity change when a 1:1 Inspection is used and who performs the Moderator's tasks. In this table PL is Project Lead, P is Producer, and I is the inspector.

Moderator Task	Required?	Who Performs
1. Inspection Scheduling	Yes	PL
1.1 Determine need for Overview	Yes	PL & I
1.2 Determine Inspection team	Yes	PL
1.3 Ensuring availability of materials	Yes	P
1.4 Assigning roles	NA	NA
1.5 Chunking materials	Yes	PL & P
1.6 Defining activities schedule	Yes	PL & P & I
1.6.1 Overview	Optional	PL & I
1.6.2 Preparation effort	Yes	PL & P & I
1.6.3 Inspection Meeting duration	Yes	PL & P & I
1.6.4 Analysis Meeting	Optional	PL & P & I
1.6.5 Logistics	Yes	PL & I
2. Overview	Optional	P & I
3. Preparation	Yes	P & I
4. Inspection Meeting	Yes	P & I
5. Data Recording	Yes	I
6. Analysis Meeting	Optional	P & I
7. Rework	Yes	P
8. Follow-up	Yes	P & I

Tasks Assignments in 1:1 Inspections
Table 4.2

We see from this table that, while there is only one inspector, all Inspection activities and tasks are still performed.

4.7 Online Inspections

The widespread availability of intranets has enabled cross-group communications and access to documents. Online Inspections should, therefore, be considered. The process is about the same as the face-to-face Inspection, but when there are multiple inspectors in different locations, the Moderator must stay on top of communications synchronizing all participants. It is not always a problem, but remoteness leads to a higher risk of lack of participation. Of course, the inspectors do not need to be remote to use online facilities.

Despite the accessibility to documents and even when voice and video services are available, remote Inspections are culturally just not the same. If an inspector wants to hide, it is easier when remote. The Moderator can poll inspectors to permit more active participation and reduce any hiding or lack of participation that may occur. As video capability is more widely deployed, online Inspections will benefit so that inspectors can see each other and the artifacts they are discussing. Video will bring them closer, but it is still not the same as face-to-face Inspections.

The Moderator must also ensure that everyone is using the same reference version for the work product. One way to ensure a common version is to place the work product in its own directory versus allowing read only access to development libraries. Yes, I know programmers can ensure they are using the right baseline if they want to, but why introduce another variable where mistakes can be made. Imagine what the Inspection would be like if different versions or baselines were used between inspectors!

One advantage to web-based Inspections is that it allows recording of Inspection data during the Inspection. Everyone can see the recording as it happens. Another advantage is that the minor logs can be visible and transferred even before the session starts. If this protocol is followed, the Moderator can get a good and immediate impression of the preparation performed. Not all recording needs to be done in real-time, but where online capability is possible, it should be used. An alternative is that the Recorder completes recording at the end or immediately after the Inspection session and makes the records available for all inspectors to review, as appropriate. Work product documents can also be highlighted or annotated and these could also be distributed before the session start.

Concurrence, when online sessions are not voice-enabled, will require a polling mechanism that all inspectors would input to when electronically discussing defects. Mechanisms like Instant Messaging can make the polling move faster, but it should be assumed that an online Inspection would go slower than face-to-face Inspection Meetings regardless of the available technology.

Since the inspectors are using an online facility, they could have an integrated set of services that would in real-time take the data at the end of the Inspection Meeting and calculate control charts. These would provide the team with a graphical presentation of the Inspection performance and to make better decisions about Re-Inspections. See Chapters 6 and 8 for examples.

Online technology is not yet fully enabled to permit the best of Inspection Meeting environments, but online technology presents an important alternative when teams are at multiple locations and geographically distributed.

There have been some implementations of tools to try to package an online integrated solution; e.g., Scrutiny. [GIN93] Other tools will be discussed in Chapter 14.

Advantages when using web-based technologies for Inspections include:

- Shared and commonly accessible libraries of work products, standards, report templates, and checklists
- Annotation facilities to capture questions, issues, and potential defects during the Preparation
- The ability to easily forward the Preparation list to the Moderator and Producer
- Online recording of defects and Open Issues as they are discovered during the Inspection Meeting
- Easy filing of the Inspection Meeting report
- Use of quantitative analysis tools to help decision making on the quality of the Inspection
- Use of quantitative techniques for making decisions about Re-inspections

4.8 Moderator's Checklist

Once a Moderator has been chosen, the following should be done for Inspections:

- ❑ Schedule the detailed dates of the Inspection, unless already set
- ❑ Designate the Inspection team with the Project Lead and Producer
- ❑ Ensure inspectors have everything needed to perform a proper Inspection; i.e., Overview Meeting, time to prepare, work product material, room, forms to be used during the Inspection Meeting, reference material, ancillary material
- ❑ Prepare for the Inspection
- ❑ Serve as an inspector to find defects
- ❑ Ensure the Inspection Meeting is performed effectively and efficiently by observing performance and taking any necessary actions to facilitate the success of the meeting
- ❑ Manage the meeting, including announcing breaks as warranted
- ❑ Ensure the Inspection Meeting does not execute under disagreements or personal attacks
- ❑ Maintain an objective and unbiased Inspection Meeting
- ❑ Conduct the Analysis Meeting unless defects have already been classified with causes during the Inspection Meeting
- ❑ Ensure the Inspection data is entered into the Inspection database and produce the required reports for management
- ❑ Follow-up with the Producer to ensure closure on defects and Open Issues
- ❑ Provide input to the Inspection Coordinator or SEPG from Analysis Meetings

Some of these items can be delegated, but they are the responsibility of the Moderator.

4.9 Moderator's Inspection Meeting Checklist

After a while the Moderator should not require a checklist for the Inspection Meeting, but in the beginning they could use the following:

- ❑ Take headcount
- ❑ Ensure participants are on time
- ❑ Make introductions, as necessary
- ❑ Determine preparedness of all participants
- ❑ Ensure the Reader gets concurrence on reading style before or at the meeting
- ❑ Ensure the Reader is properly pacing the reading
- ❑ Ensure the Recorder is sufficiently recording defect information
- ❑ Make a decision on Re-Inspection
- ❑ Decide if an Analysis Meeting will be used
- ❑ Ensure exit criteria are satisfied

End Quote:

"Indeed, inspections appear to be the most efficient form of defect removal yet developed, and only formal inspections tend to consistently exceed 60 percent in defect removal efficiency"
Capers Jones

CHAPTER 5
OTHER ROLES

"The skillful commander selects his men and then exploits the situation."
Sun Tzu in The Art Of War

5.1 Introduction

In the previous chapter the role of the Moderator was discussed. In this chapter an explanation is given for the roles assigned to other inspectors in the Inspection process. All the roles begin when an inspector has been notified of participation in an Inspection and complete when the defects have been resolved during Rework and after the final recording of the Inspection data. Each participant in the Inspection process will be assigned one or more of the roles defined below. This chapter is written assuming multiple participants in an Inspection. Gilb, among others, requires that special checking assignments also be assigned to each inspector. I discuss these assignments as assigned viewpoints in Section 5.7.

In 1:1 Inspections, role assignment has no meaning, except that the one inspector must perform all the roles in a different fashion than in Inspections with multiple inspectors. See Table 4.2 in Section 4.6 for definition of roles performed in 1:1 Inspections. See Chapter 14 for Solo:Inspections, where one inspector performs all roles without direct Producer involvement.

In the VTAM study and as documented by Fagan, we used a different set of defined roles. The roles were Moderator, Designer, Coder/Implementer, and Tester. The Moderator usually served as the Recorder. Additionally a Reader was "chosen by the Moderator (usually the coder)." [FAG76] While these roles served us for the study, it was learned by others that roles did not necessarily need to correspond to the project life cycle. Today, most Inspection users speak of the Moderator, Reader, Recorder, and Producer as the primary roles for team Inspections. Others speak of the Author as Producer or the Scribe as Recorder, and some have dropped the Reader role.

All inspectors must know the required Inspection procedures and what is required for their role.

5.2 Primary Inspector Roles

The primary roles besides the Moderator are:

- The Producer
- The Reader
- The Recorder

See Chapter 3 for suggested procedures.

PRODUCER

The Producer is the individual who produced or modified the work product to be inspected. The Producer can also be referred to as the Author when the work product is initially produced. The Producer may have worked with others to produce the work product, in which case the Producer is one of the producing team members and represents the team's work.

The role of Producer should be taken by the person chiefly responsible for creating the work product to be inspected, but can be any member of the team that produced the work product. The Producer must respond to questions and areas identified as potential defects during the Inspection. Some organizations have used teams of Producers during Inspections for large work products. My own view is to keep the team as small as necessary for an effective Inspection, so ask twice before adding participants.

The Producer should be the person who will make the changes to the work product as a result of the Inspection.

The Producer can help the other participants by focusing their attention on known Open Issues and problem areas where he or she is concerned or wants special attention paid by the inspectors.

Primary responsibilities during Inspection activities include:

Planning:

- Identify when the inspectable work product will be available for the Inspection team and will satisfy the Entry Criteria to proceed for scheduling; see Chapter 3
- Decide with the Moderator, Project Lead, and inspectors if an Overview is needed

Overview:

- If an Overview Meeting is required, prepare the presentation to be given to the Inspection team
- Note any Open Issues
- Present the Overview
- Review the rationale and relevant history behind the work product
- Discuss questions, noted problems, defects, and issues raised
- Confirm that the Overview met the needs of the inspectors

Preparation:

- Make copies of the Inspection materials available to the Moderator for distribution, or distribute directly to the participants via, for example, online capabilities

- Prepare as an inspector for the Inspection Meeting, especially if the Producer is not the primary representative of the producing team for the work product under Inspection
- Ensure the distributed material is the correct version for the Inspection

Inspection Meeting:

- Identify any remaining Open Issues at the start of the Inspection Meeting
- Answer questions raised during the Inspection Meeting
- Participate actively during the meeting
- Offer clarifications, but don't debate
- Take notes that may help with defect fixing
- Stay positive; remember it was the process that got you here
- Serve as another inspector to find defects
  - NOTE: While the Producer is most familiar with the work product, the Preparation and Inspection Meeting activities can lead to defect discovery even by the Producer
- Come to agreement on all defects found and have new Open Issues introduced for tracking and resolution when agreement cannot be achieve at the meeting

Rework:

- Resolve all accepted defects
  - Major defects must always be resolved
  - Decide on which minor defects to repair and for any not repaired maintain the Inspection input for when next working on the work product
- Resolve Open Issues, as possible
- Update work products for all resolutions of defects and Open Issues
- Write Change Requests for any defects or Open Issues not resolved

Follow-up:

- Concur with the sign-off of the Inspection report to note the Inspection as Closed
- Prepare for a Re-Inspection, if one was decided upon by the Inspection team

Possible Problems with Producers

Is defensive: Some Producers may feel they are being appraised by the Inspection team and in turn try to defend against any identified defects. This behavior will tend to slow down the effectiveness and efficiency of the Inspection.

Does not actively participate: Some Producers, especially during early organization adoption, may feel that Inspections are a waste of time. They may not say so, but their behavior may demonstrate their view. This behavior will work against efficiency. If the Producer is a reluctant participant, but does not cause overt problems, this behavior can normally be tolerated.

Was not the Producer: It will happen sometimes that the individual serving in the Producer role was not actually the Producer; e.g., when the actual Producer has left the organization. In these cases, as long as the assigned Producer participates actively, the Inspection can proceed. However, agreement on defects may need to be relegated to the Rework activity in more cases than would have happened with the actual Producer.

Responds in a hostile manner to identified defects: This behavior cannot be tolerated and must be controlled by the Moderator. This can be difficult, so both the Project Lead and the Inspection Coordinator must be informed when this happens and counsel the Producer.

Begins to make repairs at the meeting: The Producer may be motivated to solve some problems as they are identified, despite the fact that the process calls for this to be done during the Rework activity. Should solution making or hunting occur, the Moderator must ask the Producer to defer this to the Rework activity.

Biased Producer: The Producer may want to select the inspectors, which is fine, since the Producer probably has a good understanding as to who can best contribute. Be careful, however, that the Producer is not choosing friends who will help him look good. This is more likely to occur in organizations starting out with Inspections or when management inappropriately uses data.

Unprepared: This Producer submits incomplete work products as complete and changes work products after the Preparation has been started. Then if a defect is discussed he typically responds, "I've already fixed that defect."

Producer Types to Watch For

The Gamesman: There is the syndrome of "winking" at Inspections between the Producer and other inspectors; i.e., "We don't find many defects in my Inspection, and when it's your turn we won't find many there." This attitude comes about when team members still do not sufficiently trust management's use of the data from Inspections.

The Controller: You know this type. He is good, real good, and so good he is intimidating even if this is not his nature. He is a controlling Producer, who wants to get things done right away. Some team members, especially new or less experienced may hold back at Inspections with this type. This is another reason for Preparation, which is a safe space for each team member. If the Preparation was done well, this type of Producer will not have as strong a footing to make his case that defects are not defects.

The Intimidator: There is the Producer who purposely intimidates, because this is his nature. An Inspection meeting provides a focused setting for this type to fill their need of power through intimidation. The best defense for the Moderator and other inspectors is to remain objective. The most enlightening cases are when defects are found that this Producer type *knew* were not there, but must admit the possibility when they are found.

The Debater: Another Producer type accepts all queries of possible defects as an opportunity to either over explain (the Teacher) or explore countless possibilities. Everything is interesting to this type. Every possibility should be discussed completely. This type enjoys the intellectual exchange and believes others do also. They are not interested in the time constraints of an Inspection. This can be a difficult type to bring under control, because as the subject matter experts they need to respond whether an identified defect is to be considered valid or not. The Moderator needs to keep the timing focused as the team passes through the material. The Teacher sub-type is a bit easier to control, as he usually will accept from the Moderator that his "lecture" should be cut short. The debater, will debate even the suggestion to move on.

The Unbeliever: This type may not believe in the value of Inspections, but shows up because the organization requires it. This reluctant Producer may not diminish the value of an Inspection, but sure does not do anything to make it more enjoyable.

The Elitist: This type participates weakly, may be late, may leave early, and usually becomes defensive when a defect is found. This type usually engages in too much discussion and is often negative. Most people would rather not engage in endless discussion, so you can see that this type of Producer requires a strong Moderator to keep the objectives clear and directed. If the elitist simply didn't debate, then an Inspection could proceed effectively despite other behaviors. The harder issue is when they do not show up at all. This behavior requires management attention, which should come as a result of the Inspection being postponed.

READER

The IEEE standard states "The reader shall lead the inspection team through the software product in a comprehensive and logical fashion, interpreting sections of the work (for example, generally paraphrasing groups of 1-3 lines), and highlighting important aspects." [IEE98] As a guideline this makes good sense to me.

The Reader is the inspector who will lead the team through the material during the Inspection Meeting. The purpose of reading is to focus on the Inspection material and to ensure an orderly flow for the inspectors.

Guidelines for selecting the appropriate reading approach should be defined as part of the Inspection process by the organization. Multiple approaches may be used in any work product. The decisions should be reviewed with the Moderator before the Inspection Meeting.

Reading can be verbatim or paraphrased depending on the parts of the material under Inspection by the team. The Reader should keep in mind the potential problem areas identified by the Producer at the Overview or at the start of the Inspection Meeting. These areas should be read more slowly than others in the work product.

For code, the reader not only "reads", but also should give some interpretation of the related design and code. The reader should try to avoid focusing on the comments when doing this task, since the comments may be correct and the code incorrect. Other inspectors could compare the Reader's interpretation with the comments to assure correct mapping.

For design, the reader should give some interpretation stating how the design could be implemented, since the design must be implementable to satisfy the functional requirements.

For requirements specifications, the Reader should address whether there is visibility on how the design could represent the requirements in a lower level of detail definition. Basically, the Reader should be reading to ask whether the requirements are complete, correct, consistent, whether they can be implemented, and whether they can be tested or not.

If there is an individual who will be receiving the work product from the Producer for further work after the Inspection, they will best serve as the Reader. The Producer should not be the Reader as they may:

- Read as though the material is correct
- Not hear the defects being described
- Read too fast due to foreknowledge

Primary responsibilities during Inspection activities include:

Preparation:

- Prepare for the Inspection Meeting as an inspector
- Make a decision how the material will be best read
  - NOTE: consider reviewing this decision with the Moderator
- Prepare with the reading decision kept in mind
- Prepare anticipating potential questions the other inspectors may ask when reading the material
- Annotate the work product material to facilitate reading in the selected approaches during the Inspection Meeting

Inspection Meeting:

- Confirm the reading approach with the Inspection team at the start of the meeting
- Read the material as agreed with the team
- Serve as an inspector

Possible Problems with Readers

Reads too fast for the team: This could be due to the Reader's prior knowledge, lack of understanding, or just wanting to get through the Inspection as fast as possible. The Moderator should calibrate with the team at periodic points on the pace of reading and ask the Reader to adjust as necessary. Each inspector should feel comfortable with giving input to the Reader on the reading style and pace.

Reads as if the material is right: The Reader interprets the intent, rather than reading what is written. This again may be due to prior knowledge. The Moderator and inspectors should draw the reader's attention to this problem as it is encountered. Don't wait to get this changed after too much of the Inspection has proceeded. The Reader should get this input as soon as it is determined.

The Reader is not used: This is often because reading is not understood as contributing to a successful Inspection. It often seems as an overhead and waste. I suggest you start with a Reader. Then as you have evidence of a high effectiveness from the Preparation, you can move to other choices for the Inspection Meeting.

Some writers have suggested dispensing with paraphrasing or reading as taking too much time during the Inspection Meeting. See Wenneson [WEN85], Humphrey [HUM89], and Gilb [GIL93]. I believe some form of reading is necessary to pace the material and assure coverage. If, however, the organization is consistently above 90% effectiveness, they could chose to drop the Reader role and may even choose to dispense with the Inspection Meeting, but I suggest they first have the analysis that proves a consistent 90%+ Inspection effectiveness.

Votta found at AT&T that less than 5% of the defects were found at the Inspection Meeting, with 95% being found during Preparation. [VOT93] Unfortunately he did not show how many defects leaked past the Inspection and to the user, so we do not have a known measure of the true Inspection effectiveness in this study. Nonetheless, he presents a point worth further analysis, and if the Preparation can contribute 95% of the total defect discovery where test and the users find less than 5% of all defects, one has no need of a Reader or an Inspection Meeting.

What is the best way to start the reading? I suggest that the team get a consensus on style and that verbatim be permitted when the group sees value in it for pacing the Inspection Meeting in key areas of the work product. Otherwise, some form of paraphrasing should be used. Paraphrasing can take many levels; e.g., a few lines at a time to whole sections. The team should be comfortable with the styles chosen. I do not suggest dismissing reading as a technique, unless your data suggests otherwise.

If you do not have the data, then by not reading you may leave more defects in the work products, than with reading. The principle to keep in mind before making modifications to the Inspection method, such as dropping the reading, is to focus on effectiveness first. After the Inspections are shown to be effective then focus on efficiency. As the inspectors become better at Preparation and the programmers practice more Defect Prevention and fewer defects need to be found in the Inspection Meeting, you can even consider dropping the Inspection Meeting. We will discuss this possibility later in the book.

Ways to Read:

- **Verbatim**
- **Paraphrase**
- **Mixed styles:** The material can be both read verbatim and paraphrased at the same meeting based on the section under Inspection. Basically, the Reader treats each section in a way that ensures that each inspector understands it well enough to find, identify, and concur on defects.
- **Section-by-section enumeration:** The Moderator simply asks "Does anyone have any discussion on page 1?" "On Section 1.5?" This approach provides the minimum interaction and intended synergy between team members. I do not recommend this approach unless effectiveness is very high. When the ratio of defects found during Preparation is high as seen in Votta's study, this way might be appropriate, but in these cases one might even consider doing away with the Inspection Meeting and just getting the defects lists from each inspector
- **Perspective-based:** The reading is facilitated with guidance questions or scenarios; see Chapter 14 for additional discussion of this technique
- **Not read:** With this style there is no reading, but defect lists must be provided to the Producer from the Preparation.

Within these styles of reading, the Reader must also decide how to flow through the work product. Some approaches are:

- By Function
- Data flow
- Scenario flow
- Test paths based on test cases, especially when unit test is expensive

The Reader may read too fast or too slow. In the first case, the Inspection team cannot benefit through an effective interaction. In the second case, the team can become bored with the Inspection. The Moderator must address both cases. The Reader should get consensus on the reading style and be careful not to paraphrase too much or too little, but do it just right, like in Goldilocks. The suggested planning rates in Table 3.1 include the time needed for reading, which is often not considered during planning of the Inspection Meeting, so understand what tasks are included in any rates you compare with.

Why would a team permit reading too fast? Perhaps there is a temptation to accept the speed because the team members are overworked and want to get on with the Inspection, or perhaps they do not want to offend the Reader.

If the team permits reading that is too slow, perhaps they do not care enough about the Inspection.

While the Moderator may signal the Reader, it has been known that the Reader might ignore or discount the signal, either not understanding or believing they are doing the right job. This is where a strong Moderator should re-signal the Reader and the team can help. Normally when a signal is given, it will be enough to correct the Reader. But keep listening to the Reader's style even after the signal is given.

RECORDER

The Recorder is the inspector who will record the data for defects found and data about the conduct of the Inspection. See Chapter 6: Inspection Data. As noted previously, the Recorder could be the Moderator. For Inspections where there are more than two participants I suggest that the Recorder be someone other than the Moderator.

There may be situations where the Moderator should serve as the Recorder; e.g., no one else will do a good job recording or when using 1:1 Inspections.

Many Inspection practitioners would say that the Producer should not be the Recorder, since they may bias the defect write-up. Others have found that, when the Producer records the defect data, including the problem, the list of defects has more understanding for the Producer when making repairs. Both approaches have worked. Choose what works best for you, but make a conscious decision and in either case confirm the recording with the team members.

Some Inspection practitioners suggest rotating this role across inspectors. I suggest otherwise, as this approach often leads to mixed input with too much variation in the recorded data unless there is a well-defined online form to use.

It is possible that the Inspection room will permit dynamic recording of defects with a PC or workstation. This type of support environment is recommended, as it tends to facilitate capture in a more consistent way and everyone can see the wording. If it is not possible to record with a PC or workstation, the Moderator has the responsibility of ensuring the transfer of the notes/minutes/form and data from the Inspection into the Process database. I suggest that the best recording is done once, so try to develop a system that facilitates easy entry during the Inspection Meeting. I also do not recommend using a scribe or secretary to record the defects. These individuals are often not technical, they add another person to the group and add to the cost of the Inspection. They may also ask for clarifications that slow down the meeting, they may reword the defect incorrectly without knowing, and they cannot contribute to defect discovery.

The Recorder role is not particularity exciting and when some writers ask that this role be called "Scribe", I tend to be concerned. Scribe just sounds less worthy, and my concern is that this role is always relegated to the weakest inspector on the team. This would be wrong.

Now that I've introduced this concern, I would add that I do not like assigning role names to any but the Moderator and Producer. Everyone else is an inspector and some will be asked to perform additional functions for the team.

Primary responsibilities during Inspection activities include:

Preparation:

- Prepare for the Inspection Meeting as an inspector
- Review the defect types that may apply for the subject Inspection to enable efficient recording during the Inspection Meeting
- Review the checklist to ensure awareness of defect types
- Identify the recording mechanism
- Get familiar with the recording process

Inspection Meeting:

- Serve as an inspector to find defects
- Record the data about the conduct of the Inspection Meeting and defects using the Inspection Report (see Appendix C for an example)
- Listen to the identified defect as it is identified
- Do not interpret or rewrite the description without team consensus
  - If the defect is unclear, ask for clarification
- It is helpful to read the description to the team after it is written
  - Try for a media type for defect recording that is visible to team members; e.g., projection from a PC
- If defects are being found too quickly to record them well, tell the Moderator
- Review the major defects with the Inspection team at the end of the Meeting
- Make the defect report available to the Moderator and Producer immediately after the Inspection Meeting

Possible Problems with Recorders

Records too slowly: If this happens, the Moderator needs to determine how much of a bottleneck this causes. If it is too much, perhaps another inspector could take the role. Recording is a skill and can be learned. Inspector Training should focus on how to write defects for clarity and correctness.

Interprets the defect or records incorrectly: This cannot be known if the recording is not visible or restated to the team members. It is best to have visible recording or a restatement after each recording. Some Inspection practitioners wait until the end of the meeting to restate the major defects, but this can be a problem if indeed the recordings were incorrect. It is better to trap any misreporting as it happens.

Records something not understandable: This is basically the same problem as recording incorrectly and the same action can help prevent this from becoming a bigger problem at the end of the meeting.

Does not record: Here the Recorder just flat out missed recording the relevant details. This is another reason why review of the recording after each defect is more useful.

INSPECTOR

All participants are inspectors whether they are the Producer, Moderator, Reader, or Recorder.

All participants are trained to be inspectors, including the Moderator, Recorder, Reader, and Producer. This means all participants will prepare for the assigned Inspection and serve as inspectors to find defects. This was our intent during the VTAM study and was carried forward by other organizations, but is not practiced by all. I suggest this approach be used and that it leads to more effective Inspections. It is helpful if all participants have been trained to be Moderators as well as inspectors.

Primary responsibilities during Inspection activities include:

Preparation:

- Prepare for the Inspection and especially review the defect types that may apply for the subject Inspection to enable efficient identification during the Inspection Meeting
- Record minor defects in the minor defect list or clearly in the work product inspected
- Record any questions or potential defects found during the preparation to be used as discussion points during the Inspection Meeting

Inspection Meeting:

- Serve as an inspector to find defects
- Avoid style issues about how a solution could have been done
- Keep in mind that the work product is being inspected, not the Producer
- Stay in pace with the Reader and the team
- Do not offer solutions unless they are obvious and quick
- Listen to defects found by other inspectors and reflect on how this might offer new insights about the work product; try to hitchhike and see if you can find another defect based on the new information offered by other inspectors
- Review the defects with the Inspection team at the end of the Meeting and verify for consensus
- Make a copy of the minor defect list available to the Moderator at the start of the Inspection Meeting, or if a list is not used, give the marked work product to the Moderator at the end of the meeting
- Keep the Inspection Meeting findings confidential

Analysis Meeting:

- Serve to brainstorm probable causes of defects

Possible Problems with Inspectors

Is not prepared: This is the most likely problem to occur during early use. It is also the one that can cause Inspections to fail the most. Freedman and Weinberg state "At least 80 percent of all review failures can be traced to lack of advance preparation." [FRE90] The question that must be answered is how unprepared. There will be a variance in preparation times. While one inspector may be outside the limit, this could be OK, but if the average for the team is outside the limits, then the Moderator must make a decision to proceed or postpone. Just being outside the limit is not reason enough, but it is a signal that must be discussed.

Does not actively participate: This happens for many reasons; e.g., timid inspector, disbeliever. Moderators must use their skills to try to draw out all participants, but if they won't play, they won't play. The question becomes how effective the rest of the team is during the Inspection. If there is a significant lack of participation, this must be considered as a factor when deciding on a Re-Inspection.

Comes late to meetings: This will happen sometimes, and the Moderator must make a decision to start or postpone the meeting after 15 minutes or so. Keep in mind that if the meeting starts late, it will finish later also and this may have an effect on who is next in the queue for the room the team is using. If the decision is taken to start, then if the latecomer does show up, I suggest that the team continue from their present point to the end. Do not go back to the beginning for the latecomer. This would only reinforce their view that they are "important" and can be late. It is possible that the latecomer has something to contribute in the material already inspected, but this can be picked up at the end by first recounting the defects the team found and then asking if the latecomer has anything in addition.

Not focused: Inspectors will come to the meeting with all the current baggage of their personal life and work life. This is natural, and includes the Moderator. This is one of the reasons why there will be variation in Inspection performance. Unless focus becomes an issue, the Moderator should move the team forward.

5.3 Other Roles Which May Be Useful During An Inspection

Some Inspection practitioners have designated other roles for inspectors. In general individuals can serve these other roles as part of the primary roles defined above.

These other roles are included only to provide the reader understandings of what other Inspection practitioners are doing. The use of these roles is optional.

MAPPER

The Mapper is an inspector assigned the responsibility for ensuring that the work product under Inspection sufficiently maps back to the previous work product; e.g., code to Low-level design, Low-level design to High-level design, High-level design to requirements specifications. This individual would then ensure mapping during Preparation as a primary responsibility and also provide mapping, as needed by the team, during the Inspection Meeting.

NOTE: This role can be required of all inspectors. With this alternative each inspector would do the mapping during the Preparation. This is the preferred approach from my experiences.

Inspectors will always have a better understanding by comparing the work product under Inspection with the previous work product state; e.g., the Low-level design when inspecting the code. I see little value in this as an assigned separate role, and question the coverage of the work product and how complete the preparation is if an inspector does not map back to a previous state representation of the work product.

RECEIVER

While the Receiver is not a role as such, this inspector is the individual who will receive the work product for other project activities after the Inspection; e.g., the designer from the analyst, the coder from the designer, the system test planner from the requirements analyst. This individual should be one of the most active inspectors, since their work will depend on the quality of the work product under Inspection.

When the Producer is also the Receiver, this role has no significance and is not assigned.

NOTE: The Receiver can serve as Recorder or Reader.

5.4 How To Choose Participants

The Producer should be an obvious choice when there is only one person who worked on the work product. Where a team has participated in a work product, try to pick the individual who will best represent the team's contributions. When this cannot be done, then try for the next best representative.

All participants must have been trained in the Inspection process. They should be knowledgeable of the procedures required for both Inspections and the creation of work products. Most importantly they should be open and team players, as this is a team exercise.

When new members are added to the organization, even if it's only one new member, they need to receive training on the Inspection process and procedures applicable to the organization.

While it may not be possible to hold the same training that other team members have had for one new individual, some effective alternative must be used; e.g., an assigned mentor and guiding them through a copy of the training material.

When the training is less than a formal class or workshop, the Moderator should pay special attention to this individual during their first few Inspections. The Moderator should also facilitate transfer of expected behavior.

Criteria for selection of inspectors should include:

- Domain knowledge in the work product under Inspection
- Experience and expertise
- Language knowledge, if the Inspection is for code
- Whether the inspector will have responsibilities to continue with the work product; e.g., the coder for a design, a tester for the code
- Have the time to participate
- Trained in Inspections
- Know how to work well on teams
- Have a view of quality
- Willingness to participate

Expertise will be the predominant criterion for effective Inspections. This does not mean that Inspections cannot be effective with less than expert talent involved. There have been different approaches taken to try to overcome the availability of experts. One approach is to use more inspectors, pools of inspectors, or assign core groups who are focused on Inspections.

Raytheon defined what they called Diverse Inspection Teams that would serve as the "same core team (typically 3 or 4) throughout the project life cycle." [BEU94] While this approach seems to have worked well, I wonder about the efficiency of the approach. It was intended to include three sets of individuals:

- Problem domain expert to provide specific expertise
- Senior engineers to provide general expertise
- Junior engineers to grow experience

This approach may be more costly and require availability of people who may be in short supply; i.e., the domain expert, but it is a choice.

The question of how much the domain expert affects Inspections has been on the table since the first Inspections. Studies still continue to be performed to determine the relationship between the expertise of inspectors and the effectiveness of the Inspection. For example, "behavioral theory helps us to answer three questions .... First, it tells us that the most important factor in determining the effectiveness of [technical reviews] is the level of expertise of the individual reviewers." [SAU00] and "The implications for current practice are that the best available reviewers should be used." Don't get me wrong, I like research in Inspections and defect removal effectiveness, but I think this issue is settled.

We know that experts will perform more effective Inspections, and we know that experts may not always be available for an Inspection. Despite the expertise, the Inspection can still be held, but make sure that all inspectors on the team are not novices. The results may be disappointing and may give a wrong impression to the novices. More experienced team members should mentor novices, and the mentoring should include Inspection practices. Mentoring can often be the best training on Inspections.

5.5 Training for Participants

Is it a necessary precondition that all participants have been trained in the Inspection process in use by the organization? Yes! No inspector should participate without having been trained in some acceptable way to ensure they can perform as expected on Inspections.

When an inspector participates for the first time, both the Moderator and Project Lead need to provide guidance through an on-the-job extension to the formal or informal training received. They should meet as noted with the new participant after each Inspection activity to discuss what went well and what could be improved. These first Inspections are the best time to reinforce the expected behavior at Inspections. The on-the-job extension can continue for more than the first Inspection, based on the Project Lead or Inspection Coordinator's view.

When 1:1 Inspections are performed, it is especially important that the Project Lead or Inspection Coordinator observes and comments on how a less experienced inspector is performing the Inspection.

5.6 Other Possible Participants

While I prefer fewer inspectors, there may be time when more is necessary or will lead to more effective Inspections.

USER OR CUSTOMER

The user/customer may be a participant; e.g.,

- When the Project Lead or Moderators believe that the customer will add value to the team's ability to find defects
- When the customer contractually requires representation at an Inspection Meeting
- When a customer believes they can help the team during an Inspection and suggests participation
- When the software project requests the participation of the customer to ensure clear understanding of the requirements

In Rapid Application Development (RAD) projects, the customer's participation is essential. This participation should occur in any other project types where the customer is actively involved.

NOTE: Customers can be either external or internal to the software project or organization.

MANAGER

While I have discussed how managers can sometimes interfere with the desired intent of Inspections or inhibit a good Inspection, there are times when they are needed in attendance; e.g.,

- The manager is the lead technical person on the team
- The manager has the best domain knowledge for the work product to be inspected
- The team requests the manager's attendance
- The organization's culture has matured where the manager's attendance is not an issue
- A manager is invited to an Inspection on a different project

NOTE: Despite the concern with managers at Inspection they should be considered for participation in Overviews and in Requirements Specification work product Inspections. This will provide them with an opportunity for technical understanding of the work.

SOFTWARE QUALITY ASSURANCE

When Software Quality Assurance (SQA) representatives serve as auditors/reviewers of project processes, there will be times when they should attend Inspections to see the process as performed and practiced. The Inspections they attend should be chosen randomly or when an Inspection is of special concern. SQA should not be at all Inspections, but they might monitor the data from all Inspections. As an SQA representative in this role as assuror, the SQA individual will not be an inspector, but an observer of the Inspection process.

Of course, if SQA is the coordinator for Inspections, the auditing of Inspection processes will need to be done by someone other than SQA to ensure objectivity and independence.

5.7 Viewpoints To Consider for Role Assignment

There will be situations when specific knowledge areas should be focused at an Inspection. The Moderator, Project Lead, and Producer should identify these specific knowledge areas. All efforts should be made to ensure that at least one of the assigned inspectors has expertise in the specific knowledge area so they can focus on this "viewpoint".

Examples of specific viewpoints are:

- Standards
- Interfaces
- Maintainability
- Usability
- Complexity
- Security
- Efficiency/Performance

Freedman and Weinberg include these viewpoints in their suggested Technical Reviews when they speak of chunking by form. These viewpoints can be combined into sets of viewpoints that can be assigned to inspectors, including the customer.

Knight and Myers used phased Inspections where a series of partial Inspections each addressed a desired property in a work product; e.g., maintainability, reusability. [KNI93]

5.8 Rules of Behavior for Effective Meetings

- Start on time
- No last minute substitutes for any participant
- Participants have sufficiently prepared
- If it has not been decided, get agreement on reading style
- Be polite
- Participants understand conflict resolution and team work techniques
- Allow all to participate in their own way
- Do not interrupt
- Participants maintain their assigned role and viewpoints throughout the Inspection
- Chunk the Inspection Meetings into approximately two hour segments
- Give a break during a segment, if needed
- Do not criticize the work product style or the Producer
- Defer discussion on less than obvious solutions, but capture the suggestions
- Avoid threatening, challenging, sarcastic, or in any way antagonistic remarks between participants
- Keep other agendas outside of the meeting
- Remain objective and businesslike

5.9 Small Projects

Assigning roles and even assigning inspectors will be difficult in small projects. In this context, "small" refers to the number of people available on the project, not size of the work product.

Will Inspections work in these projects? Well, experience says yes, but the process must be tailored; e.g., you may need to:

- Use people who do not know the project, but who may be able to find defects
- Have the manager be an inspector

5.10 Psychology of Inspections

Once management has shown a commitment to Inspections, the primary factor determining successful Inspections is the people participating in them. Certainly the other preconditions such as training, management support, adequate time, and materials provided must be satisfied, but it is the people who will ultimately make the major difference for successful Inspections.

People can overcome inadequate training, if they believe enough in the value of Inspections. People can overcome insufficient management support and sometimes they even may use Inspections in spite of management's lack of support. People will find the time to do Inspections once they learn the value; somehow they always find the time to do the things that help to make projects more successful. People can overcome inadequate preparation time when the unit being inspected requires them to find the time. Don't get me wrong; I am not suggesting that we simply rely on good people to make Inspection miracles. In fact, people can also make Inspections fail despite all the preconditions being satisfied by the organization. Good people are not enough, but with them we stand a chance in the face of obstacles. Let's now examine some aspects about organizations and people within the organization's culture that can affect Inspection performance.

5.11 Organization Types

Constantine defined four organization types or paradigms — closed, random, open, and synchronous. While his intent was to define these differences to facilitate effective teamwork in organizations, we learn that these types do behave differently. They can all be successful, but each has its own strengths and weaknesses, which enable them to thrive or struggle based on environmental conditions.

The defining characteristics for each type are shown in Figure 5.1.

Paradigm	Coordination	System regulation	Priorities	Decision making
Closed	Traditional authority hierarchy	Negative feedback, deviation attenuating	Stability, group; secure continuity	Formal, top-down, by position
Random	Innovative independent initiative	Positive feedback, deviation amplifying	Variety, individual; creative innovation	Informal, bottom-up, by individual
Open	Adaptive collaborative process	Combined feedback, flexible responsiveness	Stability and change, group and individual; adaptive effectiveness	Negotiated, consensual, by group process
Synchronous	Efficient harmonious alignment	Shared programming, efficient uniformity	Harmony, mutual identification; effortless coordination	Unnegotiated, predefined, implied by vision

Characteristics of Organization Types [CON93]
Figure 5.1

Constantine states, “These models provide a powerful tool for understanding and shaping working groups within software development organizations.” [CON93] He acknowledges that these are discrete “reference paradigms” and that most organizations will have more than one of these characteristics. So we should not try to force any organization into one of these boxes. However, the thought process should lead us to understand that different organizations do have different personalities.

The strengths and weaknesses for each are shown in Figure 5.2.

Paradigm	Strong suit	Weak areas	Best application	Failure mode
Closed	Stable security, preserves resources	Genuine innovation, full use of individuals	Routine tactical projects	Rigid enmeshment, mindless over-control
Random	Creative invention, promotes personal best	Dependable stability, efficient resource use	Creative breakthrough	Chaotic disconnectedness, destructive competition
Open	Practical adaptation, informal sharing	Efficient process, smooth, simple operation	Complex problem solving	Chaotic enmeshment, endless processing
Synchronous	Quiet efficiency, smooth operation	Response to change, open communication	Repetitive critical performance	Rigid disconnection, drifting deadness

Strengths and Weaknesses of Organization Types [CON93]
Figure 5.2

In a later paper Constantine says, “Thus the same goal, such as, increasing code reuse or reducing bugs reported in the first 60 days after release, may have to be approached very differently in two different organizations.” [CON94] So too with Inspections, I would add.

Given then that we can approximate an understanding of these organization personality types we should come to understand that asking each type to do the same thing the same way might lead to failures. This is to say that if we do not allow tailoring of a defined approach for a policy, process, or procedure, we may find that the definitions work for some and fail for others. Basically one size does not fit all, again.

For example, with Inspections as they were defined in IBM in the 1970’s I could argue that the method worked well because it was defined for what IBM was at that time; i.e., a *closed* organization type. I would expect that if Inspections, as defined for IBM, were tried without adaptation, in the early Apple, Xerox PARC, among others as *random types*, that it would have failed or not even been tried. Does this mean that the Inspection process cannot or does not

apply to these types of organizations? No! It means that the process would need to be tailored. In at least one case that I know, we needed to permit more discussion during the Inspection Meeting in a random type organization. Had we not, the participants would have thought we did not want their participation or insights toward a better solution, and would have discounted Inspections.
It is not my intent to go further here and define how Inspections should be tailored for each organization type, but to invite the reader to make this additional consideration when introducing Inspections and when trying to make them more successful where Inspections are in practice.

Inspections are a common sense approach for defect removal, but what is common for one organization may not be acceptable to another.

So rather than try to force fit one definition as one size fits all, I suggest that adaptation of the Inspection process is perfectly acceptable.

The test of how well the adaptation was made will be in the effectiveness of the Inspections, which should not be traded off.

5.12 Participant Personalities

Every organization has its culture and within every culture there are types of personalities. These are independent of Inspections, but perhaps Inspections provide a venue for some personalities to become more visible. We are, after all, dealing in a focused group environment regardless of the organizational personality types, where strong feelings can exist regarding defects and the consequences of making defects visible. Let's take a look at some of these types and their characteristics.

AGGRESSIVE INSPECTORS

This is the type of individual who we all like to dislike, at least when they are giving us input about our work. They remind me of the Jackie Gleason character in The Honeymooners. He took satisfaction in telling others of their mistakes, but was not easily capable of accepting input for improvement himself. This personality seems to get satisfaction in loudly calling out defects in someone else's work. They probably mean well. Either that or maybe they just like to take pot shots.

During Inspections this type can be annoying to everyone, but mostly to the Producer. It is not that this type is overtly disruptive, but they can be annoying. They seem to lack sensitivity to others or maybe they don't care. They may contribute greatly to finding defects, which is the intent, so they can be effective participants from this perspective. We want what they are identifying. We just wish they would be more graceful in their approach. The team may simply have to live with this situation. When a judicious opportunity presents itself, the Moderator or other team member should try to explain to this type that there is another way to give input. Sometimes, even if rarely, they get the message and do change. Mostly we need to put up with them.

In other cases, an aggressive inspector may be trying to make the Producer look bad. While the Moderator may not be able to see into potential personality clashes so as to try to prevent them, or may not have a choice, the aggressive attitude, when it becomes evident during a meeting, must be controlled. It may not be possible to eliminate it, but tolerating it is not productive.

AGGRESSIVE OR INTIMIDATING MODERATOR

These are the types who can't wait to shout, "Oh boy, another defect!" See the Major Don anecdote in Section 4.1. Major Don was an aggressive Moderator; because this was what he thought would lead to more defects being discovered. All he did was to annoy everyone and was ignored as a future Moderator. Maybe the organization does learn to cull out the Moderators who are too aggressive. We all do this in varying degrees in other parts of our lives and work. The Major Don types may be aggressive but rarely are intimidating. We learn to ignore them.

There are Moderators, however, who do have rank and when they are aggressive this can be perceived as intimidating to some of lesser rank; e.g., time in the organization, peer acceptance, or title. These Moderators may go unnoticed by the organization for a period of time. These types try to control the meeting too much, or push in their pet areas, or can even push too much on one individual at the meeting, or can pursue a witch-hunt for some reason. None of these are desirable and can lead to less effective Inspections. People will do almost anything to try to get the meeting to close when this type appears.

How can they be controlled, removed, or changed? Well, team member input sometimes helps, since these Moderators may not even be aware of what they are doing. Good old peer pressure can work on some of these Moderators. If the meetings were too out of control I would even suggest that the team members ask that it be adjourned or call the Moderator on his behavior. Sometimes it may be necessary to get to the manager of the Moderator or the SEPG lead and ask their help.

Moderators, especially the more technically inclined, may find that the discussion on a defect or solution is interesting. They may actually get lost in the discussion and forget their role. This will be costly, as the team will pick up on this and may keep the clock running on discussion rather than the purpose of the meeting, which is to find defects. It is useful if one of the other team members serves to call the Moderator's attention to this behavior. When this is not done, then hope for the best. Hope that the analysis at the end reveals some points about the effectiveness of the Inspection.

WEAK MODERATORS

Moderators can also be weak and become overwhelmed either by other developers or by the work. If they cannot contribute except as administrators, they may not have been chosen correctly. The best developers often make the best Moderators, but they are often on other project work with little time to moderate.

There are people, who are asked to be a Moderator, but cannot adequately function in the role. They want to contribute, but they haven't learned what is needed to be effective. They either do not understand the concepts well enough, do not know how to manage an Inspection, are not accepted by the team for some reason, want to get through the Inspection as fast as possible for one of many reasons, or never bought in to Inspections.

When a Moderator is found to be weak or not suited for the role, he or she must be counseled, trained, or dropped from the list of Moderators. If, after counseling and training, they still are not suited, they must be dropped. One of the worse things that can be done to handicap the success of Inspections in organizations is to put weak Moderators into the role and keep them there.

If weak Moderators are permitted to continue, others in the organization may begin to think that management is just paying lip service to doing Inspections. From there you can trace a probable deterioration of Inspections in the organization. Don't let this happen in your organization.

LACKS COMMITMENT

What do you do when you sense that one of the team members lacks commitment to Inspections? First look at the data; e.g., are they preparing with sufficient time, are they noting defects found during Preparation, are they contributing actively during the Inspection Meeting? If they are meeting expected requirements, then their seeming lack of commitment should be discounted. Maybe they just think Inspections are stupid, but they'll do their part anyway. Fine, we should always be so lucky to have inspectors who can contribute to a successful Inspection.

If, however, they are not meeting expected requirements during Preparation, then the Moderator must factor this into the decision to postpone the Inspection. If the Inspection is postponed, then management must get involved to counsel the individual. After all, if the organization has declared Inspections to be an organizational policy, then employees are required to contribute to the success of Inspections.

You will need to proceed carefully here, as you do not want to set a tone that when Inspections go bad, individuals must be singled out for counseling. The job of the Moderator is to look at the situation, including the data, and make a decision for the organization. The Moderator or Project Lead may choose to let slide some Inspections that should be postponed. These will more likely be at the initiation of Inspections in an organization, but the Moderators must become surer and over time move to the postponement decisions when necessary.

PREFERS INTELLECTUAL ARGUMENT

Some inspectors like an intellectual debate and will bring these up at the Inspection Meeting; e.g., "There is a better way to do this." And then they proceed to explain how they would have done it. These people are not necessarily trying to show that they are right, although these types exist too, but they really want a perfect solution. They take pride in working on perfect solutions. Almost right is just not good enough for them.

We need to respect their input and rephrase the issue to "Is it a defect or not?" The answer to this will sometimes be obvious in that it is not a defect, but the solution could be done another way. In this case the Moderator asks the Recorder to take a note for suggestion and move the Inspection along. If, however, it is a question of performance in a key area of program execution, then this probably is a defect under the type of Performance. Due to the way these issues come up during an Inspection, there is probably a solution that is also being proposed. This too needs to be noted by the Recorder. If the Producer agrees, then we have both a defect and a potential solution.

The worse type of inspector is one who wants the intellectual debate, but does not have the technical stuff to back it up. Be as kind as you can when you shut them down.

DEFENSIVE PRODUCERS

Producers take pride in their work. Programmers especially seem to attach themselves to their work products. [WEI71] Thus when their work is inspected and defects are found, some programmers may take it as a personal attack. They seem to discount that they have been given a mission impossible and that defects were almost predestined. Perhaps this is due to the highly intellectual nature of programming, wherein if we even suggest that there may be a defect we are challenging someone's intellectual capability. This attitude is at least partially a factor of maturity. The nature of the software business is that young blood is always in demand due to the ever-increasing need for more software solutions.

Programmers do seem to be different enough in that thinking about and writing software is compelling to them. Not everyone can or wants to write programs. The programmers who are good at programming may have a need for detail and solutions that work "right."

Of course these are generalizations and subject to many arguments and there are probably other reasons I could posit as to why programmers would be defensive, but the point is they will sometimes get defensive about their work product, selves, or jobs. So management and inspectors must make every effort to not play into these defensive traps. Treat a defect objectively and move on. When Inspections are kept at an objective business level, defensiveness will be defused, but it will never entirely go away. Don't fan the fire. Be sensitive that the Producers are giving up their baby when other eyes are looking at it for defects.

It may not be an easy frame of mind to come to, but if the Producer can come to accept that the inspectors are helping as a team to make the product better, then learning and progress will be easier for all involved.

Capers Jones captured the feeling that may exist, especially when an organization is starting Inspections when he said, "Prior to first using this method, there will be a natural reluctance on the parts of programmers and analysts to submit to what may seem an unwarranted intrusion into their professional competence. However, this apprehension immediately disappears after their first inspections, and the methodology is surprisingly popular after the start-up phase." [JON91]

AGGRESSIVE OR IGNORING PRODUCERS

A typical way Producers may react when being defensive is to be aggressive in their counter attacks on the inspectors at the meeting. "What do you know? You couldn't code your way out of a paper bag!" These tactics are used to attack rather than defend. If the inspectors are weak and if the Moderator lets this tactic persist, the Inspection will deteriorate into just a meeting with bad memories for all attendees.

Other Producers will blithely seem to accept everything that is given as input without clear acceptance of the defects. "Well, record it and let me work on it." Later during the Rework activity the Producer will do as he sees fit and may even ignore the defects he disagrees with. The Moderator will need to ferret this out during the Follow-up, but it may be difficult, since the Producer may try to talk around the defect solution.

Sometimes you may encounter Producers who feel their work is above Inspection. The problem is that in some cases they may be right. So rather than debate the issue, try to get these individuals to agree to the Inspection so the rest of the organization can learn from what they did. Let the data speak for itself. If no defects are found and it was a proper Inspection, and if later in test no defects are found, then the organization should try to understand if there are systemic characteristics of this work product, including who the Producer is. Also, if data shows that an individual consistently produces defect free work products then maybe their work shouldn't be inspected.

I do not recommend in the early application of Inspection that some Producers be excused from Inspections, but as the organization gets data and the results suggest it, you might choose to be selective. I have seen this work successfully in mature organizations. For other organizations, this may be a mistake as it may smack of elitism.

QUIET OR LAID BACK PARTICIPANTS

It will sometimes happen that the Inspection team is too laid back during the Inspection Meeting. Often this is due to lack of preparation or lack of domain knowledge. In the early stages of the organization's use of Inspections it can be a reflection of the hunker down attitude; i.e., "Let's go through the motions and maybe they'll go away."

Regardless of the cause, it will be the Moderator's job to call a halt to the Inspection. Hopefully there is data that backs up the decision; e.g., little time in Preparation, few defects found in Preparation. Again the Moderator must be careful to not be viewed as arbitrarily calling off the meeting, but a decision must be taken when the signals are active.

If this laid back behavior is permitted and effectiveness is not high, it will only lead to poorer and poorer Inspections.

HOSTILE INSPECTORS

I keep hearing about hostile inspectors, but I have never personally encountered any in the twenty-eight years that I have been involved in Inspections. Maybe I have been lucky, but I do believe this type is a rarity.

Should they occur at one of your Inspections, the Moderator or team members must take clear and immediate action. Call the meeting off and talk with the management. Hostile behaviors of any type in any work situation are just not acceptable.

When it becomes evident that a behavior is not desirable, the Moderator should not always jump to action, unless the behavior threatens the success of the Inspection or is dangerous. Sometimes a more orderly approach can help by:

- Noting the behavior and the circumstances
- Assessing if there is impact
- Taking some action without embarrassing anyone, as may be warranted

5.13 Culture Change

We all need to keep in mind that an organization that is first learning to use Inspections will be going through an important culture change. Therefore, all management must support all policies and practices visibly and clearly. The organization may adapt effortlessly and quickly or with time and pain. The path is dependent on too many other factors. Regardless, we should try to understand how ready the organization is for accepting Inspections and then track the evolution and success.

Successful change will follow the typical S-curve shown in Figure 5.3 shown by curve A. Some people — the early adopters — will be with you from the start. The key point of rapid acceleration will occur when the mass — the followers — see that the change is safe and important. Some may never come on board — the laggards.

Figure 5.3 shows three S-curves. The first (A) is a more desired curve with the shortest timeframe to full deployment. The second (B) gets to the same result but over a longer timeframe. The third (C) probably never gets there and flounders in the ramp-up stage.

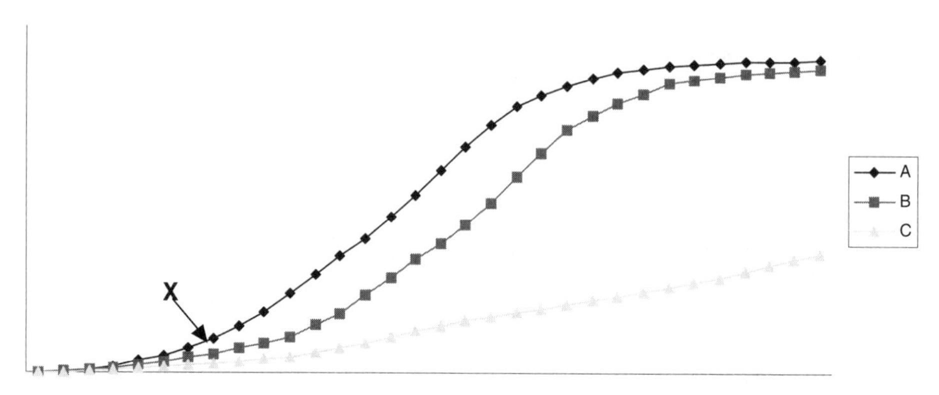

Change Variations
Figure 5.3

The Inspection Coordinator should know how to facilitate change and should demonstrate constant support to all organization members, including the laggards. I strongly suggest that the SEPG not spend a lot of time or energy with them, however. Laggards will only consume your time and energy, and should you have a failure they will be the first to shout about it. Acknowledge them, but move to the early adopters and followers.

Point X where the rapid acceleration begins in the S-curve can be moved earlier by the use of feedback of results, testimonials, handholding, and never letting up. There are three things an SEPG must do with any change program: 1. Be persistent, 2. Be persistent, and 3. Be persistent. We know that Inspections work. If the SEPG pulls away, so will the organization.

Martin found that, if he had to do something different to have made Inspections more successful faster at MCI, he "would have listened to the advice of Casey Stengel the former Manager of the New York Yankees and the New York Mets: *Keep those who hate the change away from those who haven't made up their minds*.'" [MAR97]

5.14 Personal Agendas

In the early stages of Inspection adoption, and especially if a manager is invited to Inspection Meetings, be aware that some team members may have personal agendas. These can include shooting down a technical direction or making another team member, including the Moderator and Producer, look bad. When there is any indication that personal agendas may be in play, the Moderator will have a more difficult job, but must manage the process and eventually may need to postpone the Inspection Meeting.

Sometimes the personal agenda is not obvious to all team members, but when it is suspected it needs to be dealt with. If the team has established rules that allow personal agendas to be called out, then any team member who senses one can put it on the table. Be aware that this behavior is an indication of a high maturity team. Not all personal agendas are malicious, but they do work against the team's objectives. Not all team members will be able to call out a personal agenda or get it acknowledged. Some may not even see them or care. If dealing with personal agendas is difficult in families, think how difficult it can be in a work environment.

How might you sense a personal agenda? If you see the following *smoke*, there may be fire:

- Someone who tries to get the meeting to end faster
- Someone who tries to keep the meeting going longer than is necessary
- Someone who has a need to discuss or give solutions for defects
- Someone who has a need to philosophize about organization problems
- Attacking the Producer
- Defending the Producer beyond what is necessary for a successful meeting
- Discussing non-related issues
- Nitpicking

Nitpicking is the most common personal agenda that will occur in Inspections despite training. Sometimes it is due to a type of person who is a born nitpicker in any task assignment. Sometimes it is due to revenge taken on someone who is a nitpicker himself. Regardless of the reason the team and Moderator should call out when nitpicking is occurring. No one, except the nitpicker, appreciates this act. At best it is frustrating. At worse it wastes time and is unproductive.

One suggestion we received during a training session was to classify defects into important and nits. The nits would then be quickly addressed by putting them on a nit list. This was the same intent for major and minor defects in the IBM study. I really hate to think that perhaps there should have been a third category called nits.

The issue can be addressed, and the Moderator should do it quickly, by reminding the nitpicker of the purpose of Inspections, but not to imply that the nits should be ignored. Simply take them quickly and move on. This is another reason why I prefer a list of minor defects being submitted at the start of the Inspection Meeting. Then these defects have been noted as received, but do not require time for discussion. The Producer can handle the minors or nits as necessary during Follow-up.

End Quote:

"Nobody should be in a review who lacks the qualifications to contribute to the review."
Daniel P. Freedman and Gerald M. Weinberg

CHAPTER 6
INSPECTION DATA

"Data collection is not a science, it is the first step in moving toward a science."
Jay W. Forrester

6.1 Introduction

So far we have learned about the meaning, purpose, and process of Inspections. Now let's explore how to make Inspections work to best advantage.

Management commitment will get Inspections started in the right direction. Training the participants to understand the process and their roles will enable consistent performance. Performing according to a defined policy and procedures will position the organization for consistent application. But how can we really know if we are performing as consistently as we want?

How can we know if we are meeting effectiveness objectives? Without gathering and analyzing data that result from Inspections, the answer is we cannot. We can only make assumptions, we can have opinions, and we can even debate the contribution of Inspections, but none of these are acceptable if we wish to have more discipline and better engineering of software.

In order to do analysis we need data. Let's look at why data is such an important foundation for developing excellence in Inspection practice.

6.2 Why Gather Data?

We might gather data for a number of reasons that would add value to managing software projects; e.g.,

- Benchmarking to learn how well the project compares to similar projects
- Tracking performance to learn if objectives can be met
- Using lessons learned to reduce the possibilities of making the same mistakes
- Transferring of information and knowledge
- Performing historical analysis to learn how to improve
- Performing dynamic analysis to take actions to help achieve goals

Without data we cannot objectively reflect on past performance, we are limited in how we might improve our actions in a purposeful manner. We cannot establish meaningful goals, and we cannot improve our effectiveness in a directed manner. Data is required to improve any discipline, including Inspections. To get data we must measure and to measure we must have a definition of what should be measured. The definition should have acceptance by those being measured, and this historically has been a major problem with most measurement systems. As an example, the definitions of the metric system date back over 200 years, they were in some use in Europe during the time of Thomas Jefferson, but even today there is still not worldwide acceptance or practice, not even in Europe where it originated. Napoleon, an emperor, could not make the metric system an accepted practice across all his empire. Today Britain is still inching into the metric world and the United States has barely begun the changeover.

ANECDOTE

WHAT DOES MANAGEMENT REALLY WANT?

During one SW-CMM assessment, one of the interviewees stated, "Management here doesn't really care about data." Well, this invited a follow-up question to explain what the interviewee meant. He went on to give an example to explain his statement.

"We are required to fill out task effort sheets each week." "Yes, most organizations require something similar." I said. "Well, Charlie here wrote a UNIX command that, when invoked on Friday, will scan the file that has the valid charge codes for the week and then randomly distribute forty hours for each of us and then submits the task sheets." "Really'", I replied. "How long have you all been doing this?" I asked. "Well, I'd say for over a year now." was the response. "And no one has questioned the filed task sheets?" I asked. "No! We file over 200 sheets in less than five minutes where it took us about 10-15 minutes per person before. So management's happy that the sheets are filed, and we're happy that we don't have to waste our time filling out those useless sheets. We're more productive now!"

"But this means the task sheets have garbage information." I said. "No," I was told, "They have numbers, and that's what management wants. Do you think they really care about how good the numbers are? They are numbers, they are not data, and management doesn't care."

This was sad to hear, and we can fault the programmers for being creatively malicious. Management, however, in this particular case was working on a government contract and could be held liable for misapplication of funds.

Anecdote 6.1

In the software community we do yet not have consistent agreement on measures for basic concepts of importance such as size or defect. It is not my purpose to choose one specific definition for these two primary measures, though my opinions may be evident. For me it is more important that an organization use consistent definitions when it looks to improve its practices. If an organization maintains consistency of definitions within itself, it can get a sense of its change and improvement.

Comparing to external organizations, while tempting, is more difficult and must be done with great caution. Not every organization has the same meaning for terms. We have already discussed this for terms like Inspections and walkthroughs. Definitions and terminology for defects, size (KLOC or Function Points), time, or duration etc. vary widely across the software community. So start by being consistent within your own organization. One might even question how much added value there is in comparing with external organizations given these problems with terminology, definitions of terms, exactness of the data, integrity of data, etc. across the software community.

When we gather data we want good data, not just numbers. If the data is contaminated or corrupted for any reason, the analysis can be a fruitless exercise at best and lead to dangerous conclusions at worst. Imagine going to a medical doctor who has faulty measurement devices or who is lax about how well the measurements are taken. Would you trust the diagnosis? Why put up with poor data in software projects? There are many causes for poor data, including fear of the data use, disbelief in its value, doubt that it really will be used effectively, lack of discipline, lack of tools and infrastructure support, and just not wanting to be measured. These reasons and others lead to poor practice or even malpractice in the software community.

With data and numbers, we must be careful. It is a cliché, but it has truth, "Be careful what you ask to be measured, because that is what you'll get." If management asks for measures to show change, they may see numbers that show change, but is there real change! We must ask deeper questions. We must look harder at the organization culture and its views about data.

Measures can contaminate the system in which the measures are being taken. For example, the 3rd Marquis of Salisbury, Queen Victoria's longest-serving Prime Minister, found that one gets what one rewards when he learned that the Governor of Jamaica, in an attempt to make the island free of snakes, offered a bounty on the number of snake heads brought to him. The Governor only succeeded in increasing the number of snakes by inadvertently encouraging their breeding for the bounty reward. One gets what one rewards.

For Inspections we do not just want numbers, we want data with integrity. In order to achieve good, reliable, and consistent data we will need to ensure the following:

- Clear definition of policy regarding the Inspection data and its use
- Management commitment to maintain a safe environment for Inspections
- Visible commitment to reliable Inspections by all in the organization
- Clear training on how to collect, analyze, and use data
- Accepted definitions for the measures; e.g., size and defect
- Infrastructure and tools to support collection and analysis
- Feedback to individuals participating in Inspections and all in the organization
- Visible use of the data

Once we understand the business goal we want to achieve, there are three activities related to data that are key to all software processes:

- Goal Setting for process performance
- Data Gathering or Collection
- Data Analysis

Let's explore these data activities.

6.3 Goal Setting

As we've seen, Inspections will have an effect on cost reduction, schedule improvement, and quality improvements. I would go further and suggest that as these three business parameters improve, customer satisfaction will improve, as well as employee satisfaction. These are all compelling business objectives or goals, if an organization is not satisfied with any one of them. Therefore, once an organization has decided which of these business parameters it wants to improve, Inspections can be put to use to help achieve the objectives. How much and how fast an organization can improve is dependent on its present capability and achievable benchmarks.

When first starting with Inspections, the organization should use data from the literature or benchmarks that may be available from comparable organizations. Then as the organization proceeds with Inspections, it should revise the goals based on its data and business objectives. These goals for continuous improvement will require good data collection and analysis. The goals should be revisited every six months or whenever either the customer or the data tells us we should have new goals.

Before an organization can set meaningful goals for Inspections, it needs to have analyzed data from its Inspection performance.

One could use data from the literature as preliminary goals, but in this section I want to explore how an organization sets goals for itself using its own process data. The organization will continue analysis as the process is performed and the goals will then be modified over time based on organization data. Analysis allows the organization to know with confidence that a process is stable and capable, or under control from both the organization and customer perspectives. If an organization continues a process, gathers data about it, but does no analysis, the process will deteriorate over time.

Once we have sufficient data analysis we can set meaningful goals. Initially the goals may only be to bring the process under control.

For example, if you found that your overall Inspection effectiveness was 50%, you might set a goal to improve it to 60%. You could take actions to improve in all Inspection types or just selected types. Setting a goal without an action plan is almost meaningless. It's an example of *management by prayer*.

If you found the defect density ranges were consistently met and within the defined limits, you might set a tighter specification limit, as a stretch target. Then each outlier, or Inspection data point above the new stretch limits, would require analysis for process improvement.

Goals are best set using historical data from the organization. Sometimes using benchmarks from other organizations can be useful, but keep in mind that others may not use the same terms, have the same environment, or keep data that has full integrity. Be cautious when using other organizations' data as benchmarks. Be especially leery about databases that purport to provide baselines that anyone can use.

After we have a sufficient volume of good data and have performed analysis we will have a picture or snapshot of how our Inspection process is proceeding. We may not like the picture, but if the data has integrity, we have a picture that we can improve. We can decide what should be improved and how fast we want to move.

At a minimum I suggest that organizations have goals by Inspection type across similar projects for:

- Defect density
- Inspection Meeting rates
- Preparation rates
- Inspection effectiveness
- Inspection Meeting efficiency

I do not suggest goals for Inspection Meeting efficiency when Inspections are being started in an organization. When organizations focus on efficiency first they tend not to have effective Inspections, and since the purpose of Inspections is to find defects, why handicap that objective. The goal should be effectiveness first. Later as effectiveness is proven to consistently exceed 80% one should set goals for efficiency.

Low-level maturity organizations may not be able to advance easily to 80% effectiveness. See Figure 1.7 where it was shown that level 3 organizations would probably experience between 65-75% effectiveness. Does this mean that these organizations should now focus on improving efficiencies to increase their benefits from Inspections rather than continue to focus on improving effectiveness? I leave the choice to them, but my advice is to always focus on effectiveness first. Only after effectiveness has been proven should an organization focus on efficiencies. Cleary at 75% this might be a toss up, but at or below 50% I believe focusing on efficiency before effectiveness will lead to erosion in the Inspection process.

6.4 Specific Data To Be Collected for Inspections

In the original process assessment method defined in IBM during the mid 1980's there were 12 attributes versus the 18 Key Process Areas (KPAs) in the SEI's SW-CMM and 24 process Areas (PAs) in the CMMI. Three of these attributes were Data Gathering, Communication and Use of Data, and Goal Setting. [RAD85b] I firmly believed then, and still do, that data focus in these three attributes was essential to improvements in software processes. Admittedly it would be wasteful if we gather more data than we will use. We want the essential data that will give us the best value for improvement.

Is there a minimal set of data that we can use on all projects? What is the minimal set of data that are available today in all software environments, and which should be gathered into process databases for analysis on software products?

Collecting the data and especially inputting the data should be made as easy and transparent as possible.

Today, with web-based environments, this is much easier than in previous years, but ease of input should always be an objective. If the input required is too difficult or too much, the data will tend to become corrupted or not useful. We all will remember for a long time the Florida vote recording problems in the year 2000 Presidential elections. This should keep us aware of how easily data integrity can become a major issue.

So we basically collect data from Inspections to:

- Correct the defects found
- Classify them for learning
- Ask if there will be any downstream problems based on what we have learned
- Improve the process to prevent defect types
- Better manage downstream activities; e.g., testing

The four major types of data for which we need to collect data during Inspections are:

- Defects
- Size of the work product inspected
- Effort invested in the Inspection process
- Time spent during Inspection activities

Whatever metrics one uses for these types, they should be clearly defined and consistently measurable, including the scale of the measure. Let's briefly explore each of these types.

6.5 Defects

Since we are interested in finding defects, we need to collect information on defects. This sounds simple, but there is not full agreement on what a defect is in the software community.

I suggest that a defect is something that is not satisfied in a work product per requirements and if found in a customer environment would cause a problem for the customer.

Fagan said, "*the objective is to find errors*. (Note that an error is defined as any condition that causes malfunction or that precludes the attainment of expected or previously specified results. Thus, deviations from specifications are clearly termed errors.)" [FAG76] and later "A defect is an instance in which a requirement is not satisfied." [FAG86] While we can use any of these definitions, they are not crisp enough for everyone.

The software literature uses other terms for *defect*; e.g., bug, error, anomaly, fault, non-conformance, or trouble. There are subtleties of semantics, but they are all basically the same thing; i.e., something is not working, as it should. Some writers go further and define defects as visible; i.e., to the customer, or not visible. [HUT92] [WEL93] AT&T called them faults or demerits. [GRA85] Someone even apparently suggested "Don't call them bugs, call them quality improvement opportunities."

While these give us some common notion of what a defect is, none of these definitions address:

- How the defect was found
- When it was found or caused
- The severity of the defect
- The impact on the customer

Choose your own term to suit your needs, but be consistent. Regardless of what you call them, each defect must be separately logged. Otherwise the data will not be consistent. In the VTAM study we decided that every instance of a defect was to be separately logged as a countable defect, even when it was commonly caused in one work product. Our reasoning was that each could result in a user problem if it were not fixed. Counting each instance will lead to a higher defect rate, but since each is a defect that could escape during an Inspection or test, I suggest that each be counted. The cause may be the same for each, but each is a separate defect that could lead to a problem in the delivered software. Not all organizations count multiple instances of defects within a work product as separate defects, so when you are comparing yourself, ensure you know the counting scheme.

While counting the number of defects tells us something of interest, we need to go further and classify the defects. This is often a sore point with some programmers when starting Inspections. They claim it is bureaucratic, and indeed it can be and has been made bureaucratic by some. We don't want bureaucracy, we want data that will add value to the organization, but we must ask for some classifications to enable improvements and to learn what we are really doing. So let's classify and try to keep it to a minimum.

Defects can be in the work product or in the process to produce the work product. In this chapter I am speaking to defects in the work product. Later in Chapter 7 I will address defects in the process.

This discussion on defects is an admission that we as software engineers do unfortunately create defects while we create work products. It is not apparent to me that this will ever be otherwise on a broad scale in the software community, so let us acknowledge that defects do result during the development of software. We call these defects created during work product production *injected defects*. Given this admission, we should then begin capturing at a minimum the number of such defects discovered in Inspections, reviews, tests, and by users. These discovered defects are the *detected defects*. With combined knowledge of defects injected and defects detected, an organization can make rapid strides toward improvement. Defects are any error that would cause a program to work other than desired; i.e., a deviation from the work product requirements.

6.6 Defect Classifications

Defects can be classified into:

- Severities; e.g., major or minor
- Class; e.g., wrong, missing, extra
- Type; e.g., interface, logic, performance
- Cause; e.g., resources → training → timing of training
- Where caused and where found

Severity and *type* classifications tell us something about the product and where it can use improvement, while *class* and *cause* tell us something about the process and where it can use improvement. *Where caused* tells us about the defect injection activity and *where found* tells us about the detection activity.

Severity: to separate the defects that have high significance from those of lesser significance

> **Major** is a defect that requires repair due to a failure it could cause to occur in operation with the software; it could have been found in test or customer use
>
> **Minor** is a defect that would not cause a failure to occur in operation with the software; it can be a problem to a customer, but typically it is one of format or representation

Again, not all organizations use the same term or even the same definition for the same term, so we must be careful when comparing against others. Russell, for example says, "Major errors are serious defects that would prevent or significantly degrade the product's normal function. Minor errors would not compromise essential operation, but would still be seen by the customer as a fault. Commentary errors represent inadequate or incorrect code comments." [RUS91] Ed Weller says, "defect means major defect that would result in a visible failure if not corrected." [WEL93]

Some writers partition severity into minor, major, and super major. [DOO92] Yet other writers go to the other end of classification with major, minor, and trivial. [KEL92] I personally think three partitions are not necessary, but if it helps, then why not. So we see again, we should be careful when making comparisons with external organizations and published literature.

My preference is to keep severity classification simple and use two categories only, major and minor. If these are good enough for music, they should be good enough for software.

Class: to identify one attribute about the cause, as follows:

> **Missing:** something is not in the inspected material but should be; i.e., it was addressed as required in a predecessor document; e.g., it is in the design, but not the code
>
> **Wrong:** something is incorrectly shown in the inspected material; i.e., it was addressed in the predecessor document but in the inspected material it is transformed incorrectly; it does not meet the intent of the predecessor document
>
> **Extra:** something is in the inspected material but has no prior approved basis for being there; i.e., it was not addressed as required in a predecessor document; e.g., it is in the code, but not the design

Type: one of the valid major defects sub-classified according to a predefined taxonomy. See Appendix C for descriptions of defect types; e.g., logic, performance, interfaces. Type is used to classify defects for learning and analysis in future improvements.

I suggest not defining too many defect types. Classifications should be easy to make and at the least possible cost while getting maximum benefit for learning. This is admittedly a foggy way to limit the number of types. Decide for yourself, but listen to your people about the time, cost, and benefits from classification details. I suggest no more than 6-10 types and they should represent those where you have the highest frequencies of occurrence; e.g., logic, performance, interfaces. If you find that some types are not used often, then you may not need them.

If you ask for the data, you had better show the people how it is being used. If you do not, you will see a decrease in data integrity. What's worse is that you don't see the regression in integrity while it is happening. In these cases organizations begin to *believe* the data even when it is garbage. From there process improvement will regress and decisions made based on the data may have unexpected results.

Note that the IEEE standard has extended the number of classes from the traditional 3 to 10 under their category of *anomaly classes.* [IEE98] They do not ask that type be classified which becomes one less attribute to provide data for during an Inspection, but by doing so they cause loss of information. Type will add value when one is doing Causal Analysis and Defect Prevention.

To further complicate the issue on what a defect is, customers and users will sometimes submit requests for a modification. These, as it turns out, can actually be defect identification, or a suggestion for improvement, or request for change. Without some screening of modification requests, later data analysis can lead to incorrect conclusions. Customers may want more function, but these are not defects, rather they are suggestions or requests for new function. However, be careful not to interpret a valid defect as a suggestion just to make the quality level look good.

While we in the software community cannot come to resolution on what a defect is, it seems we are not alone.

ANECDOTE

WHAT'S A DEFECT?

I remember reading in Business Week a few years back about a Japanese automobile manufacture that had made quality a major thrust in all that it did.

They would apparently test every aspect of the car's use in extreme situations to validate that there were no defects that customers could experience. They wanted to assure that they built it right. As an example, they designed one test to open and close the sunroof on one model 100 times successively at sub-zero temperature. If the sunroof opened and closed repeatedly 100 times, and it passed this one of many tests, the sunroof was deemed defect free.

Then one day, one worker asked, "Who opens the sunroof at sub-zero temperature?"

Good question! A project's test team may try to find defects where the customer never will go.

So what is a defect?

Anecdote 6.2

The defects we have been discussing so far are product-related defects, but we can also have defects in the process of developing the product. This is to say that if the process causes a defect in the product, it is not a product-related defect, even though it manifested itself in the product. It is for this reason the Causal Analysis becomes important for process improvement. Fagan to some extent suggests process defects. "A deviation from exit criteria is a defect." [FAG86] These are related to the Inspection process, but there are other causes of process defects.

It is also possible that during an Inspection a defect is found in other material; e.g., a defect found in the design when the code is being inspected. These defects must also be recorded and addressed for repair.

Other users get concerned that not enough defects are logged during Inspections. If this is true during early Inspection use, it could suggest that the participants do not yet feel safe about the data; e.g., too few defects indicate the inspectors may not have done a good Inspection. As the organization becomes more mature we should hope to find that fewer defects are being logged due to process improvements prior to Inspections and that there are indeed fewer defects.

When few defects are reported this could be an example of a good product development using good process. Under these conditions a low defect find is a perfectly good position to be in. This is what we want with process improvement!

CAUSES OF DEFECTS

We will see in Chapter 7: Causal Analysis that there are four major areas of cause; i.e., People, Process, Technology, and Funding/Resources. These major areas can be further divided and subdivided into more specific causes where eventually we will choose what we believe to be the most probable cause. For example, resources could be a first level cause, training a second level cause, and finally the timing of the training is the real cause. The classification divisions and subdivisions are chosen by the practicing organization to address their environment.

See Chapter 7 for more detail on Causal Analysis and Defect Prevention, both of which build from the cause classifications made by the Inspection Team during the Analysis Meeting.

WHERE CAUSED AND WHERE FOUND

The classification is easy for *where found*, since it is obviously the stage in which the defect is found; e.g., code Inspection, unit test, system test. The *where caused* part is limited to the production processes; e.g., requirements specification, High-level design, Low-level design, code, and fixes. An issue is how can the Producer decide where the defect was caused. A rule of thumb is to ask what work product requires a change as a result of the defect. If only the code must be changed then it is a defect caused in the code stage. If the High-level design must, or should, be changed then it is a High-level design defect.

This classification will enable analysis for defect leakage from one activity to another and for calculating the effectiveness of each Inspection type performed by the organization; e.g., requirements, code.

6.7 Size of Work Products

This is not a favorite subject with many programmers. But yes, we need to count size in Inspections. Why, you may ask?

Size is volume and the volume of the work product will correlate with the amount of time and effort needed for the Inspection. There will also be a correlation with the number of defects injected; i.e., the higher the volume or size, the greater the area of opportunity, then the more defects probable. It will take longer to inspect 1000 pages than 500 pages or 1000 LOC than 500 LOC or 100 Function Points than 50 Function Points. Pick a size measurement that serves you, be it LOC, Function Points, or your own invention; e.g., complexity or nominal task elements, but you must estimate and measure size consistently.

For code, there are many arguments regarding how size in software should be determined. The argument is especially focused on the value or meaningfulness of Lines of Code (LOC) as a data variable. The arguments will not be extended or discussed in this book. Enough has already been debated on that subject. Furthermore it has been shown that alternate metrics such as Halstead's Volume, Function/Feature Points (FP), and McCabe's Cyclomatic Number, among other metrics, roughly correlate to Lines of Code. Thus all these proposed alternatives seem to be only considered or opinionated alternatives to the admittedly weak measure of Lines of Code. But LOC afford something these other measures do not; i.e., they are easily counted. FP, which started out as a rather easy metric to calculate, has evolved into a Ptolemaic and too complex counting system. But choose what works best for you.

For the time being, I propose we use what is readily and easily available for code. Therefore, for our first variable I will propose that Lines of Code be estimated and captured, which for this book means specifically non-commentary source lines of code added and modified for the product in question. As an example, if we were looking at C code these would be lines delimited with a semicolon.

For documents, size seems to be more easily accepted as number of pages.

For design, it can be anything from number of pages, to number of design statements, to number of elements in, for example, a data flow diagram or flow chart. Equivalent lines of code have also been used for design.

It is not my intent to prove the value of or find fault with any of these size measures. They all have advantages and disadvantages. Despite the enthusiasm of Function Point proponents, LOC seems still the most widely used size metric, within high maturity organizations. [RAD00] The bigger issue is to be consistent in the use of a size metric.

You will need to be careful when trying to make comparisons with other organizations or across products, as there are many different ways of calculating both LOC and Function Points.

Remember, we want to learn how we are improving and this starts by measuring yourself against yourself, then setting improvement goals, and then measuring against those goals, and so on.

I have seen organizations use development person hours as a size equivalent. While size and the hours needed to do the work will have some correlation, they are different attributes. Worse, I've seen organizations use planned hours as a size substitute. This only compounds the issue, since we are not just interested in estimated size, but in the actual size. If one estimates a work product to be 100 Function Points and the actual was 75 or 125, the defect density is different in each case, and the time to do a good Inspection will vary. We need estimates to plan, but we must calculate with the actual results to get a true picture of the work performed and the related quality of the work.

For documents, even the term *page* can have various definitions; e.g., JPL states, "A typical page of JPL documentation is 38 single spaced, 10-point lines per page. A page containing a diagram was considered a page of text." [DOO92] The page you are reading is 44 single space, 12-point lines per page, but the point size will reduce when the pages go to book form. The amount of white space and use of figures will affect the number of pages and the complexity will usually be affected based on the number of figures and how well they represent the thought to be communicated. Pages as a size value in design and requirements specifications will provide a sense of time required for an Inspection, but I suggest that the code size also be considered for these work products, as this will be an indication of complexity that the number of pages may not completely represent.

For work products, other than code, pages are the most commonly used metric. However, there is some use of estimated LOC or FP for the requirements specification or design. When an estimate related to code size is used during these types of Inspections for defect density calculations, it will need to be recalculated after the actual code size is learned. The Inspection Coordinator will have defect density calculations using both estimated and actual sizes. The number of pages can be converted to LOC or FP at the end of the project or dynamically during the project as more is learned about the actual code size. It will be the final actual count that shows how well one really performed.

Size is a denominator used to normalize defect density in work products. If we find 10 defects in a work product this only tells us part of the story of quality. There is a difference between finding 10 defects in 1000 LOC or in 100 LOC. The area of opportunity (size) is factoring how many defects may be found and may remain after Inspection.

ANECDOTE

WHY SIZE?

Let's suppose you were a civil engineering contractor and you wanted to respond to a proposal that required building a poured concrete highway that was to be 100 miles long, flat over these 100 miles, had the same environmental conditions, and in fact had no appreciable environmental or engineering differences for a builder of highways over this defined length.

There is one major factor you still need to know before you could submit your bid. You need to know the number of lanes.

Lanes will affect volume of the poured concrete and in turn the effort and duration required. Lanes are a size factor for civil engineering and LOC or FP are a size factor in software engineering.

Anecdote 6.3

In Chapter 8: Re-Inspections we will explore how we can use size as a signal to improve the effectiveness of Inspections.

Size affects planning, since the time required should be based on the volume of the work products. Organizations that dislike the idea of size estimating or believe it cannot be done will have problems planning well. Some organizations assign a percentage of the project time estimates for Inspections. This is faulty and not good enough, since it assumes the size is known, when all that's been done is to assign a percentage portion of an unknown volume on top of an estimate of development time. This cannot be reasonably done well without knowing the size. If Dante knew of software and size estimates, he could have added another circle to Hell

6.8 Effort, Time, and Cost

As we saw in Chapter 3, effort for tasks is required in every Inspection activity. The activities that are of major interest for effort are Preparation and the Inspection Meeting. However, we will also want to know how much effort is invested in other activities; e.g., Overview, Rework.

Effort is a cost factor, and since we should be interested in controlling costs, we need to estimate and measure the effort invested and spent in Inspection activities. We will also need to compare the costs of Inspections to other defect removal activities such as test and customer use. Thus, we will need to gather data on both the estimates and actuals for effort in Inspection activities.

ANECDOTE

HOW MUCH EFFORT?

One organization that I worked with had a cost accounting system that literally prohibited the recording of more than 8 hours on the job in any given day.

When asked why they did this or why they couldn't change it, they responded, "If we record more than 8 hours then because of contracts on campus we would be obliged to pay overtime, but since our people are professionals they are not due overtime pay. They are told this when they hire on and they have no issue with it. So rather than cause unneeded problems on campus with the unions, we record what we pay; an 8 hour day."

You know, this actually seemed like it made some sense to them, but this organization really had no idea of what they use as work hours on software service. What makes it absurd is that they published yearly reports stating their productivity. I don't get it.

Anecdote 6.4

This variable of effort is for the work spent by the engineers to create the software work products. It should include all personnel hours from requirements through delivering the product to the user. Additionally, we should be interested in the effort spent in maintaining the software once it is delivered. We should want to know both required (estimated) and spent (actual) effort to perform the work. We should also want to know how much effort would be allocated to plan, track, and manage Inspection activities

The measure for effort is often in hours, but can be in days, months, or any portions thereof. For hours we have a reasonably consistent definition; i.e., 60 minutes. However, I have run into a few organizations that define hours as something less to allow for miscellaneous tasks, much I suppose as a psychiatrist's hour is billed at 50 minutes. For day and month, while these seem obvious, there are variations. The measure of a day becomes interesting when we see organizations that measure day as a unit regardless of the number of hours an individual might have actually been on the job; e.g., if 8 hours is the "normal" day and someone clocks 12 hours one day, it is still measured as one day. We even have differences of hours in a "normal' day. For some it is 8, others 7 ½, and for still others a 7 hour day is what they are officially paid for.

For all these reasons, I prefer the measure to be in hours, since there is less distortion and there is at least a chance to capture the overtime hours. These do not always get captured, so we should constantly be asking if we are comparing the same thing when we say "hours."

There are three forms of time we are interested in when gathering data from Inspections:

- Clock time or duration
- Activity time or effort
- Schedule time

An Inspection activity may take only two hours of clock time from start to finish, but if we have four inspectors, then the activity time or effort was eight hours.

If we wish to understand how well we might do on our next project, we should capture time or duration spent in producing software. This variable is different from effort in that we wish to measure linear time for the entire schedule used to develop the project, including all activities within the project. This should include all time from the day we begin to work with the user requirements to the day we deliver the software to the first users. There are other views of time invested in a project and sometimes they are called activity time, task time, cycle time, or schedule.

Preparation may only require two hours of clock time, but an inspector may only be able to perform the activity in fits and spurts over two days. The schedule time in this case should be two days, not two hours. We want to know both schedule time and activity time. We also need to know estimated and actual time in both cases.

Schedule time especially becomes important when planning for Inspections. Votta found that the delay time between Preparation and the Inspection Meeting could be as much as two weeks for a work product in AT&T's environment. He goes on to show that if the Inspection Meeting can be dropped, then schedule latency can be avoided and thus the productivity of the project could be increased. [VOT93]

To round out this section: cost will be directly related to effort. But when we are evaluating the effectiveness and efficiency of Inspections we may want to know both defects/KLOC removed and $ / defect found.

Again we must ensure we are calculating with a well-understood definition of $'s as these can be labor $'s, non-labor $'s, or both.

6.9 Other Inspection Data

While defects, size, effort, and time will be the major data types we must measure and analyze; there are other data that will facilitate improving Inspections and other processes. These data include, but are not limited to:

- Date of Inspection
- Number of inspectors
- Moderator
- Material identification or type

See Appendix C for sample Inspection data forms and the suggested data to be collected.

Some organizations capture data about inspector experience. I suspect they believe that less experienced inspectors will lead to less effective Inspections. This relationship may exist, but this is not the primary issue or concern. Since the inspectors will vary on Inspections, we want to know if any one Inspection fell within acceptable bounds for the process as defined and practiced. If not, then we need to understand why. The conclusion we reach may be lack of inspector experience. This now can be factored back to management who has the responsibility for assigning the qualified, trained, and available inspectors, and at least assigning inspectors who can satisfy the Inspection requirements.

After the Inspections we will also need data for the number of problems and defects found by tests and customers. This will allow us to calculate the effectiveness of the performed Inspections.

6.10 How Precise Must the Data Be?

Many process advocates get overly focused with precision. I see this when analysis is carried out to meaningless numbers of decimal points in reports.

**While precision may be an admirable goal,
it will be costly to achieve and probably provide little
additional value in the software environment today.**

Accuracy will be just fine, if we can achieve it. If we need precision in some measures, this will be learned as we progress. To achieve accuracy we should do some checks that the data entered is entered correctly. This can be done by looking at the data, looking at relationships between data, and reviewing outliers; i.e., data points outside of expected boundaries, limits, or expectations. Simple data entry problems will occur, and often they will be obvious; e.g., outliers often are due to bad data entry when organizations are starting Inspections, including situations where people enter bad data as in Anecdote 6.1.

Weller found that the two data entries "most often in error are the size of the inspected material and defect severity (major vs. minor)." [WEL93] If it is found that size is too often entered incorrectly, a process check can be added when the data is entered. The person entering the data can be asked to check twice when entering the size value, or asked to enter it twice, similar to what is done with new passwords. This can easily be done with web-based data entry. Alternately another inspector could check entry. Weller gives some other lessons we should keep in mind about data:

- "Lesson 1 about data collection is *you may have to sacrifice some data accuracy to make the data collection easier*." I believe he means data precision is not necessary; e.g., 300 LOC/hour is as good as 307 or 295 for measuring the rate of a code Inspection Meeting and Preparation time captured in 15 minute chunks should be satisfactory.
- "Lesson 2 about data collection is *avoid metric definitions that are similar to previously used metrics, or that are loaded terms*." In other words make data entry user friendly and check with your users about the ease and correctness of use and terminology.

In all cases, accuracy will be aided by clearly and simply defined terms. Listen to the people in your organization to ensure the definitions are easily understandable to them. If not, improve or change the definitions or terms.

Remember also that some problems with data are due to lack of appropriate classifications. Apples and bananas are fruit, but it may be useful knowing how many apples and how many bananas are in the basket. Stratification or sub-setting of data for fruit and defects into subtypes is often helpful, but avoid too much sub-typing, as it can add to errors in the data by making classification too difficult.

We do not want people taking more time trying to classify a defect than they do finding it.

The data that is provided by the programmers will have better accuracy when it is:

- Defined in understandable terminology
- Easy to apply
- Kept simple
- Facilitated with tools

6.11 How Long Do We Have To Wait To Get Customer Data?

Since most products will be in use for a number of years, does an organization need to wait until the final use of the product before it can determine true effectiveness? Clearly this will be too long a period to be helpful for most products. While the numbers will vary based on product type, the number of expected users, and their ramp-up rate, we can expect to find a relationship between the number of defects found in the first three to six months to the total that will eventually be reported.

The number for any one product will need to be learned. If you have more than a dozen active users during the first six months, you might assume that they will find a reasonable percentage of the total latent defects that will be reported during the product's life in use.

You could use percentages from other organizations as a start, but it will be better that you learn from your own product data. Remember other organization's data is only a starting point for use if you do not have your own data. You should estimate the first six months of defects in customer use, then after the product has had an initial 6-month use, you can verify your assumptions and re-estimate as necessary. There have been various internal company studies related to the subject of defect latency and calculating remaining defects that customers may find. These studies all make the same conclusion; i.e., the number of defects will be higher early in the product life, especially with significant usage, and diminish over time after a sufficient user ramp up is seen.

6.12 Inspection Data Tools

There are almost as many ways to capture data as there are organizations. There are also an increasing number of tools marketed for recording defect data. It is your choice as to how and in what form you gather your data. Web-based solutions seem the easiest to use and links are available for most common database management software, such as Access or Oracle. Relational database management software packages are best for analysis where there are many different views of the data that the organization wants to have, but if you like good old flat files, that works too. The latter will have some restrictions when you want to do data analysis, but they do work when imported to other tools such as Access or Excel.

All organizations today should be able to use web-based technology to enable data gathering. Where an organization is already capturing data today, it should be able to create bridges or filters from existent databases to a web-based interface.

Regardless of your choice, you will need a database to house the data gathered during Inspections. The SEI and the SW-CMM refer to this database as the organization's process database and it contains more than Inspection data. For ease of use, you should develop one database, feed the data items from existing databases into one prime database, or have bridges between the databases so they are integrally linked as one. These will enable the analysis to be easier and more complete. Any of these approaches will facilitate comparisons and analysis of data from multiple sources and will enable both effectiveness and efficiency of Inspections and other software activities.

And remember, once again, do not try to create a database that has more than you need and will use. Keep it as simple as possible and as necessary, and to paraphrase Albert Einstein, "No simpler." The database exists to facilitate improvement, not for itself. One should always be looking at the costs of data collection and analysis. These too can and should be improved since they are part of the Cost of Quality, which I will discuss in Chapter 9.

6.13 What Data Should Be Analyzed?

The short answer is that, if you've gathered data tied to your business goals, then you must analyze it. You are obliged to analyze it. Otherwise, why are you gathering it? Also, as mentioned earlier, inspectors will tend to more loosely record numbers versus data if they do not see the organization making use of the data for improvements. People will contribute to success and improvement, but they will tend to abhor or move away from waste, and data gathering without use is a waste. If you cannot analyze the data for an extended period of time for whatever reasons, let the people know when the analysis will be made and the reason for the delay. Let them know you still need them to get good data and not just numbers. Let them know they are the enablers of success and improvement in the organization. Let them know how the data and analysis relates to the goals of the organization.

As Inspection reports are filed to the organization's process database a record of Inspection performance is being developed. The data must be analyzed to ensure:

- Inspection data is being sufficiently and correctly provided to calculate and calibrate Inspection performance goals and capability
- Inspection performance is meeting expectations for Inspection process goals, as defined by the organization
- Exceptions in performance are investigated to determine the causes and to learn how to prevent them from occurring in the future
- Defect density discovery is within expected boundaries

I suggest that data analysis should occur at periodic intervals:

- Monthly and quarterly at the organization level
- Weekly at the project level, as appropriate

Typically the SEPG or an Inspection Coordinator is responsible for analyzing the Inspection data and reporting to senior and project management. However, in some organizations the analysis is either performed by the SQA function or SQA assists the Project Leads in doing the analysis.

When the analysis is required of the Project Leads, it should be facilitated not only by SQA, SEPG, or the Inspection Coordinator, but also with tools that make this task as transparent as possible to them. While managers and technical personnel will be interested in the results of the analysis and are responsible for taking effective actions based on the results, they should not have to get mired down in the details of data processing to see the analysis results. We want them to think about the analysis and take necessary actions based on the data, not to have to think about the algorithms for computing the data. Today there are many commercial off-the-shelf solutions to aid whoever is doing the data crunching and analysis. Many organizations have learned that spread sheet tools like Microsoft's EXCEL have ample functions to perform most of the data analysis needed and produce reasonable charts that can be graphically viewed for analysis of the results. Data should not normally be presented as numerics but rather as graphics. People seem to relate better and faster to graphic portrayals of the data.

Regardless of what mechanism is used to do the analysis, the results are fully dependent on data that has integrity. Therefore, some correlation analysis must be made by whoever is doing the Inspection data processing and analysis.

Data integrity must be a primary focus in an organization using Inspections or any process.

To achieve data integrity the following will help:

- A culture that agrees with the value of data
- Non-threatening use of data
- A system for data gathering that is made as transparent as possible
- Support for data gathering
- Assurance of data at and after entry
- Data analysis is presented back to all in the organization in a timely manner

The organization must develop a culture that allows data to be used safely and one where it is understood that improvement is vastly enabled through analysis of data from past performance. This is much easier to say than to do. Cultures do not change overnight, so if an organization has been around for many years and does not have a culture that appreciates the value of data, be prepared to nurture and support the evolution. Be prepared for resistance and even sometimes backsliding, but never give up. We've seen some anecdotes throughout this book where the "Ah Ha" comes to different people at different times. When it comes, the change is more deeply rooted.

Moderators are responsible for entering or delegating the entering of the completed Inspection reports and data into the organization's process database. The Recorder is responsible for entering data for the Inspection and Analysis meetings on the Inspection report forms. When web-based forms are used, the data could be entered directly at the meetings. Otherwise, the Moderator will need to transpose the paper report or notes into the organization's database.

The SEPG or Inspection Coordinator should audit the contents of the process database and the Inspection process to assure correctness. Anomalies and outliers should be investigated to check for data integrity. SQA should audit to assure that correct and consistent data is being provided.

Project Leads should be able to easily generate analysis reports, so that they can show and discuss data analysis with the project teams. This capability should permit regular chart generation as warranted.

I suggest that some data analysis can be immediately available at the end of the Inspection meeting; e.g., defect density, Inspection rate, Preparation rate. We will discuss examples of these reports shortly in this chapter.

On a monthly basis the SEPG or Inspection Coordinator should be generating analysis at the organization level. This will permit:

- Assurance of the data, analysis, and trends across the organization
- Establishing organization baselines for expected performance on future work
- Establishing stretch targets for further improvements

Over time, as the organization becomes more effective with Inspections, the monthly organization review could be moved to quarterly meetings.

So what types of Inspection process analysis should the Project Leads and the organization be doing?

The primary data analysis that should be performed for Inspections include:

- Defect density
- Defect distribution
- Inspection meeting rate
- Preparation rate
- Inspection efficiency
- Error prone work products
- Inspection effectiveness

6.14 Defect Density

The number of defects found is the numerator and the size of the work product inspected is the denominator.

Defect Density = # of defects / size of work product

The relationship is the defect density calculation. Thus, one may learn, for example, that a particular Inspection yielded 9 defects/KLOC. This information is interesting as it tells us something about both the work product and the process of the Inspection, but we would need to look deeper to learn how much the ratio is due to the product entering the Inspection and how much is due to the Inspection process.

The organization and projects should establish goals for the expected defect density they believe will result from Inspections. Expected means what the organization and projects are capable of finding based on historical evidence. If goals can be established, the organization and projects then have a basis to make a decision regarding the Inspection results.

The first step to determining goals is to plot the data as it is derived for each Inspection. For example, in Figure 6.1 we see that for fifteen Inspections there are varying defect densities discovered. This chart is a simple run-chart showing the Inspections in order of occurrence of 1 through 15 and the related defect density for each occurrence.

Run charts are helpful to see if there are any wide variations and to look for trends over a reasonable period of time, but they do not sufficiently tell us if the process is under control. Run charts should not be used for point-to-point comparisons. For example, it would be meaningless to say that the difference in points 5 and 6 suggest a trend of increasing defect density. Likewise it would be meaningless to say that the difference in points 10 and 11 suggests a decreasing trend. We would need to do other analysis such as with control charts before we could make such conclusions. Given sufficient data points on a project; e.g., fifteen or more for an Inspection type in code or Low-level design, then a control chart can be derived to statistically understand the capability of the Inspection process and the signals given by any Inspection instances.

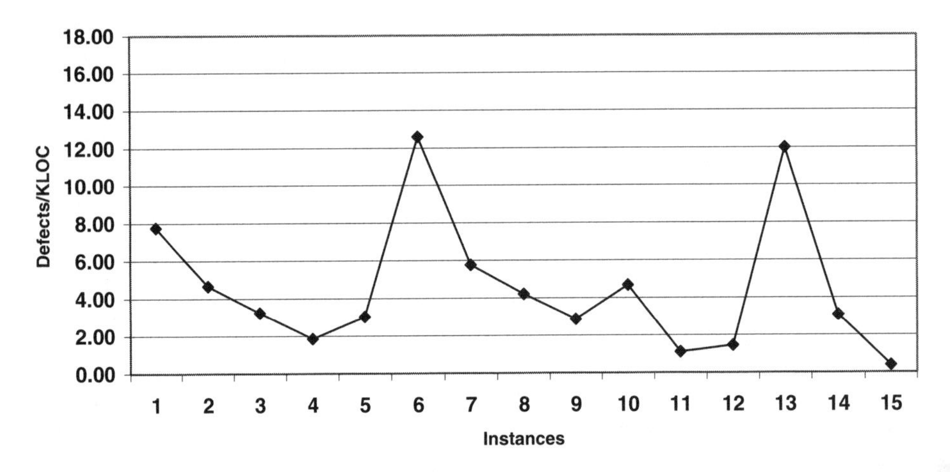

Run Chart for Inspection Defect Densities
Figure 6.1

While the use of control charts is a higher level of maturity technique for data analysis, I believe any organization with sufficient data can begin to use them. Organizations may prefer to wait until their Inspection process is practiced with some consistency before using control charts, but to not use them after some period of practice is to miss an opportunity to learn.

Control charts can be used to help understand if the Inspection process is performing in a reasonable and consistent way across a series of Inspections. See Figure 6.2 for an example of such a control chart showing a *stable process* using the same data as in Figure 6.1. A stable process is one where the Inspection occurrences are within a boundary that is determined by the data to be within 3 standard deviations from a calculated mean or average. These 3 standard deviations then define the process limits for the data. When all data points occur within these limits, they give us confidence that the process is repeatably performing within a boundary and that we have a *controlled process*. Furthermore, we can assume that if we continue to practice the Inspection process in the same repeatable way that we will see a similar pattern of performance in the future. This is a powerful conclusion, as we'll see.

In this example the average defect find rate is calculated to be 4.58 defects/KLOC. We see that no Inspection in this example exactly meets the average, and in fact we do not have any expectation that any Inspection will be exactly average. We see variation in performance and it is reasonably random. Some Inspection instances are greater than the average, which is calculated by summing all defect find rates and then dividing by the number of Inspection instances, and some are less than the average. Every process will demonstrate variance in performance, but we now know the range of variation we expect to see repeat, if the process continues to be performed as it was when the data shown in this example were gathered.

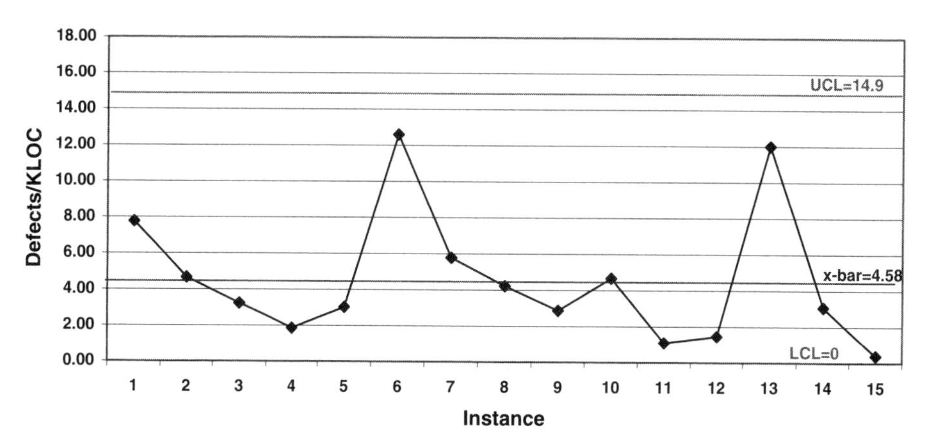

Rudimentary Control Chart Showing Defect Find Rates
Figure 6.2

This knowledge is powerful in that it allows us to control the quality of the work product and final product.

The first calculation is for the upper and lower limits defined by the data as is shown in Figure 6.2. It is not the purpose of this book to discuss statistical calculations or control charts in detail, but only to introduce some concepts. The upper and lower limits defined by the data are more specifically called the *upper control limit (UCL)* and *lower control limit (LCL)*. These are derived through various algorithms specific to the type of data being analyzed.

In the case of this example the UCL is calculated as 14.9 as is shown in Figure 6.2. The LCL is calculated to be a negative value (-5.7), but a negative value is meaningless for defects/KLOC, so the LCL is set at 0 (zero). One cannot have a negative defect density. These limits are statistically defined to be 3 standard deviations around the average when the distribution of the instances is random, as they were in this example.

I'll go no further in this book except to say that the chart shown in Figure 6.2 is an example with only one half of an XmR chart, one of the types of control charts, and this half is only addressing the variations in the measured process data. The second half would address variations in the calculated ranges from point to point. XmR charts tend to be easier to read, have been used by a number of software organizations, but may not be the best for defect data. More appropriately for defect data we should be using a u-chart, where the control limits are re-derived after each instance. The control limits tend to be tighter with u-charts, but many people do not like to use them, as they seem more complex. So if you do not like u-charts, start with XmR, but use control charts. As you become more comfortable and confident with your data and processes, then move to u-charts for defect density.

From my point of view, the LCL for defects/KLOC should always be zero. Anything greater admits to a production process where defects will always be created and are expected to be created in work products. This should not be acceptable production practice and definitely should not be an objective or assumed as a specification limit. An organization may not want or need to set a goal for zero defects in each work product, but to set a goal of more than zero defects in all work products does not acknowledge good quality or reward improvement. An LCL greater than zero will also tend to increase the average defect density seen in a product.

So what do these limits tell us? If we have a stable process; i.e., one that is under control or repeatable, then approximately 99.73% of the Inspection instances should be between the UCL and LCL. We see in Figure 6.2 for an example where all points are below the UCL. This gives us some assurance that the Inspection process is stable and under control; i.e., consistently repeatable within the calculated UCL-LCL bandwidth, but we should always ask if this is acceptable. Maybe we should have a UCL that is a lower number. Wouldn't this be proof of higher quality? Well, this is a more complex question to answer.

The question one must first ask is whether the spread between the UCL and LCL is acceptable. In other industry sectors, the customer might give specifications or quality limits that must be met to be acceptable. In software this rarely occurs, so the software organization should set its own limits of acceptable quality. To answer this question we start by making some simple calculations.

For this example, let us first assume that we are perfectly satisfied if we did not find more than 14.9 defects/KLOC in any Inspection. This is another way of saying that we have a goal or a specification limit that defines for us acceptable quality in this production process and the related Inspection process. Since, in this example, all our instances are below the UCL, which is also the specification limit, we can make another statement; i.e., that our Inspection process is both *stable and capable*. A capable process is one where the data falls within the specification limits and is stable.

If we had a goal or a required specifications limit of say no more than 10 defects/KLOC, then in this example we would have two points outside of the specification limit; i.e. points 6 and 13. In this case we would not have a capable process even though it is still stable. We need to improve the production process before we could claim it is capable and meeting specifications at no more than 10 defects/KLOC.

For any limits set (data and specifications) if we had an instance that was outside of the UCL and LCL and/or the specification limits, then the process data is giving us a signal that something exceptional or not expected is occurring. We must then look deeper into the data and situation about the specific Inspection to learn if we have a problem, whether we believe this problem could recur, and what actions we should take to prevent recurrence. A signal to investigate has been sent by the process data!

Of course, we could get some understanding about how we are doing in our Inspection process without calculating UCLs and LCLs and continue to use simple run charts as in Figure 6.1, but the information provides less insight into the process while it is being performed, and therefore is not as helpful. Besides it is not difficult to make calculations using control charts. There are many tools available that make them easy to create, and once we have them we can make other decisions and set goals for orderly process improvement.

I could discuss more about how to use these charts, but that is not the purpose of this book. One point to keep in mind is that real-time use of data analysis is more of an advantage than analysis at the end of the month or quarter. If we have an instance where the defect density is too high, we have a better chance of taking action during the current Inspection rather than a month later when it may be too late.

After you have demonstrated that the process is both stable and capable; i.e., behaving in a repeatable and consistent manner within expected boundaries for both the data and specification limits, you can set goals that stretch your capability. For example, we might choose to improve the production process and reduce the average defects as in the case of setting a USL to 10 defects/KLOC. Assuming that we had an effective Inspection process, this is a natural quality improvement step we can take. If, however, the Inspection process is not under control and is not effective, then setting this type of improvement goal would be premature and tend to confuse rather than help. The effectiveness of the process will evolve incrementally and is best done when analyzing the data and making incremental and achievable goals through process changes.

6.15 Issues versus Defects

Some writers and organizations using Inspections prefer not to use the term *defect* during the Inspection meeting, but rather *issue*. An issue can be any thought or question that an inspector has about the inspected material in the belief that it might be a defect. It is possible that an issue will result in a defect, but not every issue becomes a defect. An *issue* in this sense is not the same as the *Open Issues*, which are used to reduce unnecessary work by the inspectors and Producer, as discussed earlier in the book.

Open Issues come in two types:

1. Known or unresolved problems that the Producer identifies coming into an Inspection; they are declared outside the scope of the Inspection; if there are too many, an Inspection may need to be postponed; the intent is to allow a work product to proceed while the Open Issues are being worked; after the Inspection they will be tracked using Change Requests
2. Unresolved discussions about potential defects at the Inspection Meeting; these must be resolved by the Producer during Rework; any unresolved during Rework are tracked using Change Requests.

It is believed by those who use *issues* that the more issues written up during an Inspection, the more possible defects will be determined during the Rework by the Producer.

Issues "are not recorded as 'defects' at this point because they may not be defects. They are simply 'matters requiring attention'." [GIL93]

The Producer has the responsibility to resolve all issues raised. Since there will be more issues than ultimate defects in the work product, every issue that does not become a defect is basically non-productive work for the Producer.

All issues are logged at the Inspections Meeting, and many organizations get into a race for logging more and more issues. For example, Barnard states, "With one notable exception, I was unable to exceed 1.0 or 1.1 issues per minute." [GIL93] This is not what we should be focusing on with Inspections. Certainly Inspections help to remove defects earlier, but our goal should be to have fewer and fewer defects injected into work products. In my mind the perfect Inspection is one where the process was effectively followed and zero defects are discovered in a work product. This is much like the perfect game in baseball where a pitcher gives up no hits during a game.

Finding more issues should not be the end game objective. Let's look at an example of my concern with issues versus defects. If a two-hour Inspection finds 120 issues and the nominal size of code during two-hour Inspections is between 200-400 LOC with an average of 1.0 issue per minute, this Inspection will log 120 issues. This is not good news. This is a work product that is not under control. This Inspection should have been postponed until the Producer makes the work product right.

We should not use Inspections to compensate for poor production processes.

If we continue with this example, then if each issue became a defect, there would be 300-600 defects/KLOC. I have never seen code with such a high defect rate of 300-600 defects/KLOC in one code Inspection. I have seen an average of 20-30 major defects/KLOC in code Inspections for organizations of maturity Level 3 or less.

If recording issues becomes the goal then recording issues will make the data noisy; i.e., too many of the issues will become false-positives or issues that are not defects. For every false-positive issue, the Producer has extra work to do dealing with issue resolution and not defects. The producer will have to come up with acceptable reasons why an issue is not a defect. In this case the Producer must deal with 270-570 issues that are a waste of effort. Yuk! How many of these issues are worth the time and trouble during a project?

We should reflect on what is needed to improve the production process to inject fewer defects rather than creating a race to write more and more issues. For the organizations that suggest that more logged issues are a reflection of a good Inspection, I totally disagree and ask that they rethink their position on issues.

The objective of an Inspection is and has always been to find defects not issues. If you reward high issue volumes, you will get high issue volumes, but do you get high value? Do you find defects or issues? What's the effectiveness for defect removal when focusing on issues?

The objective should be to use Inspections in the best possible, controlled, and effective manner, and when zero defects are found to celebrate and understand how the organization can produce more work products with such high quality.

When high defect rates are found, the production process is out of control. Inspections cannot fix this pathology by simply finding defects, but the defect volume can be used as an input to focus on the source of the problem; i.e., a poor work product production process.

6.16 Defect Distribution

Defect severity, class, and type recording will provide input for us to analyze how defects are distributed. If we had sufficient data we could then make defect density calculations within each distribution. This type of analysis can lead to what statisticians call stratification, which is basically partitioning data into subsets to learn at a deeper level about the data and the related process.

Figure 6.3 shows an example of defect distribution by type of defect. We could also do an analysis by severity or class. For severity we might find that there is a ratio between major and minor defects. What this tells us needs to be analyzed. For class we have three categories and it might prove interesting to know the percentage of defects categorized as Wrong, Missing, and Extra. When we are performing causal analysis to help Defect Prevention, class analysis might give us some insights into the causes of certain defect types. For example, we might find that for Logic types 90% are categorized as Wrong. This might suggest something about how the predecessor documents were created. The analysis will help Defect Prevention activities.

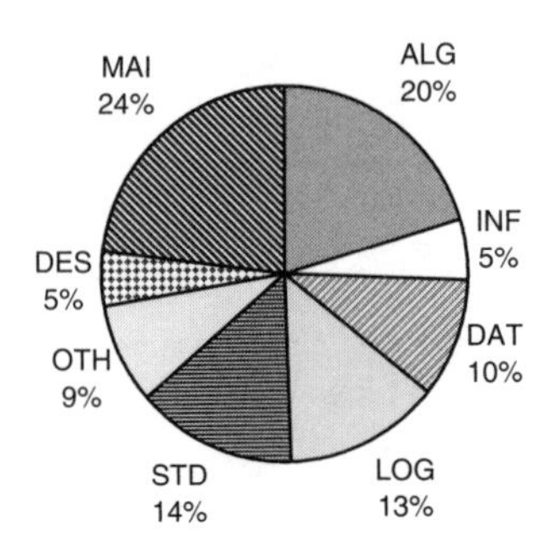

Defect Type Distribution Example
Figure 6.3

In the example in Figure 6.3 we see that 24% of the defects were categorized as Maintainability (MAI) defects, 20% as Algorithmic (ALG), etc. This type of analysis provides a picture of defect types and when we perform causal analysis we may get insight into what actions we should take to prevent these higher frequency types from recurring. In this example, we would probably start with the top two types since they represent 43% of the defects.

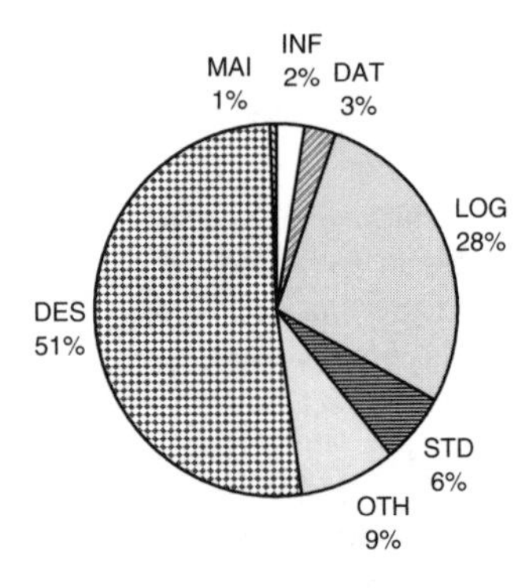

Another Defect Type Distribution Example
Figure 6.4

In Figure 6.4 we see another example, but the distributions are quite different even though these were projects in the same organization. The top defect type is the design base (DES) at 52%; second highest is logic (LOG) at 20%. If we focus on these two defect types for causal analysis, we are dealing with 72% of the defects. Clearly these two projects have different defect profiles. What this means and the actions to correct, change, and improve will vary between the projects.

6.17 Inspection Meeting Rate

As we capture the Inspection Meeting time and compare it with the size of the work product inspected we can derive a size/hour measure; e.g., LOC/hour or FP/hour.

What we want to know is how fast the Inspection Meeting proceeded compared with other meetings for this type of Inspection. Once we calculate the Inspection Meeting rate we can determine within an acceptable band of capability if any meeting went too fast or too slow. See Figure 6.5 as an example.

In this example we see that the average is 256 LOC/hour for code Inspections. While there is only one instance outside the UCL of 647 LOC/hour, the rates with this average and the UCL seem aggressive. The literature suggests between a 100-200 LOC average. Also the calculated LCL for this data is negative 134 LOC/hour, which gives a planning rate of negative 134 to 647 LOC/hour. This clearly is not a rate that can be used during the development of the project plan. This process example is not in control.

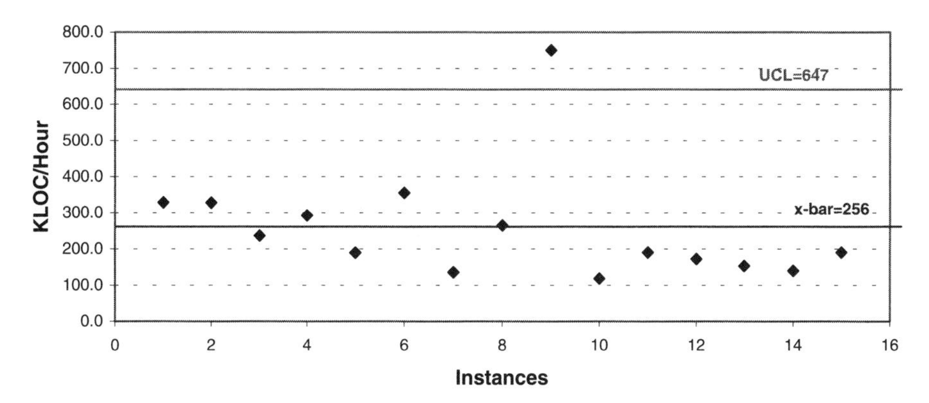

Inspection Meeting Rate Example
Figure 6.5

If we put specification limits on this data of 100-200 LOC/hour we would see something like Figure 6.6, where we see that the process does not meet specifications, as we have 7 of the 15 instances outside of spec. This is a process that needs improvement.

We need to investigate why the rates are outside the applied specification limits and understand what actions we can take; e.g., perhaps the inspectors were not trained on how to perform Inspections. If we were able to bring the process under control within the new specifications, we would then have a useable planning rate of 100-200 LOC/hour. This rate range could be applied for planning Inspections for other projects.

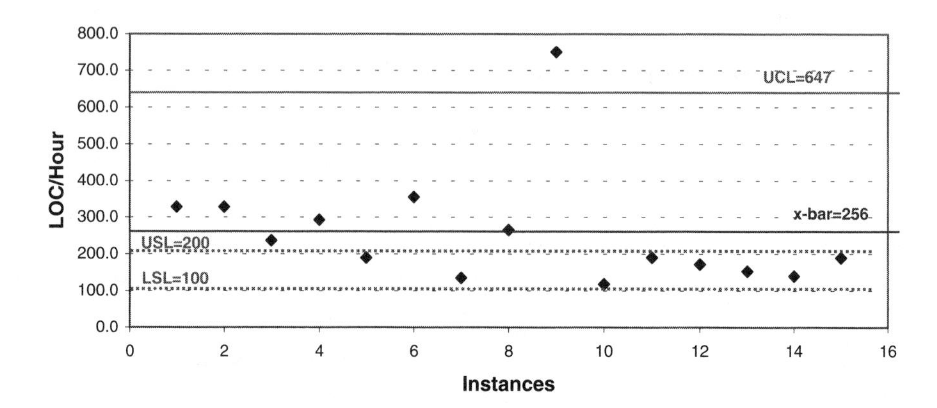

Inspection Meeting Rate Example With Specification Limits
Figure 6.6

This is another example demonstrating that Inspections are one process in software where control charts can be easily and well applied with minimal effort. There is increasing use and more understanding about the value of control chart use during software production and test. Each year more is published showing the value and how to apply control charts in software organizations and projects. See for example Graden [GRA86], Hutchings [HUT92], Weller [WEL93], Grady [GRA97], Radice [RAD97], Florac [FLO99], and Florac [FLO00]

When Inspections are monitored during real-time performance using control charts, they can provide process signals about the Inspection instance while the Inspection is still in session; i.e., until it has achieved Closed status. During early use in an organization there may be many signals since the Inspection process is probably not yet stable. Do not let this deter your use of control charts. They are giving you the information that says you must take action to bring the Inspection process under control. Do the analysis and take appropriate actions for improvement. If the data varies too much and the charts show vast instability, wait before briefing management and the teams using control charts. Over time fewer and fewer instances will be outside the control limits. Now you can show the charts and make note of the improvements as the process becomes more stable.

As mentioned previously, you should have a minimum of 15 data points before you try to draw conclusions from control chart analysis. Statisticians will debate the number of necessary data points. More traditional statisticians say 30, some 15, and lately at least one suggests 12, but as we all know statisticians never need to be certain or in consensus, and they say so themselves.

We in software do not produce chemical batches, where the process must be monitored in very real time by taking frequent samples and immediate actions when the process has gotten out of control. We have more time to react, but we still want to know as early as possible when there is a problem. We can use control charts, though we may need to be a bit more tolerant in their use than other industries. Control charts are a useful tool for software projects; use them, but don't become pedantic about them.

There are other statistical techniques that will be useful for analyzing Inspection data, or as Garden said, "Classical statistical techniques have application in monitoring and controlling the software development process." [GRA86] These techniques that are helpful include control charts, histograms, Pareto distribution, scatter diagrams, regression analysis, correlation analysis, and run charts, among others. Examples are shown in this book. Use what works best for you.

6.18 Preparation Rate

We could make similar calculations for the Preparation rate, and again we would expect to see that the Preparation rate was not only stable but within reasonable specification limits based first on industry data and then on the organization's data.

A real-time advantage is that we can calculate where a new Inspection instance stands relative to the organization's and project's control and specification limits for Preparation rates. If the instance is too far outside, a signal has been given to postpone or, if the Inspection Meeting proceeds, to discuss the needs for a Re-Inspection at the end of the meeting. See an example of a Preparation control chart in Figure 6.7 derived from client data.

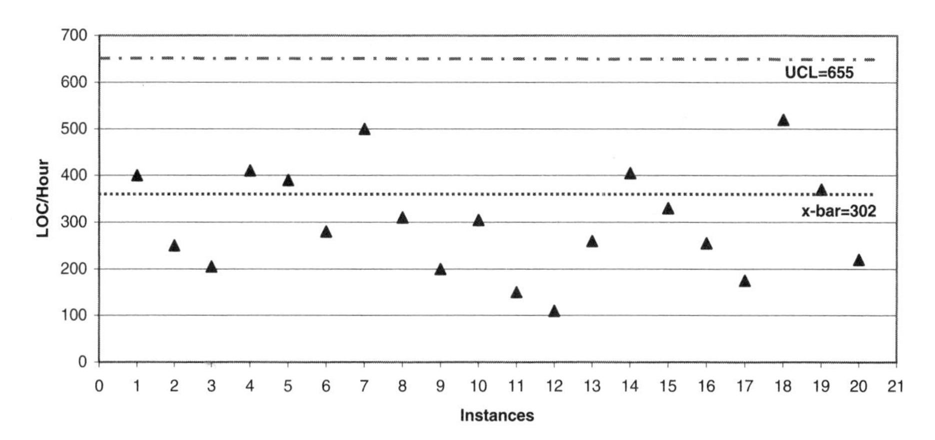

Example of Average Preparation Rate
Figure 6.7

Here we see the project's actual average rate and UCL are much too high. A Preparation at 650 LOC/hour would be within the UCL, but this means that the inspector is preparing at the rate of almost 11 LOC per minute. I don't know about you, but I cannot read and understand code at that rate. The literature suggests a specification range of 100-200 LOC/hour, but this example shows few instances within this range; there are only four such points. This suggests that the Preparation is proceeding too fast. To understand how this may affect the Inspection process we would calculate the effectiveness of the Inspection; see Section 6.21. If the effectiveness is less than desired, then the inspectors must be especially coached and guided to prepare within the defined rates.

6.19 Inspection Meeting Efficiency

Given we know how many hours the preparation and meeting took for all participants, we could calculate the cost per discovered defect, and as with the previous analysis examples, we could do this immediately at the end of the Inspection Meeting. Then if the instance shows data points outside the limits, we have immediate information that can be used to determine how well the Inspection might have been performed. We could use these signals to consider a decision to re-inspect, if the work product displayed other signals indicating a Re-Inspection. See Chapter 8 for Re-Inspection indicators.

A small concern is that the actual defect count may change during the Rework activity. But this is a minor concern for our purpose, as we could calculate efficiency at the time of the meeting and at the end of Rework. The difference is usually small. Or we could calculate an extrapolated range. If issues rather than defects are logged, the real-time analysis is not as helpful, as we must wait until the Rework is finished to evaluate this indicator for Re-Inspection.

Once we have efficiency calculated for an Inspection instance we could compare it with the expected efficiency in the organization for this type of Inspection. If we are within the limits of the organization, we can note this and move on. If we are outside of the limits we should try to understand why and whether this signifies anything about this instance; e.g., was the work product substantively different or could we have done a better Inspection? We may come to the conclusion that we did the best job possible and that process improvement is the probable reason why we have a difference; i.e., we are building it more right than before.

The types of analysis we can make for efficiency are:

- Total Invested hours / defect
- Preparation Invested hours / defect
- Inspection Meeting Invested hours / defect

As I noted in Chapter 1, Table 1.1, the costs run within a reasonable boundary across different organizations when they are starting to use Inspections. You should see similar results when you start Inspections. Over time, however, you should see changes. Initially the change might show your efficiency is improving; i.e., you are spending fewer hours per defect found. This is probably due to the inspectors learning how to be more effective during Preparation and the Inspection Meeting. Later you may see a decrease in efficiency; i.e., it is costing more to find defects during Inspections, because the volume of injected defects is decreasing.

See Figure 6.8 for an example of tracking the efficiency of Inspections. Here we see only one data point outside the UCL, which signals that more time is being spent to find defects in this instance than history has previously shown in the organization. However, literature suggests that costs for finding defects should be in approximately 1 hour/defect for an organization of this maturity level. We would need to investigate why these costs may be occurring here; e.g., are these work products less defective or is the Inspection team less capable of finding defects in these work products? We will know how well these Inspections performed when we see the test results. If test finds more than 25% of the defects, this organization should investigate how to improve effectiveness during Inspections. Effectiveness improvement will reduce the costs for defects per hour.

Is it bad to find defects that have a higher cost than the UCL suggests? If the programmers have begun to practice Defect Prevention formally or even informally then fewer defects should be entering an Inspection. Therefore, fewer can be found. Therefore, if the costs remain the same, the efficiency measures will show an increase. This then can become a signal for other types of process improvements to be considered; e.g., executing sample Inspections at faster rates. This is an opportunity you should be glad to have in front of you. This is the type of opportunity that data analysis can present to you.

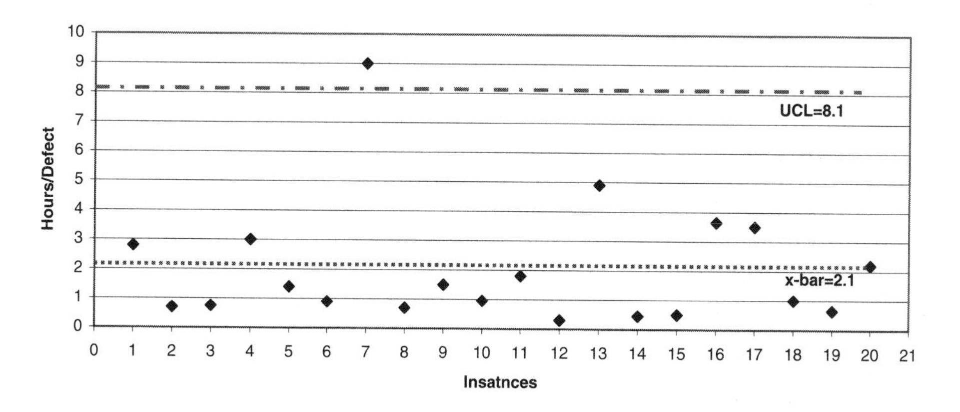

Example of Hours per Defect
Figure 6.8

Imagine the situation where the production process has been improved such that very few defects are passed into the Inspection. As fewer and fewer defects are passed into Inspection, and assuming the Inspection costs for the size of work products remains the same, then the costs per defect found by Inspection will increase. If zero defects entered and the Inspection was performed, the costs per defect would be infinite. This would be the time the organization must give serious consideration to selectively performing Inspections and perhaps not using Inspections for work products with certain characteristics. I'll discuss these possibilities in Chapter 14.

Figure 6.9 shows a representation of the relationship of cost per defect as the injected defects coming into an Inspection decreases. As the defect density approaches zero, the cost approaches infinity.

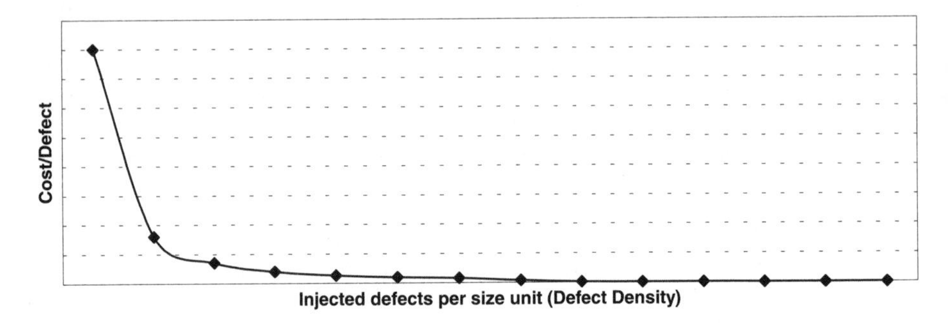

Increasing Costs per Defect As Zero Defects is approached
Figure 6.9

We could calculate efficiency using cost factors, such as dollars, and effort, but often these are tightly correlated and thus do not provide added insight. Yet in some organizations dollar measurement is preferred.

6.20 Error Prone Modules

Not all modules will have the same defect density. There will be variation as I discussed. However, some modules can be much more defective than we might consider reasonable. In these cases, we may need to make a decision for further action before proceeding into test. The decision ranges from a Re-Inspection to re-engineering the module.

Of course one could choose to do nothing. In these cases, I suggest that the module be given special attention during test. This could include additional testing, but at a minimum should include a management review of the quality as seen during test. If the module still reflects undesirable quality, then management has other decisions to make. I could argue that management should have taken action sooner, and this is often true, but they will at least now know the risk when the module is shipped as part of the product. This type of action is hardly quality management, but more like quality praying. We can hope that some lessons are learned and integrated so similar bad decisions are not made the next time a module is demonstrated to be error prone.

Figure 6.10 shows an example of a frequency distribution ordered for modules grouped by defect density into sets of 10% or deciles. In this example, the defects were counted for Inspections, all tests, and six months of customer use. The size was the final size at delivery of the product. This distribution looks like a Pareto chart, and behaves like one. But it is an ordered distribution from most defective decile to least defective decile. Each decile represents 10% of the code. As might be expected since we are trying to place discrete modules in each decile, the module sums do not add neatly into 10% clusters. Therefore, we will have approximate deciles.

When a module crosses two deciles, we put the module in the decile where most of the module's LOC fit. The module placements are thus not precise, but it's simple and gives us something easy to work with. One needs a reasonable number of modules to do this analysis. If there are not enough modules, then rank ordering by module is recommended. An easy way to start is to take the module with the lowest defect density and place it in the 10th decile. Then pick the next lowest defect dense module and place it on top, as in a stack. Keep placing modules in this fashion. After all modules are stacked, then indicate the deciles.

In this example, we see that some deciles are defect free, and isn't that good news. Yes, some modules are defect free! Later in Chapters 9 and 14 I'll explore how we might increase the volume of defect free deciles. Look at the decile with the highest defect density. Shocking isn't it.

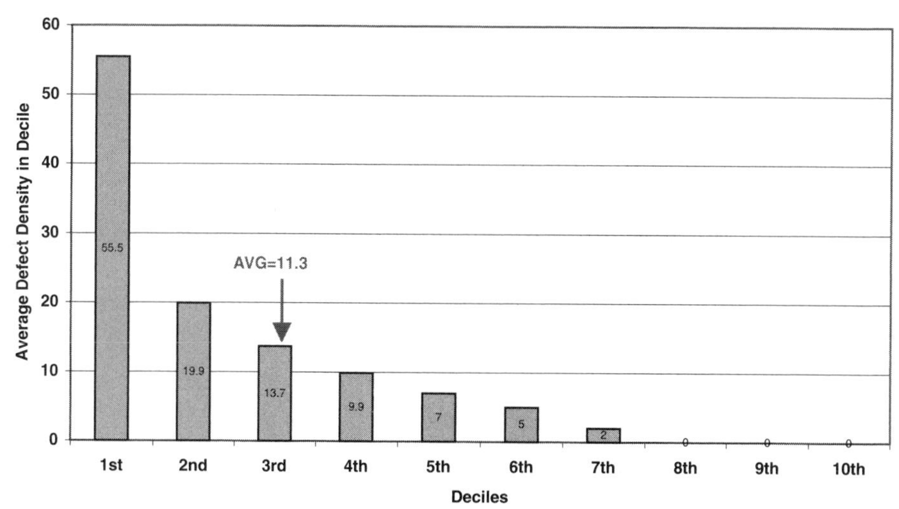

Distribution of Modules by Defect Density As Decile Sets
Figure 6.10

The average of this decile is 55.5 defects/KLOC, but if we examined the most defective module in this decile we would find that it was almost 200 defects/ KLOC. This means one defect for every five LOC.

If this module is not a subject for corrective action to improve quality, then I cannot imagine what criteria one would use. This is one error-prone module and as was learned with this module, it remained an error-prone in test and when delivered to the users as part of the product.

Inspections, therefore, can provide an early indicator of modules that have a high probability to continue to cause trouble during test and with users. The choices of action vary, but the signals are given by the Inspection process data.

Boehm and Basili also found this pattern and noted in their *Software Defect Reduction Top 10 List* "About 80 percent of the defects come from 20 percent of the modules, and about half the modules are defect free." [BOE01]

When the decile ordering analysis is performed after Inspections, it can provide signals that can help focus decisions for re-engineering or test. We could also analyze the modules in the bottom 30% to try to learn characteristics that could be used in future projects to enable lower defect injection rates.

6.21 Inspection Effectiveness

I discussed effectiveness in Chapter 1. In Figure 1.7 it was shown that the more mature an organization is, the better its effectiveness is in removing defects via Inspections. As I discussed, a higher effectiveness will lead to lower costs in the project. In Chapter 9: Economics of Inspections we will discuss how effectiveness can be used to manage project quality. For now, we need to remember that:

Inspection Effectiveness = Number of defects found during Inspections / Total number of defects found in all activities

Thus if we found 65 defects via Inspections and 100 defects in Inspections + all tests, Inspections would have a 65% effectiveness before delivery. We'll see later how we factor into our effectiveness calculations the defects that customers find. I will discuss in Chapter 9 how we can analyze and determine effectiveness by Inspection type; e.g., design Inspections, code Inspections. As we'll see each of these can have a different effectiveness. We should want to know both the full effectiveness of Inspections and the effectiveness by Inspection type to learn how each contributes or can be improved.

One pattern that continues to repeat itself is that the faster an Inspection is executed the fewer defects are found. This has been found and documented by Buck [BUC81a] and Wenneson [WEN85] among others. Thus the rate of Inspections is one factor that affects the effectiveness. We will learn about others later in the book.

6.22 Feedback to All in the Organization

The organization and projects will be providing data for each Inspection. These data need to be analyzed and presented back to the organization and projects to enable learning and process improvement. The types of reports, feedback, and frequency of feedback are choices of the organization and projects.

I suggest that reports and feedback be provided monthly at the organization level. In many situations weekly or fortnightly discussions should occur at project meetings. The ease of feedback is directly tied to the database recording system. Web-based solutions make reporting and analysis easier and quicker.

There are many opportunities for feedback:

- After the Inspection Meeting
- Periodically during the project
    - Monthly to the organization
    - Monthly with the Defect Prevention action teams
    - Weekly or fortnightly with the project team

The feedback at the end of the Inspection Meeting is real-time and enables a reaction to process signals as close to the source as possible. Feedback to the organization enables goal setting and is necessary for goal tracking. Analysis is provided to the Defect Prevention action teams for improvement considerations.

At the organization level, the SEPG or Inspection Coordinator usually coordinates the analysis and suggestions for new goals. At the project level, the Project Lead discusses the analysis with the team during weekly or fortnightly team meetings.

Reports, required by the organization's management, should be produced for management review every month. These reports should be shared not only with management but also with project team members beforehand to avoid surprises and incorrect conclusions, and to further the buy-in. These monthly reports will allow the organization to reflect on organization status and progress.

The project team and the Project Lead should discuss outliers and improvements when reviewing the latest set of Inspection performance. Once the process becomes reasonably stable, in most cases there will be no action required. However when results are outside of defined limits, thresholds, or norms, then the team should be asking what could be done to prevent the occurrence in the future. Then actions can be assigned to remedy the issues and to establish changes to defined processes. These actions should be coordinated with the Defect Prevention action teams. I will discuss more on process improvements resulting from Inspection data analysis in Chapters 7 and 8. Feedback to the team members not only gets them involved, but also reinforces the management commitment to Inspections and shows the importance of analysis for continuous improvement.

At the conclusion of each Inspection, the Inspection team should discuss and review the primary Inspection process measures:

- Inspection rate
- Preparation rate
- Defect density
- Efficiency; e.g., hours/defect
- Effectiveness

Reasons for immediate discussion at the Inspection Meeting are:

- The results may suggest a Re-Inspection

- The Producer has immediate input for consideration during Rework

Actual effectiveness will only be learned later in the project, but projections can be made as a result of other Inspection process indicators. I'll discuss this more in Chapter 9.

I discussed earlier that data integrity is essential if the analysis is to have meaning for the project and organization. Feedback of the analysis will help improve and maintain data integrity. Generally people will fill out forms when asked to, but people are typically overextended in software projects, so filling out forms tends to fall to a lower priority for them. Low priority is OK, provided the data entered are correct.

People will work with the management system in the beginning, but if they do not see any results or feedback from the data they provide, they may become lax and the data starts to lose integrity. People will do what is required, but only if it is really required and they can see the value.

The system of data gathering and analysis supports itself through visible use.

Feedback also enables people to learn how to improve and set goals for themselves. If, for example, the average found in an organization is 9 defects/KLOC, then Producers with Inspections below the average get a sense of accomplishment. If their rate is above the average, they can give thought to how and what to improve.

In early use of Inspections, data reports showing differences may be difficult for some programmers and managers to accept. They may find the reports as an affront to their ego, a personal attack. They think the analysis is incorrect, or they just believe this type of analysis is meaningless. Therefore the senior management, Project Lead, SEPG, and Inspection Coordinator must support feedback without challenging the questions asked. The message must be clear that the organization is willing to learn, including from mistakes. The message should be repeated that it is better to find a defect earlier than later. Then as the data has integrity, let it speak for itself.

When the report is flawed, apologize, thank them for their input, ask how this could have been avoided, and take corrective action to assure it won't happen again, and then ensure it doesn't occur again.

If the data lacks integrity, the reports will be flawed, and if the programmers or management find the flaws, they will rightfully challenge not just the data and analysis but the Inspection process itself.

The transition to accepting and trusting the data and reports may take longer in some organizations, but it will come. In the meantime, all data must be non-attributional and not threatening to any individual. All efforts must be made to keep the data safe at individual levels. There still may be situations where it is known who the Producer was for the most defective module inspected, but the message must be repeated that, while this could be true, there may be system reasons that contributed to this fact. Then focus on the system changes that are required. Never let it happen that an individual can prove or even suggest that they were punished because of Inspection results.

Over time, people will come to accept that this is a learning experience and the data can help them learn. For some organizations this may take a longer time than one might expect, so keep at it. In higher-level mature organizations, I sometimes see surprising differences in how the data is perceived. See Anecdote 6.5

ANECDOTE

WHO WAS IMPACTED?

During an assessment, I once asked a programmer how he felt about the fact that everyone knew his recent module was the most defective and well outside the upper limit of expected results.

I asked this as I was already sure that this was not a threatening question for the individual and I have found that sometimes a question that is unexpected tells me more about the organization, its culture, and its institutionalization of practices, than typical assessment questions do.

In a heartbeat, the programmer told me, "I felt I let the team down."

To say the least, I was surprised by the answer, but it made perfect sense for this Level 5 organization where the data was not threatening and the project team worked as a team to deliver almost defect-free solutions. He went further to explain actions he personally took to help prevent this from occurring in the future.

I wish we had more of this attitude in the software community.

Anecdote 6.5

Management needs to get feedback to understand how well Inspections are proceeding. But, as always with Inspections, management should not be using the data in any negative manner. Once they do, the data will begin to deteriorate. Management must never even suggest that they know the defect rates for individuals. They also should not shoot the messenger when it is reported that Inspections are not proceeding well. In early use the organization will see situations where Inspections may not proceed as well as desired or expected. Management must reinforce that while this occurs, the Inspection process will be improved through learning how and where to improve. Keep the focus on the policy and objectives. This will be difficult in some organizations, but it is necessary.

6.23 Early Use Types of Reports

We have already discussed a number of report types in this chapter. Some other reports that may be useful include:

- Plan versus actual status
- Defect trend
- Defect summary
- Where Caused – Where Found
- Defect Leakage
- Major to minor ratios
- Regression analysis

PLAN VERSUS ACTUAL STATUS

These can be a simple report of actual versus planned Inspections. In early use of Inspections, this report is helpful. When an organization is mature in its use of Inspections, this type of report is less interesting. Figure 6.11 is an example of such a report. I suggest that the report be presented weekly when first adopting Inspections, as monthly tends not to be frequent enough to manage problems as they occur. Once an organization chooses Inspections, they should keep the focus on the objectives and plans.

The example in Figure 6.11 shows that the organization started out meeting plan in the first couple of weeks, and then started to fall behind plan. There can be different interpretations or reasons for why the actuals are not in line with the plan, but the fact remains that the project is not on plan and is falling further and further behind, at least with respect to Inspections. We could intuit that the project is also falling behind in other milestones also.

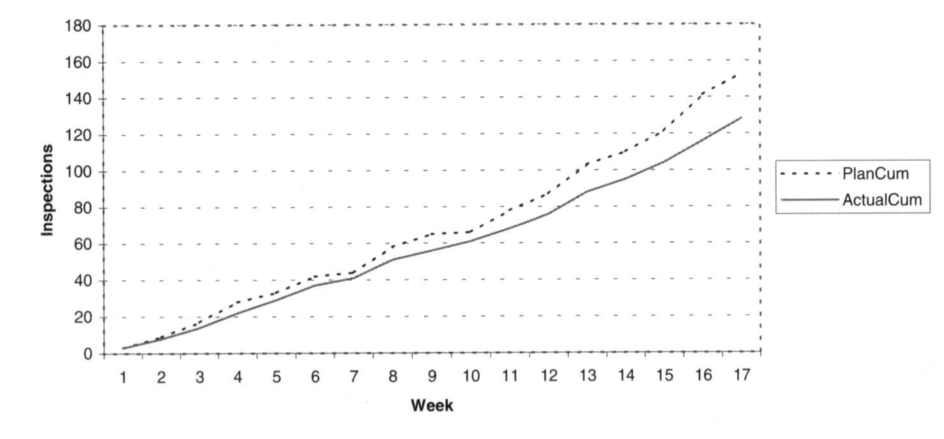

Example of Tracking Actual Inspections Versus Planned
Figure 6.11

The project plan may have been too aggressive despite the Inspections, but it would not be unexpected to hear from some critics that the project is late due to Inspections. Should this happen, ask why the Inspections did not occur on plan. Usually it is because the work products were not ready. Help management to see the problem, since the signals occur quite early; e.g., Inspections are not occurring on plan starting in week 2 in this example. Other milestones in the project will probably slip also, so signals from Inspection status could provide an early indicator for other slippages. Corrective action should be taken and it is better to know this in week 3 than later post week 17 when test begins.

This type of report can be shown for KLOC or FP planned versus actually inspected if a more granular view is wanted. KLOC or FP can give a picture of how much has been completed and how much remains with respect to resources that may be needed. Tracking only at the event level of Inspections treats all Inspections at the same nominal weight. Either form can provide a sense of earned value as Inspections are completed. When an organization is running behind plan, this detail may prove more helpful. When the plan is reasonably being met, the additional detail does not offer more insight.

ORGANIZATION DEFECT ANALYSIS AND SUMMARY

Defect summaries should be made available for each specific Inspection type, for periodic summary reports to management, and on an as needed basis. We saw some examples in Figure 6.3 and Figure 6.4 where pie charts were used for defect types. If you do not like pie charts, use histograms or tables. Figure 6.12 is the same data as in Figure 6.4, but as a histogram.

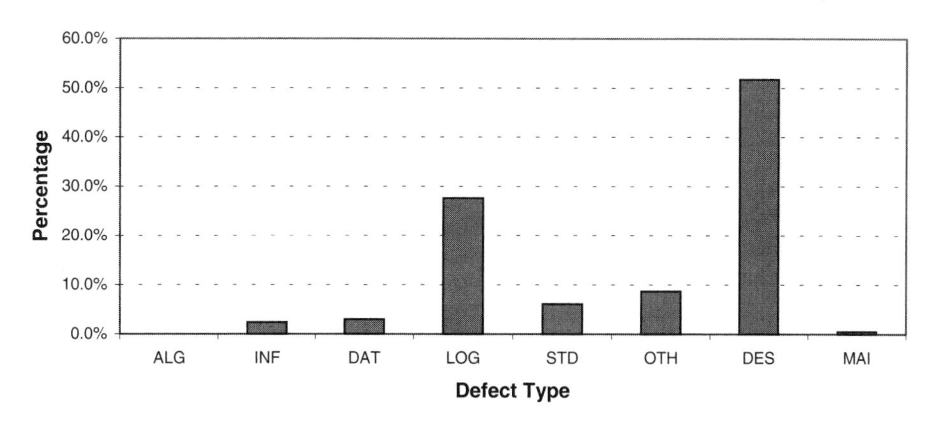

Example of Defect Types as a Histogram
Figure 6.12

These reports can include a summary of defect class by defect type by severity. For example, in Figure 6.13 the same data is shown for Figure 6.3, but here it is tabular for major defects.

Type	Missing	Wrong	Extra	Total
Algorithm	12	180	14	206
Interface	42	12	0	54
Data	36	66	4	106
Logic	5	128	3	136
Standards	49	96	0	145
Other	33	37	19	89
Design Base	34	3	10	47
Maintainability	121	101	13	235
Sum	332	623	63	1018

Tabular Presentation of Defect Types
Figure 6.13

While this tabular form may have use, graphics are always easier to read. See Figure 6.14 for the same tabular data graphically. Make the choice that works for you.

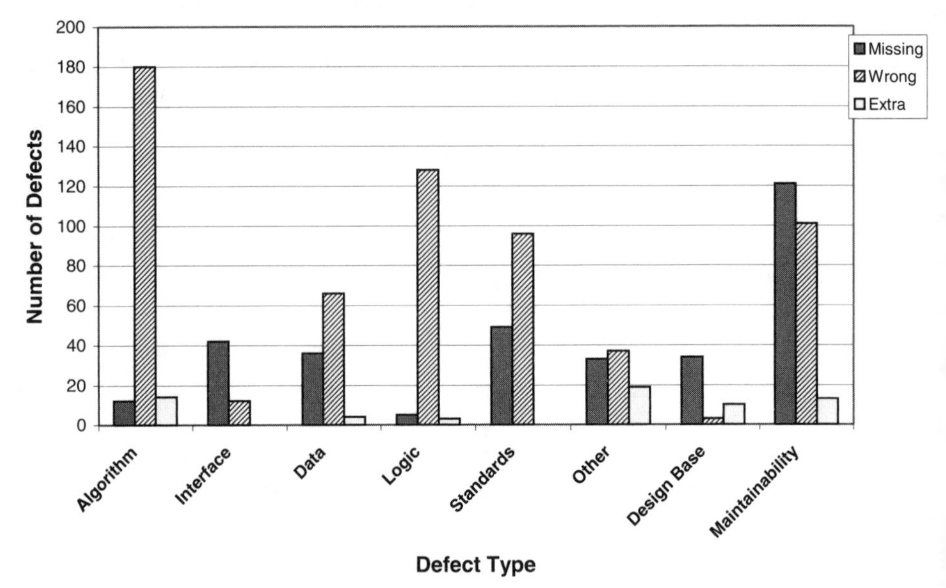

Example of Graphic Form of the Tabular Data
Figure 6.14

If we wanted to get an understanding of where to focus our improvements, we might use a Pareto chart, which is shown below in Figure 6.15 for the same data.

A Pareto distribution allows us to quickly see the most frequent contributors for defect types. In this case it is Maintainability and Algorithms.

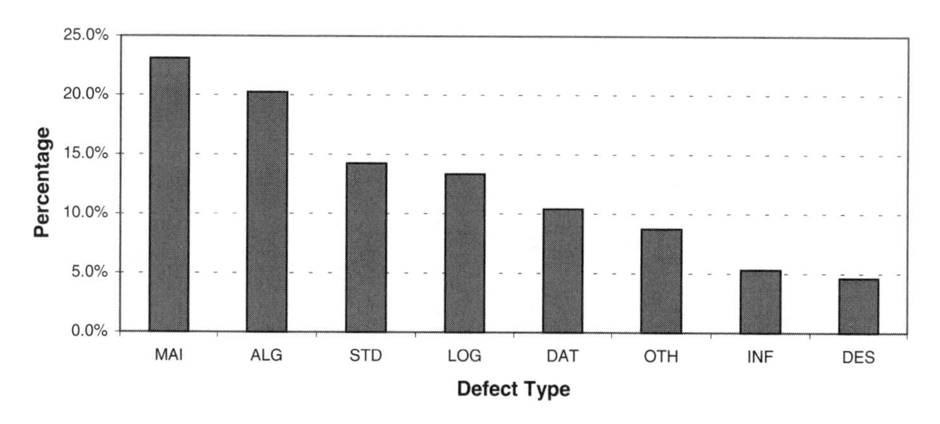

Example of A Pareto Distribution
Figure 6.15

Another report might show the relationships between defect types and defect removal activities as shown in Figure 6.16. While this table may be complete, it is difficult to read and understand. Too much data may not be useful for the organization. It could be useful for the SEPG when doing analysis for defect trends across the organization, but I tend to vote for simple reports that are easy to read and understandable for the people who need to use them to take actions for improvement. Choose what is useful to you, but confirm the usefulness with the organization.

Type	REQ	HLD	LLD	Code	UT	FT	ST
Maintainability	2	36	39	55	31	48	24
Algorithm	7	23	45	62	14	47	8
Standards	1	9	27	76	12	27	11
Logic	44	21	8	12	3	16	14
Data	1	7	26	34	22	12	4
Other	17	6	14	21	19	8	4
Interface	2	12	25	3	1	9	2
Design Base	0	5	21	15	0	6	0
Sum	74	119	205	278	102	173	67

Example of Defect Types by Inspection Type
Figure 6.16

This type of report just has too much data to be used easily. Partitioning of the data may be more useful with a graphical representation. See Figures 6.17 and 6.18 for examples of subsetting this data into types of defects across defect removal activities.

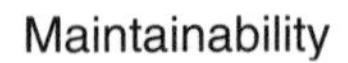

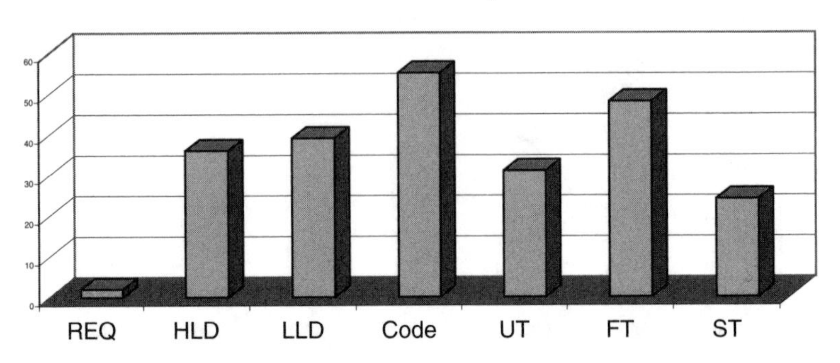

Example of Maintainability Defect Type Distributed by Defect Removal Activity
Figure 6.17

- § -

Algorithm

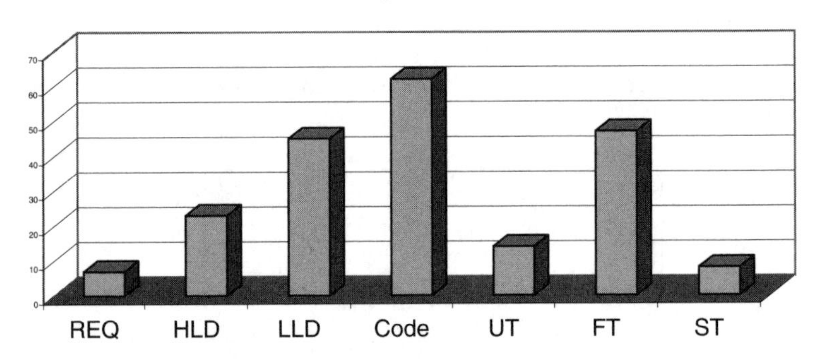

Example of Algorithm Defect Type Distributed by Defect Removal Activity
Figure 6.18

WHERE CAUSED AND WHERE FOUND

In any Inspection we will obviously know where and when the defect was found; e.g., in requirements specifications, design, code. We will also know in which test a defect was found. To get more information for defect analysis we should also identify where we believe the defect was caused. This can be done immediately at the time of defect discovery and acceptance, during the Analysis Meeting, or after the Analysis Meeting. Once we have a history of where found and where caused, we can begin to build our defect injection and detection curves. See Figures 6.19 and Figure 6.20 for examples of defect injection and detection.

These distributions can be derived within one product release (or project) cycle. They should be started as soon as Inspections are started. In early use of Inspections, people may complain that this is hard to do, that it is difficult or arbitrary to try to decide where a defect was caused. This is because they may not yet see the value; so keep asking them to do their best when deciding where a defect was caused. There may be some errors in placing the cause, but this will tend to clear up as people learn that it is not so hard after all. Over time the issue goes away.

A simple test for where a defect was caused is to ask, "What must and should be changed to correct the defect?" Then pick the earliest stage where change is required. Yes, I know we sometimes fix the code to correct a design defect or fix design to correct a requirements defect. This is why the "should' part of the question needs to be answered also. This is not a perfect way to determine where a defect was caused, but it helps.

Figure 6.19 shows an example of how defects from various stages contributed to the total set of defects attributed or injected in a production stage. This figure shows where defects were found; e.g. some defects caused in REQ were found in requirements analysis (REQ), High-level design (HLD), Low-level design (LLD), and System Test (ST).

Note that not all defects are found in the activity where the defect was caused. For example, some REQ defects are found in HLD and LLD.

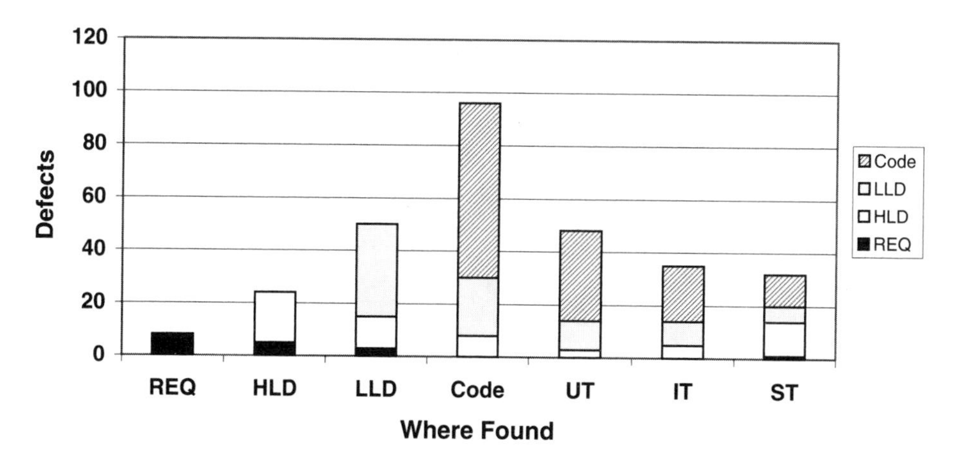

Example of Defects Found By Activity
Figure 6.19

In Figure 6.20 we see the reallocated cumulative volume of defects shown as *where caused*. Here we see that HLD injected 60 defects, but that during the Inspection for the HLD only 19 were found. Thus the effectiveness pre-ship was 32% for this Inspection activity. See Figure 6.19.

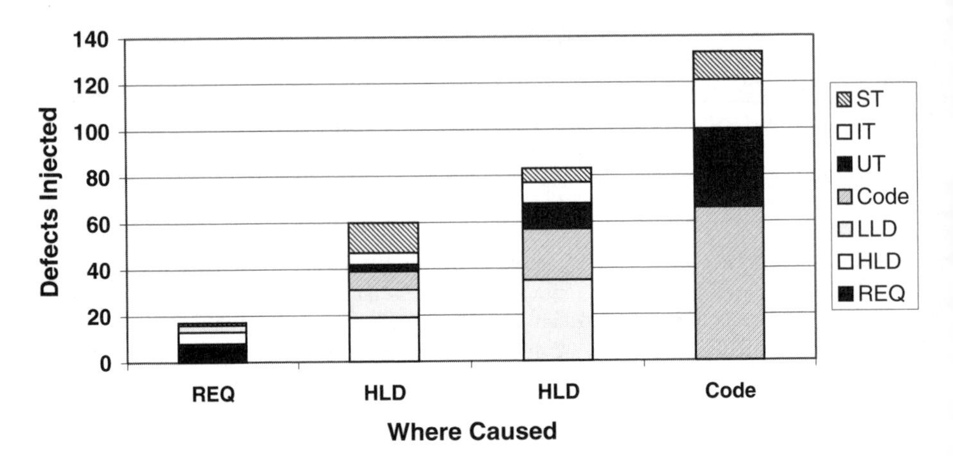

Example of Defects Caused By Activity
Figure 6.20

DEFECT LEAKAGE / DEFECT CONTAINMENT

Defect leakage from design to code or code to test is something we will want to analyze. Defect leakage is a measure of the percentage of defects not found by a specific defect removal activity. The analysis is directly related to *where found* and *where caused* analysis and reflects defect containment; i.e., how well the Inspection activity performed in removing defects.

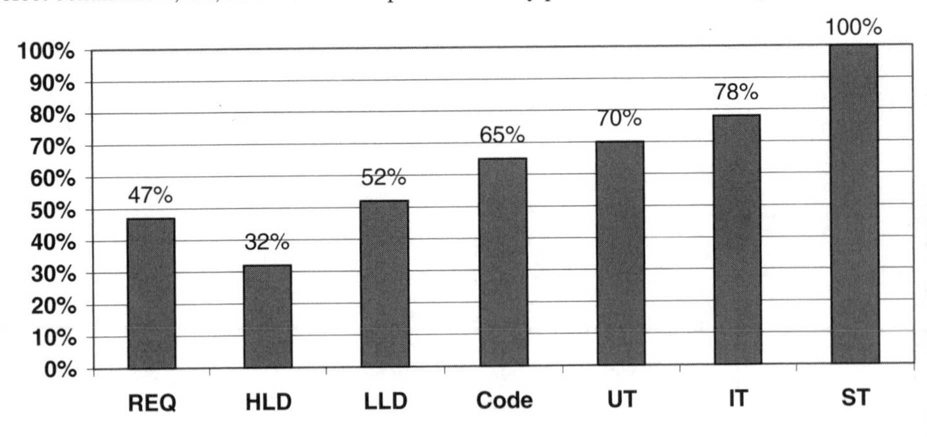

Example of Defect Containment Percentages
Figure 6.21

Some organizations call this *defect leakage*, which is a reverse measure and others call it *defect containment*; i.e., how many defects were contained in the Inspection rather than leaked from the Inspection activity. It will take at least one cycle to know the percentage leakage from activity to activity, and again it should be started as soon as possible. Both are views of the effectiveness of the Inspection process. See Figure 6.21 for a brief example.

n this example we see that no Inspection type is near 100% effective. For example, REQ is only 47% effective, HLD is 32%, LLD is 52%, and Code is 65% at the respective Inspections. Effectiveness of ST is 100% since in this case we did not count the defects found by customers. When we do, the effectiveness of each defect removal activity, including ST will decrease.

MAJOR TO MINOR RATIOS

There is a ratio between major and minor defect found in Inspections, but I am not sure if this has any significant meaning. Some organizations do analyze and present these ratios. Clearly minors should be addressed and resolved. We might also suspect that a high rate of minor defects would suggest defective work and we might see a high major defect rate, though I am not aware of any study that has proven this.

Some view minors as equivalent to majors by some ratio they've determined; e.g., "We assume that every 25 minor defects would have resulted in the generation of one extra fault report. " [DOO92] Doolan derives this relationship to look at ROI, and while this makes some sense, it cannot sufficiently have an effect on the ROI or make or break Inspection success in an organization. My vote is to count the minors, fix them if there is sufficient time, but spend as little time with them as possible.

If the code executes successfully without repair to minor defects, it may be counterproductive to fix the minors and potentially introduce other defects during the repairs. This is a caution to be especially considered when only minor defects are found in a work product.

Some Inspection advocates would object to this recommendation. They believe that all minors should be repaired and that potentially some minors will be in fact major defects. If you too believe this is a potential, then you should choose to fix all minors in all Inspections. The choice is yours. Fixing all minors will address these concerns.

REGRESSION ANALYSIS

Figure 6.22 shows a simple regression analysis, which is a linear relationship between two variables determined for a series of Inspections. Defects/KLOC is the variable we would like to understand in relationship to LOC/Inspection Hour. In this particular case there is a relationship that suggests when the rate of Inspection proceeds at a faster rate fewer defects are found. While this will be true in almost all Inspections, each organization should prove this for itself. Fortunately is does not take look to see the same pattern.

This analysis is one of the first that should be made in every organization. Tools such as EXCEL make the calculation fairly straightforward.

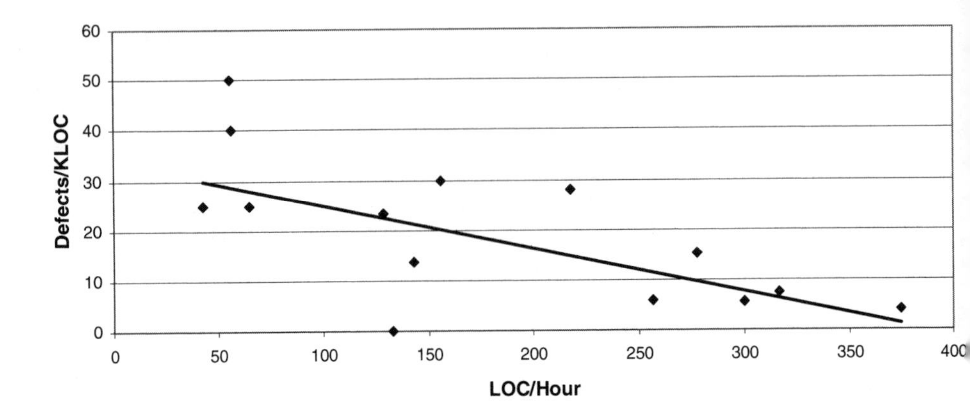

Example of Regression Analysis
Figure 6.22

6.24 Still Other Reports

There is a limited set of ways to look at Inspection data, but many ways to portray it. Some reports that others have found useful include:

- Average size of work product inspected
- Average effort/KLOC per Inspections
- Percentage Re-Inspected
- Preparation rate compared to Inspection Meeting rate
- Preparation rate compared to Inspection Meeting defect removal
- Size of work product compared to defect density
- Number of Open Issues converted to Change Requests

The examples discussed have predominantly focused on size of code, but the same examples could be applied for documents where pages would replace KLOC or FP.

While we can create many different types of reports and they may look interesting in some way, the most important question is what is being done with this information. For example, it may be interesting to know how many defects by subsystem were Wrong, Missing, or Extra, but by themselves these reports mean almost nothing. One can seriously ask, so what?

If this information is, however, used to prevent types of defects and if these reports are tracked to see if improvements are actually occurring, then they have value, because they are used to improve and reduce the number of defects injected.

End Quote:

"The introduction of appropriate measuring techniques does not cost. It saves. It is not a luxury. It is a necessity."
Robert G. Ebenau

CHAPTER 7

CAUSAL ANALYSIS

"Teach a highly educated person that it is not a disgrace to fail and that he must analyze every failure to find its cause. He must learn how to fail intelligently, for failing is one of the greatest arts in the world."
Charles F. Kittering

7.1 Introduction

Causal Analysis and Defect Prevention existed as quality management techniques before Software Inspections were defined. The original Software Inspection method did not address Defect Prevention but rather early defect discovery and correction. Carole Jones in Raleigh, IBM, introduced extensions to the Inspection method including Defect Prevention actions in 1985.

Tom Gilb has been a major proponent of coupling Defect Prevention activities with the Inspection activities since Jones' work was first published. He notes, "It has shown at least a 13-to-1 ratio return on investment. [GIL98] Raytheon coupled both Inspections and Defect Prevention by addressing both the costs of conformance and cost of non-conformance through institutionalizing of both Inspections and Defect Prevention. The result was a staggering 7.1 to 1 ROI. [HAL95]

With these examples how could any organization not want to couple Defect Prevention with Inspections? The techniques are simple and easy to introduce. When Defect Prevention is coupled with Inspections, we have a strong approach to controlling and reducing the Cost of Quality (COQ). I will later posit that with effective Defect Prevention, the volume of Inspections can be radically reduced, if not eliminated, in some situations.

7.2 What Is Causal Analysis?

In its simplest form Causal Analysis is nothing more than trying to identify the probable cause that led to a defect in a work product or process. The method is sometimes referred to as the cause and effect relationship; i.e., an identified probable cause is presumed to have led to the defect or effect. Causal Analysis is one quality technique that is included in the Defect Prevention suite. At the heart of Causal Analysis is the willingness to learn from failure and mistakes.

ANECDOTE

WHO MAKES MISTAKES?

In my early career, I cubed with an individual who told me once, " I've never made a mistake. Well actually I once thought I did, but I was wrong about that." He was joking, of course, but he was also good. He set a goal for himself to become a VP within 5 years, and he did it. I should go further and add that he was more than willing to learn from his mistakes and sought feedback from everyone at all levels to learn how he could improve. This openness allowed him to grow quickly as a key contributor and have his contributions rewarded by rapid, well-earned promotions. He kept his learning channels open at all times.

This is our objective; i.e., to have everyone learn from themselves and others in the organization so that fewer and fewer defects are made and goals are achieved.

Anecdote 7.1

While quality models such as the SW-CMM and ISO 9000 address Defect Prevention and Causal Analysis, they do so to different degrees and have a different focus on what is to be performed. This has led to some confusion in the software community, but the bigger concern is that not enough software organizations practice rigorous Defect Prevention or Causal Analysis. Oh, they do to some degree, but I am now talking about a structured and consistent approach to learning, Causal Analysis, and Defect Prevention.

Reasons why the software community has not yet fully embraced Causal Analysis vary from reluctance due to lack of understanding on how one even starts such a process, all the way to outright refusal for any of a long list of emotionally charged reasons, including the view that it is a quality technique for quality's sake. Fortunately there is a growing trend toward software organizations using this technique.

The results of defect Causal Analysis are exactly what any sound business wants; i.e., improve quality to better control its costs to get more sales. This is an example of the Deming Chain Reaction as was shown in Figure 2.9. Given that there exists a repeatable process for accomplishing a task, be it developing software or building homes, the only ways to increase profits are to build the work product for less cost or sell more of them. Quality drives both of these and Causal Analysis with Defect Prevention feeds both.

Performing defect Causal Analysis for software will affect all business issues; i.e., quality, costs, revenues, profit. To fully benefit, identifying the causes of defects requires that one also identify a proposed solution to prevent a defect type in future work. Reducing the defects caused results in lower development costs and fewer defects delivered with the product. Products that have fewer defects will be accepted by the users and marketplace and will lead to higher sales volume. The Deming Chain Reaction plays out once again.

Let's assume that, in your environment, the data shows one hundred different defect types. Let's further assume that the cost to remove these defects is evenly distributed across the one hundred defect types. Then, for each defect type that is prevented in future software development, the costs of quality can be reduced by approximately 1%. Not much you suggest. But when ten defect types are eliminated the savings can approximate 10%, and as we begin to eliminate one type after another we can observe how our costs may be reduced dramatically. Some types will account for more than 1% of costs. These are the important drivers, so we should gain more by addressing them first. Furthermore, if we eliminate the causes of these errors, the costs are removed in all future products. Defect prevention can lead to a lower Cost of Quality for products in the organization.

Carole Jones, in her seminal article "*A Process-Integrated Approach To Defect Prevention*" [JON85] integrates Causal Analysis and Defect Prevention into a methodology that is based on three concepts:

- Programmers should evaluate their own errors
- Causal Analysis should be a part of the process
- Feedback should be part of the process

She then proceeds to define the methodology as an extension to the Inspection process.

In another paper Robert Mays and Jones found that the number of defects entering work products could be reduced by as much as 50%. [MAY90] Clearly this kind of ROI should get our attention.

It is interesting that while Fagan used an Ishikawa or Fishbone diagram, one of the Causal Analysis techniques, to demonstrate the value and contribution of Inspections to software quality, he did not make the easy leap taken by Jones to apply these techniques to the Inspection process. [FAG86] Although he does state in the same article "An outstanding benefit and control of inspections was that designers and coders through involvement in inspections of their own work learned to find defects they had created more easily. This enabled them to avoid causing these defects in future work, thus providing much higher quality product." But it was Jones who showed us how to integrate the processes of Inspections, Causal Analysis, and Defect Prevention.

The Causal Analysis process is rather straightforward:

- First you identify classes, types, or even instances of defects that you would like to prevent from recurring in the future
- Then, assuming that the team of people reviewing the defects has been trained in Defect Prevention and Causal Analysis, try to identify the probable cause in the environment in which the defect was found

In the case of software the environment is the software development system.

In this chapter we will explore both Causal Analysis and Defect Prevention. Briefly stated, we perform Causal Analysis so we can determine what actions we might take for Defect Prevention. Defect Prevention involves changing the development process to systematically eliminate the cause of the defect types. We start by understanding that people do make mistakes when they work and that we empower them to improve their work quality using both Causal Analysis and Defect Prevention.

7.3 The Systems View

The process of developing a software product is in essence a system, and each activity and task within each stage of the product process cycle is a subsystem. All have inputs, subtasks, states, and outputs. If we now accept that as part of our inputs we must address and understand the four basic factors within this system, then we will be better able to ascertain which of these leads to the root cause element. This is what we must change if we are to also change the effect; i.e., prevent defects.

The system or environment varies from organization to organization and, within an organization, from project to project. Each organization should be understood in its own terms and on its own ground if defect Causal Analysis is to have maximum benefit. It is this environment that should be evolved into a more repeatable and controllable discipline. We are, however, a long way from that objective in the software community today, although I am sure there are numerous experts who would argue we are better off than I suggest. Nonetheless, we will incrementally come closer to the objective as the software community matures into the business it should become.

When we look at the environment within which software is produced, we note a few major aspects which intersect and which have an effect on how well the other aspects will contribute to a successful software product solution. These aspects are shown in Figure 7.1, and include the following: people, technology, resources, including software and hardware, processes, including information of various types, and funding. Jay W. Forrester of MIT, when writing of systems dynamics called this set the four M's: Men, Machines, Materials, and Money. All four of these are common to almost any system.

In the software environment these sets become, people, technology, processes, and funding, and it is these elements which we must model into our process definition and which in combination with the tools (hardware and software), personnel, practices and methodologies will define our environment. If we refer to the SW-CMM, these are the Commitments and Abilities required for a Key Process Area. In the ETVX model, these are the Entry criteria or preconditions.

The interaction of these aspects defines how well the system performs and how well it meets its objectives. [FOR61] For our interests the system is the environment in which software is produced. If we understand how these factors relate to one another and how they relate to the end product, then we can begin to understand how we might change them to achieve a more desirable effect or result.

THE SOFTWARE DEVELOPMENT ENVIRONMENT

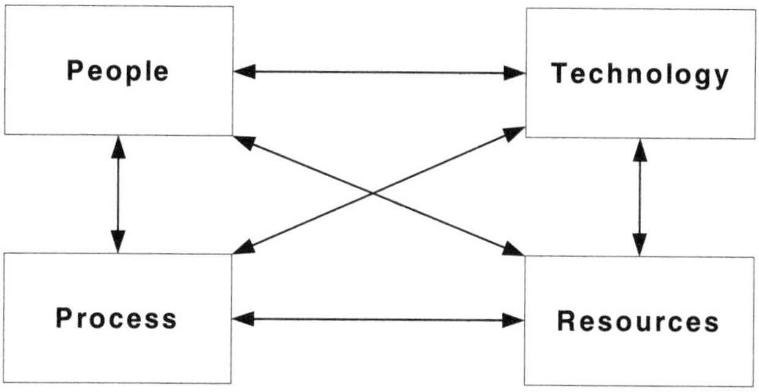

People ↔ Technology
People ↕ Process
Technology ↕ Resources
Process ↔ Resources
People ↔ Resources
Technology ↔ Process

Relationships In A Production Environment
Figure 7.1

THE ECOLOGY OF SOFTWARE

In the world of software production, just as in the world at large, everything seems to affect everything else to some degree. This means that in the environmental relationships shown in Figure 7.1 each of these aspects can have an effect on each of the others through interaction. It also suggests that in the more granular view of the system of software production that there may be data variables that reflect how these aspects affect each other. There are only a few relevant data variables that we will use to analyze software projects. Then we can learn how their relationships suggest the probable causes for defects injected into the system. These data variables were discussed in Chapter 6.

7.4 How To Do Causal Analysis

First we start with a problem or, for our purposes, a defect found in an Inspection. Then we need to understand the problem in an objective way, so we can learn the cause and what we might do differently. The cause is determined by iterating through and down to the most specific and isolatable root element which will map to the effect; i.e., the defect.

The first time it is tried it will not be as easy or as simple as I have suggested getting to the root cause. The team may default to choosing what seems obvious rather than the real cause. As the programming team continues to employ Causal Analysis it will find that the process becomes easier and more effective. After a while the team will take pride in being able to identify causes to help prevent future defects.

In the world of quality control and in the specific area of Quality Circles this method has been introduced under the name of Cause and Effect diagrams or Fishbone diagrams or Ishikawa diagrams, after the innovator's name. [ISH68] Combined with brainstorming sessions the method has proven to be highly effective. See Figure 7.5, for an example of a fishbone diagram. Other techniques that can aid Causal Analysis are listed at the end of this section.

In Figure 7.2 we see a process flow for Causal Analysis combined with a high-level view of Defect Prevention. Note that during Causal Analysis we will iterate until we believe we have selected the most probable cause. We will also iterate if the proposed solution needs tuning before deployment. Then we will implement an action for prevention. These actions can be in any of the aspects in the project or organization environment/system; e.g., people, technology, process, funding.

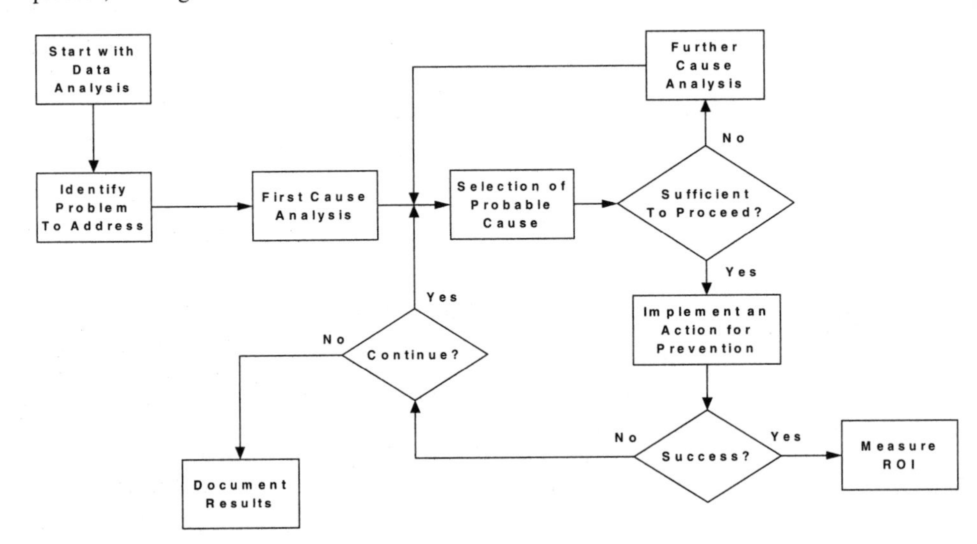

Causal Analysis and Defect Prevention Process Flow
Figure 7.2

7.5 An Example

The only requirements to begin defect Causal Analysis are:

- A defect
- Knowledgeable programmers involved in the development software process
- Time for them to assess possibilities for the actual cause of the defect

Let's follow an example of what might happen for a specific defect.

A program in system test, while executing Test Case TC123, takes the operating system into a loop that hangs up the operating system. On first analysis it is not clear why the loop is occurring (it never is) and furthermore the loop is occurring in an area that should not have received execution and is also outside any code that the module calls or interfaces with. After debugging the problem, it is found that the last instruction of module ABC is a BC 7,

OTHERLOC; i.e., branch under seven conditions out of a possible fifteen to OTHERLOC. This program had been run many times before and this loop never occurred. The branch obviously had always been successfully taken before.

However, in one execution none of the seven branching conditions were satisfied, and execution fell through to the next immediate instruction in module XYZ that was next to module ABC in memory. From there execution in the operating system simply got deeper and deeper into trouble until the loop occurred somewhere within a set of instructions that had all the registers and conditions to enable the loop. The comment attached to the BC 7, OTHERLOC instruction reads, "WILL ALWAYS TAKE THIS BRANCH". See Figure 7.3.

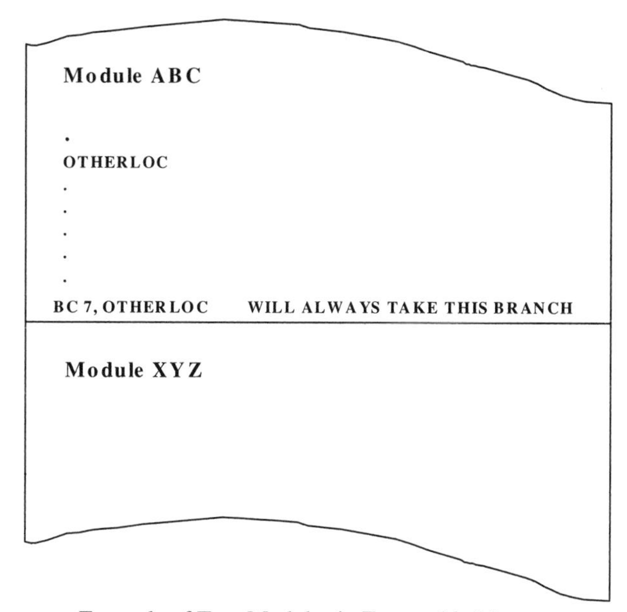

Example of Two Modules in Executable Memory
Figure 7.3

This particular bug is interesting because the code says one thing and the comment says something different. One of them is wrong, but which? Should the branch be conditional, or should it be unconditional? Which did the original designer/programmer intend? What is required?

If the former is correct, then code might be missing after the BC 7, OTHERLOC — code that would process the situation when the conditions are not met. We may have an opinion that there should be no additional code, but we have no hard evidence one way or the other. If the comment is correct, then the branch should be changed to an unconditional execution. After assessing the design materials, if any exist other than the comment, or discussing the problem with the last and hopefully original programmer we might learn that it really should be an unconditional branch; i.e., always take the branch regardless of conditions.

To this point we have done no Causal Analysis.

We have done nothing more than problem determination:

- Isolate the instructions in error
- Debug the error to ascertain the fix we choose to apply

Often the process of defect repair stops after three steps:

- Find the problem area; in this case where the branch was incorrectly taken
- Choose a fix
- Apply it and deliver to the user

History is forgotten because it is not recorded or not thought to be important enough to spend time on and the programmer moves on to the next program, or the next job, and the next set of bugs. Clearly individual programmers may integrate some of the knowledge for themselves as to what they should pay attention to in future assignments. Typically, too much is lost in the haste of getting on with the next piece of work, and most certainly the knowledge is not transferred to other programmers in the organization. This is not Causal Analysis. It is bug fixing.

Problem determination or defect analysis is obviously necessary for a defect to be properly repaired, but we have more that can be learned about this defect and others like it. We can through Causal Analysis begin the step toward preventing future instances of a defect type.

If we continue with the defect analysis in our example we may find the following possibilities for causes after a Brainstorming session:

1. The design materials were in outright error.
2. The code materials are contradictory.
3. The programmer doing the code did not understand the conditional branch instruction or the conditions that could occur while the program was executing.
4. The documentation incorrectly defined the meaning of the conditional branch instruction.
5. The training provided to the coder was insufficient.
6. It was undetected in earlier Inspections.

Now that we have enumerated some possibilities, let us assume that these are the complete set of valid possibilities for the environment in which this defect occurred. We can now try to ascertain which is the probable cause in this particular case. It is important to note that any of these causes might have been "the" specific cause, and only by looking deeper into the environment can we determine which one is the true cause.

Each of these possibilities requires a different solution as to how the defect type or instance might be prevented in the future.

For example:

1. If the design were in outright error, perhaps holding design Inspections would have helped. If design Inspections actually were held, then we must dig deeper, and try to understand why this defect was not found at that process checkpoint. Each of these sub-possibilities in turn offers other possibilities that must be evaluated to determine the real cause in this environment.

2. If the programmer was given inadequate training or documentation, then a correction in the training and/or documentation may be needed for this specific case. Additionally we should determine if this is a unique, endemic, or wide spread problem. If the latter, we may have to take a more global action with other programmers.

If we developed a Fishbone diagram for this example we would start with something as follows in Figure 7.4.

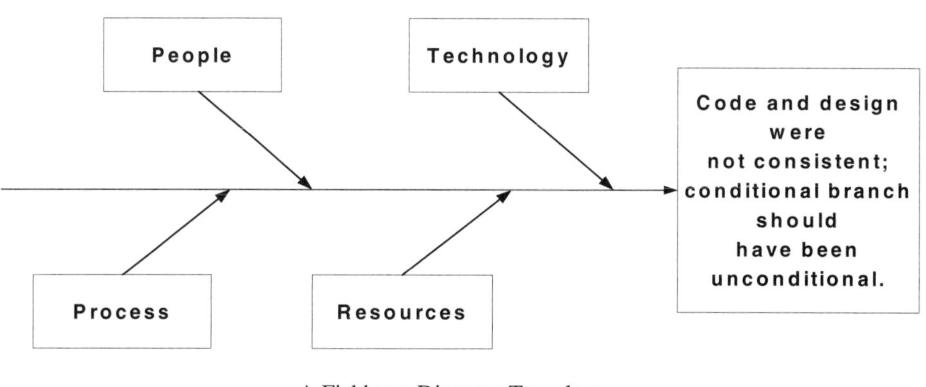

A Fishbone Diagram Template
Figure 7.4

Once the actual and specific cause is decided, then actions can be put in place to try to reduce or prevent future occurrences of the same or similar errors coming into test. For example, if inadequate training had been provided to one programmer, then we should investigate the possibilities that this is true for other programmers who could be making errors from the same cause. If the Inspection checklist was not addressing the defect type, perhaps it should be updated; e.g., “Comments and code must match.” We could also apply Causal Analysis and Defect Prevention to prevent defects entering Inspections.

As we take the analysis to a deeper level, we might see the following in Figure 7.5 where probable causes are highlighted. We would still need to decide which of these probable causes was the most probable.

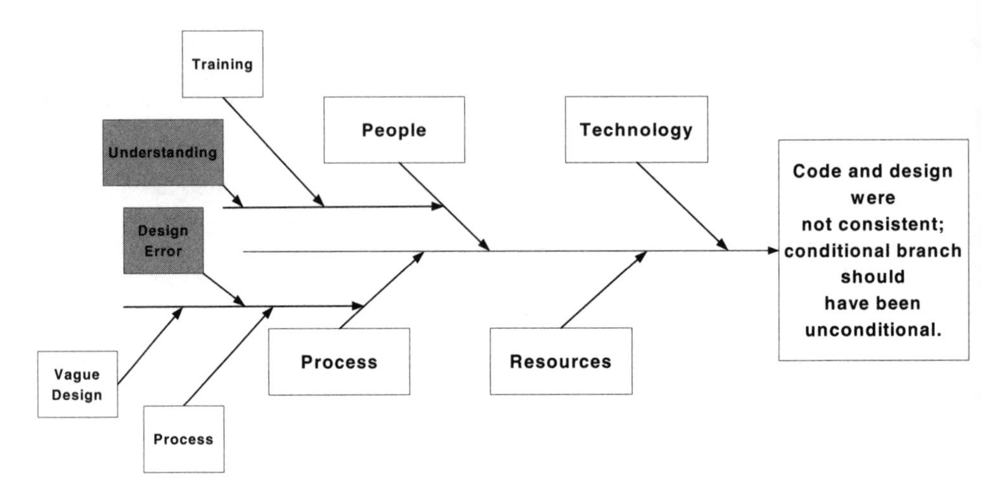

An Example Fishbone Diagram
Figure 7.5

Fishbone or Ishikawa diagrams are one technique used in Causal Analysis. These diagrams are sometimes called cause and effect diagrams. Other techniques that could aid Causal Analysis include:

- Affinity Diagrams
- Fault Tree Analysis
- Brainstorming
- Force Field Analysis
- Interrelationship Diagrams
- Matrix Diagrams
- Nominal Group Technique
- Pareto Analysis
- Prioritization Matrices
- Storyboarding

All these techniques are aided by data analysis using what we discussed in Chapter 6. While all of these techniques have value, I will only address one other, Pareto Analysis, as it is such a strong technique for data analysis.

7.6 Pareto Analysis

Pareto analysis gives information in an ordered frequency of defect type occurrences. Pareto helps focus where to start by presenting graphically the high frequency or critical defect types. We saw a similar form of frequency distributions previously in Chapter 6, Figure 6.15.

See Figure 7.6 for another example of a Pareto distribution. In this example we see different defect types classified by frequency of occurrence with a summation curve going to 100%.

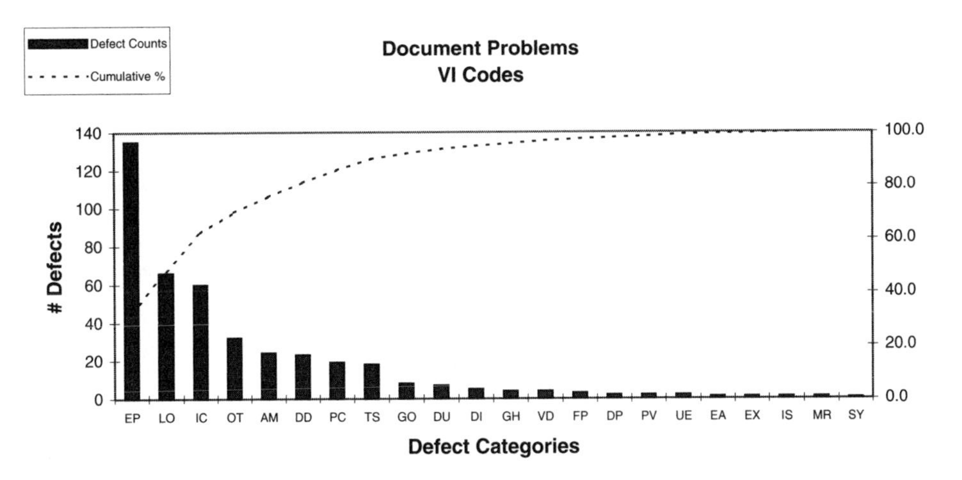

Example of Pareto Analysis of Document Problems [HUT92]
Figure 7.6

In the next example in Figure 7.7 we see that we can even do Pareto analysis on the determined causes of the defects in an organization.

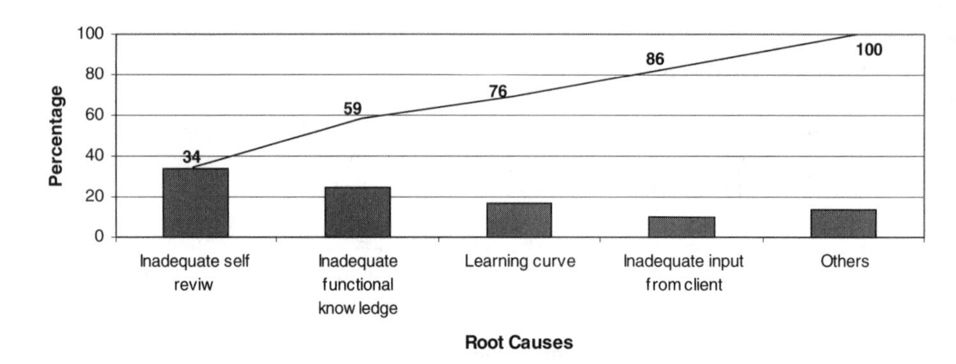

Example of Pareto Analysis of Causes
Figure 7.7

These charts are interesting as we can compare them over time to understand if we are actually seeing defect volumes decrease; i.e., prevention is paying off. For example, we would expect that the EP type in Figure 7.6 would decrease in volume if we took action to prevent this type. Over time we would also expect to see a reduction in the costs to produce a product when doing COQ analysis.

7.7 Which Errors Should Be Analyzed First

If data has been gathered on defects found in a project or an organization, we should determine which defects are the most frequently occurring, and then we should turn the focus to these first. A solution for the most frequently occurring defects could have a significant chance of affecting a larger savings. Juran calls this focusing on the vital few. [JUR88]

For example, if 30% of the code defects manifest themselves as incorrect use of defined global data areas, then possible solutions exist in:

- Programmer training to make them aware of this fact, including changes to checklists
- Training as to what can be done to avoid these types of errors
- Improving or completing documentation about these data areas
- Tooling to help the programmers to better understand the effects of using a specific field in a global data area (static analyzers and cross reference listings are examples)

Again the solutions will vary based on the environment in which these defects occur.

If data has been gathered but not analyzed, then clearly the analysis should be done first. This may appear to the reader to be an almost trivially obvious statement, but there are many projects that have taken the first step in gathering data and unfortunately they do nothing with it except rankle the programmers who are told to provide the data. The message here is: if one does not use the data, then be prepared for unhappy data providers. Eventually you are likely to find that the data integrity has eroded.

If the data has not yet been gathered, then turn to the people who know best where to start; the programmers themselves. Ask them which error types should be addressed first. If you cannot get started this way, then pick the next defect that occurs and begin with it.

The answer then is very simple. Start now and start with the best available information that you have. But most importantly, start.

7.8 Propagation of Causal Knowledge

It is clearly our objective to perform defect Causal Analysis and to put in place a solution that will address the problem cause. At the micro level this is quite satisfactory, as it will satisfy our objective. In the macro sense it is not satisfactory. We should propagate this knowledge first through our organization and later, perhaps, throughout the organization's company. If we hesitate to do so within our organization and limit our knowledge to our project alone, then we are merely chipping away at the global issue of trying to understand how people think and in turn how people make errors in their thinking and working.

If we look only at the cause of a problem for one department but fail to ask ourselves if it applies to other departments or people in our organization we are not getting the full benefit. Doesn't it make sense to propagate this newly found knowledge to the other groups for their use also? As we do so we will begin to see a compounding effect for our efforts, and in turn maximize our return on our investment of the original defect Causal Analysis. To do otherwise seems foolish, and certainly it does not make good business sense.

If we were willing to be more open in our behavior, then propagating this knowledge through the software community would lead ultimately to better tools, methodologies, processes, practices, and education. In turn this may contribute to a more productive environment in our organization. Can you imagine how much better our lives would be if we each added to the knowledge of our organization and software community in preventing defects?

Organizations practicing Defect Prevention using web-based publishing or knowledge management facilities make both Lesson Learned and Good Practices available to all personnel almost immediately. When a new item is added to these databases, news of it is posted so anyone can look at it.

7.9 Can You and Should You Analyze All Defects?

Well, the answer depends on how many defects you have. Juran and others tell us to first focus on the vital few. This is fine if we have a high numbers of defects. As we get defects under control we should have fewer and fewer defects. In these cases I would suggest analyzing all defects. I've worked with organizations that perform Causal Analysis on every defect found at Inspections; they have few defects to remove, but also have a very high effectiveness with Inspections.

If we focus Defect Prevention to include data from all defect removal activities, we will see that earlier discovery becomes more likely. Then, as we shift the defect discovery closer to the point of injection, we want to shift to fewer and fewer defects being injected. These two actions will demonstrate Defect Prevention in its best form; i.e., actual prevention.

Not all prevention solutions can be implemented. For example, if we determine that the best solution lies in developing or modifying a tool for which the technology does not yet have an answer or is too expensive as a choice, then we simply should address the problem with another solution. Perhaps education would be an alternative solution until the tool can be developed or changed.

7.10 Analysis Meeting

So how does all this relate to Software Inspections, you might ask. Remember that optional, but recommended, Analysis Meeting discussed in Chapter 3? In this meeting, if we choose to perform it after each Inspection Meeting, the Inspection team will discuss and categorize the potential causes for each defect identified in the Inspection. I suggest you seriously consider using the Analysis Meeting, except in situations where it would add to further rejection by people in the organization during early Inspection adoption; i.e., some may feel under attack as defects are discussed and the prevention actions seem to point toward the Producer or there is a strong view that the invested time will not pay off.

Gilb took up the baton for Defect Prevention in a more deliberate manner. For this specific meeting he states, “A process brainstorming meeting (optional) is held with the aim of getting at the root cause of some of the major issues logged, and to generate suggestions for improving the software development process.” [GIL93] Gilb uses the Analysis Meeting for both Causal Analysis and a bit of Defect Prevention.

I differ slightly in my practice. I fully endorse the Analysis Meeting, but not for brainstorming to the solutions related to the root cause. I suggest rather that the Analysis Meeting be used primarily to assure the defects have been properly logged and that this logging include probable cause from the team's point of view. This meeting should last less than 30 minutes and should proceed at a reasonably quick pace. Of course, this meeting can take more than 30 minutes depending on how many defects are found. If we assume a typical code Inspection of about 300 LOC, then finding more than 10 defects is a serious situation with such a highly defective unit. But even with 10 defects, each defect should not need more than 2-3 minutes for discussion and cause classification. Only major defects should be analyzed. The output from this meeting will be input to the SEPG or Inspection Coordinator for Defect Prevention analysis and suggestions. See Section 7.13 below for discussion on the Defect Prevention Meeting that includes Defect Prevention activities.

I suggest that the Analysis Meeting should not be focused on trying to determine the suggested solution to the probable cause. But if the solution is obvious, it should be captured and submitted with the data to the SEPG or Defect Prevention Coordinator. Keep the Analysis

Meeting short and remember that the ultimate true cause may not be known until the Producer corrects the defect.

If you choose to not hold the Analysis Meeting directly after the Inspection Meeting, that is your choice, but hold one for each Inspection at some point in time.

7.11 Defect Prevention

Defect Prevention and Causal Analysis are related but different. With Causal Analysis we determine what we believe is the probable cause for types of defects. Causal Analysis helps ensure we identify highly probable causes based on data. Given we have made this determination, we then proceed to take action to prevent these types of defects from occurring in the future.

I must note one caution: we must first assure ourselves that it will be less costly to implement the actions than to continue to live with the defect causes. There should be a return on investment (ROI) that is good enough for us to continue. We certainly do not want to spend $1,000,000 on prevention of defects that, if they continued to occur, would cost us only $100,000 to repair. We may address this defect type later, but it should not be among our early defects to prevent unless the defect is safety or life critical. You should have criteria for selecting which defects to address first. This is one reason we use Pareto Analysis to pick the defect types of significant frequency. Analysis of defects does not constitute a commitment to change the process or development environment for each defect type. But when we perform ROI analysis on Defect Prevention, we may find some exciting results.

When we prevent a defect, we not only prevent the next instance, we prevent all future instances. It is this multiplying effect that makes Defect Prevention a significant ROI contributor.

Results can be outstanding when both Causal Analysis and Defect Prevention are practiced well; e.g., 50% of defects were reduced within one year [JON85] [MAY92] and in another organization 70% over a 2-3 year period and 95% over 5-6 years. [DIO92] These are impressive returns and I've seen similar quick returns with other organizations.

Shirey at HP makes the point that "the larger, long term payoff is not in merely getting better at finding the types of faults that inspections do so well, but in identifying the process error that generated the fault in the first place." [SHI92] So we can extend the power of Inspections by using them with Causal Analysis and Defect Prevention actions as logical extensions to reducing the COQ.

7.12 Personal Defect Prevention

Prior to completion of a work product and before it is submitted for an Inspection, the Producer should be performing a self-check to assure that common types of defects are not propagated to the Inspection. The Producer's objective should be to propagate zero defects. The Producer should be using a checklist for guidance on what to look for and prevent as common defects.

The same checklists used for the Inspection could be used to preview or self-check the work product, even while creating the work product. An individual can also keep their own checklists based on their own known and repeatable mistakes; e.g., I often type "form" when I mean "from", and Spell Checker does not help me prevent this defect.

At another level each programmer should do analysis on each of their defects found during Inspections and ask what could have been done differently to prevent the defect. When organizations are practicing the Analysis Meeting, this analysis should be a natural fallout for the Producer.

With or without the Analysis Meeting, the more important task is that the Producer does the reflection and thinks through what could have been done differently. This reflection will require a deep and honest look into ourselves if we want to find the most probable cause. It may not be easy to admit to the cause or we may just be blind to the real cause. This soul-searching analysis is not easy to do, but it can be done. It requires a willingness to accept that a defect was made and we made it. The cause of how we made it is a different issue. Once we have determined a cause, there should be an action we will take to eliminate the cause. If we can remain objective and distance ourselves from our egos, we stand a good chance of learning the cause and removing it in future work.

Sometimes we may choose to invite input from others. This is a mature approach, but we need to be prepared for what we may hear. If you are willing to learn, and I sincerely believe we all are, then we should invite all input that can help us improve.

The actions that may need to be taken can range from being as simple as doing a self-check to as complex as an action that is not in the immediate control of the programmer; e.g., asking management to provide the training needed before the project starts. Some actions are directly controllable by the programmer, such as ensuring that one gives sufficient time to understanding the requirements or getting the answers to vague requirements before performing the self-check. Other actions may be out of your direct control, like getting access to the design being developed at another location when you have a dependency or need to provide an interface.

Previously we discussed the four major influencing factors (People, Process, Technology, Resources) that affect systems and in turn may lead to defects. These factors can be further partitioned into commonly repeating cause categories. Not all of the categories will distribute equally across all systems factors, but they do distribute.

These categories as Jones suggests [JON85], are at least:

- Education: where the Producer failed to understand something
- Communication: where there was a breakdown in communications between groups or team members
- Oversight: where something was not considered or handled
- Transcription: where the Producer knows what to do, but "for some reason simply makes a mistake"

- Process: where the process somehow misdirected your actions; this category was added by Gale, also of IBM [GAL90]

These categories are useful in that they give insight into the cause that requires action. But they are not sufficient for complete Causal Analysis. For example, if education is the determined category, was this because a programmer did not receive the education, the education received was not effective, the education was not in time, or the programmers were overworked when they were given the education and could not absorb the learning, etc. As you see, we need to go deeper than these five categories to determine the actionable cause. If we give you the same faulty education again, it may not address the real cause.

Watts Humphrey addresses personal Defect Prevention in his Personal Software Process (PSP) method where it is integral for personal learning. Humphrey does not view adding items to checklists as Defect Prevention. "Suppose that in a Defect Prevention review you find that variable initialization was a frequent problem. You could add an entry in your code review checklist, but doing this would be a detection and not a preventive action." [HUM95] Humphrey's purpose is to prevent defects from occurring at their source of creation via PSP. I support this and we'll come back to PSP in Chapter 14.

For the purpose of this book and this chapter, I argue that if one can take an action to prevent a defect from being found during an Inspection, this is a giant step toward the prevention of defects going into work products that are declared ready for Inspection.

Often the change in the process results in a change to a checklist for either the task or activity where the work product was produced or for preparing and inspecting the work product. This is an important first step to inculcating the knowledge and thought process that will in fact lead to Defect Prevention in its purest light; i.e., not making the error in the first place. So checklists have a key role in leading to Defect Prevention, but we should want to wean ourselves away from them over time and practice Defect Prevention by learning how to build a work product right the first time. I am not sure if this could ever be done completely; i.e., I do not see checklists going away. But I do believe that an expert is not fully dependent on checklists. This is a gray area, I agree. Imagine if an airplane pilot told you he no longer needed to use pre-flight checklists because he had years of experience and knew what was on the lists. He may be good, but there is room for error here that might be prevented if he uses the checklists. Would you choose to fly with this pilot?

The direction in software engineering is to put more responsibility on the programmer for building it right the first time. Believe it or not, however, there once was a time when it was believed that having the compiler find the defects was more effective and efficient! This was clearly a short-term view about costs. Go figure! Compilers will find certain types of defects, but why have programmers continue to work in a way that produces these defects? Poor practice with defects that a compiler can catch begets poor practice with other defects.

7.13 Defect Prevention Meeting

Defect Prevention Meetings can be held independent of Inspections, but certainly would use data derived from Inspections; e.g., defect analysis, Analysis Meeting results. Defect Prevention Meetings are meetings conducted well after an Inspection and use data from multiple sources, including Inspections.

The purpose of the Defect Prevention Meeting is to determine probable actions that would reduce the possibility for certain defects recurring.

Jones [JON85] built upon the ETVX structure and added a rigorous Defect Prevention kickoff meeting to the Entry sub-activity of the Inspection process. At this meeting the Inspection team:

- Reviews what is available as input
- Reviews process/methodology guidelines
- Reviews error checklists
- Sets team goals for quality

While this meeting can be held separately and should be considered by organizations starting up an Inspection program, for mature organizations the new tasks could be required of each inspector to complete with the help of the Moderator. It may not require a separate meeting as Jones suggests or it could be included in the Overview meeting or at the startup of the Inspection Meeting,

In the Validation/Verification sub-activity Jones adds a preliminary Causal Analysis Meeting. Her preliminary Causal Analysis is to ensure that data is captured to enable her final Causal Analysis Meeting that includes Defect Prevention actions.

In the Exit sub-activity she adds the final Causal Analysis Meeting where the following is performed:

- Analyze defects
- Evaluate results against team goals
- Evaluate the processes used

Questions Jones suggests be asked at these meeting are:

- "What stage originated the error?
- Category of cause or error?
  Communications
  Education
    New functions
    Old functions
    Other
  Oversight
  Transcription
- How was the error introduced? What caused the error?
- How could it have been avoided?
- What corrective actions are recommended?" [JON85]

Later, action teams are assigned to address suggestions for Defect Prevention and process improvement. At the time Jones wrote her article on Defect Prevention the SW-CMM, as we know it today, did not exist with the Process Change management (PCM) Key process Area. [CMM93] PCM is an excellent process for fielding input from Causal Analysis Meetings and other improvement generating methods. A well-define PCM process will address all the activities required of Action Teams by Jones; e.g.,

- Prioritization of all action items
- Status tracking of all action items
- Implementation of all action items
- Dissemination of feedback
- Data base administration
- Generic analysis
- Visibility of success stories

To these I would add that some actions should be piloted before deploying. While most actions from Causal Analysis may be small in nature, some require resources and if implemented incorrectly could generate other defects.

All of the process steps that Carole Jones includes in her final Causal Analysis Meeting are consistent with what I would expect to see in the Defect Prevention Meeting.

End Quote:

"Without analyzing statistics, defects, or trends, we fail to utilize the most valuable information we have at our disposal for fine-tuning the development process."
C. L. Jones 1985

CHAPTER 8

RE-INSPECTIONS

"If it's worth doing right, it's worth doing twice."
Anonymous

8.1 Introduction

It hardly seems fair to ask you to do another Inspection of the same material right after you have just performed an Inspection. You have followed all the guidelines; you are now a believer in the effectiveness of Inspections, and look at all those defects you have found without using the computer to test the defects out.

Why re-inspect you may ask. Well, we re-inspect for the same reason that we inspected; i.e., to find defects earlier and at lower cost.

What we may have learned from an Inspection is that:

1. There were more defects in the material than expected
2. There is a reasonable probability that there are more defects in the work product
3. There are indicators from the process performance that are signaling potential problems with the inspected work product

This may sound to you like an admission that Inspections are not 100% effective in discovering all latent defects in a work product. In the vast majority of Inspections this is true. There are instances where Inspections have proven to be 100% effective and I will discuss this in Chapters 9 and 14.

There are a number of documented cases of Inspections above 80% effectiveness. See for example Fagan [FAG86], Kolkhorst [KOL88], Tackett [TAC99], McCann [MCC01]. Regardless of the effectiveness of any particular Inspection, removal of defects earlier will always be more economical than when testing or when users find them. Refer again to Figure 1.3 where the cost to find and correct defects is shown as increasing with each activity after Inspections. See Figure 8.1 for a relative cost curve based on varying effectiveness of Inspections compared with removing defects in test and by users.

This simple curve shows that when no Inspections are performed, there is an explicit Inspection cost of 0%; i.e., all defects are found without Inspections. All costs to remove defects will all be in test and with users. The cost in these other defect removal activities by definition is 100% of defect removal costs. This then becomes the baseline we compare against as Inspection effectiveness increases. The actual costs will vary by organization.

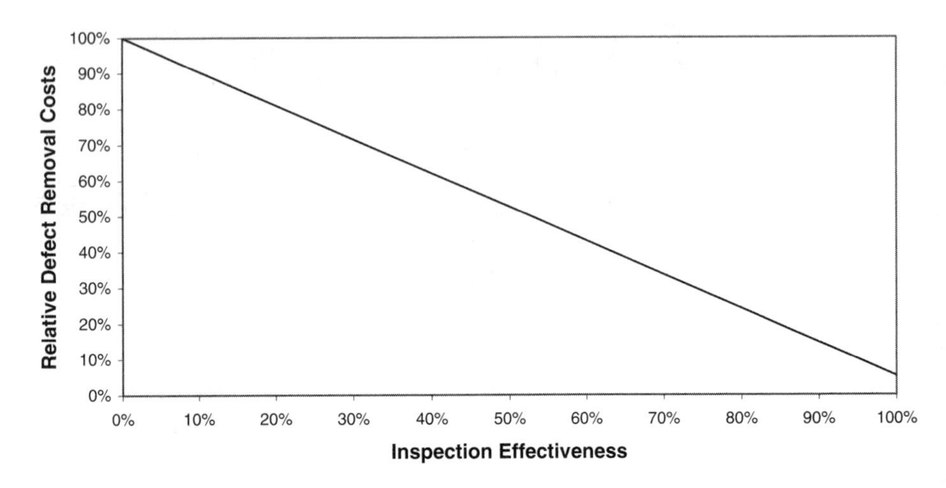

Relative Defect Removal Costs
Figure 8.1

When Inspections are 50% effective, the total relative cost to remove defects becomes 53%. This means that total defect removal costs have decreased by 47% in the project and there is a corresponding savings. When Inspections are 80% effective the relative costs become 24%. This translates to a 76% savings when Inspections are 80% effective. For an understanding of how this curve was derived refer to the calculations made in chapter 9 for Section 9 Calculating Cost Savings where it is shown how total costs for defect removal decrease as Inspection effectiveness increases.

As Inspections are practiced and the effectiveness of Inspections increases, the total relative costs to remove defects decreases.

When we see this cost relationship and know that there are more defects to be found after an Inspection, we should appreciate that a similar cost savings relationship may apply if we did another Inspection or a Re-Inspection in this case. We will need criteria to help guide us to make good decisions on when to re-inspect. We do not want to re-inspect for the sake of re-inspecting. We re-inspect to find more defects at a lower cost than in test or with users. Re-Inspections will increase the yield from Inspections, but we should ensure ourselves that there would be a ROI.

Fagan originally suggested, "If more than five percent of the material has been reworked, the team should reconvene and carry out a 100 percent Re-Inspection. Where less than five percent of the material has been reworked, the moderator at his discretion may verify the quality of the rework himself or reconvene the team to re-inspect either the complete work or just the rework." [FAG76]

As noted, there are situations where the Inspection team should recommend a Re-Inspection for a work product that was just inspected. The recommendation should not be arbitrary. It should be guided by a set of criteria that is repeatable and can be evolved based on data and experiences from previous Re-Inspections. These Re-Inspection criteria are part of the exit criteria for all Inspection Meetings.

If any of the Re-Inspection exit criteria are not satisfied, a signal is being sent by the Inspection as just performed. For example, if the Re-Inspection criteria signals that a code module should be re-inspected and it is not, then there is an increased risk that test will not proceed efficiently. Test processes will have a lower probability of completing on time, completing coverage, and therefore they will likely leak defects into the next life cycle phases, including leaking defects to the users.

An informal survey of Inspection practitioners suggests that very few organizations significantly use Re-Inspections. When they do, it is more of a randomly practiced event. One would hope that the decisions are based on data that show:

1. They do not need to re-inspect
2. Their Inspection effectiveness is consistently over 80%
3. Their test activities proceed orderly to completion as defined in the test plans, are under control, or show cost reductions

The use of Re-Inspection criteria based on data will move an organization further along the path of a disciplined, effective, and efficient Inspection process. Let us now look at some Re-Inspection criteria used in software projects.

Re-Inspections can occur at any time based on signal input; e.g., immediately after an Inspection Meeting or even after a work product has been delivered to the users.

8.2 Criteria To Trigger a Re-Inspection

There are various criteria that have been used to signal a consideration for Re-Inspection. I suggest that these signals are to be given careful consideration rather than rigidly followed. We do not yet have criteria that are absolute. The signals must be listened to and then a decision taken based on the signals and other data for any Inspection.

For example, we might have criteria to re-inspect any code work product where the defect volume is greater than X defects per unit of size; e.g., LOC or Function Points, or where the number of defects discovered per page exceeds X. If we then have an instance where X has been exceeded, should we then automatically re-inspect? Well, it depends on other factors; e.g., who were the participants, the relationship to the time taken for the Inspection, the number of participants.

We should listen to the signal and ask the participants if a case can be made against a Re-Inspection. If a case can be made and the participants judge that the risk is low, then a Re-Inspection might not be proposed. The decision taken should be reviewed during test to ensure that it was an effective decision. Here effective means that when a Re-Inspection is proposed and executed that a return on investment is found to be positive. If so, then the Re-Inspection criteria can be modified to include this knowledge. If the decision was wrong, then the organization should also consider updating their criteria to integrate the learning for future Re-Inspection decisions. Thus we are performing dynamic Causal Analysis and Defect Prevention on our Re-Inspection criteria. In both cases the signals (criteria) can be refined to be more helpful and correct in the future.

When organizations practice Re-Inspections it seems to be done for less than 1% of all Inspections. It is a rare exception when as much as 5% have been re-inspected. Perhaps these percentages are as they should be, but the real test is how defective were the work products in test and with users. In Bull, we had an experience where Re-Inspections were at 25% and the total effectiveness of the Inspections was 95%, but this high Re-Inspection rate is rare. My view is that some Re-Inspections are always warranted, and that the percentage of Re-Inspections is directly related to the effectiveness in the organizations with Inspections.

In a heuristic process, the participants will learn to make more useful decisions for Re-Inspections in the future. While we will want to perform Re-Inspections when warranted, we want them only when we have confidence that they will help remove more defects at a lower cost than test will. A false Re-Inspection could add a higher cost at a less than expected return on investment. Just because we choose to re-inspect does not mean we will find sufficiently more defects. We believe we will, but only the Re-Inspection will prove it.

**Fisherman return to waters
where they have successfully landed fish.**

Now let's look at some criteria that have been used in the last twenty-eight years:

- Defect density
- Large work products
- Inspection rate
- Preparation rate
- Change volume from defects found
- Complexity
- Error removal history
- Small changes with a history of high defectiveness
- Change history
- Logistics
- Quality of the Inspection
- Moderator decision
- Group consensus

8.3 Defect Density

The early applications of defect density as a Re-Inspection criterion worked from the assumption that a bad module of code remains a "bad module", or that error prone modules always are error prone. This suggests that when there is a high defect rate in Inspections there will probably be a high volume of defects found in test and with users. While there is some evidence suggesting this to be true, it would be better that we learned why these bad modules became bad in the first place. And this is just what the learning process is all about. We cannot get to that understanding overnight. We must learn our way toward it. So let's start by gathering good data (see Chapter 6: Inspection Data) and now study some indicators that result from the data analysis.

Given that a work product has defects discovered during an Inspection, one question we need to consider is "What is the density of the defects found?" For example, if we found 10 defects in a code unit, is this what we would expect? First we need to understand the size of the unit. In case A, if the unit were 100 LOC, then we have 1 defect in every 10 lines of code or 100 defects/KLOC. In case B, if the unit were 1,000 LOC, we have only 1 defect in every 100 LOC or 10 defects/KLOC. This latter is a much different situation and clearly a better one. This type of clip-level or threshold to pick off units that should be re-inspected is better than not having any criteria, but there are other ways to use defect density criteria.

If we knew the average defect density for code in our organization we could make an immediate comparison. If an Inspection instance were greater than the average, this could be a signal for us to consider a Re-Inspection. For example, if the average for code in our organization is 15 defects/KLOC and we found 100 as in case A, the signal has gone off. The difference in these defect density rates strongly suggests that we consider a Re-Inspection. However, if the instance had been 16 defects/KLOC we would still be above the average, but just barely. We would need to apply other information. We would probably not re-inspect in most cases when the difference is uninteresting.

So an average is only one indicator to help guide our decisions. If we knew the range of defect densities in our organization that accounted for 99.73% or a 3 standard deviations spread of all code inspected, then we could use the boundaries that contain the 99.73% as criteria. Then when an Inspection instance fell outside of these boundaries we could consider a Re-Inspection.

See Figure 8.2 for an example in an organization where the data points show 18 defects/KLOC for the lowest and 84 defects/KLOC for the highest Inspection and calculated UCL-LCL of 86.2-6.4 defects/KLOC. I briefly discussed in Chapter 6 why and how these boundaries or upper and lower control limits are calculated and how we use them. From a Re-Inspection perspective, we could choose to re-inspect for each instance outside these limits. This is an example of real-time use of Inspection data; i.e., at the end of the meeting a comparison could be made for the work product just inspected using the control charts for the respective work product. Then if the defect density calculation is outside the control limits, a signal has been given for us to consider a Re-Inspection.

In Figure 8.2 we are only viewing the data points with respect to the data and resultant control limits. Let's assume that the organization decided that the defect rate was much higher than desired; e.g., the average is 44.8 and the LCL is not zero. The organization might then apply specification limits, in which case we would need also to compare to these limits to decide on a Re-Inspection. Let's assume the organization chose 65 defects/KLOC as the upper specification limit (USL) and 4 as the lower specification limit (LSL). In Figure 8.3 there are 5 instances above the USL. Clearly the 5 are of interest, since when defect density is high there are probably more defects waiting to be found. There are no points below the LSL, but what if there were? Would this signal a Re-Inspection possibility?

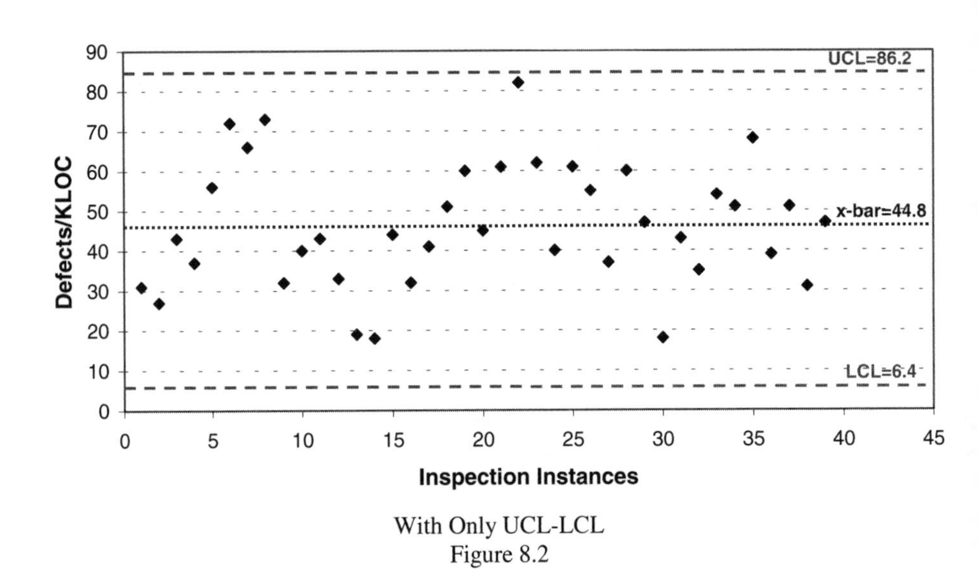

With Only UCL-LCL
Figure 8.2

When any point is outside of the UCL-LCL or USL-LSL boundaries it would be signaling that something is potentially different and we should try to understand what is different. It could be that all is well or it could suggest a problem. For example if the data points were outside of the LSL, it is possible that the defect rate was so low because the team was not experienced and did not find all the defects. This could be a candidate for Re-Inspection.

It is also possible that the defect rate is low for other reasons; e.g., a high quality work product. We should try to identify what those reasons are so that we can learn from them. Perhaps there is something in the process or the environment that is leading to this low rate. If so, wouldn't we want to try to ensure the same process or environment in future work? Isn't this process improvement? I discussed in Chapter 6 how to calculate the UCL-LCL, but you could set thresholds without limits that are defined by the data. The main difference is that a threshold is usually based on a gut feeling or less rigorous data and may have more error with the conclusions it leads to, but it is a reasonable place to start. In the SW-CMM, use of thresholds appears at Level 3, control limits at Level 4.

In Figure 8.2 the LCL is 6.4 defects/KLOC. This should not be acceptable to the organization, since it suggests that all units will have defects. I suggest that the LCL should always be zero when we are working with defect density. As an organization begins to use control charts the

LCL often is not zero for defect densities, even when the process is stable, as in Figure 8.2. I suggest that this is a signal that quality is not yet under control.

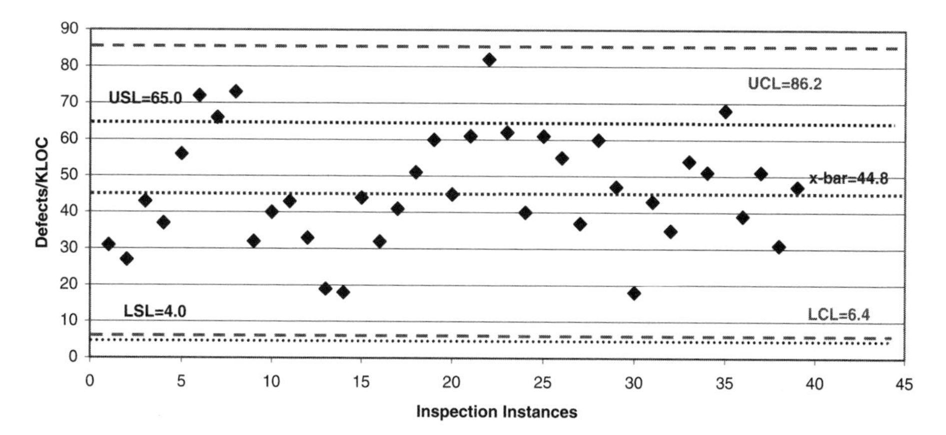

With USL-LSL
Figure 8.3

Defect density is a better metric than just the number of defects for obvious reasons, but some organizations do use the number of defects as an indicator; e.g., "we suggest that if more than 90 faults are detected in a single inspection ….. the reworked code must be re-inspected." [BAR94] If we assume that these faults are 90 major defects and that the average Inspection is about 250 LOC, then the defect density in this environment would be 360/KLOC. Even if only 1 in 4 of the faults were major this would be 90 defects/KLOC. You can see that defect density is a much more telling metric than just the number of defects found.

So far we've addressed using the data limits (UCL-LCL) and the quality limits (USL-LSL) as indicators to look for process signals to re-inspect. Recall that UCL-LCL are calculated at 3 standard deviations from the average and USL-LSL are either specified by the client or decided by the organization.

Major defects are the focus when we do defect density analysis. But what about all those minor defects? There are two other analyses we might consider when for example:

- The major/minor ratio is different than the organization's average and limits. Let's assume we may be typically finding that the major/minor ratio averages 2.2 and has normal boundaries of 1.6 to 2.8 defects/KLOC across the organization. If we now have an instance that is different than the organization's patterns, we should ask why this could be true. For example, are minor defects really major or are too many major defects really false-positives that later prove to not be defects at all?

- The defect density or volume found during Preparation is different than the organization's average and limits. Let's assume we typically find between 50% and

75% of the defects during Preparation across the organization. If we have an instance where 25% or one where 95% of the defects were discovered during Preparation, we should investigate to learn why. Perhaps there is a signal that suggests a Re-Inspection is warranted. Or perhaps, there is good news and we should try to learn from it.

An approach that some have used to estimate the number of defects in a work product is capture-recapture wherein the defects captured by each inspector during Preparation are analyzed to learn which were commonly found and which were uniquely found by each inspector. Then based on a derived equation the actual maximum number of defects in the work product is calculated. Based on the derived number a decision can be made to re-inspect or not. [EIC92] The approach is compelling in that it uses more discrete information about the work product rather than history for similar type work products to help signal a Re-Inspection. The calculation can provide an alternative view for remaining defects and hence signal the need for Re-Inspection. I have not personally used this approach, but it would be interesting to learn how accurate the predicted residual defect volumes are. Defect density, however it may be calculated, is a key Re-Inspection criterion as it can signal that more defects remain than may be desired.

8.4 Large Work Products

Do larger work products units have more defects? Well, of course, you say. Larger code units have more code; therefore they will have more defects! The same is true for documents.

This is where normalization becomes important. Normalization is a way to view different size work products from a common perspective. While it may not be perfect, the normalization of defects with a size factor gives us some insights. See Figure 8.4, where the data within one project drawn from a set of code units with varying sizes shows something interesting; i.e., after normalization there is a larger density of defects in units greater than 200 lines of source code. Why might this be true?

I am not sure we fully understand why, but it seems that complexity may have something to do with this pattern. It has been demonstrated a number of times that as the complexity increases in a code unit so too does the defectiveness. In Figure 8.4, we note that above 200 LOC the defect density is almost doubled that of units below 200 LOC.

This pattern is not always doubled nor does it always show at the 200 LOC level, but the relationship of a set of modules within a specific size range having a lower defect density than units in a larger size set does repeat many times across software projects. In this example the average defect density for the first 12 modules is 15.6 compared to 29.3 for the next 13 modules, all of which are over 200 LOC. Important to note is that the defect density in this figure is calculated after test is complete. As it turned out, the volume of user found defects was less than 1% and did not change these numbers with any significance.

Module Id	Size	Defects	Density	Cum Size	Cum Defects	Cum density
1	55	1	18.2	55	1	18.2
2	67	2	29.9	122	3	24.6
3	89	2	22.5	211	5	23.7
4	101	1	9.9	312	6	19.2
5	114	2	17.5	426	8	18.8
6	129	1	7.8	555	9	16.2
7	142	3	21.1	697	12	17.2
8	155	2	12.9	852	14	16.4
9	173	3	17.3	1025	17	16.6
10	188	2	10.6	1213	19	15.7
11	197	3	15.2	1410	22	15.6
12	209	8	38.3	209	8	38.3
13	231	5	21.6	440	13	29.5
14	266	13	48.9	706	26	36.8
15	308	7	22.7	1014	33	32.5
16	371	12	32.3	1385	45	32.5
17	414	17	41.1	1799	62	34.5
18	448	14	31.3	2247	76	33.8
19	503	9	17.9	2750	85	30.9
20	598	19	31.8	3348	104	31.1
21	603	18	29.9	3951	122	30.9
22	677	9	13.3	4628	131	28.3
23	717	22	30.7	5345	153	28.6
24	751	16	21.3	6096	169	27.7
25	802	33	41.1	6898	202	29.3

Defect Density Varying With Size
Figure 8.4

Kitchenham came to a conclusion that there is not a discernable pattern of higher defect volume above a given size due to size alone, but that other factors such as the amount of testing those large modules may receive affects defectiveness. "The results indicate that the large programs which received least testing were those that revealed most faults after release." [KIT83] Important to understand is that she is not summing the defects to determine true defect density throughout development and test, but only defect density as the users see it. She suggests that the defects would have been found with proper testing, thus the defects were there and could have been found by Inspection, test, or the users. The defect density we can assume may actually have been due to size differences.

Different studies may show different results with Inspections or test; therefore, we need to look for:

- Dominant patterns of behavior across studies; e.g., size correlating to higher defect densities is one from my experiences in commercial studies; lower discovery rate when Inspections proceed too quickly is another pattern
- Environmental differences that may account for the results; e.g., Where were the actual defects found? What is included in the counting for any variable? How effective was testing?

Size is a factor affecting how well people review and inspect materials; i.e., if a work product is large, people spend less normalized time per unit and consequently find fewer defects. This is human nature and an organization must either work knowing it to be true and get less than the best results or try to give more time to review, Inspection, or test when a work product is big. Alternately, the large work product can be chunked or partitioned into smaller units that can be properly inspected.

How might we use this characteristic for Re-Inspections? First you should try to learn how the pattern manifests itself in your organization. Given that you see the pattern, then you should analyze how the larger sets of modules behave in test. Are more (normalized) defects found in this set than with the set below some size value? If so, you now know that the pattern exists and could repeat in the next project. It may now prove beneficial to re-inspect units above the trigger size value.

If this pattern is not found in your environment, then size may not yet be an indicator of consideration for you. The objective is to analyze our data and draw conclusions and come up with criteria that apply. Studies that are published may be useful, but they need to be confirmed, as environmental differences across organizations are still not well understood or sufficiently stated in some published studies. Not all software or software organizations are the same and university case studies are not the same as a live production environment.

Does this mean you should re-inspect all modules above the trigger size value where the criterion suggests that the pattern may repeat? Again we should allow the Inspection participants to discuss the need for a Re-Inspection. Regardless of the team's decision, you should track the results in test and with users to see how well the decisions were made. Then tune and learn to improve the Re-Inspection decision criteria.

As the world of software seems to be inconsistent in published findings, there should be no surprise that there is yet another relationship about size; i.e., that at least one study found that smaller modules were more defective. Both Basili [BAS84] and Shen [SHE85] found just that. Shen said, "The observable trend, that there is a higher mean error rate in smaller modules, is consistent with that discovered by Basili and Perricone. They attributed the trend to the distribution of interface errors, the extra care taken in coding larger modules, and the possibility of undetected errors in larger modules."

I vote for the latter, as this is what I have repeatedly seen. If the possibility is undetected errors, then there is an admission that they may still be there, so we would need to see the data from the users, which was not provided in these studies. But it is possible that all three relationships can exist and that the organization's environment defines the pattern and relationship.

How then are you to know which relationship is true in your environment? Keep the data and follow what it tells you. Your history will more likely repeat itself in your environment. If this is more data analysis than you want, then ignore size of modules and related complexity and use another indicator to decide on Re-Inspection.

In Figure 8.5 we see a correlation where as a work product's size increases the average number of defects removed decreases. Is this because the large units have fewer defects or because people get tired and don't do as good a job? What's your guess? You know mine. I would also suggest that a similar relationship exists during test with modules of varying size.

This seems to be a repeating pattern where the defect density found at an Inspection decreases as the size of the work product increases. This does not necessarily mean that larger work products have a lower defect density. What we may be seeing is that an Inspection team's ability to stay with a large work product for the consistent intensity of defect discovery is difficult to sustain. The team members may have taken shortcuts, but I also believe that they may feel that they've done the job since they've found a number of defects. It is hard to sustain interest on large work products. This is why chunking becomes so important for effective and successful Inspections.

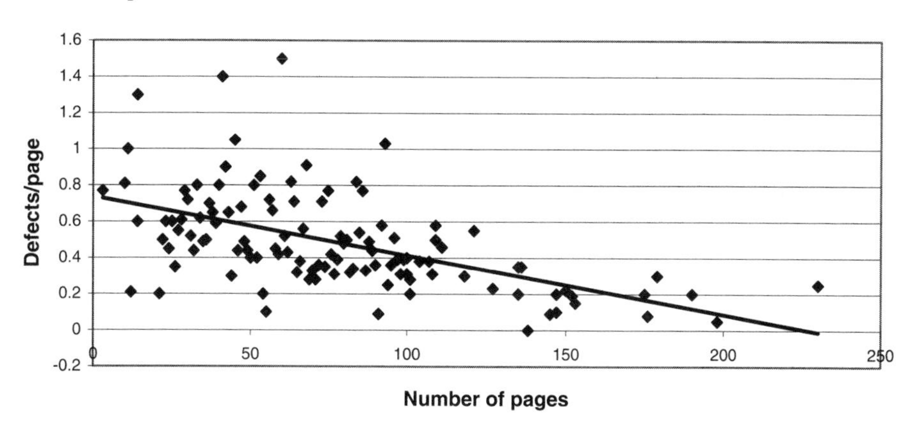

Example of Defect Discovery Compared to Number of Pages Inspected
Figure 8.5

If this phenomenon recurs in an organization, management may want to understand why and, in some cases, require Re-Inspections. Others may choose to proceed into test, but the feed forward signal should be sent to the testers. Buck first noted this pattern as seen in Figure 8.5. Others have also documented the same pattern; e.g. Grahame Terry at Racal. [GIL93] See also Kelly [KEL92] and Barnard [BAR94] among others. There is no systemic reason why the injection rate would be substantially lower for larger work products, unless the work products are of different types. The correlation of defect density seems to repeat for code size and document size, as shown in Figure 8.5.

Le at IBM Raleigh found a number of patterns regarding size:

1. "Small modifications, particularly modifications less than 4%, are highly error prone in the field environment
2. Modules that have high defect rates during testing will also have high defect rates in the customer environment
3. Large new modules cause higher TVUA (total valid customer defects) rates than small modules." [LE85]

Small modifications here were classed as those with less than 5% of the code modified; e.g., less than 10 LOC in a 200 LOC module. The defect rate was over 8 times higher in this set than for modifications over 5%. Large modules were classed as those greater than 250 LOC. In another study the same authors found that for another product the clip level was better defined at 400 LOC.

While some would argue that making more modules would only increase other problems; e.g., overhead of maintaining more units, interface issues, I posit that these added "problems" are less of a concern than the defects that we would have otherwise. Since the advent of OO technology, we see units are of even much smaller size, with no apparent ill effects in increased defects.

So what can you do knowing this? Set goals to try to keep modules in a manageable size range. Don't make modules small for the sake of being small, but try to instill the practice of chunking functional units into an appropriate size, rather than putting as much function as possible in one unit. If you do prefer larger units, then design for self-contained sub-units within the larger unit. This will aid readability also. But whatever you decide, listen to the signals and patterns from your data correlating size and defect volume.

8.5 Inspection Rate

There was some early work in this area by Frank Buck at IBM where he showed that there is an optimal Inspection rate; i.e., the number of LOC that can be sufficiently inspected for each clock hour. [BUC81a] See Figure 8.6. In this case a rate above 125 shows a rapid decline in defects found. Here NCSS means non-commentary source statements, another version of LOC as a measure.

Buck, using a code module with a fixed set of defects in it, discovered this relationship. All inspectors were trained and asked to perform an Inspection exercise using this code module. What was learned was that some Inspection teams went too fast, some too slow, and some about right. Just as with the Three Bears, the results speak for themselves. This pattern has been repeated since Buck's study.

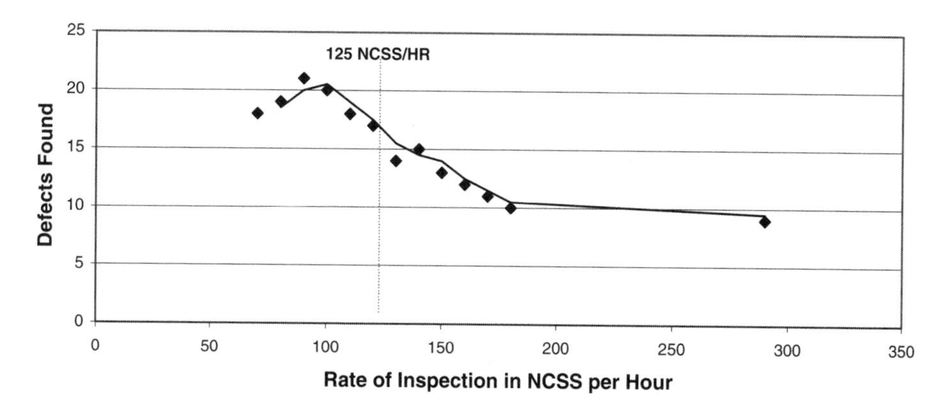

Defect Removal Compared to Inspection Rate [BUC81a]
Figure 8.6

In Figure 8.7 we see another relationship that has repeated itself many times in many organizations.

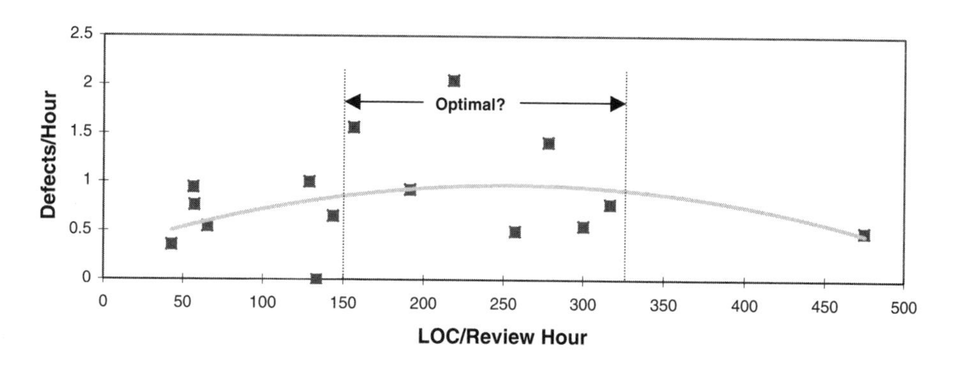

Polynomial Regression Analysis for Defect Removal
Figure 8.7

This example is from a client, but had its origins in IBM during the 1980's in some later releases of VTAM. Even with a few data points we can see the relationship after calculating a polynomial regression curve. Now if we apply the idea of thresholds that could lead to improved performance we might chose 150-325 LOC/hour in this environment. Of course, the test if whether this range is really optimal depends on how effective the Inspections are with defect removal using this boundary.

See Figure 9.23 where McCann found a similar relationship when Preparation rates differ from a derived optimal of 91.26 SLOC/Labor Hour. [MCC01]

I suggest that the reader plot data for Inspection rates in their organization. The pattern is not always as clear as shown here. In this case, a polynomial regression analysis shows the interesting correlation that when an Inspection proceeds too fast or too slow, the defect detection rate is less than optimal. This is the same pattern Buck and Weller found. [BUC81a] [WEL93]

See Figures 8.8A and B for similar patterns that have been discovered in a number of Inspection studies. In these figures the values for defect density are different on the two projects in the same organization, but the pattern is the same. This pattern is now so repeatable that it is almost one of the laws of nature about Inspections; i.e., the faster an Inspection, the fewer defects removed.

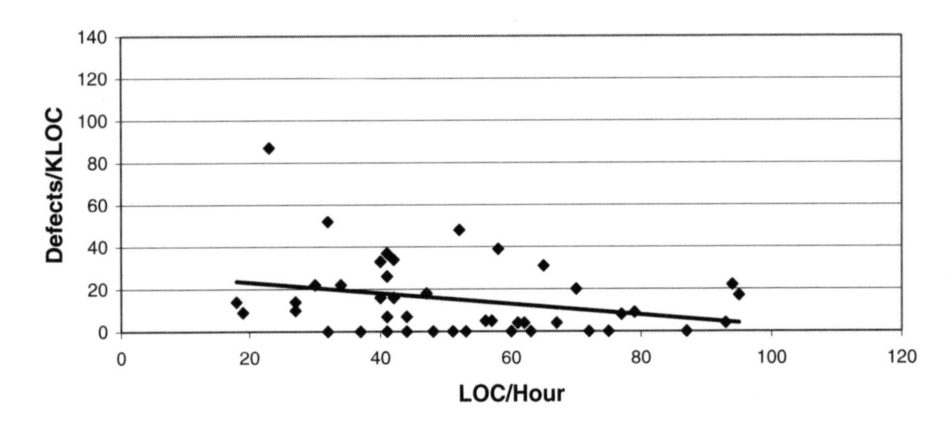

Different Removal Rates With Pattern of Removal
Figure 8.8A

Notice that while the scales are the same that the correlations are somewhat different. Organization B has higher defect discovery rates. This can be due to a poorer quality set of work products, a higher quality Inspection process, or some combination of these two. The important pattern repeats in both; i.e., as one goes faster, fewer defects are found.

Defect removal rates will vary by organization and project, but are correlated to the effort applied, as noted. There are many models that have been derived for predicting defect removal or density to be expected when a process is reasonably repeatable, but all seem to follow the same pattern. See Buck [BUC81a], Graden [GRA85], Christenson [CHR88], and Radice [RAD90], among others. All of these models are useful when applied in their specific environments.

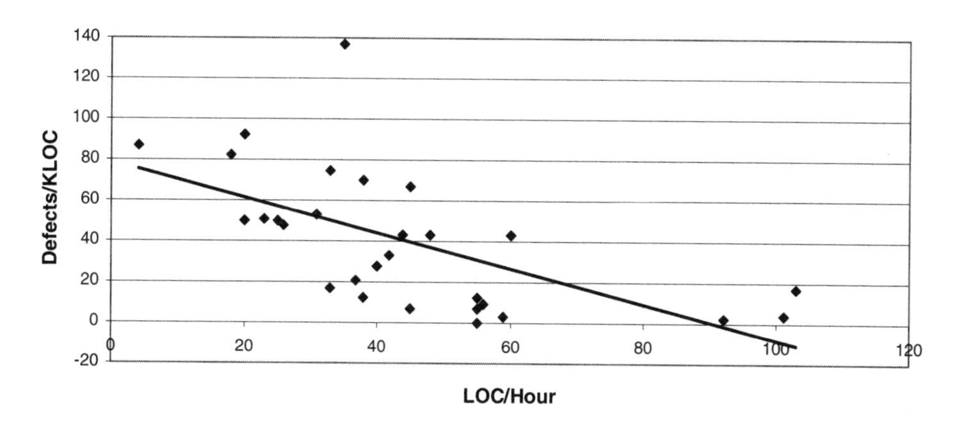

Different Removal Rates With Same Pattern of Removal
Figure 8.8B

Russell showed a similar relationship at BNR as shown in Figure 8.9. Interestingly here the same pattern shows for minor defects also.

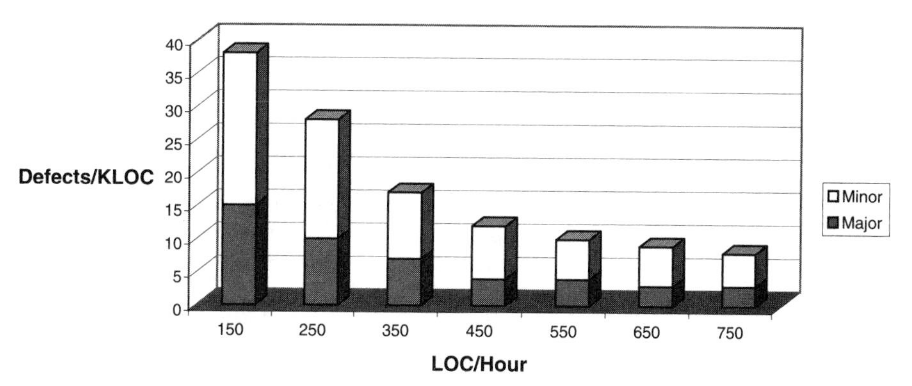

Defect Removal Rates Compared With Size of the Work Product [RUS91]
Figure 8.9

8.6 Preparation Rate

Preparation rate is a factor in the effectiveness of Inspections. For example, Buck noted "The more preparation time expended by the team, the more likely that the Inspection will be held at the planning rate coverage." [BUC81a] Buck goes on to explain that when the planning rate is satisfied, a higher error rate is correspondingly found to be true. My experience also suggests that this is true. Given that Preparation rate does correlate, we could then use this as a factor to decide for a Re-Inspection. By itself, this factor may not be compelling enough, but in concert with some other signals, it could help to make the decision for Re-Inspection.

Buck's study showed that there were normal distributions for two populations; those that exceeded the recommended preparation rate (E/R) and those that fell within the recommended planning rate (P/R). While there was an overlap in the two populations, which is what we might expect since the rates are continuous, he found that "The most efficient Inspections (20 majors found or at least 74% of the maximum number found) were all conducted at the Planning rate coverage." [BUC81a] Buck first discovered this relationship when using a control module with a known defect density during training sessions. Later he found that the relationship repeated during production.

The planning rate was 125 LOC/hour, which is a rate we used during the VTAM study, prior to the Buck study, and one that reasonably persists today.

From another perspective, we can easily conclude that when no Preparation is made, the Inspection Meeting (if held) will take more time. This is because participants are not prepared, so they need time to orient themselves. Additionally, in these cases, the minor defects tend to get discussed and consume time that could be better spent toward major defects discovery.

So as the clock ticks and the Inspection Meeting proceeds, the Inspection Meeting will come to an eventual closure based on some nominal agreement that the "right" amount of time was used and the material was "fully read." Typically, we see that these meetings find fewer defects. This pattern recurs far too often to say these are unrelated events.

There is probably some ideal amount of time to spend in Preparation to enable the best use of the Inspection Meeting time. In Chapter 3 the planning rates shown are the same for Preparation and for the Inspection Meeting. Your numbers may not be exactly the same for both as you progress with Inspections, but they should be close rather than widely different.

The amount of Preparation time will affect the amount of Inspection Meeting time and in turn its success in discovering the highest volume of defects. Therefore, we should use the Preparation rate data to help understand if the Inspection was effective.

Preparation rate may be helpful to decide for a Re-Inspection, and it will always be a primary factor in a successful Inspection. It has been noted earlier in the book that Preparation could find at least 50% of the defects that will be found. There is evidence that this can be as high as 96%; e.g., where teams at AT&T were found to be more than highly effective during Preparation. [VOT93] Votta concluded, "Is the benefit of ~ 4% increase in faults found at the collection meeting (for whatever reason) worth the cost .... and the reviewers' extra time. The answer is no."

My experience even during the initial VTAM study shows that as much as 75% of the defects can be discovered during Preparation. We will revisit this in Chapter 9 when we discuss how an organization might tune its Inspection process and perhaps eliminate the need for an Inspection Meeting, when Preparation is done effectively.

Preparation rate can also be too slow. Effectiveness will decrease with each increment of time, so we need to find the balance that best works for an organization. Until that balance is learned for your organization, I suggest you begin with the standard rates quoted in Chapter 3 as specification limits.

As an illustration of how the Preparation time and success of an Inspection Meeting are related let us look at the following example:

> Four programmers spend 2 hours each preparing and they mutually discover 8 defects. These same programmers participate in the Inspection Meeting, which runs a total of 2 hours, and they find another 4 defects. For this Inspection they have found 12 total defects at a cost of 16 programmer hours or .75 defects per programmer-hour.
>
> Let us now assume that these same programmers did no Preparation. Again they are scheduled for a 2-hour Inspection Meeting. What do you think are the chances that they will find 12 defects; i.e., triple the rate in the previous situation? More than likely they will find less than the 8 found during the previous Preparation example. Why? We do not know exactly, but it sure has something to do with not being prepared. It is also possible that independent work to find defects; i.e., Preparation, is more effective and more efficient.

8.7 Change Volume from Defects Found

In the original study, Fagan suggested that we use 5% as a guiding factor to call a Re-Inspection; i.e., when the defects found would cause change in volume of 5% or more of the material inspected, that a Re-Inspection would be called. We never substantively proved that 5% was better or worse than some other percentage, but we all accepted that when a sufficient volume of change was necessary, a Re-Inspection should be recommended. Since that time no one has come up with a better percentage criterion, so I would suggest starting with it. The decision for Re-Inspection may need to wait until the Rework is completed, but it could be anticipated at the end of the Inspection Meeting.

Again, by itself this indicator may not be compelling, but together with some other indicators it could help us make the decision. And again, as in all cases with data, we need to track to learn how effective our decisions were, good or bad.

Percentage of change is one way to look at the impact of discovered defects. Another is rather straightforward: if even one defect will cause a substantive rewrite of the material inspected, then the material should be re-inspected after the rewrite. This decision can sometimes be obvious to all and in other cases will require time for discussion and getting team consensus. Here is where good moderation helps to achieve the most likely right decision.

8.8 Complexity

Complexity measures exist in many forms, but the simplest is to look at the work product. A work product that is complex tends to shout that message. In many cases these work products should be candidates for re-engineering, but that always seems to be a difficult decision for management to make.

Next easiest to use for code is the McCabe Cyclomatic Number [MCC76], and some organizations ask for this value on the Inspection form. When supplied, it is another data value that can be correlated during data analysis.

Harder to calculate and now out of favor are Halstead metrics. These seemed to have only proved the point that what was apparently complex was complex. This is then the tautology of complexity. Various analyses had been performed in the 1980's trying to find the grail of complexity predictions. While they all seem to have proved that "that which is complex is complex" these studies did open thinking that with complexity knowledge one could make decisions to improve quality. For example, "Based on our analysis of three program products and their error histories, we have discovered that simple metrics related to the amount of data (η_2) and the structural complexity (DE) of programs may be useful in identifying *at an early stage* those modules most likely to contain errors." [SHE85]

This suggests that at a code Inspection one could calculate complexity and then use this value with other information found at the Inspection to decide for a Re-Inspection.

8.9 Error Removal History

In a nutshell, this criterion is based on the knowledge that when a code unit has been error prone in the past, it will stand a high chance of being error prone in the future when it is modified and then inspected. If the data or team knowledge shows this to be true for a particular unit under Inspection, then based on this and other indicators from the Inspection, we should consider a Re-Inspection. Use of this criterion assumes that the unit has not already been substantially rewritten or re-engineered since its last Inspection and release.

The working premise here is that if you found a high volume before, and unless something has changed, there will be good chance of finding more defects now. This phenomenon seems to persist in the best of software organizations, since rewriting, while an obvious choice, rarely seems to get done until there is no other choice. This is a management decision usually, and I sometimes think they really do believe that next time will be better despite the recurring pattern.

When a rewrite has not been done and the indicators are that this unit has a recurring history of defectiveness, the next best play is to allocate more time for Preparation and the Inspection Meeting. Here we can at least try to give more time to the removal of defects in the Inspection and perhaps not need to call for a Re-Inspection.

In the AS/400 software system, Kan found, by applying a problem index to each component and applying a frequency analysis, that a subset would clearly stand out as the most problematic and that actions should be applied to these to reduce their error proneness. His problem index is calculated after reviewing all post release defects in the new and changed code for the new release. [KAN95]

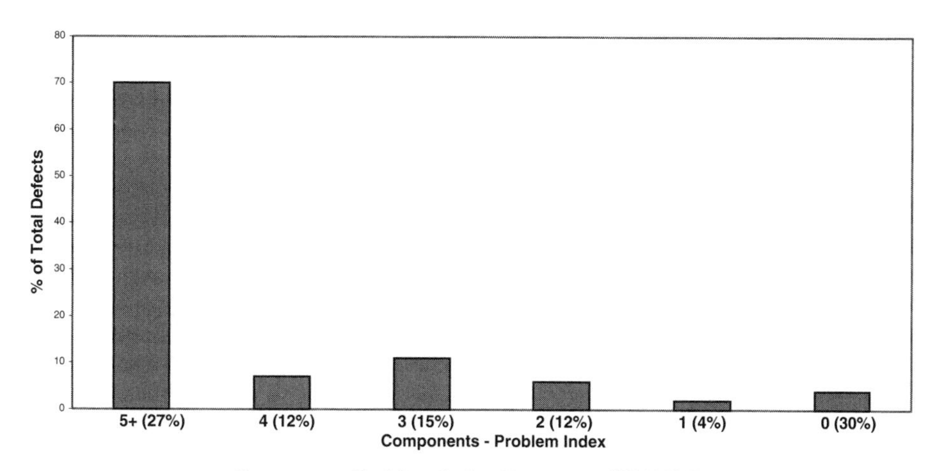

Component Problem Index Frequency [KAN95]
Figure 8.10

After the components are scored with index ranges from 0 to 9, a type of Pareto analysis is performed with rank ordering by index values rather than by frequency. The result might look something like Figure 8.10. With this knowledge, various actions could be proposed; e.g., "component restructure, module breakup, complexity measurement and test coverage, intermodule cleanup, and so forth." Let me suggest that the "so forth" for our purposes could include Re-Inspection, especially if no other actions were taken for the component.

Needless to say, this criterion has no significance on the first release of a product.

8.10 Change History

If a work product has a history of active changes, then the changed units might be considered for Re-Inspection when other indicators are in evidence. Changes include both requests for change by the customer or from internal sources and changes due to defect repairs. This is similar to error removal history, but now includes changes in addition to repair.

We would be most interested in the current release change history, but we could include change from prior releases when it is significant. This type of indicator is not quite the same as a "bad module stays a bad module", but an indicator where the work product volatility is telling us something about that unit. Perhaps it is poorly structured or is too big, or it was not understood, and these all lead to its being more difficult, hence more defect prone.

Change history will come from two sources: requirements changes and fixes to prior releases. For example, we could decide if three or more fixes were made to a work product within the last 12 months that it would be a candidate for consideration, especially when other Re-Inspection indicators were in evidence.

8.11 Logistics

Most of the time the logistics will not be a consideration for a Re-Inspection. However, when a room is less than useable or when telephone conferences are used, I suggest the team be canvassed to understand if, in their view, the logistics inhibited effectiveness or efficiency. Regardless of their response, if the effectiveness or efficiency is out of limits, the question should be asked again whether the logistics was a probable cause. If so, then a process change may be in order regarding logistics, but a Re-Inspection may also be in order.

8.12 Quality of the Inspection

This criterion is more qualitative, but just as important. At the end of the Inspection, the Moderator should be able to score the following questions with input from the team:

1. Were entry and exit criteria sufficiently satisfied?
2. Were there any problems found during the Inspection that caused the Inspection to lose efficiency or effectiveness?
3. Was the complete work product covered sufficiently?
4. Were roles assigned prior to the meeting?
5. Were human factors impacted by fatigue, hostile behavior, or defensive behavior?
6. Were other Inspection process aspects compromised?

8.13 Moderator Decision

In Chapter 4: The Moderator, I stated that the Moderator had the authority to call for a Re-Inspection. This authority goes with the role, but it should not be used indiscriminately for it could cause the programmers to view the call for Re-Inspection as arbitrary. Nonetheless the Moderator does reserve the right to call for a Re-Inspection when warranted.

Hopefully the Moderator will not stand alone in the decision, but will have team consensus based on various indicators. If not, then it is the role of the Moderator to try to help team members learn why a Re-Inspection may be the right decision. This may take time, but this also is part of the Moderator's responsibilities; i.e., a successful Inspection, which involves helping team members to learn. This will more likely occur with new teams or team members.

There can be times, however, when the team cannot reach consensus. For example, a Producer who does not have the time for a Re-Inspection and therefore does not see the need, or a Producer who has been reassigned and believes the work on the inspected unit is now history or for someone else to deal with. Whatever the reason, when the team cannot reach consensus in a reasonable time, the Moderator can cast the deciding vote. Management may overrule this decision, but the Moderator will have given the input for a Re-Inspection.

8.14 Group Consensus

As noted, there should be group decision for Re-Inspection, so the Moderator should always be working in that direction as a facilitator on the team. The team consensus can be based on one indicator or the summing up of a number of indicators. See a Re-Inspection checklist in Figure 8.11.

Since Inspections and Re-Inspections are more successful over time when we analyze the results and learn from them, all decisions to re-inspect or not should be correlated with defect data from stages after the subject Inspection. A Re-Inspection is a feed-forward mechanism to try to avoid more costly defects in test or with users. Correlation after Inspections is a feedback mechanism to help tune the process for future use in the organization. We want to do both.

8.15 When To Decide for a Re-Inspection

Re-Inspections are a tool to be used when signals about either the quality of the work product under Inspection or the quality of the Inspection process are less than expected. The organization performing Inspections should, at a minimum, be prepared to ask the question, "Should the work product be considered for Re-Inspection?" The answer is a recommendation to the organization.

The decision to re-inspect or not is guided by the organization's policies and procedures on Re-Inspections. For example, one organization might always choose to re-inspect when more than a specific defect density has been found during an Inspection; let's say when more than 5 defects/KLOC were found. For another organization the threshold might be 10 defect/KLOC. Your organization should determine its own criteria.

Re-Inspection Criteria	**Evidence Available**	**Group consensus?**
1. Defect density is high		
2. Larger than average unit?		
3. Inspection rate out of range?		
4. Preparation rates out of range?		
5. Defect repair impact is high?		
6. Prior unit defectiveness history?		
7. High change volume affecting the unit?		
8. Were logistics a concern?		
9. Quality of the Inspection		
10. Moderator suggests Re-Inspection?		

Re-Inspection Checklist
Figure 8.11

One organization might treat these limits as signals for consideration; another might require them to be used as fixed criteria. In the former, if the decision to re-inspect is not taken, the risk should be noted and tracked on the respective work product throughout test and customer use. If a decision is taken to re-inspect, either via a decision criteria or as a fixed criteria, the tracking should still occur, to facilitate the organization learning from its process decisions.

Certainly when one or more of the indicators (criteria) are sending signals that this work product is outside the norms, it should be given serious consideration for Re-Inspection.
The question to re-inspect or not is required to be asked at the end of the Inspection Meeting. This is part of the Exit Criteria. But should the team always wait until the end of the Inspection Meeting?

A Re-Inspection is another Inspection of a work product and all reworked defects. If it is clear when the Inspection Meeting is in progress that the work product really is not ready, I suggest that the Moderator stop the Inspection. The Producer needs to make the work product ready for a new Inspection. I believe this is best especially when the work product is large, as the team will need to have two Inspections if the first is not cancelled.

Some organizations use discovered defect density with a decision quadrant related to Inspection effort as shown in Figure 8.12 to guide a Re-Inspection decision.

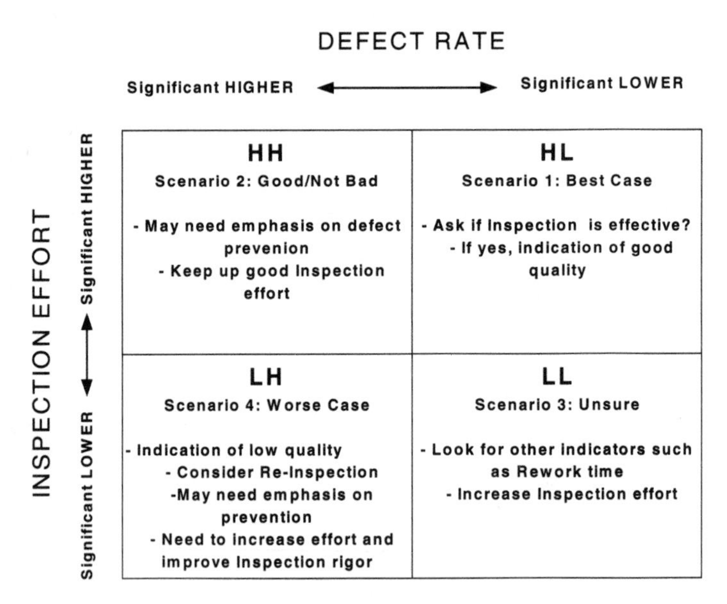

Error/Defect Matrix [Kan95]
Figure 8.12

If the decision is taken too early during the Inspection Meeting, the potential downside is that the early signals may get neutralized after some time in the Inspection and the signal would no longer clearly exist. I feel it is worth this risk, as I have seen Inspection teams get weary of finding defects after too large a volume has been found because there are so many to find. They do not seem to look as hard after a while. From their point of view they've found a work product that is a dog so why keep beating it.

The Moderator should still assess the set of Re-Inspection indicators and ask for consensus. Why force everyone to do an unnecessary Inspection?

Re-Inspections should also be considered any time after the work product was inspected and new data suggests a higher than desirable defect rate in the work product.

8.16 When To Stop Re-Inspecting?

I noted earlier in this chapter that few organizations make any substantive use of Re-Inspections. At the other end of the spectrum, I have seen a few (fortunately) organizations that think Re-Inspections are to be done and redone until there is evidence of a depleted defect pond. This is similar to fishing until the fish have disappeared or it is too costly to fish in the pond again.

The concept makes sense to a point. If an organization has data that shows Re-Inspections are finding defects at a lower cost than test, then they should continue. I worked with one organization where some units had been re-inspected four times. When I ask to see the data, so I could learn, they had none to offer. When I asked why the decisions were made for Re-Inspection, I was told the Moderator suggested it. Fine, but for what reasons? In fact, when we derived the effectiveness and efficiencies for these cases, the Re-Inspections should not have re-occurred after the first one. I would suggest these were not quite wasted efforts, but not the best use of resources. The Re-Inspection should find a defect density rate above the established LCL for a first-time Inspection of a work product type. If not, the Re-Inspection may not be the best way to find remaining defects.

So the short answer is:

1. Re-inspect as long as the indicators suggest this is a good decision
2. Do not re-inspect if you don't have substantive data that it will be effective and efficient compared to other defect removal activities

8.17 Re-Work versus Re-Structure Recommendations

When defects are found, they must be repaired in the Follow-up activity and verified to have been repaired. This is normal process.

When there is a high volume of defects or high impact defects to rework on an inspected unit, not only should the recommendation be made for a Re-Inspection, but in some situations a recommendation should be given to rewrite or re-structure the unit; i.e., start over. Management and/or the Producer may not want to hear this recommendation, but it must be given when there is sufficient evidence. Management must determine whether the decision is accepted and will be implemented.

I hesitate to give guidance as to when the Inspection team should make work product rewrite recommendations, as I think these decisions should be made in the context of the organization and the work product. Both of these are so variant, that I believe the organization will do best to judge for itself. When it is clear that defect rework will have a significant cost, a decision should at least be made to calculate the cost of a rewrite and make an economic comparison.

I do recommend that the exit criteria for stating an Inspection is Closed include a check that the team has at least considered this recommendation. While this is not a perfect answer, it at least causes the team to think about the question.

8.18 Re-Inspections After Delivery to Test or to the User

When a product is in the test cycles and the defect rate is found to be higher than desirable, it may be appropriate to re-inspect parts of the product. Management is often reluctant to do this when the product is in test and the ship date is in view. Management are reluctant to do anything they think will jeopardize that date. But if the defect volume is too high, they are already in jeopardy.

We found such a situation of high latent defects in one product area while they were in test, so we made a proposal to the management.

A Case Study

> Our objective was to get the overrun in defects removed as soon as possible; we began to build a case that would use a subset of the full product as a sample to determine the remaining error density.
>
> Based on where the product was at this point early in the test cycle, we had projected a remaining defect volume of 24/KLOC or latency of this amount in the product. We now needed to prove that this projection was credible. We argued that if the sample Re-Inspections would find ten defects per KLOC against the projected 24, the effectiveness would then be 41% or about what it was for the primary Inspections in this release. So this would probably be a best case given that they had already inspected once. If it would find 12, it would be 50% effective. If it would find 16, it would be 67% effective, which was the best this product had historically been able to show two releases ago. We, of course, had no way to pre-determine the effectiveness of these Re-Inspections. We were in a sense building upon sand to make these projections, but we needed some way to get management to make a "quantitative" decision. Effectiveness higher than 41% would be suspect without reasons to demonstrate why it should now be higher, especially as these were Re-Inspections. With this number we had a boundary that could be used to test the projection of 24 defects/KLOC.

In order to try to achieve a maximum effectiveness and minimize the debate about how effective the Re-Inspections really were, we asked that the Inspection moderators be chosen from a list of people we knew managed effective Inspections. We asked that each Inspection team member be properly prepared for the Re-Inspection, that they had been trained as Inspectors, and that they understood that the objective was to find as many defects as possible in the allotted Re-Inspection time. Thus we were trying to ensure that rigorous Re-Inspections were performed and minimize the affect from other variables.

We frankly tried to force the level of effectiveness. This was done to try to get a consistent approach to the Re-Inspection process. Without this we felt we would be contending with too many unknowns to draw acceptable conclusions from this sample. We asked that the Moderators try to execute the Inspections at the then recommended Inspection rate of 125 LOC/Hour for Preparation and 100 LOC/Hour for the Inspection. We also had to contend with the possibility that any finding below 10 defects/KLOC would indicate that the product was indeed under quality control in this part of its life cycle.

We additionally wanted the Re-Inspections to represent a cross section of the complete product rather than to choose from only the highest defect dense modules. The sample had to be representative of the product. Nothing else could suffice.

After about four weeks, nineteen modules representing 4,030 LOC had been re-inspected. In these modules, 59 major defects had been found. This represented 14.6 defects/KLOC, which was above what had been deemed the lowest signal indicator at 10 defects/KLOC.

The product management team accepted that an additional 200 defects needed to be removed immediately to achieve a desired level of quality for stability in the remaining tests. We were asked to re-evaluate our rank ordered list of modules and to resolve with the engineers an agreed to list for Re-Inspection. We never achieved a list that fully satisfied all the engineers, so the Project Lead asked each development team to find a percentage of the 200 defects based on the percentage of the code for which they were responsible. They were also told they could use any method they determined would find the defects over the next four weeks; unit test, Re-Inspection, or whatever. Most chose Re-Inspections. [RAD90]

This study proceeded with additional Re-Inspections, the defect removal targets were more than satisfied, and the product shipped on time at an acceptable quality level.

So Re-Inspections are a decision that should not only be taken at the end of an Inspection. They can add value anywhere along the project life cycle when other signals suggest quality is at risk. In this study we used Re-Inspections as a sampling technique to verify a projected defect density.

8.19 Cost To Re-Inspect

Since there is a cost, we should only re-inspect when we have conviction that:

- We will find more defects at a lower cost than the alternative approaches of testing
- We have clear data signals which work products may have a high remaining volume of defects
- The work product has been substantially reworked after an Inspection
- The data signals for the Inspection suggest a Re-Inspection

We do not want to re-inspect cavalierly.

Re-Inspections tend to have a reasonable ROI when an organization is not a mature practitioner of Inspections. As Inspections become more effective and integrated into the culture, I tend to see fewer Re-Inspections. In these more mature organizations the Inspection process does not send the signals to re-inspect, since fewer defects are injected and the teams tend to perform within expected capability bandwidths for effort expended and defects removed in Inspections.

In the case study discussed above in Section 8.18 it was established that for this organization the Inspection preparation rate was 125 LOC/hour, the Inspection rate was 100 LOC/hour, and the average Inspection for code required four people. Therefore, for every 1 KLOC of code re-inspected the project would need to expend 88 engineer-hours for planning, Preparation, Inspection, Rework and follow-up. We had projected that a minimum of 200 additional defects should be removed prior to the start of the next test stage. This would bring the product back under quality control and would reduce the impact to test.

Case Study Continued

We assumed that we would not be able to find defects at the rate of 14.6 as was found with the sample, because the sample Re-Inspections had a rigorous environment with selected moderators. This situation would not necessarily exist throughout the project's now larger set of planned Re-Inspections. Therefore, we assumed that the general population would find about 10 errors/KLOC or that they would function at about 41% effectiveness for their environment as they had done in the primary Inspection for this release.

Thus, 1760 engineer-hours would be needed to re-inspect the 20 KLOC to find the additional 200 defects. This was a cost that was not easy to accept, even if it was only an upfront cost and, if sufficiently productive, would save time later. We estimated after interviewing a number of engineers that for each defect it cost about 10 hours in test to isolate a fix, to make the fix, to test it, to reship the fixed code to the code control group, to retest it in the test environment, and to carry out other necessary controls. We determined that the cost to fix the average defect found through Inspections ran at less than 2 hours per defect on average. This difference was primarily due to the random nature of encountering errors during test. During an Inspection or Re-Inspection all errors are found in the same logical period, there are no retests as the problems have not been found in a test. There are no patches or temporary fixes to carry and control, and the code has only to be shipped once, not every time as when each test error is repaired.

Accounting for the savings in fix time for the 200 errors, 1600 hours of time would be saved. This savings comes later in the cycle during test. The apparent cost for the Re-Inspections, therefore, was 160 hours, but 1760 had to be invested now. This may not appear a savings, but recall that many defects would have leaked past test to the users. We would only have had to have two defects leak to the users to make the savings positive beyond anyone's doubt. Also the test schedule would probably have been impacted if quality were not brought under control. The testers had a saying that communicated this situation: "Pay me now or pay me later." The challenge then was to demonstrate that an upfront cost now was in the best interest of the product. At worse the Re-inspections were a break even in cost. More probably they would enable test to proceed under more stable conditions and fewer defects would be delivered with the product. Product management accepted the recommendation and committed to find the 200 defects prior to starting the next test activity. The savings due to defects not having to be found by customers would have been much greater and was not included in these estimates.

Interestingly, if the effectiveness of the Re-Inspection were equivalent to the sample Re-Inspections with 14.6defects/KLOC, the costs would only be 1284 hours to find 200 defects. This would have been a real and immediate savings of 316 hours during test alone.

This example is provided only to give some indication of how one might calculate the contribution Re-Inspections can make toward quality objectives. You'll need to make similar analysis should you find yourself with the opportunity to recommend large scale Re-Inspection.

The Re-Inspections will always proceed more efficiently when the same team is used. Of course a new set of eyes with a new team might find something the original team could not see, but in some cases the necessary inspectors are not available, so your desire for another team may not be a choice. Both approaches work.

End Quote:

"The reason we don't have the time to fix it today
is that we didn't take the time to do it right yesterday."
H. James Harrington

CHAPTER 9

ECONOMICS OF INSPECTIONS

"The surest foundation of a manufacturing concern is quality.
After that, and a long way after, comes cost."
Andrew Carnegie

9.1 Introduction

In this chapter I discuss the economics related to Software Inspections and how to control the costs while focusing toward more effective results. We will explore some models for viewing effectiveness and efficiency. As we saw earlier in the book, Inspections have repeatedly proven to be effective in removing defects and thereby reducing the costs of the project. Now I want to explore with you how we can keep, and indeed improve, the effectiveness while reducing the costs of the Inspections themselves.

Models give us a way to understand a complex problem that may be too confusing with all the details. Models may not be perfect, but they allow us to see aspects that are difficult to see without the aid of the model. Christenson and Huang, I think, express this thought well about some equations (models) they used at AT&T when they say, "then several things are possible:

1. Estimates for the remaining coding error density can be made for each inspection, and for the entire release/feature.
2. A cost model can be derived which would give guidelines on the appropriate level of effort per thousand non-commentary source lines.
3. A prediction of the quality of the release/feature can be made using the resulting estimated effectiveness and the density of errors found in later testing phases." [CHR88]

Models permit these and more:

1. Models make it possible to control the software process economically while consistently achieving quality objectives.
2. Every field of business has used models.
3. Models give power to the user of the model. Models help managers set goals and control the achievement of the goals.

So let's investigate how some models may be used on software projects with Inspection data.

9.2 The Cost of Defects

Software project costs can be partitioned into two sets: Production Costs and the Cost of Quality (COQ). Every dollar spent in COQ is one less dollar available for Production or Sales. COQ is the overhead to deliver a solution that hopefully will satisfy the customer. Since COQ is a drain on profits and production capability, we should want to keep Cost of Quality to a minimum. Production is what is necessary to create the solution, and customers want solutions; they just assume quality will be in the solution. Sad to say they are often surprised otherwise.

What should the COQ be for a software organization? Is there a reasonable amount that should be spent? After all, it would be foolhardy to think that one could or should try to reduce COQ to zero for all projects.

A more difficult question to answer is "Do you know the COQ for your organization?" Most software organizations have little idea, and those who do know tend to be at the higher maturity levels in the SW-CMM. Philip Crosby shows the following COQ data for non-software organizations in his Quality Management Maturity Grid (Figure 9.1).

	STAGE 1	STAGE 2	STAGE 3	STAGE 4	STAGE 5
Reported	Unknown	3%	8%	6.5%	2.5%
Actual	20%	18%	12%	8%	2.5%

Cost of Quality as a Percentage of Sales [CRO79]
Figure 9.1

This Quality Management Maturity Grid is not the same as the maturity scale used by the SW-CMM, but it was an input to the creation of that scale. [RAD85a] Crosby defines six quality measurement categories and COQ is one of them:

- Management understanding and attitude
- Quality organization status
- Problem handling
- Cost of quality as a percentage of sales
- Quality improvement actions
- Summation of company quality posture

Of these I will only address COQ in this book, but the others are recommended to the reader for future study. Before continuing with Crosby's grid, let's take a look at possible COQ in software projects. Cost of Quality is traditionally broken up into prevention, appraisal, and failure categories. In any business, we should want to keep to a minimum all of these COQ factors, but especially appraisal and failure. Test costs are a major contributor to both appraisal and failure costs.

Answer the question, "Do you know the test costs as a percentage of your total project costs?" after the brief description on the next page.

Break your pre-delivery project costs into two sets, Production and Test.

- In Production include all costs for requirements understanding and analysis, prototypes, design, code, and project management. For our purposes we will include Inspections as part of Production costs, for the time being. Later we must remove these costs from Production, as they are an element of appraisal costs in COQ. At this time I simply want to explore cost relationships between production and test.
- In Test include all costs for test planning, test case development, test environment design and development, running the test cases every time until successful completion, defect discovery, repair, and re-test. Include costs for all tests performed from unit test through Final Test. These will include all costs related to defects, executing test cases every time after the first execution until they run successfully, all related costs to determining what the defects are, fixing them, and re-delivering fixes into test.

Note that for this question I am not including any costs for maintaining the product after it is delivered. I'll come back to the costs for maintenance later.

Now if we say that project cost is the sum of Production and Test, "What percentage is Test in your organization?" It is amazing how many software organizations cannot readily answer this question. With a little coaxing I typically hear numbers between 35-65% in organizations below Level 4 maturity. When I analyze the data it is more likely they are at 65% than at 35%.

This means that for every $100 spent on a project $35-65 is for test and related activities. This translates into a COQ of at least 35-65%. Well you might say that's the cost of doing business. But for what reasons, we might ask?

Now let's look further into the costs of Test. Leave the costs of Production aside for this analysis. Break the costs of test into two sets:

- **Fixed**: includes costs for test planning, test environment, writing test cases, and executing each test case once.
- **Variable**: includes executing each test case every time after the first execution until it runs successfully, all related debugging costs to determine what the defect is, fixing it, re-delivering it into test.

What percent is fixed and what is variable in your organization? I've seen fixed as low as 10% and more likely 20%, but it is always the smaller of the two subsets in organizations below Level 4. In an ideal case where effectiveness of defect removal pre-test would be 100%, we could see 0% variable cost in test. To date this has not been shown via case study or anecdote. I suggest that the 80-90% variable costs in test can and should be significantly reduced.

What drives the variable costs? The cost driver is defects! The more defects, the higher the variable percentage and cost to the project.

So to control project costs, we need to control the variable costs in test. To control the variable costs in test, we need to control the defects leaked into test. To control defect leakage, we need to control the effectiveness of Inspections. To control the effectiveness of Inspections, we need to use best practices in Inspections.

If 65% of costs were for test and we assume the fixed cost for test as 10% of the test costs, then 58.5% of project costs (65%-6.5%) are due to injected defects during tests and relate to the variable costs. Not a trivial amount!

Now lets look again at Crosby's Quality Management Maturity Grid in Figure 9.1. In the worst cases he states the Cost of Quality (COQ) is 20% and in the best case it is 2.5% of sales for non-software organizations. For software we are seeing typically a COQ 35-65% pre sales costs. When we extrapolate to Crosby's approach and assume project costs to be equivalent to the cost of sales, then we have 17.5%-32.5% COQ as a percentage of sales. But we have not included all elements of COQ; e.g., maintenance or even Inspections. So far in this discussion we've only included test costs. Due to the costs of maintenance alone, I believe we can safely double the software numbers to 35-65% and I have seen maintenance actually higher in some organizations. Let's look at some documented examples of COQ and how it was reduced.

Prevention and appraisal costs are sometimes lumped into cost of conformance and failure is restated as cost of non-conformance. Haley showed how COQ decreased from about 61% to about 23% over a 7-year period at Raytheon. This is about a 62% reduction in COQ. See Figure 9.2. [HAL95] Raytheon tracked the cost of nonconformance (CONC) and costs of conformance (COC) to achieve better quality. As can be seen the path is not constantly reducing since investments; e.g., training, must be given to reap the benefits, but the trend is down and the sum of CONC and COC is reduced.

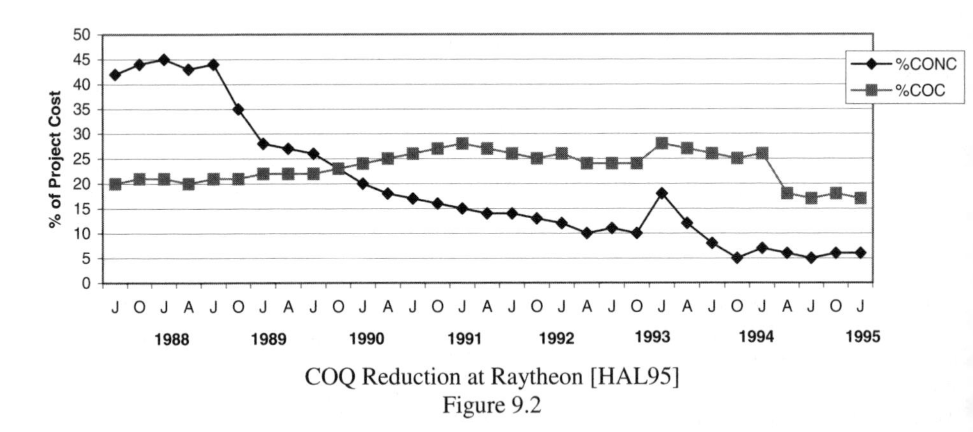

COQ Reduction at Raytheon [HAL95]
Figure 9.2

Slaughter et al. calculated COQ and nonconformance costs for BDM International as starting at \$46/LOC and \$32/LOC respectively and then reducing to \$23/LOC and \$9/LOC over a nine-year period or about a 60% reduction in total COQ. Conformance costs remained fixed at about $14/LOC. [SLA98] Clearly this is an investment that paid off, and the payoff repeats as long as the emphasis on quality remains in an organization.

Knox estimated that Level 5 SW-CMM organizations could reduce the COQ by about 67% and then extrapolated the probable COQ by four sub-elements for each SW-CMM level performing organization. [KNO93] Knox splits failure costs into external and internal costs. See Figure 9.3.

Krasner provided a summary of the status of what he called Costs of Software Quality (CoSQ) across the software community and concluded, "Initial uses of CoSQ show that it can be a large percentage of development costs – 60 percent or higher for organizations unaware of improvement opportunities." [KRA98] Can any CEO, CFO, or CIO accept such a high COQ in their organizations without doing something aggressively to reduce it?

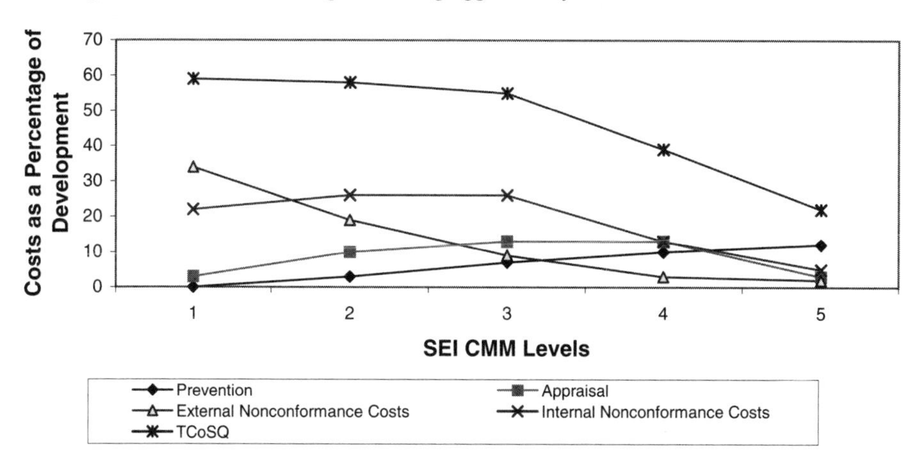

COQ in Level 5 Organizations [KNO93]
Figure 9.3

COQ includes appraisal costs and Inspections as part of that cost factor. Costs attributable to defect removal in Inspections seem to run within a reasonable bandwidth as noted in Chapter 1 Table 1.1. This phenomenon is especially true in similar environments or where multiple releases are delivered in a short timeframe. For example, Russell showed data for 8 releases over a 2-year interval at Bell-Northern Research for defects/man-hour invested at code Inspections. [RUS91]. See Figure 9.4 below. This is an example demonstrating that where an environment for production is not sufficiently changed, that history will tend to repeat, Here, Inspection costs remain constant within a narrow bandwidth, and the COQ will not be reduced. We will see later that focusing on the effectiveness of Inspections will reduce COQ and after we have effectiveness under control that we can further reduce COQ by addressing the efficiency of Inspections.

Defects also seem to correlate from one defect removal activity to another; i.e., a high volume early in the development cycle results in a high volume later. [GRA85] Christenson and

Huang found that this also reflected the environment at AT&T. [CHR88] This suggests that by analyzing early Inspection results we can focus in-process improvements that change the volume leaked to test and therefore reduce COQ.

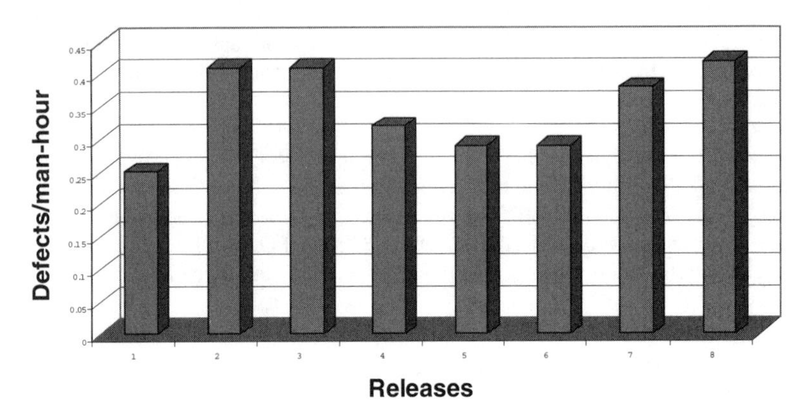

Defect Costs Over Eight Releases at Bell-Northern Research [RUS91]
Figure 9.4

9.3 How Defective Is Software?

Usually when this question is asked, people are looking for a number to compare against. I am hesitant to give a number or even a range, though in some places in this book I have suggested ranges that should be considered when an organization does not yet have its own data. The reason I hesitate is that someone may use the number as something that is absolute. We have so many different types of products and we do not use terminology the same way in the software community, so we need to be careful when quoting and using quoted numbers.

We must be careful when making comparisons and using someone else's numbers. One could use these as reference points, but I strongly suggest creating your own baseline as soon as you can. Numbers will vary across organizations and products because the environments are variable in software production. Use ranges from published sources to get started with Inspections and control of quality costs, but move aggressively to getting the data from your organization. See Chapter 6 for discussions about data.

The volume of defects or defect density in a project is a variable of, at least:

- Processes defined
- Adherence to defined processes
- Tools used
- Experience of the programmers
- Experience of management
- Complexity of the project

- Clarity of the requirements
- Stability of the requirements
- Reasonableness of the schedule
- Newness of the technology in the solution
- Size of the project
- Quality of the base the new project is built upon
- Measurement definitions; e.g., defect, LOC

9.4 Can Inspections Replace Test?

As noted earlier, Inspections are low tech, labor intensive, and rarely fun. These among other factors cause people to question the value of Inspections. A frequent challenge is put forward that some form of testing; i.e., unit test, will be just as effective and efficient or that Inspection cannot catch all defects.

I previously discussed that the solution for a defect is usually evident when it is found during an Inspection, thus the costs for repair are minimized. Tests after unit test do not make readily identifiable the area requiring repair and thus the costs increase. The countless attempts to prove that unit test is more efficient have failed and I know of no study that has been repeated where unit test has been demonstrated to be as effective as Inspections in removing defects.

If it is accepted that Inspections have value, the next challenge voiced about Inspections is that unit test in combination with code Inspections will lead to better results. Again, every trial I know of has failed in this regard. Russell gives two other reasons for not testing before Inspections: [RUS91]

1. As Inspections require a motivated team, testing first may lead to a view that the code is reasonably stable and the team will be less motivated to perform the best Inspection.
2. With the investment of test the Producer may be less receptive to major rework on an "already-stable program image" which will also require retesting.

Ackerman found that the savings from defect detection costs in Inspections was 2.2 hours compared to 4.5 hours in unit test. A two to one savings is a good place to bank. In another organization he states a 1.4 to 8.5 staff hour relationship in finding defects with Inspections versus testing. [ACK89]

Weller states that there are disadvantages of inspecting after unit test: [WEL93]

- Unit test leads programmers to have false confidence that the product works, so why inspect
- It is a hard decision to inspect a large batch that has been unit tested and there may be the view that there is no longer time to inspect

He also gives reasons to perform Inspections first:

- You may actually be able to bypass unit test if the Inspection results are good
- You can recover earlier with lower cost to serious design defects found in Inspections versus unit test

Denise Leigh implied that unit test was dropped at SEMA Group because it was no longer cost effective. [GIL93]

There is some evidence that Inspections find defects that cannot be found by test. For example, Yourdan stated that 5 of 25 defects found in Inspection could not have been caught in testing. [YOR79]

Gilb furthers this view, "Inspection does not replace testing. They both perform some unique functions, which neither can replace for the other. [GIL93]

Jalote found that "such published data from organizations around the world often fail to convince engineers that reviews can be good for their organization. One reason for this skepticism is the Not Applicable Here (NAH) syndrome – people believe that reviews are good for other organizations, but that the situation in their company is different and thus the reviews are not applicable." [JAL00] So at Infosys, when Jalote was with them, they performed an experiment to demonstrate how code Inspections compare with unit testing.

		Inspections		Unit Testing	
SER	Size (LOC)	Total Effort (Hours)	Total Number of Defects	Total Effort (Hours)	Total Number of Defects
1	968	8.0	8	2	4
2	432	5.0	8	1.5	3
3	85	4.0	4	1.5	1
4	667	6.5	26	1.5	7
5	50	12.5	3	1.5	0
6	408	2.5	5	2.5	5
Total	2,610	27.5	54	10.5	20

Experiment Results Using Inspections and Unit Test [JAL00]
Figure 9.5

The experiment used two teams; one that performed an Inspection and another performed unit test with the module leader. Inspections found 2.7 times more defects than did unit test (see Figure 9.5), and even while the costs per defect found are approximately the same, Jalote concludes "if we spend one additional day in code inspection, in this product we can expect to save three to six days in defect fixing later in the development cycle!" This is primarily due to the serial nature of finding defects in unit test and that, when defects are found in Inspections, the fix is often understood as soon as the defect is identified.

Does this mean that both testing and Inspections will always be needed? Inspections cannot replace systems or environmental testing, since this is where the full system comes together before customer production use. Inspections will probably not replace Integration Test, at least in some environments, but I believe with a well thought out test strategy that includes knowledge from Inspections that Integration Test can become more efficient, as can System Test also. I do believe that Inspections can replace unit testing, as do other writers; e.g., Ackerman, Weller, and Jalote. [ACK89] [WEL93] [JAL00] When the data from Inspections shows an effectiveness of over 90%, this should open serious consideration for dropping unit test. When there is 100% effectiveness, then we should seriously ask what value unit test provides. This latter question should be even considered when Inspections are less than 100% effective but more than 80%.

Despite this clear evidence, to this day many will suggest that unit test should be done before Inspections. Always this has proven to be less efficient. When I run into people who are hard to convince, I suggest that they try a simple experiment to see what the data tells them. I remain fully objective and state, "If the data proves that unit test before a code inspection is cost effective, then by all means proceed." Twenty-eight years of requests and I have not been given proof that unit test is less costly. This does not mean the experiments should never be tried again. I'll discuss more on this in Chapter 14. For now I'll leave the door open suggesting that as technology evolves, so too might the best way to remove defects.

9.5 Adjusting Test Based on Inspection Results

Since Inspections occur before test, the results from Inspections can be used as a feed forward to rethink how tests should best proceed. This includes both reduction and enhancement changes to test.

Not all projects will get the opportunity to drop testing, but we have increasing instances of this. While in most cases these are maintenance or enhancement projects, it is a growing possibility in development projects. Of course, your customer may have a different view and require exhaustive testing; e.g., in safety critical environments.

The point is not that all projects should strive to remove testing, but that all projects should strive to have 100% effectiveness with Inspections so as to reduce the costs for test.

We want to enable the possibility, and if it reveals itself, to consider taking it. So for reduction of testing as a feed forward, we might remove a planned unit test if we had high conviction that Inspection quality was high. Or we could do sample unit testing to verify our conviction about the high quality before dropping unit test. We could even extend the sampling of tests to the integration test environment. In both of these cases we would be choosing to reduce the costs of test based on Inspection performance. I suspect it will be a long time before projects choose to remove or sample in Systems Test, but it too has possibilities for efficiency improvements. If the only tests that were performed in the future were system test to validate the product, we will have come a long way to reducing COQ and wouldn't that be grand. Is this a dream?

Well then let's dream on, as those who do not are doomed to live only with the past, and the past with software COQ is not a pleasant picture.

ANECDOTE

TEST ELIMINATED

One client in a maintenance project found that test was not finding any defects. They investigated further and found that only one bad fix had been delivered during the last year.

They made a decision to remove testing, since it was apparent that Inspections were removing practically all injected defects. One could argue that the one bad fix was still not zero-defect delivery, and they would be right. Where would you choose to improve your processes to have caught the one bad fix?

This project chose to improve Inspections, not test. Upon investigation they found that they could have caught this bad fix in Inspections with an improved checklist and training and that discovery in test would have been more difficult and costly.

Anecdote 9.1

Another feed forward effect from Inspections to test would be to increase the volume or focus of test. Whether a Re-Inspection was called or not, if the Inspection defect results suggest that some units are error prone or that the rate or volume of certain types of defects are other than expected, then the testers could be asked to include this knowledge and modify their test approach. They could add some tests if time allowed or they could ensure that focused attention was given when certain units were tested.

9.6 Can The Number of Defects in Test Be Predicted?

If we make assumptions about how effective Inspections are, we can extrapolate the remaining defects to be found in test. If you found 1000 defects and have, or believe you have, a 50% Inspection defect removal capability, then test and users would discover another 1000 defects.

This simple ratio calculation can even be made when only part of the product has been inspected. For example, when we mandated Inspections in Bull most projects were already in progress. One was about 25% completed when they started Inspections. A volume of defects had been found and two levels of test were completed, with defects having been found in each level. The product manager wanted to know if he could predict the number of defects that would be found in the final test. As we explored this, we needed to make some assumptions; e.g., how effective were these first time Inspections. We boxed the estimates as shown in Figure 9.6. The projected defects were determined based on the percentage of code inspected, the defect density in that code, and the possible effectiveness (40-60%), and then extrapolated the number that might have been found if 100% of the code had been inspected.

The defects found in the Inspections were 480, but only 75% of the code was inspected. A calculation was made assuming100% of the code were inspected and then this figure was further extrapolated based on the postulated Inspection effectiveness. For example, if the Inspections were 50% effective then 480 defects represented a possibility of 1280 defects in the code. This number was then compared to the actual total number of defects found through integration test and the difference was the projected defects that would be found during system test.

Defect Removal Activity	**If 40% Effective**	**If 50% Effective**	**If 60% Effective**
A. Defects found for 75% of code inspected	480	480	480
B. If Inspections were 100% of code = A / .75	640	640	640
C. Extrapolated for varying Effectiveness = B / % Effectiveness	1600	1280	1067
D. Unit Test (UT)	288	288	288
E. Integration Test (IT)	195	195	195
F. SUM pre System Test = B + D + E	1123	1123	1123
G. Projected System Test defects = C - F	477	157	(56)

Bounded Defect Prediction
Figure 9.6

Since 60% effectiveness clearly was not possible with these numbers and 40% seemed too low given the rigor applied on the project, the Project Manager chose 50% as the probable performance.

Then the Product Manager made a wager with the System Test manager that about 157 problems, give or take a bit, would be found. The System Test manager lost the wager and, as agreed, subsequently made a public presentation about this use of data and projecting defects.

Harding states a similar relationship where he suggests that based on the number of defects found in Inspections you could calculate the defects to be found in test based on 40%, 50%, and 60% effectiveness values for organizations starting with Inspections. After Inspections are completed he states, "You now have a quantifiable target for the number of defects that should be found in test." [HAR98] He suggests the 40%, 50%, and 60% as a relationship that is "consistent across many different software organizations." From my experiences, this is consistent with SW-CMM level 1-2 organizations. If one had multiple test activities, Harding suggests the use of techniques such as depreciation algorithms wherein decreasing volumes are found in each subsequent activity as is shown in Figure 9.7.

The depreciation results assume that the test activities are reasonably well performed for their purpose with sufficient test case coverage of the product as an area of opportunity in which defects exist.

I include these two examples for defect prediction not as definitive approaches but only as examples that show that we can predict and that we do not need large volumes of data to begin. It is the willingness to try to predict that is important.

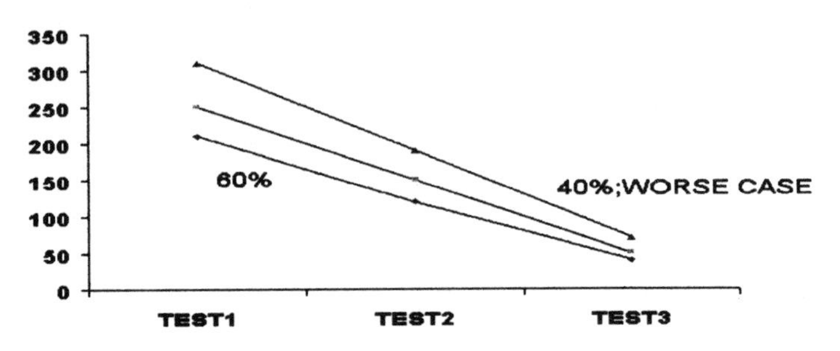

Depreciation of Defects Over Multiple Tests [HAR98]
Figure 9.7

Using Inspection results to predict test results, Graden and Horsley at AT&T performed a study in the 1980's, which demonstrated that defects found in Inspections were not evenly distributed. They found a correlation that defects found before code (e.g., requirements, design) were a good predictor of defect volume to be found during test of sub-systems. They stated, "There is about 10 chances in 100 that a subsystem or feature will be mistakenly identified for concern." [GRA85] Another way to say this is that they had 90% confidence that they could identify areas of concern in test before test started. They proposed to their management "we recommend re-evaluation of documents for features and subsystems identified as concerns before proceeding to the coding phase." This is a good example of feed forward use of Inspection data.

Christenson and Huang found a number of relationships between Inspection effort and error density found during Inspections. From this relationship they could calculate remaining error density. They maintain that from these derived curves they could "estimate the remaining coding error density in a unit of code following inspection." And that "The underlying model fits the data fairly well." [CHR88]

Later, Christenson, Huang, and Lamperez showed analysis of preparation rate and Inspection rates for varying size units of code. They found, as have others, that when a unit is larger, Inspection teams move at a faster than desirable rate in both Preparation and the Inspection Meeting. The result, not unexpected, is a lower error detection rate. Based on these findings they established new goals for Inspection performance. They reported, "The increased preparation and slower inspection resulted in a twofold increase in the density of the errors found for larger units of code." [CHR90] This is a good ROI.

The authors proceeded to define a model that would permit Re-Inspection based on defect density experienced and projected remaining defects. An important point they made after their analysis and included in their model was, "if few errors are expected, little or no effort is justified." I will discuss more on this in Chapter 14. Their conclusions were based on attributed improvements made to the coding process, so that "It was now possible to have very clean code go through an inspection with moderate effort, and be fairly confident that the code was of high quality."

This should be the first objective for a project, followed by an objective to remove the need for Inspections.

9.7 Inspections Viewed as an Up-Front Capital Cost

It has often been argued by management that a project that is already in trouble cannot afford to take more time with Inspections. On the surface this almost seems to make sense. It also depends on where the project is in its schedule. There is probably not much to be gained training everyone in Inspections on a project when 90% of the code is complete. These unfortunate project people will have to continue to suffer along until they finally deliver the product. We can, of course, make sure we train them as they become ready for their next project.

Look at Figure 9.8 below. Here I make an assumption that a total of 60 defects/KLOC enter the work products during analysis (12), design (18), and code (30). There is a typical pattern wherein a higher number of defects tend to be injected during the coding compared to design, and more in design compared to analysis. Use your own numbers to get a picture that represents your organization, though these numbers were representative of software systems products.

If you do not use KLOC, this analysis will work with other size denominators such as Function Points. I am not accounting for bad fixes caused during the test stages in this example.

	Analysis	Design	Code	UT	IT	ST	User
Latent	0	6	12	21	10.5	5.25	2.6
Injected	12	18	30	0	0	0	0
Total Opportunity	12	24	42	21	10.5	5.25	2.6
50% Effectiveness	6	12	21	10.5	5.25	2.65	NA
Residual	6	12	21	10.5	5.25	2.6	NA

Defect Depletion with Inspections at 50% Effectiveness
Figure 9.8

Latent defects are those carried forward from previous project stages. *Residual defects* are those not removed by the last defect removal activity. These defects are still in the work product, since effectiveness is not 100%. Therefore some defects leak from activity to activity. For example in this figure, when analysis begins there are no latent defects. While the analysis

work injected 12 defects and the related Inspection removed 6. There are still 6 latent and carried over to the next activity, design, as residual defects.
The assumption in this example is that each test is executing at about 50% effectiveness, which seems to be reasonably consistent in the software community.

Each Inspection removes a volume of defects. In this example I assume 50% effectiveness. The delivered quality to the users after ST is 2.6 latent defects/KLOC.

In Figure 9.9 when Inspection effectiveness increases to 75% we see that the delivered quality to the users has improved from 2.6 defects/KLOC to 1.1 defects/KLOC. This is a 2.36-fold improvement to the customer by improving Inspection effectiveness alone. In a 200 KLOC product, this translates to 300 fewer defects that customers may encounter.

	Analysis	Design	Code	UT	IT	ST	User
Latent	0	3	5.25	8.81	4.4	2.2	1.1
Injected	12	18	30	0	0	0	0
Total Opportunity	12	21	35.25	8.81	4.4	2.2	1.1
75% Effectiveness	9	15.75	26.44	4.41	2.2	1.1	NA
Residual	3	5.25	8.81	4.4	2.2	1.1	NA

Defect Depletion with Inspections at 75% Effectiveness in Inspections
Figure 9.9

Can you imagine what the quality would be if no Inspections (0% removal) and only tests were practiced, as is still the approach in too many organizations? See Figure 9.10 for the unfortunate result as delivered to users.

So far we see that Inspections clearly improve the quality of products delivered in measures of defect reduction. Now let's look at the effect on costs when we introduce Inspections. Take a look at Figure 9.11 below. If we calculate costs to remove defects using the relationship of 1:10:100 we learned in Chapter 1 (Figure 1.3), we see some interesting results. We find a compelling cost reduction as Inspection effectiveness increases.

	Analysis	Design	Code	UT	IT	ST	User
Latent	0	12	30	60	30	15	7.5
Injected	12	18	30	0	0	0	0
Total Opportunity	12	30	60	60	15	7.5	7.5
0% Effectiveness	0	0	0	30	15	7.5	NA
Residual	12	30	60	30	15	7.5	NA

Defect Depletion without Inspections
Figure 9.10

Recall from Chapter 1 that when we normalize the costs of defect discovery in Inspections to 1 unit per defect, the costs increases to 10 units in test and then to 100 units when customers find defects, as shown in column 2 in Figure 9.11.

Given this relationship, we have reduced defect removal costs from 1275 to 483.5 units when we introduce Inspections at only 50% effectiveness. Here we removed 39 of the 60 defects injected when using Inspections. Hence the cost is 39 units for Inspections. Test removed 18.37 defect units (10.5+5.25+2.65), and at 10 costs units per defect, this becomes a rounded 184 cost units. 2.6 defect units were delivered to the users; thus the costs are 260 units. See Figure 9.8 for the defect removal rates in this example.

For Inspections at 50% effectiveness, this is over a 60% potential savings in the project for defect removal costs. Look at the savings when Inspection effectiveness moves to 75%; there is over an 80% savings in defect removal costs!

	Relative Cost per Defect	With No Inspections	Inspections @50% Effectiveness	Inspections @75% Effectiveness
Inspections	1	0	39	51.2
Test	10	525	184	77.1
Customers	100	750	260	110
Total Cost	NA	1275	483.5	238.3

Example of Savings in Defect Removal Costs Using Inspections
Figure 9.11

So if we net out what Inspections and the COQ measurement ask us to think about; it is not a question of finding the defects that have been injected into a product during production, we must find them. They are there waiting to be found. The issue is where we find the defects and the related costs to do so. Example after example shows that it costs more to find them later. Therefore, we should give strong consideration to reducing COQ by using Inspections to find the defects earlier and at a lower cost to the project. After we have Inspections under control, we can move to Defect Prevention to further reduce the COQ.

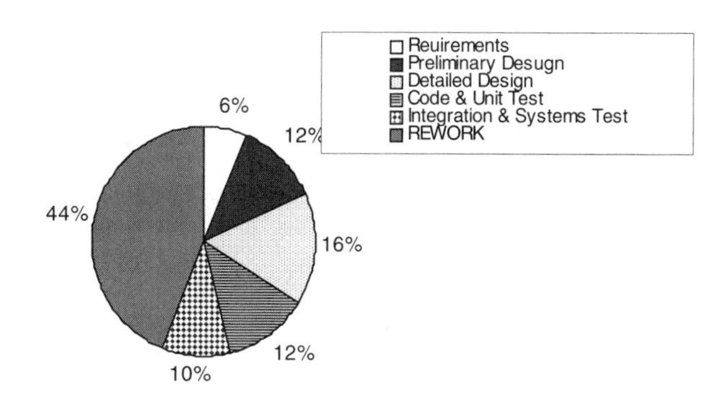

Rework Costs in Software [WHE96]
Figure 9.12

Wheeler stated that 44% of software development cost is rework, but rework is only a part of the COQ story. [WHE96] Using their figures, when all test costs are included in appraisal costs, I estimate COQ would be a minimal 60%, if we assume that code and unit test costs are split 50:50. See Figure 9.12 for Wheeler's breakout of costs. When maintenance costs are included, which is not addressed in these costs of rework in Figure 9.12, the COQ becomes higher.

Since the effectiveness of Inspections is a COQ driver, a solid Inspection program will go a long way toward establishing effective Inspections. How effective have others been? See Figure 9.13 for some documented organizations with high effectiveness.

An organization should see the results of effectiveness manifest as either savings in costs as indicated in Figure 9.11 or as a reduction in cycle time to deliver a solution, and it may be seen in both areas. I'll define the first type of savings as cost reduction and the second as productivity.

ORGANIZATION	EFFECTIVENESS	SOURCE
IBM VTAM	65%	[FAG76]
AETNA	82%	[FAG86]
IBM RESPOND UK	93%	[FAG86]
IBM Space Shuttle	85%	[KOL88]
JPL	75%	[BUS90]
BNR	80%	[RUS91]
LORAL	74.8%	[KOE94]
FA-18	86.6%	[OLS96]
LOCKHEED	67%	[BOU97]
ITT INDUSTRIES	99%	[TAC99]
INFOSYS	75%	[JAL00]

Some Published Effectiveness of Above 50%
Figure 9.13

9.8 Inspection Cost Curves versus Alternate Detection Stages

Fagan notes "Experience has shown that Inspections have the effect of slightly front-loading the commitment of people resources in development, adding to requirements and design, while greatly reducing the effort required during testing and for rework of design and code. The result is an overall net reduction in development resource, and usually in schedule too." [FAG86]

By this time there were other papers written suggesting similar cost reductions and with Fagan's restatement in his 1986 paper, we have clear and repeated evidence that Inspections do not add costs, but reduce costs. Figure 9.14 from Fagan's article shows a graphic representation of these savings in cost and schedule.

The two curves in combination suggest that with an approximate 15% higher up front cost, the overall project costs will be reduced 25-35%. [FAG86] Not a bad investment, but one that is still not taken in most software organizations. Some skeptics believe it intuitive that skipping an Inspection will save time, but evidence consistently shows it is quite the contrary.

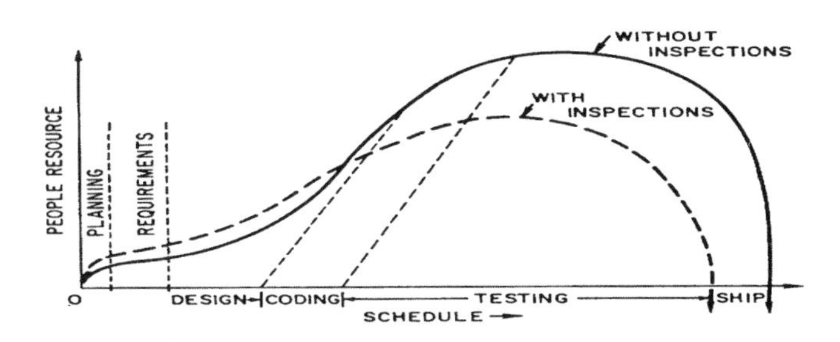

Cost Curves With and Without Inspections [FAG86]
Figure 9.14

9.9 Cost of Inspections as a Percentage of Project Costs

How much of a project's budget should be allocated for Inspections? The answer is ultimately related to how effective the Inspection process is and how effective it should be as determined by the customer's or business needs.

I have seen budgets with as much as 20% allocated and used for Inspections. Why would these projects spend such a high percentage? They do so simply because it has proven to be an advantage. Keep in mind that the 20% in these cases is of a smaller overall budget than the budget of those not using Inspections for comparable work. The project costs are more efficient with Inspections

What becomes interesting is that as organizations move to higher levels of maturity; their total project costs reduce, so the percentage of Inspections might get higher.

The numbers vary across the software community, but again we find that there is a repeating range between 8-20% in project investment for Inspections. Fagan says, "Typically all design and code inspection costs amount to 15 percent of project costs." [FAG86] The costs would clearly be higher when other types of Inspections are included; e.g., requirements specifications, external documents, project plans, test plans, test cases.

Let's look in Figure 9.15 at relative percentages of Inspection to project costs as maturity levels increase with the use of well-performed Inspections. I am assuming that at Level 1 when Inspections are used they could find 50% of the defects and that at higher maturity levels the percentage removed by Inspections would increase.

This would in turn reduce the variable costs in test. I also assume there are fixed costs for Inspections and test that remain constant across all maturity levels. This figure assumes that production costs are not reduced when using Inspections, where in fact they are, as we saw in the VTAM study. See Fagan. [FAG76]

SW-CMM Maturity Level	Production Cost Units	Inspection And Test Cost Units	Total Project Cost Units	Inspection Cost Units	Inspection As % Cost
1	1000	760	1760	150	8.5
2	1000	625	1625	165	10.2
3	1000	535	1535	175	11.4
4	1000	400	1400	190	13.6
5	1000	310	1310	200	15.3

Relative Cost of Inspections at Maturity Levels
Figure 9.15

So while the percentages for Inspections increase, as does the absolute cost; i.e., these organizations spend more on Inspections, the total project cost decreases. It is the project cost that is important not the cost of Inspections.

Investment in Inspections simply results in reduce project costs, better schedules for delivery of solutions, and higher quality.

The Inspection Coordinator role will also require resources. These costs will vary by size of organization, but I have found that a reasonable rule of thumb for coordination (see Chapter 10 for responsibilities of the Inspection Coordinator) requires about ¼ person year equivalent for every 100 people in the organization. This was nominally true during the VTAM study and seems to remain true today.

Barbara Spencer of Applicon, Inc. states, "The ongoing cost of maintaining Inspections is approximately 25% of one full-time job in the software process group. The cost covers minor improvements, maintaining a statistical database, and training of Inspectors and leaders." [SPE94] There should be a higher cost per 100 people during start up for training. Then it should settle into a fixed cost as new people come onboard. You should assume about two days training investment per team member.

Since we find that organizations investing in Inspections spend between 8-20% of project effort, when Inspections are used successfully, your organization cost should be within this range. A lower percentage may signal that Inspections, while in operation, are not yet sufficiently effective.

A good way to start is to use the planning rates noted in Chapter 3. Then based on the work products and value of what is to be inspected an approximate cost can be calculated. First ask if you are inspecting what is necessary. Then ask what it costs. If the costs seem too high, then some serious decisions must be made. I, of course, recommend that management bite the bullet and spend the money for good Inspections. The cost trade-off is always in the favor of using

Inspections. This may be easier for me to say than for some to do, so at least note the risks and try to manage them.

9.10 Calculating Cost Savings

If it cost 10 hours to hold an Inspection and 10 defects were found, then given the 1:10 ratio of costs in Inspections to costs in test we have saved 90 hours (100 hours in test versus the 10 hours in Inspections). This is an ROI of 9:1.

Return on Investment (ROI) in its simplest form is savings divided by costs.

Fagan in his 1976 paper gave us the first public view of comparative cost; i.e., inspected code versus non-inspected code. This calculation has been repeated often and basically shows that there is a higher cost in test than with Inspections and even higher costs when the user-discovered defects must be resolved. The numbers vary, but as a rule of thumb we see the 1:10:100 order of difference previously noted. Given this pattern, it does not take sophisticated mathematics to show that the more defects found by Inspections the lower the costs for a project. See Figures 9.16, 9.17, and 9.18 below.

Defects Found Without Inspections			
	Found	Relative Cost/Defect	Full Cost
Inspections	0	1	0
All Tests	90	10	900
Users	10	100	1000
Sum	100	-	1900

Example of Costs for Defects Found Without Inspections
Figure 9.16

In this simple example, where I assume tests will cumulatively be 90% effective and that Inspections are only 50% effective, we see a savings of 900 cost units. This is not trivial. This is a potential ROI of 14:1. Furthermore, if we have cost data for defects found in test and by users, we could quickly extrapolate savings attributable to Inspections. Figure 9.17 shows a conservative effectiveness with Inspections at 50%.

Defects Found With Inspections at 50% Effectiveness			
	Found	Relative Cost/Defect	Full Cost
Inspections	50	1	50
All Tests	45	10	450
Users	5	100	500
Sum	100	-	1000

Example of Costs for Defects Found With Inspections at 50% Effectiveness
Figure 9.17

Defects Found With Inspections at 90% Effectiveness			
	Found	Relative Cost	Full Cost
Inspections	90	1	90
All Tests	9	10	90
Users	1	100	100
Sum	100	-	280

Example of Costs for Defects Found With Inspections at 90% Effectiveness
Figure 9.18

If we look at the potential that higher maturity organizations are seeing with 90% effectiveness, we see an even more impressive return on investment with Inspections. See Figure 9.18.

After 90% effectiveness, we need to explore new approaches for reducing the COQ and we will do so in Chapter 14: Inspections Future. Here the ROI is 15.8:1.

9.11 Productivity Improvements

Examples of documented productivity improvements seen by different organizations are shown in Figure 9.19 below.

Productivity gains will not be limited to production processes, but include test processes. Larson stated that as much as 85% of time normally needed for unit test could be saved by inspecting the unit test plan and related test cases. [LAR75]

Organization	Productivity Increase	Source
IBM VTAM	23%	[FAG76]
AT&T	14%	[FOW86]
IBM Space Shuttle	50%	[KOL88]
AT&T	30-40%	[CHR88]
JPL	$25K/Inspection	[BUS90]]
FA-18	$14.4 million	[OLS96]
HP	$31millio/year	[GRA97]
MCI	$70 K/month	[MAR97]
Lockheed	70,000 hours/MSLOC potential	[MCC01]

Examples Of Productivity Improvements With Inspections
Figure 9.19

Another way to look at productivity improvement is in costs saved that could be invested in other product development. Every dollar spent in COQ uses up a dollar that could be spent in production or seen as profit. HP, a company of about 3500 programmers estimated savings of $31.1 million per year from Inspections, with a possible saving of over $100 million, as

Inspections were not yet fully deployed at the time of the calculated savings. This is an impressive number, and with large organizations the multiplying effect makes the return more dramatic. [GRA94] [GRA97]

Grady used the following calculation to determine the $31.1 million savings:

Estimated $ Savings/Year =
% Total costs saved X Rework % X Efficiency factor X Total engineering costs

Where:

- Total engineering costs were $525 million
- Efficiency factor (effectiveness) was 50% or .5
- Rework % was 33% based on an HP software development cost model
- % Total costs saved is a derived value based on increased percentage of Inspection types; e.g., if design Inspections increased in volume by 12% in one year, this value would be 12% as an additional contribution.

9.12 Calculating Effectiveness

As noted earlier in Chapter 2: Introduction, effectiveness is the percentage of defects found by Inspections compared to the total number of defects found during the life of the product. For example, if it were known, that 100 defects were in the product and 60 were removed by the set of Inspections used, then the effectiveness for the set of Inspections is 60%. See Figure 9.20. Each Inspection type would have its own effectiveness.

So how can we calculate the effectiveness? There are two ways:

- After the fact
- By estimation using historical data

After the fact, we simply need to sum the numbers of defects found by Inspections, tests, and users. For example if we found that:

DEFECT REMOVAL AREA	DEFECTS FOUND
All Inspections	60
All Tests	35
All Users	5
Total	100

Simple Effectiveness Calculation
Figure 9.20

Then we would know with full conviction that Inspections were 60% effective. This is interesting, perhaps, but not compelling. It is interesting to learn from and to compare against our projections, but it is post facto. Its best use will be to serve as a baseline for future work with similar projects. This is to say that, when we have similar projects and unless the work environment has changed, we could postulate that we would see a similar distribution of defects as we did in the past. This is an assumption that is difficult to accept for many Project Leads, who argue that all projects are different. Well they are different in that they have their own requirements and their own team members, but they may not be so different as reflected by process patterns or environments in the organization.

If we recall the discussion on environments in Chapter 7, we need to ask of new projects, "How is this project different from others we have had?" If it is another project of a similar type with similar people using the same processes, tools, and methods, then we will see similar results.

History in software projects does repeat.

If, however, some aspects of the environment have changed, then we can factor in these changes. We have a choice:

- Use the historical data without change and see how we compare on the new project, and then use this new experience to calibrate the goals for defects
- Make some assumptions regarding the new factors and correspondingly make changes to the defect distributions we expect to encounter

In this latter choice, I recommend that all assumptions be agreed to by the team to test them as much as possible. Otherwise, rash assumptions may be made for any one of many reasons resulting in garbage defect projections. Whatever assumptions are used to change the expected defect distribution should be documented and tracked. This allows the project to see if the assumptions end up being valid and will improve the organization's ability to use these kinds of assumptions in the future.

In the 1970's when Inspections were beginning to prove to be effective, these baselines needed to be learned. Fagan published results seen in the VTAM case study. Since then many articles have entered the literature that show distribution numbers. Any of these could be used by an organization that has no historical data of its own, if they are viewed as a similar organization. They could simply use the numbers as is and then make a comparison, or they could tune the numbers based on assumptions for their environment.

You may feel this will not apply in your environment, but there are patterns in how organizations perform and therefore in the defect removal distributions we see in the software sector. There seem to be repeating behaviors that organizations at higher levels of maturity see, compared to organizations at lower levels. The SW-CMM model implies that this pattern should be true when using the term maturity. The numbers in Figure 1.7 show increases in Inspection effectiveness as the levels of maturity increase. These are not based on full data analysis across the software community, but represent patterns that I have seen repeatedly.

These distributions seem to repeat themselves within reasonable boundaries and appear to be independent of language type, but more data is required to state this unequivocally. Nonetheless one could use these numbers in lieu of anything else. They have been used by some organizations as approximations to determine the latent defects for some products.

Capers Jones suggested that effectiveness (or efficiency as he called it) varied between 30% and 75% as of 1986. [JON86] This is in line with the same pattern for maturity.

Thus if your organization were at Level 1 and using Inspections, the pattern suggests your effectiveness would be 50% or less. Therefore, if you found 100 defects with Inspections, there is a reasonable probability of another 100 being latent.

Larson proposed an error detection model in 1974 based on this same thought where he assumed that code Inspections were 60% effective. Larson went further to state that each of three subsequent test activities was individually 50% effective. [LAR74] These numbers were based on the work in VTAM during the case study in 1972-74. Therefore, these numbers could be a reasonable assumption for similar types of products in IBM at that time.

In this model the user starts with one known fact; i.e., the number of defects found during code Inspections. With this one piece of information and assumptions about test effectiveness the user can extrapolate or predict how many defects are expected in each remaining defect removal stage.

If we decided to reuse this model, we could extrapolate the resultant and expected defects in each subsequent test and even predict what the users might experience. For example, as Norris shows in an early IBM analysis, when 209 defects have been found in code Inspections, the numbers in Figure 9.21 could be forecast. Defects Out is equal to Effectiveness multiplied by Defects In; e.g., 209 = 348 * .6. *Defects In* for each subsequent Phase is the residual from the previous phase; e.g. 139 = 348 - 209. [NOR78] The columns showing defects without Inspections was only a comparative to convince management that Inspections were a better approach.

Phase		**With Inspections**		**Without Inspections**	
	Effectiveness	**Defects In**	**Defects Out**	**Defects In**	**Defects Out**
Code Inspection	60%	348	209	NA	NA
Unit Test	50%	139	70	348	174
Mission Test	50%	69	35	174	87
System Test	50%	34	17	87	44
Environmental Test & Field Use	100%	17	17	43	43

Defect Prediction With and Without Inspections [NOR78]
Figure 9.21

This model while simplistic is useful when we have no other data. We can use it to make projections immediately after code Inspections are completed and then we can test our extrapolations in each subsequent test. More than likely the numbers will not match precisely, so we will need to re-calibrate the extrapolations with each subsequent set of data. Eventually we will have the full set of defects and data and can re-calibrate the actual effectiveness percentages in our environment from similar projects.

9.13 Preparation Rate as an Effectiveness Factor

In 1981 we found in IBM that, as the team size increased, the average individual preparation time tended to decrease. This is shown in Figure 9.22 below. This relationship has continued to show up since 1981 and is another reason to consider smaller teams.

Team Size	Average Individual Preparation Time In Hours
3	2.5
4	1.7
5	1.4
6	1.4

Preparation Rates Varying By Size Of Team
Figure 9.22

Keep in mind that the Preparation Rate will also affect the speed of the Inspection Meeting. In which case poor Preparation leads to poor Inspection results as discussed in Chapter 8. Buck found that when the Inspection Meeting proceeded within planning rates, 19.3 defects were found per Inspection. When the planning rate was exceeded, the defects dropped to 13.5 per Inspection. [BUC81a]

McCann at Lockheed Martin analyzed data for code Inspections "using a similar Fagan-style code inspection process with significant cost and schedule savings as well as quality improvement – in effect, better, faster, and cheaper." [MCC01]

He found, once again, that as the Preparation rate increases from 100 to 600 Source LOC/Labor Hour that the Inspection effectiveness decreases from 90-100% to 60%. He calculated a F-test with a "confidence level in excess of 99 percent with the linear fit accounting for more than 90 percent of the variation in the data."

What is more interesting is that he derives the cost in excess labor hours as the Preparation rate both proceeds faster than the recommended 100 LOC/hour (see Table 3.1) and when it proceeds slower. Refer to Figure 8.7 where a similar relationship was noted. Figure 9.23 is an approximation of his data in his calculated cost curve. When reading this curve note that his savings are normalized to 1,000,000 Source LOC.

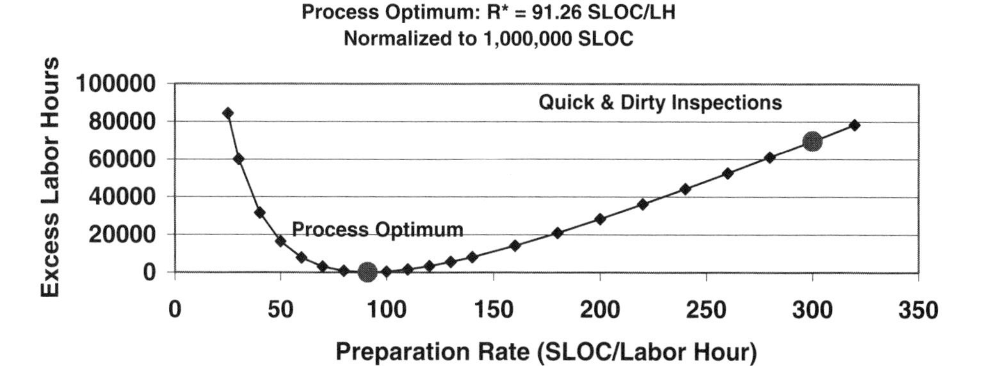

Excess Labor as a function of Inspection Preparation Rate [MCC01]
Figure 9.23

9.14 Can Inspections Be 100% Effective?

The answer is yes, yes, yes. Unfortunately not enough organizations have experienced this possibility yet, and I suspect many more think it impossible, if not unnecessary. I will discuss more on this topic in Chapter 14, but for now, let's note that it has been done.

Can it be accomplished in every environment, in every type of organization? Probably not! But I believe every organization should be able to, for at least some Inspections, experience 100% defect removal. Then if these experiences can be analyzed, I believe effectiveness can be improved in all and 100% might be achieved in more Inspections.

So how is it accomplished? Step by step. First, Inspections must be put into practice. Next, and continuously, the data should be mined to learn how the effectiveness could be improved. Then one day there may be one example, followed by other examples, of 100% defect removal using Inspections.

I've not yet seen an organization where every instance is 100% effective, but I hope to see or read about one soon. Of course this effectiveness is dependent on many factors, not all of which are easily controlled; e.g., retention of qualified staff.

In Chapter 6 I discussed how effectiveness could be calculated dynamically using *where found* and *where caused* data. See Figures 6.19 and 6.20. While the true and final effectiveness must include the defects that the users find, we can incrementally learn what the effectiveness may be for any Inspection type. Thus, in the example in Chapter 6, we see that while the REQ Inspections start at 47% effectiveness that it increases to 76% when REQ defects are found in the HLD Inspections. Therefore, we can learn the effectiveness dynamically by observing the volume of defects found by each defect removal activity and then attributing found defects to a where caused classification. By the time we finish system test (ST) we could make an assumption that all defects have been found and we can calculate the current effectiveness for each Inspection and test activity. Of course we would need to update the calculations later as we learn about the defects the users find.

9.15 Will All Inspections Find the Same Number of Defects?

The answer is No. Variability exists in all processes. One of the factors that lead to variability is people, as discussed in Chapter 7. Each person has different experiences, skills, knowledge, and capability. We cannot assume all people are equally capable even when we provide them the same training, processes, tools, etc. We can, however, bring them all into a higher range of capability. Another variable is the quality of the work product being inspected or as Buck stated:

**"The number of errors found during an inspection is not an adequate indicator of a quality inspection.
The number of errors found is just as much a function of the quality of the material being inspected as it is a function of the quality of the inspection itself." [BUC81a]**

This is an excellent observation and a particularly tricky issue in Inspections. When the defect rate is high, is this due to a good Inspection or a poor quality work product? The answer will be learned through analysis, but if we practice Inspections with well-defined processes and trained participants, we can begin to remove one of the doubts. Then as the process becomes stable in its performance, we can relate the stability of the Inspection process to the quality of the process and related training and in turn conclude that, if the process was well performed; i.e., within the calculated control limits, then a high defect rate could suggest a poor quality work product. First we must focus on stabilizing the process before we can answer Buck's observation in our environment.

See Figure 9.24 for an example of variability found by Martin during his *N*-Fold Inspections study. [MAR90] Here we see that, while there is variability across ten teams, it is reasonably centered around an average.

So we will see variability and we should expect different teams to find different volumes of defects. If multiple teams inspected the same work product there will be overlaps in what they find, but there will be differences also. Later as the organization learns how to practice Inspections effectively, the differences will reduce.

For an Inspection we should always try to pick the best available people to serve as inspectors. This just makes sense. However, those who are available may not always be the absolute best fit. Clearly we must proceed and plan for the best. The differences in people and the teams are one of the system variables that lead to a spread in performance. Not all teams will find the same number of defects, especially during startup where variation is typically wider.

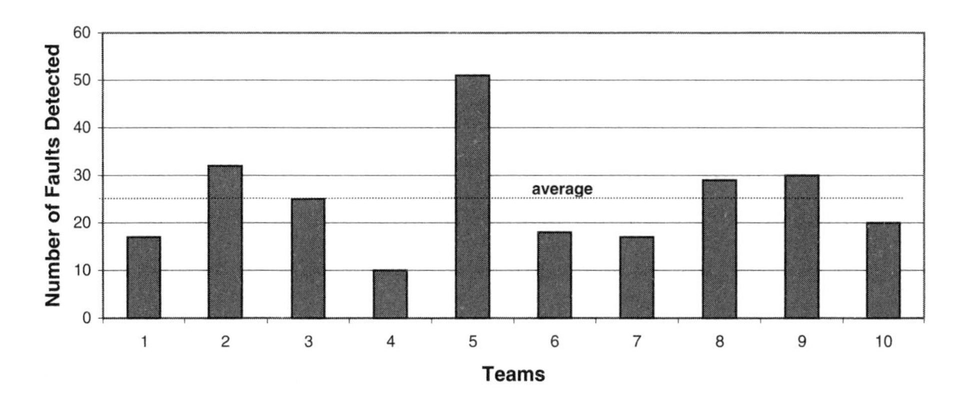

Number of Faults Found by Each Team During Inspection [MAR90]
Figure 9.24

The issues that we can control are whether the people selected have been properly trained in the Inspection process and have sufficient domain knowledge. Without training there will be too much variability in performance, and perhaps to an unacceptable degree. Training is an entry criterion or precondition to successful Inspections and reduced variability.

Without sufficient domain knowledge, the inspector may not understand what is being inspected and therefore cannot contribute beyond a surface level. This can be frustrating and annoying to the Producer. Rifkin and Deimel in a case study demonstrated that comprehension is a key factor in the number of defects detected. As they stated, "You cannot inspect what you cannot understand. This raises a new entry criteria for Inspections: inspectability – can I comprehend what you have given me to review?" [RIF94] The point they are proving is more about the readability; i.e., *inspectability*, of the material, but it applies more broadly to comprehension regardless of the source; i.e., the material or the person.

INEFFECTUAL TEAMS

How can it be learned if a team is effective with Inspections? I discussed this in Chapter 8: Re-Inspections. Initially we need to look at the results for speed of the Inspection, the defects per volume inspected, and how well the process was performed. When the results do not show that both speed and defect volume are within acceptable boundaries, then there is a signal that we need ask other questions about the Inspection. Later we should look at the defect leakage for the work product inspected. When leakage is greater than we have established as an acceptable target, then we need to do Causal Analysis to learn how to improve defect removal in the Inspection process.

Why are teams ineffectual? This could be due to any one of many reasons, but one that we should be concerned with in this chapter is where the organization permits Inspections that are just check marks; i.e., "We did the Inspection. Don't blame me if it didn't find enough defects!"

The organization must take charge immediately by reviewing the results for each Inspection and when they are outside acceptable bounds, take action to change and improve. If this is not done and feedback is not provided to teams, the Inspections can further decrease in effectiveness. Then at some point management may ask why Inspections are being used, since little value is seen from them. Eventually the Inspections are stopped.

9.16 Cost of Maintenance

Often the cost of maintenance is not factored into a project's cost. Consequently a project that ships on schedule with "committed function" is considered a success despite the maintenance costs. This is not good business when the maintenance costs are paid by the project's organization.

Today software suppliers have learned to charge the customer for maintenance. This seems almost unethical, but it does let the supplying software organization recover the costs of maintenance. During the warranty period, however, the projects could show a heavy drain on resources for rework and repair. Maintenance costs are included in the Cost of Quality. They impact the organization and the customer.

An additional cost is due to bad fixes made for maintenance repairs. Every time a fix is delivered to a customer and it either does not really solve the problem or causes another problem, the loop and costs for repair continue. The only real way out of this loop is to deliver defect-free fixes. This can be partially satisfied with good Inspections of fixes. See Weller's articles for a discussion of maintenance economics and Inspections. [WEL93] [WEL00]

Fagan was aware of bad fixes that resulted from repair to Inspection defects. He noted, "The inspection process clearly has an operation called Follow-Up to try and minimize the bad-fix problem." This check on the Inspection process is useful, but it is not sufficient. The best way to minimize bad fixes is to fix them right the first time!

Inspections can be successfully applied to maintenance. They will have some differences compared to work product Inspections, so tailoring should be considered when:

- The volume of work is continuous; i.e., the work required is not determined by a schedule, but by customer dynamic experiences with defects
- The enhancement changes are small

A team of four may be overkill on most maintenance Inspections, so 1:1 Inspections should be considered. It is very likely that one inspector can sufficiently serve for Inspections of maintenance repairs. This is usually true when the repairs are small; many fixes will be just one LOC. But we should ensure that even one LOC changes are inspected, as there is evidence that with small changes programmers make assumptions that work against quality. Weinberg reports that defective repair rates may be about 50% for one LOC changes, 75% for 5 LOC, and 39% for 20 LOC. [WEI81] Small but deadly changes shown from this data! This suggests that we cannot stop Inspection of fixes until we have evidence that proves we are making fixes right the first time.

Weller shows an analysis of improvement in fix quality with an apparent 3X improvement in bad fixes, which later settles in at 2X. He does not show the actual defect rate, but we can surmise that these fixes were defective and the rate was improved when using Inspections. See Figure 9.25.

Bad fixes can occur during maintenance, but they also occur during test. Anytime a fix is made, it is potentially flawed. How flawed is a factor of the process performed by the project and under which constraints it is performed. I have seen the pressure of time during test bring the bad fix ratio to as much as 50% the day before delivery. Fortunately at the start of test the bad fix ratio was only 10% or less. But we must keep in mind that every one of these bad fixes injects one or more defects into the product. The reason the bad fix rate increases at the end of test is that process short cuts are taken due to time pressures.

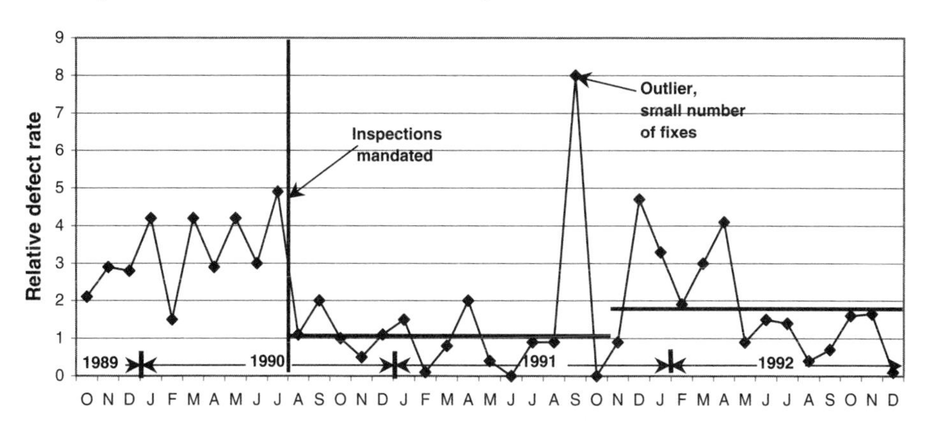

Improvement in Fixes [WEL93]
Figure 9.25

The cost of bad fixes will increase the COQ of a project, so it is suggested that bad fix volume be tracked and analyzed as part of project management, Causal Analysis, and Defect Prevention activities. An organization may have a good effectiveness with Inspections, but lose the quality due to high bad fix volumes.

The cost of maintenance is not just fixing bad fixes. Let's take a look at an example scenario of maintenance in one company. See Figure 9.26.

This example shows some interesting relationships. The valid defects; i.e., the defects that require repairs are only 3% of the total problems that the customers report. The vast majority (97%) is reported for other reasons and some of these reasons explain the high COQ in maintenance. If a product has good quality, customers tend not to report or call for other reasons. So when we see 20% of reported problems are due to user error, we should suspect that the product confuses the users and is probably quite defective also. Unfortunately in some cases these problems as well as the No Trouble Found problems get closed with offensive classifications or reporting back to the customer as "Working as designed." I don't know how you'd feel about a problem that was closed this way, but it makes me want to scream.

Take a look at the Duplicate Discovery problems at 36%. Every one of these problems is valid for the customer who found it. Every one requires effort by the supplier. Every one impacts the customer. When the number of Valid Unique defects are reduced, so too will be these duplicate discoveries. You do the calculation, but I think you readily see that for each reduction in defects leaked to the customers there is a large positive effect on COQ. If an organization does not gather this type of data they cannot analyze it and cannot see the impact. Still, too many organizations do not understand the maintenance impact on COQ.

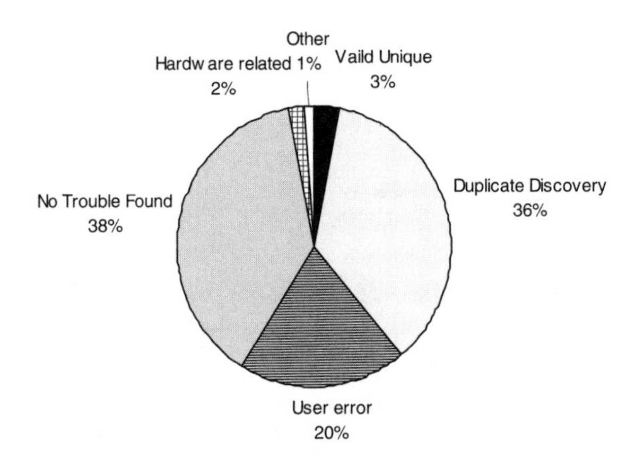

Examples of Types of Cost in Maintenance
Figure 9.26

While COQ measures may prove insightful when first calculated, this metric suffers from the same problems we have with all measures. People can game them, and since COQ drives a focus on how well management is doing its job, you should expect some gaming. There will be lots of debate about what should or should not be included in the calculations. Be consistent and allow no tailoring of the measures.

Let the defect data sort out the management rather than permitting the management to sort out the data.

One reason why COQ calculations can be miscalculated is that the costs are hidden or not visible, as we've just discussed. See Section 9.23 for elements in COQ.

9.17 Costs to the Customers

The customer is impacted every time a defect is found. Sometimes they find a work around, sometimes they just live with it, sometimes they need to get a fix from the supplier, sometimes they see downtime, and sometimes they impact their own customers.
Costs the customers see are in the following areas, at least:

- Downtime
- Workaround or repair or living with it
- Satisfaction
- Move to new suppliers
- Opportunity costs

Let's briefly explore each of these to see how they affect or are related to the supplier's business.

DOWNTIME

When a defect is discovered, there will be some downtime or lost time for the users. Downtime can be more significant with mainframe operating systems or in systems such as the Space Shuttle, airplanes, air traffic control, military weapon systems, utility suppliers, financial systems, etc, but it also affects every PC user when, for example, Word or Windows encounters a bug. In the latter cases, we usually simply reboot and move on. Other times, even a reboot is not enough. Contaminated or lost data can be very discouraging even in a PC environment. However, a reboot or loss of data on a Boeing 777 while in flight would be more dramatic.

In most cases there is no good measure for customer downtime, but we know and hear of many users experiences. When it gets to be too much or too frequent, then complaints are made. If there are contract clauses for downtime penalties, these will tend to get visibility in an organization, as no one likes to lose money. But the true and total impact to the customer or the supplying organization is rarely known.

WORKAROUND OR REPAIR OR LIVING WITH IT

Customers will often try to fix or to make do with a problem before getting the supplier involved. They have found that this is often more expedient. It may not always be the best solution, but if it gets them past the immediate issue, then they will do it themselves. Expediency is the tradeoff they prefer.

These workarounds are often costly to more than one customer. The supplier loses information on defects not reported, so a fix may not be developed that should be distributed. As we all know, these situations add up and customer satisfaction takes the loss. How often have you wanted to call the supplier of some software product, but you make more than one attempt to workaround. When your workaround works, you move on with other work. Sometimes the workaround is a "fix" that has continuing costs to the customer as a functional nuisance or performance degradation. In all cases there is at least a one-time cost and in some cases a recurring cost.

SATISFACTION

This is a subject that most suppliers say they are concerned about, that they want high customer satisfaction, but I have heard too often, especially from marketing types, "If the customer doesn't complain then they must be satisfied." Yeah, right!

Many customers, when they have poor quality, would love to have another choice and to be able to take that choice when they wanted to, but in software this is not an easy thing to do. It is not as easy as taking one's business to another deli for a sandwich order. Customers and users are held captive when they have made a bad choice with a software supplier. They do eventually move when it becomes too unsatisfactory, but by that time neither party is happy with the relationship.

Customers, as Deming said, vote with their feet. This applies to software too, even though the walking shoes are harder to put into motion for a software customer.

MOVE TO NEW SUPPLIERS

Every time a customer moves away from one supplier to another, both parties lose something. The customer incurs the cost of making the move, but often he should come out ahead after a period of time.

The supplier who is dropped, however, loses the customer and all related revenues from this customer. Furthermore, if revenues are to be retained at the same level, the supplier must spend effort to replace the loss. The common thinking is that is costs 20 times more to replace a customer than to retain one for a supplier. This is easy math proving poor quality carries a big cost.

OPPORTUNITY COSTS

When customers suffer any of the costs we've just discussed they lose the ability to use that time and money for other efforts that could better serve their needs. They cannot spend the money on opportunities when they lose it to a poor quality product delivered to them. Customers cannot usually calculate it, but they know it occurs.

9.18 Should All Work Products Be Inspected?

I always have mixed feelings when this question is asked. As a purist I can argue that all code should be inspected. Even the SEI' SW-CMM directs that "Each code unit undergoes peer review and is unit tested before the unit is considered complete." [CMM93] But I would point out, as we have seen, that not all code will have defects. So inspecting code that has no defects is clearly a waste of time for finding defects. One could beat the code with a bat and if it is defect free, nothing will be found. This latter may be the necessary insurance coverage in safety critical software. In fact one might even have *N*-Fold Inspections when a safety critical situation warranted.

Boeing decided that the approach for Inspections to be "applied to the procurement of safety-critical systems used in commercial airplanes," was that they would use not one but multiple teams. [TRI91] The process they used was as defined by Fagan and applied across 5 concurrent teams inspecting the same work product. The defects found by the teams varied from 72 to 163 and, curiously, the most experienced team found the fewest defects. See Figure 9.27 on the next page. [MAR90] See Chapter 13 for discussion on *N*-Fold Inspections.

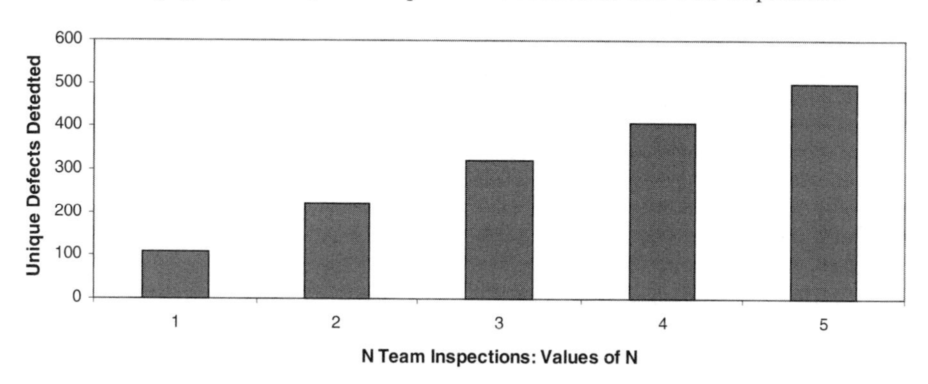

Results From *N*-Fold Inspections [TRI91]
Figure 9.27

Multiple teams represent an increase in costs, but there may be situations where they are warranted, as with Boeing.

The issues are twofold for inspecting less than all work products:

1. How to select a subset.
2. How to learn from the subset selection process.

To address the first issue one needs data with integrity. Most organizations will not have sufficient or good data until some reasonable period of time has passed with successful Inspections. Should these organizations wait and simply inspect all work products until they have data? Should they make a best-case subset selection with what they know qualitatively? This is a decision that requires that they understand, accept, track, and manage the risks, as they will be taking a risk. With or without good data, selection criteria should be stated. Otherwise whim, time pressures, and other issues that come up on a project when it is underway may control the selection. Let's explore some decision criteria.

Blakely and Boles identified two criteria in their paper, "*A Case Study of Code Inspections*." [BLA91]

"First, modules were selected only if they were modified in the course of the project." This may seem obvious, but I have often heard the complaint that for enhancement releases the Inspection of the full product is too costly, because they inspected the full product not just the modified portions. It is normally true that it would be too costly to inspect the entire product. It is not necessary and it should not be required. Unfortunately, some organizations have stated a full product Inspection as a requirement and then due to costs and resistance they chose to not employ Inspections, as too costly.

So restricting the Inspections to only the changed or new units is a good criterion for selection. However, the base release may be a primary source of defects that will become manifest when changes are integrated and some of these defects will be found when the Inspections are performed. When this happens, it can be discouraging at least and at worse may cause some to think that Inspections are finding unnecessary defects that customers never experienced. After all they were not found before, someone might argue!

I suggest that the Project Lead and the Inspection Coordinator plan out, with the help of the project team members, where additional value may be achieved by inspecting some base release units that were not changed. This approach has often paid off in interesting results and it empowers the team to improve quality, that they often know needs improvement.

"Second, the complexity of the modified modules was determined." This is an excellent selection criterion. Complexity can be determined many ways; e.g., McCabe metrics, size of the unit, number of changes to the units, including canvassing the team members for a qualified ranking of complex units. None of these approaches is perfect, but all provide insights into making the selections. I've even seen organization use multiple complexity criteria to guide their decisions.

What if you only have resources to inspect 20% of the new and changed code? Let's assume further that this is your first use of Inspections and you want to proceed cautiously.

Use of these two criteria may result in an amount greater than 20%, and if you do not have budget for more than 20% in your first use, then you will need to make a paring down decision. I recommend against this approach, since the selection criteria has sent a signal and to do less will result in less than is warranted.

But if you choose to restrict yourself to 20%, then start with error prone areas, and track the results to learn how and where you can increment higher than 20% in future projects. Keep your eye on the effectiveness. If you are not finding more than 70% of the defects with Inspection, you have more to improve and it will start with resourcing more for Inspections.

In any case, whether you inspect 20% or more, you must learn from your decision. This requires that you track the results during test and customer use, though test results will usually speak quite clearly about your decision.

For new releases, the selection will be more difficult, and you should take a much harder stand on anything less than 100% code Inspection. However, you may still have budget or commitment constraints in your first use, so you may need to select. Clearly all units are candidates since they are all new, but you could still make use of complexity measures as a criteria to hold or not hold a specific unit in Inspection or not. While this will give you a way to subset, you must have planned for a specific volume (size) at the start of the project. If you do not plan or you exhaust your planned Inspection resources earlier than expected, you have a problem in that units that could benefit from Inspection may just be passed by. I do not like this approach for first releases and first use of Inspections, but it does happen. In these cases, I recommend a minimum of 50% to be planned for code Inspections up front. This is not a perfect answer, but seems practical for some first time users.

If your selection criteria were the best whether for an enhanced release or new release, then the units that were not inspected (on average) will prove to be less defect dense than those that were inspected. If they prove to be more defect dense or if they lead to serious delay problems during test, then you should revisit your selection criteria to improve them. If you do not evolve the selection criteria, you will repeat the same process the next time and you should expect the same comparable issues in test.

It is OK to take some risk, but the risk should be understood and managed. Otherwise the risk will manage you and your project.

O'Neill gives one suggestion for selection with legacy code: "To optimize the practice of software inspections on legacy code during maintenance operations, all modules are rank ordered according to cyclomatic complexity. Candidates for inspection are selected from those with the highest complexity rating, where the defect density is expected to be high. The legacy code maintenance strategy can be extended by rank ordering all modules based upon defects encountered in the past year and by rank ordering those that are expected to be adapted and perfected in the coming year. Modules are then selected based on their rank ordering in cyclomatic complexity, defect history, and expected rework." [ONE97] And then one must track to see the results. This works for maintenance or enhancement projects, but for development projects there is no history to guide, so this criterion cannot be used. One could also ask the lead technical people to rank what they think should be inspected based on their experiences with the product.

Is inspecting changed code a Re-Inspection? No! Changed code is code that is new for the release in which it will be delivered. An Inspection for a work product is always focused on the new and changed code, since this represents new or changed function and therefore needs to be verified.

9.19 Number of Participants

As noted earlier, the fewer the number of participants the lower the costs, but the primary objective should always be the effectiveness of the Inspection. While one inspector will be the least costly, they may not be sufficiently effective during early use of Inspections. The objective should still remain to get to 1:1 Inspection practice within the organization. Track the results of Inspections by reviewing the defects found after Inspections before leaping to 1:1

Inspections. When the data shows that 1:1 Inspections are effective, then continue in this mode as appropriate.

Buck found in IBM that there was little difference in effectiveness for teams of 3, 4, or 5 participants as shown in Figure 9.28. [BUC81a] He initially found the relationship in a controlled experiment during training sessions where he used a code unit with a known number of defects and various team sizes. He later replicated the results in a project in development. In this figure the Planning Rate is the expected rate that would be applied. The Exceed Rate represents Inspections that went faster than the Planning Rate. We see that in all cases the Planning Rate Inspections found more defects that those that exceeded the Planning Rate for teams of 3, 4, or 5. We also see that the defect discovery rate is nominally the same in both cases across team sizes; i.e., Planning or Exceeded Rate.

Freedman and Weinberg give a different view. "The first principle of formal review composition is this: **Select the reviewers to ensure that the material is adequately covered.** One consequence of this principle is that there is *no* fixed optimum size of a review group. The size of the group depends on the material to be covered and the skills and review experience of the potential participants." [FRE90] I disagree with this approach as it leads to higher costs and with no appreciable improvement in results. The principle should be to include the fewest participants who meet the requirements for a successful Inspection, not the maximum. The number will vary by Inspection type, but we should always strive to have the essential few needed.

Later Freedman and Weinberg state, "Since no leader in the world is skilled and experienced enough to consistently conduct successful reviews with groups larger than seven, break down the review any time you think you need more than seven people or more than two hours." While I fully agree a review may need to be broken down due to time factors, having multiple Moderators for Inspections seems highly untenable. The coordination and memory of what is occurring at different sessions can only be confusing. Here again I suggest keeping the number of participants to the fewest possible. This can admittedly be difficult with requirements specification Inspections for large projects, but should remain the objective.

There are three controls the Moderator should invoke when an Inspection requires more than four participants:

1. Chunk the work product into logical pieces each of which can be addressed in a nominal two hours. In some cases there may be logical pieces that do not fit within a nominal two hours, but with some effort even these can be further chunked.
2. Determine which participants should be at each chunked meeting. While there will be some participants who need to be at most, and in some cases all meetings, there will be others who are naturally limited to selected chunks.
3. Plan that the meetings will need to take a slower pace to ensure all are participating and heard.

Code Inspections should almost never require more than four participants, and there is good evidence that fewer participants can be equally effective. For documents such as requirements specifications, four participants may not be sufficient, but even with these I suggest that the number be held to the fewest possible.

Weller found a similar situation with fewer participants contributing more, but only with the obvious need to have a precondition satisfied. He notes "A three-person team with a lower preparation rate does just about as well as a four-person team with the higher rate, which shows that the preparation rate, not size of the inspection team, determines inspection effectiveness." [WEL93]

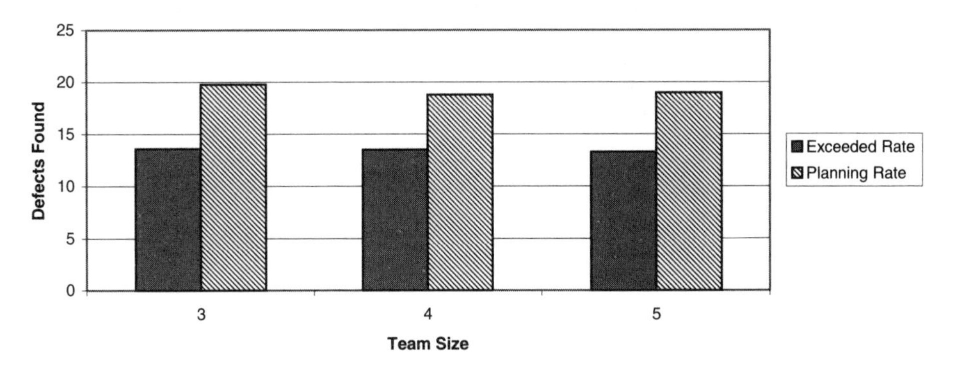

Defects Found By Inspection Team Size [BUC81a]
Figure 9.28

Porter and Votta in a study at Lucent found "While inspections with one reviewer were less effective than those with two, inspections with two reviewers were no less effective than those with four (an argument for smaller teams)." [POR97] I will come back to the one inspector question in Chapter 14.

9.20 Preparation

We see again and again that preparation is key to successful Inspections. As a reminder, it should be understood that defects will be found during Preparation, and if insufficient Preparation occurs, the defect discovery rate during the Inspection Meeting will be less.

Arskey gave data on using the Fagan approach at Boeing for 4 project areas of Inspections. As seen in Figure 9.29 all of these project areas found the vast majority of the defects during Preparation versus the Inspection Meeting.

Humphrey notes also "Experience has shown that about three-quarters of the errors found in well-run inspections are found during preparation. Good preparation is thus essential." [HUM89]

When Preparation is not performed well, it will have an effect on the length of time at the Inspection Meeting and Inspection teams will see reduced effectiveness the longer the meeting runs. It was noted in Chapter 3: The Inspection Process that Inspection Meetings should not run for more than two hours. This is a rule of thumb, so there will be some exceptions based on logical chunking of the work product inspected. Nonetheless, the Moderator needs to periodically check that the team is functioning well. If a break is warranted, then take it. If meetings must run for more than two hours, then multiple breaks may be needed.

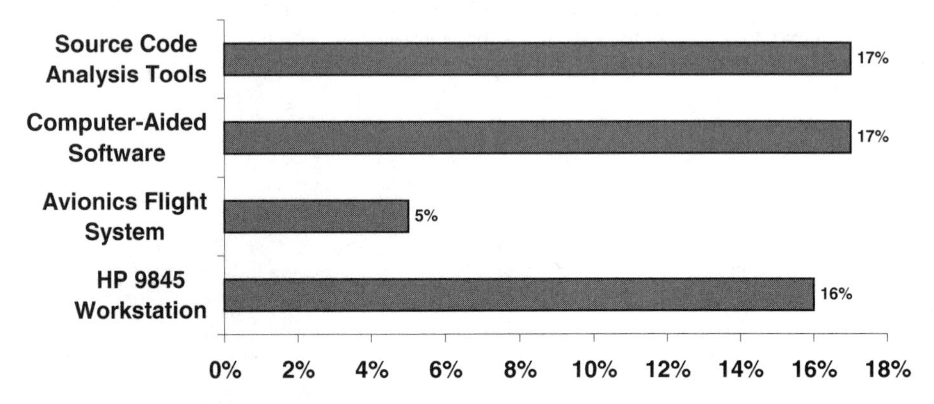

Percentage of Total Defects Found During the Inspection Meeting [ARK89]
Figure 9.29

Not only will team effectiveness decrease with longer meetings without breaks, but teams members may begin to act or react as less than a team player.

If an Inspection meeting runs too long and the Moderator is not keeping track, the team may be led into a false belief that they have spent enough time and they may speed up on the remaining sections of the work product. This is clearly not good practice, so the Moderator needs to monitor the pace and ensure that the pace is reasonably consistent throughout the Inspection. If it looks like more time will be needed than was scheduled, the Moderator needs to canvas the team for how much they think is needed. Be careful that they do not default to trying to fit the remaining sections into the time left. This could be for reasons that are not related to the work product; e.g., they have another meeting, they are going on vacation.

9.21 What To Do when Inspections Go Bad

Yes, Inspections can go bad. This can happen at the start of adoption of Inspections in an organization or there can be regression after some successful use in an organization. Figure 9.30 shows an example. Bad does not mean that the Inspection process is not used, it just is not as effective as it once was and there may be other signs of regression or erosion. This can happen for many reasons:

- View in the organization of “we know how to do it”
- Decrease in infrastructure investment
- Re-organization

- The non-believers come into management control

All processes will have difficulty for transition into use and can regress after mature and long term use. For most people Inspections are not the high point of their working day.

In Figure 9.30 there is regression from release 2 to release 3 and from release 2 to the current release in this study. The regression was from an apparent 65% Inspection effectiveness in release 1 to 59%, then 56%, and finally 41% in the current release. Management believed they were getting the benefit of Inspections, but no one was tracking the effectiveness to see how much benefit was really being achieved. The assumption actually put the product into serious quality problems during test in the current release.

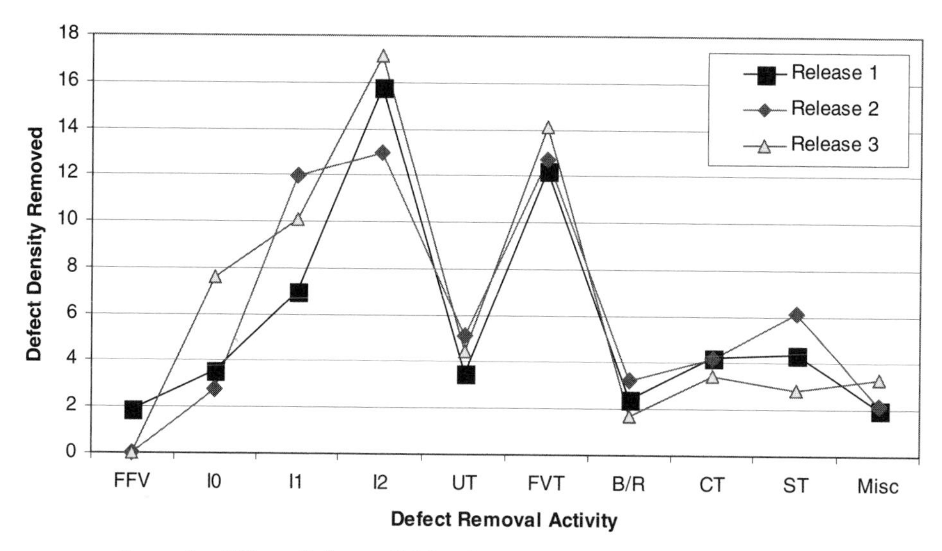

Example of Three Releases Of One Product Using Inspections [RAD90]
Figure 9.30

Going bad can also mean that Inspections are not paying off as well as expected. Shirey at HP stated that in 1990 a comprehensive review of post release critical and serious defects showed that product quality was not increasing. Further, there had been no appreciable shortening of project duration. [SHI92] This was found after extensive use of Inspections.

Shirey's article demonstrates the essence of maintaining effectiveness: consistent review of the data and results. Review after the fact, as in Shirey's case, can reveal a regression, but it is far better to listen to the process signals during the project to offset regression. Control charts and other data analysis techniques as described in Chapter 6 provide suggestions for real-time analysis of data to control effectiveness.

9.22 How Long Will It Take To Be Successful?

The answer varies based on whether one is trying to have success in one organization or across a company with multiple and varying types of organizations. We saw that the VTAM study demonstrated success within a few months and that the results established quick acceptance and deployment across the organization. Other organizations in IBM were equally successful in short periods. Yet, it took many years for most of IBM to apply Inspections, and there never was application in all organizations.

AT&T and HP applied Inspections across a large company and both took a number of years to get full adoption. Grady in his 1994 article on widespread Inspection use in HP, gives us a clear view of obstacles, stages of transition, and time required for broad application of a technology. [GRA94] First he shows that adoption of a technology goes through four classical stages.

The Experimental Stage at HP lasted between 1976-82, Initial Guidelines Stage between 1983-89, Widespread Belief and Adoption 1989-93, and Standardization Stage followed. This is a 17-year cycle, which has been seen in other technology adoptions across large populations. See Redwine [RED85] and Rogers [ROG83] where it is suggested that a typical cycle can be anywhere between 10-25 years.

The Experimental Stage provided the following insights:

- Initial use depends heavily on visionary people
- A risk-averse environment will not lead in change
- Early success is fragile; a supporting infrastructure is needed

The Initial Guidelines Stage revealed:

- Communicating success speeds adoption and improvement
- Clear definition of responsibility speeds adoption
- Management training contributes to strong, sustained sponsorship
- Goals tied to business challenges help ensure sponsorship
- Readily available training is necessary

The Widespread Belief and Adoption stage was a "blitz campaign to promote inspections and the new training class across HP." During this stage it was further learned:

- Training and guidelines are not sufficient; consulting with objectives tailored to divisions is also required
- Few divisions can start with an optimal process
- Good management process metrics are necessary

From these efforts HP saw a ROI greater than 10 in the first and subsequent years. Despite all the positive results HP still only had 26.2% adoption by 1993. Why not 100% we might ask.

Grady suggests it is due to the adoption time frame across large organizations, and he may be right. He states, "It has taken HP more than 15 years to reach this point, and we feel we still have almost 80% of the benefit to gain!" His data suggests he is right. However, in IBM we were successful within less than a 9 months from startup, including the definition of the Inspection process, to completion of the case study with the development organization, but we were one organization and one project.

Fortunately for smaller organizations or one-shop locations, the time to adopt is much shorter. There are fewer problems and fewer differences that must be addressed.

In Bull we mandated Inspections across locations and countries and were remarkably successful in getting all units to use Inspections though with different degrees of effectiveness. In a private note, Weller states that at SATCOM, "after the management edict, within 6 months the organization was fully engaged." So where there's a will, there's a way.

Standardization across diverse locations is always difficult and when units are given the choice to use or not use a new technology, it seems to take more time and may never be completed. My personal view is that when a technology is proven a company should use both a stick and carrot approach. And sometimes they may need to also hit with a big carrot. All the requirements should be addressed to train, facilitate, consult, convince, and hold hands, but forcing can accelerate adoption. It starts with commitment at the top and continues with commitment in all units if adoption is to be accelerated. Once the business value is understood, only management is at fault for late adoption, and sometimes some of the management should be taken out of the loop.

9.23 Prevention, Appraisal, and Failure Costs

The following elements in a software project are similar to Crosby's breakout of the three areas of Cost of Quality. It would be a useful exercise to learn what these costs are in your organization.

PREVENTION COSTS

"Prevention costs are the cost of all activities undertaken to prevent defects in design and development, purchasing, labor, and other aspects of beginning and creating a product or service. Also included are those preventive and measurement actions conducted during the business cycle." [CRO79]

Examples for software in no particular order include:

- Technical reviews
- Self-checking
- PSP-TSP practices
- Process definition

- Process assessments
- Defining release criteria for acceptance testing
- Quality standards
- Training
- Process improvements
- Causal analysis
- Related data recording
- Reporting of results
- Defect Prevention meetings
- Sub-contractor evaluations

APPRAISAL COSTS

"These are costs incurred while conducting Inspections, tests, and other planned evaluations used to determine whether produced hardware, software, or services conform to their requirements. Requirements include specifications from marketing and customer, as well as engineering documents and information pertaining to procedures and processes. All documents that describe the conformance of the product or service are relevant." [CRO79]

Examples for software in no particular order include:

- Prototypes
- Testing at all levels
- Software quality assurance
- Inspections
- Reviews of any type
- Status measurement and reporting
- Product quality audits
- Go-No go decision analysis
- Regression testing
- Defect analysis
- Related data recording
- Sub-contractor audits
- Software Quality Assurance

FAILURE COSTS

"Failure costs are associated with things that have been found not to conform or perform to the requirements, as well as the evaluation, disposition, and consumer-affairs aspects of such failures. Included are all materials and labor involved. Occasionally a figure must be included for lost customer credibility." [CRO79]

Examples for software in no particular order include:

- Consumer affairs
- Pre-release defect management
- Rework
- Re-reviews
- Retest of fixes
- Re-engineering
- Operations support for retesting
- Post-release technical support
- Compliant investigation
- Defect notification
- Remedial upgrades
- Fixes
- Debugging
- Defect analysis
- Related data recording
- Reporting of results
- Concessions to customers
- Product liability

End Quote:

"Quality is free. It's not a gift, but it's free. What costs money are the unquality things — all the actions that involve not doing the jobs right the first time."
Philip Crosby

CHAPTER 10
MANAGING INSPECTIONS

"Your taste in music is excellent. It exactly coincides with my own."
King Henry to Sir Thomas More in A Man For All Seasons

10.1 Introduction

This chapter is about the manager's role in Inspections, and it is especially written to the Project Lead. But since the management's role is important to the success of Inspections, it should be of interest to anyone interested in Inspections

As we have seen in Chapters 4 and 5, there are different roles and responsibilities that make Inspections successful. None, however, are as significant to the success of Inspections as that of management. Even though we generally exclude them from participating in Inspections, they will set the context for consistent and effective performance. They are responsible for setting the values and expectations for the performance of Inspections. While they should empower the organization members to fulfill Inspection performance, management can easily spoil the broth through indifference, misunderstanding, or negligence.

Management at all levels is a primary factor in the success or failure of Inspections in organizations.

Sometimes it is difficult for senior management to require their organization to practice Inspections. I have seen this so often that I wondered if there was a repeating reason why this was true. I often found that these managers did not have a completely thought out vision or strategy. When they do, they have no problem seeing that Inspections could help them achieve the vision and they quickly bring Inspections into their strategy for achieving that vision.

Above all the senior management must not be hesitant with Inspections. Senior management is responsible for the success or failure of the organization, and they are chartered to control costs, if not improve quality. Inspections will aid both. The literature and experiences are just too much in evidence now. Senior management must be bold in requiring Inspections. Middle management and Project Leads are then responsible for carrying through on the deployment. They should not be tentative. The organization needs to take action that fulfills the vision. To do otherwise is to be remiss in carrying out management duties.

Good management is necessary to the success of any business, but leadership is absolutely essential. Leadership in the context of Inspections is often demonstrated by supporting the practice of Inspections, even when the organization is resisting. For Inspections to be successful in the best of ways, we need both management and leadership. We need leadership to set the direction and management to carry out the direction. Hopefully some of the organization managers have both leadership and management capabilities.

Management must:

- Establish policy
- Commit
- Provide funding and resources
- Set and require goals
- Monitor progress
- Take action to achieve goals
- Provide feedback
- Adhere to principles

In this chapter I will also discuss the Inspection Coordinator's role in Section 10.9, Software Quality Assurance's (SQA) role in Section 10.10, and the Inspection Champion's role in Section 10.11, as these are other important roles in managing Inspections to success.

10.2 Policy

Together with the necessary organization leadership, management is responsible for establishing the culture and values of behavior in the organization, which includes Inspections. Management must understand and communicate the value of Inspections.

Culture, behavior, and value can all be reflected in a policy statement that management makes to the organization. Since the policy represents values it is more than a piece of paper. It is what management and the organization will hold to be true regardless of the circumstances. Figure 10-1 shows an example of a policy statement for Inspections.

While it is important that the policy statement be documented, it is essential that it be a thought through value statement. The paper by itself is a reference, a baseline, but the way it was created should reflect the value it states.

It is appropriate for the senior manager, who should be providing leadership and not just another level of management, to be involved in defining and stating the policy. It rarely seems to work well when senior management rubber stamps a policy written by someone else in the organization.

For the policy to be treated seriously, the management at all levels needs to reinforce it whenever appropriate, not just when it is on the agenda of some department meeting.

INSPECTION POLICY

It Is the goal of XYZ Company to continuously improve the ways we develop our products and to grow our business in the marketplace. In order to understand our capability in meeting these goals we need to produce and deliver products with high quality.

To help achieve the quality that our clients and we desire, we will use Inspections to identify and remove defects as early as possible in the production cycle.

To this end we will inspect all work products created during the production of software. Exceptions can be granted based on quantitative analysis demonstrating low risk when the Inspection is not to be performed.

XYZ will provide the environment for safe Inspections for all individuals with necessary facilities, training, and management support.

While metrics will be gathered from Inspections these are solely Intended to measure and to help us improve the processes we use during the development of a product, not to evaluate the performance of individuals. All metrics will be collected and combined so that they are personally non-threatening and non-evaluative.

Example of an Inspection Policy
Figure 10.1

10.3 Commitment

Management often believes it has demonstrated commitment by stating that they believe in the value, that they want the organization to practice Inspections, and then signing the policy statement. While these words and actions are expected, more important is how management continues to demonstrate the commitment. The words are helpful, but actions will speak louder. Good words are too often contradicted by some action to the contrary.

As the cliché says, management must "walk the talk." The proof of this will be constantly under test until the organization has developed the culture for Inspections. People will look for signals that say other than the words, and some signals can destroy the Inspection intent all too quickly. Sometimes management may not even be aware they are sending contradictory signals, but personnel and especially middle management will test the adherence to fidelity and look for cracks in the policy. Middle management, also known as the management black hole when change is being introduced, will say the right words, but as soon as they see senior management wavering, they begin to slip away and eventually the jump will be made.

Management, unless of strong conviction, can benefit by help from supporting managers and supporting infrastructures; e.g., SEPG and SQA, within the organization. The potential to see erosion in commitment is a further reason why a policy must reflect the value management expects from Inspection performance. Once stated, the policy can become a conscience to keep management focused. Stating the policy publicly will tend to make the commitment deeper.

Management can accelerate acceptance in the organization by showing encouragement to early adopters and by providing guidance should there be a mistake or some stumble in application, and there will be. Reinforcement of values can be made by stating the belief and the value when opportunity allows, by setting goals for organization performance, and by having a policy statement that is not a rubber stamp or motherhood statement.

Management can also destroy the commitment by not requiring Inspections to be an integral part of everyone's job. Or as Lee stated, "Failure to treat support of the inspection process as a major job responsibility of employees sends the message that inspection is relatively unimportant. And if programmers know that they are evaluated only on the development of their own specific product, they are less likely to be supportive of inspections for others' products." [LEE97] But there is no option, and there should be no allowance or impression that there is an option. If so, the option will be taken and this will work against successful Inspections.

Once the sound commitment is provided and passes the test of time, then the implementation will proceed with success.

10.4 Providing Funding and Resources

"Money talks" skeptics will sometimes tell us. Well in fact they are right.

If management simply expects the project teams to make Inspections happen without understanding that 1) training must be given and 2) resources must be allocated in project plans, then major risks to the success of Inspections are created at the very start.

In Chapter 2 when I discussed the ETVX process paradigm, it was noted that if the entry conditions are not sufficiently satisfied, the tasks are at risk in performance. Resources are a necessary entry condition and it is management's responsibility to get these assigned. The team members cannot assign them. Let's take a look at resource considerations Project Leads must make.

EARLY PLANS AND ALLOCATIONS

Resources must be identified in project plans at the start of the project. They are a reflection of the commitment to do Inspections.

Scheduling occurs in two phases typically:

1. Inspections types must be identified and planned in the initial project plan, and the required effort resources must be identified, allocated, and reflected in the early plans.
2. As the project evolves the detail schedules and plans should be updated to identify when work products will be inspected, including that the resources are allocated.

If Inspections are not included in the initial project plan definition, they will be scheduled only with difficulty later in the project's life. If not planned early, this can become an excuse for not doing them. If you do not know how much you may need, make assumptions with contingencies. Make use of the experience from the literature for how much you may need. Start now, even without your own history and experience. Don't wait until you have "the data." You can start even if in the middle of a project. It will always be best to start from the beginning, but you may have long duration projects, so why wait.

TRAINING

I've discussed it a number of times, but training is essential for good Inspections. If inspectors are not trained or do not know how Inspections are to be performed, they will go through a meeting and call it an Inspection. They won't know any better. The so-called Inspection may look more like a walkthrough, and effectiveness, among other concerns, will suffer. Then Inspections will be abandoned as something "we tried and it didn't work."

Management must ensure proper and effective training. If the programmers complain about the training, management must determine if it is the trainer, training material, or just Inspection start up complaints. If the latter, do the best to keep the programmers focused on objectives and admit to the learning curve. If it is the former two, make needed changes and demonstrate to your people that you are listening to them.

ENSURING TIMELINESS OF SCHEDULED INSPECTIONS

While it is essential to plan for all Inspections on any project, the actual scheduling cannot occur until work products are ready to be inspected. At the beginning of the project there can be an approximation or expected timeframe where an Inspection instance may occur, but the detailed schedule can only be known later. Therefore it is necessary that management track the project using the defined and current plan. While this tracking is proceeding, the Project Lead should look to the immediate next few weeks to understand when Inspections may be needed. When this is done, the Moderator can be appointed and the actual scheduling can proceed as the work product becomes completed.

The schedules should be timely; otherwise they may either not happen or not happen properly. The latter may be more disconcerting, since the Inspection team will invest time but may not find enough defects. They will go through the motions and the results will be disappointing.

Then they may begin to believe that Inspections are not effective, when in fact insufficient management scheduling contaminated the process.

It can sometimes happen that a Producer is reluctant to say the work product is ready for Inspection. This could be for a number of reasons:

- It really is not ready
- The Producer wants more time to make it "better"
- The Producer is the type who will never be done

All of these must be managed. The first and best way to mange is for the Project Lead to maintain steady contact with the Producers on status during the weeks prior to a planned Inspection. During this time, the Project Lead must try to determine if the Inspection date should be moved out, especially when the work product really cannot be ready. The Project Lead must also analyze why it was not ready and do some causal analysis to try to prevent future occurrences.

In the situations where the Producer is ready enough but wants more time, the Project Lead must decide whether a postponement will lead to a better work product without affecting other commitments. These can be difficult decisions, as the Producer may feel he is being forced into an Inspection. The Project Lead should remind the Producer that it is OK if defects are found, and that together the Project Lead and Producer can suggest process improvements that will make future work products less defective, but that the Inspection should proceed. Hopefully this will work, but be prepared to handhold some Producers who may be shy of the Inspection process. For the Producer who is never done, the Project Lead simply must set a cut-off date.

The Project Leads should keep data and report on how often these situations occur. Over time there should be a discernable trend that shows improvement in work products being ready as planned, so the scheduling can proceed according to plan.

A corollary to consider is that when the schedule gets tight the Project Lead should not cause Inspections to be cancelled or pressure the teams to inspect faster. Changes in schedules may be warranted when a work product is not ready. Simply canceling an Inspection versus postponement is not a valid option if one wants Inspections to be successful. Any cancellation should be tracked, made visible, discussed, and action taken to improve.

PLAN BASED ON SUGGESTED RATES

Planning should follow the suggested rates in the software community, when you do not have your own yet established. (See Chapter 3: The Inspection Process) As the organization develops its own experiences and data, the rates should be adjusted. Russell suggests that the time for Inspections is "Days = 3 times n KLOC." [RUS91] These are days in the schedule, but not full days of Inspections. If you find you need this, it is a lot of time, so plan for it.

The actual number of days will vary based on the rates of Preparation and Inspection and how much overlap can be managed. We have known since the VTAM study that Preparation is essential to success. Various studies have consistently confirmed this precondition. For example; "The study also concluded that inspections and reviews could be even more effective if inspectors were better prepared." [FOW86] So ensure that inspectors have sufficient time to prepare. I sometimes suggest during early use that the Project Leads ask each participant if they have had enough time to prepare. If not, postpone the Inspection and send the signal that you want Inspections done well, not just done. This reinforces the organization's commitment to Inspections and belief in their value.

KEEPING PLANS AND SCHEDULES VISIBLE

Planning and scheduling of Inspections, including results, should be discussed and tracked at project status meetings. This visibility sends a positive reinforcement to the organization. This is especially important early in the adoption curve. The frequency and length of these discussions can be adjusted after the organization has demonstrated institutionalization of Inspections. But they should always be discussed during project status meetings since they are a necessary task for a successful project and as I've discussed can be as much as 8-20% of project resources. Management should want to know how well these resources are used.

When the project team members see visible commitment and allocation of resources, they know that management is serious about Inspections.

ASSIGNING THE RIGHT PEOPLE

Inspections work best when the right people are made available to participate. One individual must always be made available and that is the Producer. Without the Producer an Inspection can be wasted effort. We'll see later in Chapter 14 that even in Solo:Inspections, the inspector must have access to the Producer when necessary.

Other people who have experience and domain knowledge of the work product being inspected should also be made available. This is not always possible; e.g., when the Producer is the only person with domain knowledge. In this case, provide good practical inspectors who can ask common sense questions when they don't understand something in the work product. Don't just put any available bodies into an Inspection. The selection of inspectors requires discussion among the Producer, Moderator, and Project Lead.

Where the Project Lead is the one who selects the Moderator; e.g., when an Inspection Coordinator or SEPG is not in place, try to equitably rotate the Moderator role.

The Moderator should not be a full time assignment. While it sometimes appears that this is practical, sometimes the full time Moderators are personnel who are viewed as not being able to contribute anywhere else. Putting the bottom staff in as Moderators and especially as full time assignments will work against organization buy-in and acceptance. In turn this will put the success of Inspections at risk.

It will be difficult to always put the best people into Moderator positions. Part of the answer is to not make Moderators a full time assignment. Create a pool of Moderators; again not just with the bottom staff. Give everyone a shot at being a Moderator. There may be some pleasant surprises. I have seen organizations where some of the star technical people want to moderate, but of course not full time. Use the best technical people as Moderators or Readers on the most critical work products undergoing Inspections; e.g., Requirements specifications, key functions in High-level design.

TOOLS AND DATABASES

Today it is no longer acceptable to perform Inspections without tools for data entry, analysis, and report generation. Fortunately much of what is needed is readily available with software such as EXCEL, ACCESS, or other spread sheet and database products.

Web-based input is easy today and there is no longer an excuse to not provide this environment to the programmers for use with Inspections. Forms are easily created and transfer of information and communication is almost as easy as turning on the system. With all web-based solutions, the screens should be easy to use and self evident to the users.

PROCESS DEFINITION

Process standards need to be defined and understood. If they exist or are borrowed from another organization, then they need to be communicated as being required. Of course, they should be reviewed to assure applicability before use. Standards are a precondition to effective Inspections. The responsibility for formulating the process standards may fall to the SEPG or SQA.

Management should understand that process standards are necessary and must require that standards be available and used.

I've discussed the entry criteria and one is that the work product to be inspected needs some standard, guideline, template or procedure defining what it should look like and what it should contain. If none of these exist, the Inspection can only be faulty at best. This does not mean that Inspections should be put off until the precondition is fully satisfied, as this will be an excuse to never start. Rather, management must:

- Support the development of these standards, guidelines etc.
- Understand that the Inspections will not be highly effective until the issue is addressed
- Permit the Inspection process results on both product defects and process defects to be used to improve this situation

If nothing exists, don't let the programmers flounder. Start by giving some criteria that must be satisfied for format and content of work products. Then improve and evolve.

Start with informal procedures etc., then evolve and improve them. The key is how well the programmers know what needs to be done, not how well it is documented. If there is a good understanding then begin with whatever informal procedures exist, but don't delay the practice of Inspections until the procedures are documented. This is process backwards. If what is being practiced is sufficiently correct, document it and keep it simple.

PROVIDING LOGISTIC SUPPORT

Logistic support, while less emotionally charged, if absent, can defeat or delay good Inspections. Mostly logistics will mean making space available for teams to perform the Inspections. Conference rooms usually make the best choice, but they may not always be available. Inspections can be performed in any space that permits a team of inspectors to discuss the work product and defects without being interrupted or interrupting others. Office and cafeteria spaces have been used. Library space has been used. When Inspections become institutionalized, it is not uncommon to see teams using the senior manager's office when she is out of town.

It is an excellent signal about commitment when a manager makes their office available for an Inspection. The team will get the message. Over time, the team should be given the option of using any office for Inspections when the resident is out of office. While offices should be respected as private spaces, they are company resources and should be considered when needed.

Rooms can be difficult to use when participants are in different locations. In these cases, video or telephone conferences for the Inspection Meeting may be an acceptable choice. While these alternatives have their own problems, they do work and can be as good as face-to-face Inspections. The Moderator should make this decision with the Project Lead. The participants should be canvassed to get their opinions, and the team should definitely ask at the end of the meeting whether there should be a Re-Inspection due to insufficient logistics.

10.5 Take Action To Achieve Goals

Inspections will not always proceed according to plan and even if they did there will be problems found during Inspections. Corrective actions will be required and it is management's responsibility to review the data, the progress, and the results and then to take the appropriate actions. To do less is to let the Inspection process fly without a management pilot for the project. The success or failure of Inspections will always be related to the management on the project and in the organization. When Inspections succeed, management enables the success. When Inspections fail, management is the cause.

SETTING GOALS

The goals for Inspections are to do them and do them well, but management should set goals specific to the organization that are:

- Quantifiable

- Performable
- Time based
- Consistent with other priorities and goals
- Focused on effectiveness and efficiency
- Managed

These elements are part of every Project Management book or training. For Inspections these translate into:

- Require Inspections (goal); e.g., how many and when
- Require that Inspections be planned into the project with sufficient resources and visibility
- Track how many Inspections occur per the plan
- Take corrective action when the plan is not being followed
- Support improvements as the data may suggest
- Ensure data is used to set goals for Inspection process performance

It starts with goals linked to the business objectives. At the highest level, the organization goals are to use Inspections and to see improvement in quality, productivity, and schedules. At a project level these same types of goals apply, but the specifics will vary based on project dynamics and domains.

As I discussed in Chapters 6 and 9, some goals are important to achieve effectiveness; e.g., we should know how well Inspections are proceeding according to planned rates for Preparation and the Inspection Meeting. During early use, these goals most likely will not be met as much as desired. The important next step is to do the analysis and provide the feedback to the project members for improvement. I suggest looking for convergence toward plans for the goal areas noted above. If it is occurring, celebrate with your team. If convergence is not occurring, more improvement is needed.

10.6 Monitor Progress

Monitoring progress starts with monitoring the data to ensure it has integrity. The Project Leads should review the data submitted and check that data has not been incorrectly entered. This does not mean that all entries must be reviewed, but the summations and outliers should all be checked to assure that they are not outliers based on bad data entry. Relationships between data entries should also be reviewed to help ensure integrity.

Senior and middle management should periodically monitor progress at project status meetings. During early application these reviews should be monthly and then the frequency can be adjusted over time after Inspections are meeting goals.

An area to keep in mind as you proceed, especially during early use is to understand the difference between a good Inspection and a good product under Inspection. There will be times when a good work product is produced and no defects or few defects are found. Management should get the team to be aware of these good work product examples and have the team ask how the quality can be repeated in future work products.

Progress may also be demonstrated through soft metrics, which would be readily understood by all affected, for example, how many meetings occur in the evenings, how much money is spent on pizzas, etc. These happen in organizations that have no other known choice but to work hard, long hours to deliver products. It doesn't have to be that way. Inspections will help change this situation. They can't change everything, but given a fair chance they'll affect everything.

The Project Lead should define with the Quality Assurance function how and when the Inspection process would be audited and reviewed. This agreement includes the role that SQA may have in the Inspection process.

Management should survey the project personnel regarding the effectiveness of Inspections and should actively solicit from the team members how inspections can be improved. The success that can come from these team surveys during project status reviews can be immediate by tuning the process to make it more effective in removing defects.

10.7 Feedback

When an organization is in the midst of change, it is important that continuous feedback be given to all players. When feedback is insufficient, personnel get confused either by contradicting messages or rumors. When Inspections are being deployed, it is necessary to keep everyone aware of the successes that are being seen. Nothing will breed success faster than keeping everyone aware of the early successes.

The results when quantified will be more objective and therefore less debated by the cynics or critics that exist in all organizations.

10.8 Inspection Principles for Managers

While the items we have discussed so far in this chapter are all part of the success of Inspections, there are a number of principles that management must always keep in mind. When these principles are not maintained, erosion or misapplication will occur and will defeat the value of Inspections.

MANAGING INSPECTIONS VERSUS EXECUTING THEM

Management should try to manage the project and give the team the resources they need to do their jobs. When management insists on being in Inspections or is required in an Inspection for it to be successful, then management may not be allowing the project programmers to do the job and learn. In the 1970's, when Inspections first started, management was more often distant from the technical work than it is today. It is less true today, where Project Leads are also often key technical contributors to the project. So we do not want to necessarily exclude management from all Inspections, but we don't want the success to be always determined by management participation. When the technical team believes that a technical Project Lead can help and invites them to an Inspection, the Project Lead should attend just as any other inspector.

Management simply cannot be at all Inspections. They can, where needed, participate, but the results of Inspections with and without management should average about the same measured effectiveness. If they do not and where the management has attended the Inspections and the effectiveness is significantly different, then management needs to look at the signals to understand what is being said about Inspection process performance. If the Project Lead is always the key contributor to successful Inspections, institutionalization of Inspection practices is not yet in place.

All Inspections benefit by having the right people, but if management are the only right people, there may be a problem. For example, the project may be too dependent on the Project Lead. Backup should be developed. If Inspections are significantly less effective when management attends, then the question that needs an answer is why. Are the teams intimidated? Do they fear that the defect count is too high? These are times where we must ask why management should be at Inspections.

ATTENDING INSPECTIONS

There will be situations where a Project Lead will be the best choice as a participant; e.g., they have the most knowledge based on domain experiences, they have just recently become the Project Lead but were the technical lead before. In these cases it seems foolish to exclude them, but the Inspection team should know that this is an exception.

Now the harder question: Should it be the exception? Looking at this from a different perspective: Why should Project Leads not be technical? When the original Inspection method was put together, there was intent to keep Project Leads managing schedules, resources, and personnel issues and not actively working on the technical solution. This is still true today in organizations where the projects are large or where the Project Lead has too many people to manage. There are always non-technical management tasks that assigned Project Leads must perform on a project. But on some, especially smaller projects, the technical tasks that Project Leads are assigned often take precedence. Should we leave these Project Leads out of Inspections?

I think this would be senseless, but that means we are asking that the Project Lead and the inspectors feel comfortable that Inspection results will not be used in negative ways regarding Producer performance. In many projects, the team may already be in that state of acceptance. Where they are not, they should proceed with caution and understand the risk. This is a situation where an independent Inspection Coordinator can facilitate the objective of keeping the data safe even when the Project Lead attends. Sometimes all that's needed is for the Inspection Coordinator to remind the Project Lead. Keep in mind, however, that it is in situations like these that Inspections have had a higher risk of failure.

When it is clear these "exceptions" are working well, then the process should be modified to acknowledge when they should be used.

KEEPING COMMUNICATION CHANNELS OPEN

Management must listen to the team and must send a clear message about Inspections. When the team suggests that Inspections can be improved, management should listen and explore possible improvements. But they need to keep in mind to stay the course since the process has been proven for so many others. Do not change the process simply due to issues and complaints. Rather, try to discover why the issues and complaints exist. Then appropriate improvements should be tried, but not all at once. Take steps rather than jumps. Build upon what works.

The team has a responsibility to use the process and provide input based on experiences where the process was followed. Management has the responsibility to listen to the results. Together the team and management can then tune the defined process that will best work for them.

DO NOT APPRAISE BASED ON INSPECTIONS

Never attend an Inspection to gather information as input for a performance review. If this purpose is even suggested, the behavior at Inspections will change, so management will learn almost nothing useful. If management does attend as a team member and later uses that experience during an appraisal, the integrity of the Inspection process will deteriorate.

Management must never appraise, promote, reward, demote, reprimand, or call any individual to task based on the number of defects found during an Inspection. There are too many variables, including management itself that can lead to a high defect discovery rates.

Management must reinforce that it is always preferable to find defects earlier rather than later. Management must make the defect discovery processes with Inspections safe for all participants.

You may ask how can management do this when it is obvious that a team member is injecting more defects than is acceptable. Management is responsible for developing an environment where individuals can learn how to improve and for reinforcing the concept that improvement is desirable. When this environment is created, individuals will improve their skills and learn how to reduce the defect volume going into Inspections. This environment will not occur at the introduction of Inspections in an organization, but management must focus on it as the desire and intent right from the start.

There are a few cases I've learned of where management will evaluate team members based on the number of defects found in system test under the view that the Inspections will become more effective and fewer defects will leak to system test. I have personally never used this approach and suggest that if it is used that, at a minimum, the team be in consensus with the management for this approach. There are aspects that I like about this approach, but it is fraught with land mines. If you do use it and it works, let the rest of us know about it.

MAKING BEHAVIOR CLEARLY UNDERSTOOD

Management must clearly state the policy for Inspections and the desired goals to be reached with Inspections. Management must ensure that the behavior during practice is fully aligned with the policy, goals, and process definition. Management must reward expected behavior and help the team members learn when mistakes are made. While none of us want to make mistakes when introducing Inspections, we would do worse to not learn from any mistakes that do occur. Reward does not necessarily mean monetary reward, but acknowledging expected behavior and results.

PRESSURE TO MET THE SCHEDULE

The team will be under pressure to get the work done, but sometimes a schedule goes bad. There may not have been enough resources or not enough time and the delivery date for the work product is approaching. The team may naturally choose to skip an Inspection or perform it more in name than in spirit. If management condones this behavior, it will happen more and more.

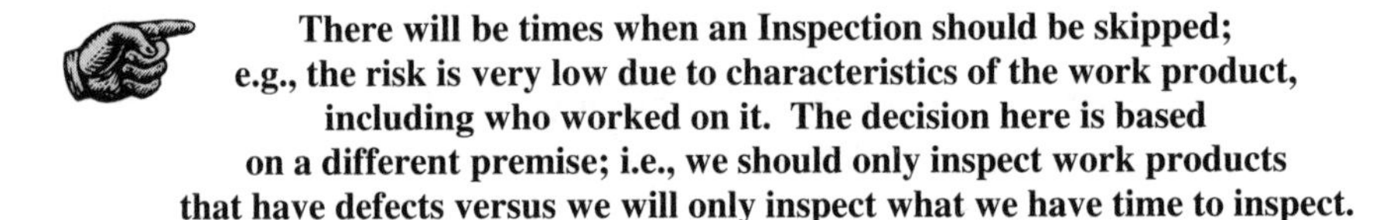

There will be times when an Inspection should be skipped; e.g., the risk is very low due to characteristics of the work product, including who worked on it. The decision here is based on a different premise; i.e., we should only inspect work products that have defects versus we will only inspect what we have time to inspect.

On the other hand, it can be hard to do, but management needs to put the cards on the table when a schedule or target date is perceived as only achievable by skipping an Inspection. The Project Lead may feel they are taking the heat when a date must be slipped and they may not want this public. Tough! Analyze why the slip occurred, suggest corrective and remedial actions, or get out of management. Show upper management that there is a way to do better in the future.

SHOWING COMMITMENT AND ENCOURAGEMENT

Successful Inspections are directly related to strong management support. So management must show its commitment even when under pressure. There are many things that should be done to support the stated commitment, but unfortunately management only needs to backslide on any one and people will begin to believe that the commitment was not real. This is hard on management, but people tend to look for the cracks and then they expand them, so the message of commitment must be constant and consistent.

There will be problems in practice. So help the team members to learn from these and move forward. Constancy of commitment will enable success. Encourage the Moderators and teams to make the right decisions, especially when an Inspection should be postponed or a Re-Inspection is recommended.

TAKING CORRECTIVE ACTIONS

When Inspections are not meeting expected goals, management must try to understand why this is occurring and then take corrective action. Management cannot accept that Inspections are not working as well as expected and do nothing to change this. The literature has amply demonstrated that Inspections work, so if the organization is not meeting objectives, management should learn why. If they cannot solve the issues in-house, then they should look at possibilities to bring in consultants from the outside who have demonstrated successes with Inspections. In this case consultants are well worth their cost.

Regardless of how management tries to address the issues with corrective actions, they must never give in and accept less than what can be done. To yield to less than what can be achieved with Inspections is to accept defeat.

NOT QUESTIONING POOR RESULTS

When Inspection results are outside of expected boundaries of performance, the team should be bringing management recommendations for Re-Inspections or process change. If they do not, then there should be a clear rationale why no actions are required. Never bet that no tuning or improvement actions will be required when first starting up Inspections.

If the team brings management input for action, then management must act. If no actions are brought to management, then the results of the Inspections must be reviewed if not questioned. To do otherwise will reinforce wrong behavior in the future. To question will reinforce expected behavior.

NOT SUPPORTING POSTPONED INSPECTIONS

This sounds easy to commit to, but then the hard part comes when a work product is recommended by the Moderator to be postponed for valid Inspection process reasons and the work product is on a key path for delivery into the next project activity. Management will be under pressure to "manage the situation." Too often this becomes making a decision that countermands all the support and commitment that management claimed up to this point. Be careful not to shoot the messenger or the principles of Inspections. Take the hint and support the decision to postpone.

OVER RIDING INSPECTOR'S JUDGMENT

When the team makes a recommendation for a Re-Inspection and management overrides this, the team needs an explanation. If management can show minimal risk in the overriding of the recommendation, this can be OK. If, however, management simply overrides without explanation, the team will have been given the signal to not recommend Re-Inspections in the future.

SELECTIVE INSPECTIONS FOR SOME PRODUCERS

Management may choose to hold Inspections for only some Producers. This could smack of being selective, and sends a message that some Producers either cannot be trusted or they make defective products, so be careful. Sometimes selection is warranted; e.g., when new people join an organization. But be careful when only a few people always must have their work inspected. If their work really is error-prone, then other actions may be warranted.

MANAGEMENT PREROGATIVE

This problem can show up in absurd ways that will kill Inspections. For example, management believes they have first rights to conference rooms, and while they have meetings and work that may need a conference room, they should be careful to not misuse this "prerogative." If a team is overrunning on Inspection time and using a conference room that management has next, don't just throw them out or confront them. See if there are alternatives that you can work with first.

If it is necessary that the team shut down and yield the room, they should decide whether they can continue and close somewhere else or if the meeting should be re-scheduled.

10.9 Inspection Coordinator

Someone should coordinate the Inspections within the organizations. The Project Lead should be working with the Inspection Coordinator. If you already have an SEPG, they should be considered for this role. If you do not have an SEPG, then assign the Inspection coordination to someone who is motivated to make Inspections successful. If you are fortunate to have someone who has been championing Inspections, they may be the choice, unless the champion is the senior manager as we saw with the VTAM study. Normally the role of Inspection Coordinator should not be assigned to a manager anyway. Recall that we need management support but we want management to remain objective with the data. Distance will facilitate objectivity in most situations.

The coordination should be at the organization level and across all projects. If your project and organization are small, then the Project Lead may need to be the coordinator. This will present some problems in regard to distance, objectivity, and independence, but with a motivated Project Lead it can work. If it is working, the results will prove it.

Regardless of who is doing the coordinating, work should be performed before rolling out the Inspection process.

Before rollout, the coordinator may need to:

- Write a policy *with* management for senior management's signature
- Determine the degree of organization buy-in and resistance; i.e., know the territory before trying to deploy
- Write procedures
- Provide training
- Pick a pilot project when first starting Inspections

After a successful pilot, Inspections should be deployed across the other projects. This will take time and resources. In the meantime management must be visible throughout, until successful deployment, and for all future use. Pilots are necessary in large organizations, and are comparatively easier to bring to success than full deployment is.

After deployment, the Inspection Coordinator will remain busy working with Project Leads to properly plan for forthcoming Inspections, analyzing Inspection data, presenting the results to the organization, and making suggestions for improvements. During early use, the analysis should include interviews and surveys with participants to understand bottlenecks and examples of success.

The Inspection Coordinator should:

- Provide or acquire training
- Develop procedures, data templates, and the process data base
- Get management signoff on policy statement and direction
- Learn who is for and who is against Inspections
- Perform surveys from time to time
- Support, coach, and consult with the practitioners
- Gather the data
- Perform the analysis
- Present the feedback
- Wave the flag
- Allow management and practitioners to claim the success
- Create the organization Master plan for Inspections
- Monitor and improve the process

KEY TASKS

1. Captured data for each Inspection is compared to the organization's Inspection capabilities for, at a minimum:

    - Defects/KLOC
    - Hour-of-Inspection/Defect found

- KLOC-inspected/hour-of-Inspection
- Inspection effectiveness and efficiency compared to other defect removal activities

2. The Inspection capabilities will be determined after the Inspection process has been performed within the organization or project for a minimum of fifteen instances for each inspected type; e.g., code, detailed design, and test cases work products in the organization. Other work products will have capability determined across projects. Capabilities for all work product type will be reviewed and updated periodically.

3. The Inspection process in its totality will be monitored to ensure it continues to meet the business objectives of the organization and the effectiveness and efficiency of the Inspection process itself. A report on the Inspection process should be made periodically to senior management.

4. A Master Schedule for Inspections should be developed. While the Project Lead performs the original planning and allocation of resources, when the coordination role is assigned to someone other than the Project Lead, they will need to develop and maintain a Master Schedule. See Figure 10.2 for sample contents within a Master Schedule. This schedule would be created by the Project Lead as part of the Project Plan and provided to the Inspection Coordinator for continued use throughout the project's life cycle.

   In this example, the **Work Product Type** is a list of all work products by type that the project commits to inspect. The **Work Product Identifier** is a detailed list of all specific work products that will be inspected. Each has a unique identifier; e.g., module name, test case number, document name. Sometimes specific Work Product Identifiers cannot be determined at the start of a project, so Trigger Dates become useful to complete the details of the Master Schedule later during the project.

   The **Trigger Date** is posted in the Master Schedule for refinement or completion of the plan. This is the date by which a decision must be made to set a specific date for an Inspection. For example in Figure 10.2, Part 1 of the Requirements Specification triggers on 1/15/01, but it was planned that the Inspection date would be between 2/15/01 and 2/28/01. However, no later than 1/15/01, the actual scheduled date is triggered to be set.

   The **Planned Inside Date** is determined when the Project Plan is initially committed and represents the earliest probable date for a work product Inspection. The **Planned Outside Date** is the probable latest date that the Inspection would occur. The **Scheduled Date** is the firm committed date for the work product to be inspected. Not shown in this example is the **Actual Date**, which would be used for tracking of the planned schedule to actual Inspection performance.

   Also not shown in the Master Schedule are the sizes of the work products or the effort resources required. These would be included in the Project Plan.

Refer to Chapter 3 for further discussion about planning Inspections and scheduling Inspections.

Master Schedule Contents					
Work Product Type	**Work Product Identifier**	**Trigger Date**	**Planned Inside Date**	**Planned Outside Date**	**Scheduled Date**
Requirements Specification	Part 1	1/5/01	2/15/01	2/28/01	2/17-18/01
	Part 2	1/19/01	2/28/01	3/15/01	
High-level Design	Main Line	3/5/01	4/2/01		
	Subsystem 1	3/19/01			
	Subsystem 2	4/4/01			
Low-level design	Unit A	5/7/01			
	Unit B	5/7/01			
	Unit C	5/7/01			
	Unit D	5/7/01			
Code	Unit A	6/4/01			
	Unit B	6/4/01			
	Unit C	6/4/01			
	Unit D	6/4/01			

Sample Contents in a Master Schedule for Inspections
Figure 10.2

5. Conduct surveys of the Inspection participants and management.

The following is an example of what the Inspection Coordinator could ask participants using an anonymous survey:

1. Is adequate Inspection planning time provided? Yes? No? Please comment.
2. Is adequate Inspection Preparation time provided? Yes? No? Please comment.
3. If an Inspection is rescheduled, what is the most common cause?

   - Materials not ready
   - Participants not available
   - Management preempts the Inspection
   - Insufficient preparation
   - Other; please comment

4. When an Inspection is postponed, how do you feel?
5. How is a Re-Inspection decided?
6. Do you believe management sufficiently supports Inspections?
7. Do you see results that Inspections are helping? How do they help?
8. Would you like more feedback?

9. Comment on the Inspection forms: Easy to use? Need improvement? Where?
10. Are there situations where an Inspection should be skipped?
11. Can this be determined in advance using data or input? How?
12. How would you improve the Inspection process?

10.10 SQA Responsibilities

Software Quality Assurance (SQA) should review and/or audit the Inspection process to assure the process is being followed as required by projects in the organization. SQA may participate in some Inspections as Moderators or as an independent assurance role. In the latter case, their time should not be recorded for the Inspection but for SQA activities.

This role is written from the point of view that SQA is not coordinating the Inspections but assuring them. If SQA is also the coordinator for the organization then responsibilities as defined in Section 10.9 for the coordinator must be merged with those defined here. This description also assumes that SQA is separate and distinct from the SEPG.

Assurance of Inspections provides feedback to the organization that:

- It is practicing the Inspection process as defined
- Project plans sufficiently address Inspections
- Inspections are occurring according to plan
- Analysis of goals versus actuals are being addressed by the projects and organization with appropriate corrective actions
- Defect Prevention activities are practiced as defined
- Reports from SQA are provided periodically addressing concurrence or not with analysis provided by the coordinator
  - NOTE: This latter item can be a concern when SQA is the coordinator. In this situation an independent view must be provided to the organization
- Suggested actions are provided to the projects and organization regarding improvements in Inspections

KEY ACTIVITIES TO PERFORM

SQA will select Inspections to review and/or audit using a random approach to selection that provides coverage of Inspections performed across the organization. This can be performed as part of the internal audits performed by SQA or SQA representatives at Inspections. These reviews/audits are focused on the Inspection process to assure, for example:

- Work products are meeting defined standards
- Project plans sufficiently address Inspections
- Inspections occur per plan
- Inspections are performed according to the defined process
- Discovered defects are resolved and fixed
- Open Issues are documented for completion

10.11 Inspection Champion

History has demonstrated that when organizations starting with Inspections have an Inspections Champion, they make quick strides for success. A champion is someone who understands Inspections and believes with a passion that Inspections can help the organization achieve rapid improvement and reduce the costs to develop software.

It is does not always happen that an Inspection Champion takes up the gauntlet to make Inspection successful in an organization, and it is not possible to anoint someone to be a champion when they are not so inclined or motivated. But when they are available, organizations have far greater success in shorter acceptance timeframes. So seek them out.

Management's job is to endorse when a champion steps forward. Alternatively management must seek out the individual who will take on the role of sheparding success with Inspections. This could be the Inspection Coordinator, but can be two distinct roles. The Inspection Coordinator role persists in the organization throughout its use of Inspections, while the Inspection Champion is needed when first starting Inspections.

End Quote:

"Management gets what it Inspects, not what it expects."
Tom Gilb

CHAPTER 11

PRACTICAL ISSUES FOR SUCCESS

"In matters of style, swim with the current.
In matters of principle, stand like a rock."
Thomas Jefferson

11.1 Introduction

Throughout this book there are examples that I have discussed where Inspections have evolved to a higher effectiveness after modifying the original method based on demonstrated value, but there are countless examples in practice where doing something different has regressed Inspections. In these latter cases, as the Inspection process regresses and its effectiveness is not demonstrated, its value is put in question, and the downward spiral begins. Eventually those who used Inspections, but did not use them well question not only in form but also in principle the very process itself. The unfortunate situation in these cases is that neither the management team nor the technical team seems to be aware of what has caused the regression, nor how to reverse it. The pathology, once ingrained, becomes intolerable in its repercussions.

In many cases the regressions or ineffective use of Inspections could have been avoided by knowledge of common mistakes that others have made or by knowing what issues occur in Inspections and how to minimize their probability of occurrence.

In this chapter I will explore issues that if managed can lead to successful and more effective Inspections, including common issues that get repeatedly raised and which have led to failure and ineffective Inspections when they are not managed.

While I have discussed some of these issues earlier in the book, this chapter is a collection of some of the more significant issues to keep in mind when practicing Inspections.

11.2 Timing Issues

By now we have learned that if Inspections are to be most effective, sufficient time to perform them well is needed. Let's now look at some practical aspects to keep in mind about time for and during Inspections.

PREPARATION AND INSPECTION MEETINGS

Both Preparation and the Inspection Meetings need sufficient time if they are to be effective. There are recommended rates for Preparation and Inspection that the organization should have accepted or established to use. It is the Moderator's responsibility to ensure that these rates are met. When they are not, the Moderator must treat this information as a signal to probe the goodness of the Inspection. It is the Project Lead's responsibility to address chronic situations where the rates are not consistent with expected performance for Preparation and the Inspection Meetings.

While the overall pace may have been within the expected rates for an Inspection, the Moderator should assure that the pace is reasonably consistent throughout the Inspection Meeting. No meeting will have a fully consistent pace, but the Moderator and team should focus the meeting on the purpose and not get lost in social discussion, asides, or agendas that are not directly related to the intent of the meeting; i.e., to find defects.

REASONABLE LENGTH

The human mind has some limitations for endurance. Long Inspection Meetings are not effective. It has been traditionally suggested that about two hours maximum is reasonable for most participants. If more time is required to inspect the work product the Moderator should plan for this and should schedule two-hour chunks on consecutive days. While this may sound like it will slow down the completion of the Inspection, the alternative is to have defects leak into the next stages of the project. If a unit under Inspection requires more than two hours but less than four hours, the Moderator with the team can decide if holding the Inspection Meeting in one day with reasonable breaks can still be effective. If the team decides to proceed, the time should be noted in the report, and analysis should be made to learn the effectiveness of longer meetings.

SUBSETS

When chunks or subsets are chosen they should be broken at logical points. Do not choose only to do two hours when two and a half are a logical break point in the material under Inspection. The Moderator should make the decision with the Producer and then confirm with the participants at the start of the Inspection Meeting. If the meeting needs to be longer than 2 hours, breaks should be factored into the scheduling.

ENFORCING TIME LIMITS

Sometimes an Inspection Meeting may run longer than scheduled. This usually happens when either the volume of the work product is greater than planned or more defects than anticipated are found. The Moderator should bring this to the team's attention and they should make a decision. If they are close to finishing, they could easily proceed to finish. If too much more time is needed, they could adjourn at a logical point and resume on another day or take a break and continue the same day, but don't plod on and declare the Inspection completed.

BREAKS DURING INSPECTIONS

The original Inspections had a ten-minute break at about the halfway point. This was both effective and a relief to clear the minds of the inspectors. Often this break is not practiced. While there is no hard data that shows the lack of a break decreases effectiveness, there is no reason why breaks should not be scheduled. The team can make the decision for where the break point should be when the meeting begins. The Moderator should include breaks in the plan when using the rates for meeting time.

SCHEDULED TIMES

There is no one period in the work day that is best for all organizations to schedule an Inspection Meeting, but here are some periods to avoid: first thing in the morning, after normal quitting time, just after lunch. I suspect the reasons for not using these periods is self-evident.

11.3 When Is an Inspection Finished?

As discussed earlier there are three states in which an Inspection can be: Planned, Performed, or Closed, where:

- **Planned**, includes any time during the project's life cycle where the schedule has been defined for a required Inspection; it concludes with the Inspection Meeting start
- **Performed**, includes all times from the start of the Inspection Meeting through Re-work
- **Closed**, is only after Follow-up when closure has been achieved and signed-off

At one level it can be argued that an Inspection is done when it is Performed, but I suggest that an Inspection is not really done until it has reached the Closed state after the defects have been corrected and the Inspection data captured. The Moderator has exit criteria to help determine if these states have been achieved. The participants have checklists to help them determine if they have provided closure for defect detection.

11.4 Best Place to Start First

Any work product can be inspected. When first starting I suggest that requirements specifications, design, code, and user documents be inspected, in that order. In situations where the software is not safety-critical or life-critical, I also suggest that you try to choose what code not to inspect. This choice is best made based on data, but can be initially based on the group experience within the project team.

Should you wait for a new project before starting Inspections? No, you can do an Inspection when any work product is completed or even when it is partially completed.

You do not have to wait until a new project begins to implement successful Inspections. When we performed the first study of Inspections in 1972-74 in IBM, they were started when most of the product was already coded.

11.5 Can Some Work Products Not Be Inspected?

Yes, but the decision requires data that demonstrates minimal risk and good data requires time in practice. As will be discussed in Chapter 14: Inspections Future, there may be situations when we might even stop needing Inspections.

There will always be a temptation to put some work product aside. This is done with risk. On the practical side, can or should you inspect all code? The decision could vary with the type of software being produced. For safety-critical or life-critical software, you should not take the risk lightly, if at all.

It is also known that some programmers are very good at what they do and produce close to defect-free code. You could choose to not inspect their work if you had good experience that showed there was minimal risk. Unfortunately in most projects we have a limited set of these programmers. Be careful when using this criterion too early with Inspections. Over time, it may prove to be the right decision to not inspect a high performer's code, but not when first starting Inspections.

So the answer is yes, there are times when a work product need not be inspected, but be careful to manage the risks.

11.6 Who Are the Right Inspectors?

Are all people equally capable of contributing to the most effective Inspection Meeting? Well, we know this is not possible. A domain expert will be far more effective in finding defects than a novice. Experts, however, are not always available when we want them. For some situations the Inspection Meetings should be planned around the expert's availability. In other situations we should look for qualified substitutes.

Does this mean we should defer Inspections when the experts or next best person are not available? Surely we will try to find the next best fit for all Inspections. Nonetheless, for some work products, the answer could be yes; i.e. the Inspection will be deferred. For others, you can proceed, provided the inspectors can contribute to some level of effectiveness and know a defect when they see one. If they can't pass this test, the Inspection effectiveness will suffer significantly. Less capable inspectors may only be able to find a certain class of defects, while experts can find deeper defects, but they all can contribute to finding defects.

The decision should be based on risk and criticality of the work product. Here criticality is not just safety-critical or life-critical situations, but work products critical to the success of the project. If experts are not available and the decision is made to proceed, then use the resultant data to decide if a Re-Inspection is warranted when the experts are available. To hold an

Inspection for the sake of an Inspection does not make sense and will, in many cases, prove ineffective. Sometimes it is better to delay the Inspection until the right people are available.

11.7 Inspections Don't Make People Feel Warm Fuzzies

Inspections are rarely the most exciting task for programmers. They are necessary and they are useful, but they can be uninteresting. Therefore, we want to do all we can to make them as comfortable as possible, such as reasonable schedules and breaks. Some organizations even provide refreshments to the participants.

In the beginning of practice, some individuals will feel stress just because this is a different method, even if they don't admit it. I have actually seen people get tense and sweat not only during an Inspection but also during training when their work is used as the practice work product in training. Fortunately this does not occur often, but it does occur. Therefore, we must make Inspections safe by ensuring they are not used to appraise or judge people. We must go out of our way to keep the Inspection environment and results safe.

ANECDOTE

HOW MANY DEFECTS?

People learn and adapt very quickly to any fear at work. They compensate in many ways to avoid these uncomfortable situations. They may even change the data.

In one organization we found that Inspection teams had an unwritten policy to find defects, but not record the full amount. They bundled the number of defects into clusters. This was done to keep the countable number as low as possible, because they believed that's what management wanted to hear.

The result was data that lacked integrity. Oh, the defects were fixed, but the data analysis was defective.

Anecdote 11.1

11.8 Helping Programmers to Learn from Their Errors

If we allow the programmers to learn in a safe environment, they generally will learn. We may need to provide some additional training to some, but this is perhaps what we should be doing anyway. Not all programmers are equal in capability, but all can contribute to the project's success. As programmers learn, they will become more effective. This will show both in the performance of Inspections and during production of work products. Programmers will learn how to build it better and make it right. Furthermore, they will take more pride in their work and work environment. Of course there will be exceptions, but we should not normalize the organization to the exception conditions of those who are less capable.

11.9 Competence Paying for Incompetence

Sometimes I hear that Inspections are the price competent programmers pay for incompetence in others. This is such an egocentric attitude that it does not bear response.

ANECDOTE

A CONVERSION

I remember once, when one of the truly outstanding programmers in our project made no bones about his view that Inspections were a waste of time. He was someone that other technical people would look to for opinion on what to do. He was most definitely a technical leader with the respect of his peers. We felt that his attitude needed to be addressed. But how?

He was invited to an Inspection of someone else's code. We decided to ensure that the Inspection team and Moderator were among the best and most motivated. You could say we rigged the team, but not the material. We had no way at that time to know how many defects, if any, were in the code.

During the break, I asked the Moderator how the Inspection was proceeding. He sadly stated that they had not found a single defect. Wow, it looked like we were in for it, and our critic was already making noises that he was right.

In the second half of the Inspection defects were found and that particular code unit was the most defective in the project. Our cynic became at least a partial believer. In any event, he did not shoot down Inspections as he did before. Sometimes the process group needs to win them over one by one.

Anecdote 11.2

Yes, programmers are not all the same, but, as noted at the beginning of this book, even good programmers make errors

Another approach to transitioning the organization is to let the non-experts on the project learn from the experts and the high fliers; then their effectiveness will increase. Inspections provide a good forum for this type of coaching. Raytheon used this approach to a good effect. [HAD95]

11.10 Small Teams

How can Inspections be applied in small teams? Sometimes a project only has one team or there may only be one person who is on a project or there is only one truly knowledgeable person for a project.

Well, we do the best we can in all these cases. While the Inspection may not have the same formality as with larger projects or teams, we can benefit by having another set of eyes look at the work product. These are situations where less rigorous Inspections may be good, practical, short-term solutions. The Inspection team may only be the Producer and Moderator, doubling as an Inspector; e.g., as in 1:1 Inspections. Data should still be gathered and used to learn how to improve effectiveness.

11.11 Do We Really Need All that Data with Inspections?

Well, you can begin an Inspection without any data and you may not analyze the data you capture. You will still see some benefits, but you cannot see the best effectiveness without data analysis and goal setting.

If the concern is that there is too much focus on data and you believe this will lead to Inspections not being accepted, then start with less rigorous Inspections. I may not like this, but I prefer that you at least start with Inspections, provided you are willing to learn how to make them more effective as you proceed.

Maturity Level 1 and 2 organizations do not have much data and seem to have concerns about capturing data. This is one reason the SEI placed the Peer Review process at Level 3. Nonetheless, we know that Level 1 and 2 organizations have achieved a level of success with Inspections.

If your objective is to have highly effective Inspections, then you'll need the data and analysis. If this is not your goal, then proceed as you see best, but maintain the objective to move to more rigorous Inspections.

11.12 Get Off to a Good Start

Not all people will accept the use of Inspections initially. Data and experience should win some of the doubters over, but holding the hands of some will be necessary, as well as taking verbal abuse from others. Learn to understand the concerns of the people who are being asked to use Inspections and you will be more successful.

Some will just naturally doubt about the value of Inspections, since after all their culture is under change, and the skeptics will not believe until there is irrefutable proof. They will ask questions like:

- Is the overhead worth it?
- Does management really support this?
- How will the data be used?

These doubts will not be limited to practitioners. Management may have even deeper doubts and issues. This is the time the Inspection Coordinator or SEPG must stay the course. Responses must be given to hold the doubters' focus, and eventually the data should win them over too. Today it is far easier with the volume of Inspection data and literature in the community. By and large the issues today are the same that existed in 1972. Each organization has a common set of repeatable issues with Inspections. Some vary by organization type, but the full set of objections is remarkably still the same.

11.13 Inspecting Changes

There is an argument that is sometimes used to blow off Inspections. It is argued that when a change is made to a previously tested work product that it is cheaper and less labor intensive to retest rather than inspect or re-inspect. This is false for three reasons:

1. If a fix or change is made and previous test cases did not flush out the defect, then rerunning them does not prove the change works. It only proves the change did not regress the work product. This is not verification of the change or fix! The test cases need to be changed or modified before rerunning; otherwise they would have found the defect.
2. When a Re-Inspection is performed it is not required on the whole work product. The change plus surrounding code may be sufficient to verify the change or fix. See Section 11.32.
3. Changes and fixes have defects in them. In fact, there is data that suggests that small changes are more defective than large changes. Therefore, there is a good likelihood that a defect will be found in test, and now we are back to the very reason why Inspections are better; it is cost effective to find the defect before test versus in test.

Then there are some who would argue that small changes, especially for maintenance, sometimes affect parts of the product a distance away from the area in the work product being repaired and that only test can expose these relationships and rippling effects. It is possible that Inspections could also find these relationships. I've seen it happen at Inspections, although I agree that this is not always easy.

But let's go back to first principles: Inspections are looking at the change in the context of the work product and relationships it has with other work products. This means the inspectors should ask what else could be affected by the change and try to ensure that the change does not ripple into another defect. No one ever claimed that test would go away because of Inspections; it just will be less costly. Therefore, we would expect that some regression testing should occur even after Inspections are finished. Test will validate that the product was not regressed by the fix; Inspections will verify that the fix is correct.

Buck suggested "Due to the overhead of getting an Inspection team together, it is recommended that several small, but related, changes be grouped together into one Inspection effort." [BUC81b] The intent was to group Inspections into one set rather than have one for High-level design, Low-level design, and one for code. He recommended the following groupings by size as shown in Table 11.1. Separate means holding an Inspection solely for the work product.

Inspection Type	**New Unit**	**Changed Function**		
		>33% and ≥40 LOC	<33% or 6 to 39 LOC	5 LOC or less
HLD	Separate	Combined	Combined	Combined
LLD	Separate	Separate	Combined	Combined
Code	Separate	Separate	Separate	Combined

Clustering Small Changes for Inspection [BUC81b]
Table 11.1

11.14 "Yes, of course, we do Inspections!"

It sometimes happens that the checkmark of having done an Inspection is tracked with a higher level of importance than performing an effective Inspection. For example, Inspections are indicated as having been completed regardless of when they might have occurred. This results in ineffective Inspections and an organization attitude that Inspections are a bureaucratic quality approach. Situations where this checkmark misuse is seen, include:

- Unit test is performed before the code Inspection, and in some cases the Inspection becomes a non-event
- Resources are not available for a scheduled Inspection, so the work continues without an Inspection and then sometime later a minimal Inspection in name is held; e.g., a requirements Inspection is held after or while the design is being competed
- Some people believe an Inspection will go faster when the bugs have already been taken out via test or some other approach

One must really wonder why these Inspections are held, as they can be viewed as bureaucratic, not effective, and a waste of time, and prove the points of the skeptics. I suspect these occur in organizations with weak management commitment, but where no one wants to be the first that management slaughters if it is found an Inspection was not held. So one will be held, even if it is after the fact, just to say it was. I feel for the people who must live in this type of organization.

11.15 Will Users Find All Latent Defects in a Product?

No. However, we have no way of knowing this with full confidence. All of the latent defects may never be found, or they may be lying in wait for the environmental condition that will trigger them.

Dijkstra and Mills have both stated that one cannot prove that zero defects remain in a work product. So it must follow that one cannot prove that a specific volume of latent defects remain in a work product. But we can more readily surmise there may be some latent defects than accept an unprovable zero-defect claim. This has been found to be true in a few cases where backward analysis was performed on products that seemingly had zero defects after customer use; e.g., the earlier Space Shuttle project. In a couple of cases a retired product was reviewed, not even inspected, for potential reuse possibilities and latent defects were found. See again Anecdote 1.4. So, as a concept, we should be able to accept this as true, but as a proof or with quantification this is near impossible.

11.16 No Previous State to Inspect Against

In Shirey's study at HP he found that in 76% of the cases there was no document to verify against. [SHI92] This situation is clearly not unique to HP, but definitely indicates that a necessary precondition for effective Inspections was not being satisfied. Would there be any surprise then that, as Shirey found, "product quality was not increasing"? This situation is roughly equivalent to putting someone into a city they know nothing about and then asking them for directions on somewhere to go in that city. They may actually try, but I wouldn't bet on their directions, or in this case on the Inspection results.

Another version of this is when a previous work product; e.g., design, may actually be updated but is not inspected as a re-baselined document. However, the code is inspected.

Yet in other cases a work product is continuously modified; e.g., code, while the design is never updated. At some point the code is declared by the producer to be ready and an Inspection is held with an out-of-date design.

How often these situations occur, I cannot say, but they are not uncommon. Why would they occur? I suspect that in many cases the Producer of the code was also the Producer of the design. At least I hope so! This allows the code Producer an understanding of the intent of the design since he created it. This is still not desirable or recommended, since a baseline document may be missing, but it slightly mitigates a worse case, when the code Producer was not the design Producer. The other common reason is lack of time. Well here we go again: a project is out of control, so it is made more out of control by skipping process steps. You fly in that plane, not me. I've been there and it's not comforting.

11.17 If You Find a Defect, Fix It

It makes no sense, but sad to say it happens, that defects found during Inspections are not always fixed correctly and in some cases just not fixed. This latter case typically occurs when the Producer runs out of time; e.g., the work product must be turned over to test, or sometimes the Producer just doesn't think it is a bug the users will find.

Later during test when the defect is found again, it is not only wasteful but also demoralizing to the people who were asked to perform the Inspection. If management does not act in these cases, they are reinforcing poor Inspection behavior.

Some incorrect fix situations will pass through to test but these should be analyzed to understand, learn, and prevent future occurrences. Other incorrect fix situations result when the Moderator does not check the Producer's rework. Propagation of defects can also occur when defects are not fixed and the Moderator has not checked the repairs.

Shirey says that at HP "the most common reasons for not fixing a defect were:

1. The inspection data was lost
2. The author didn't understand the inspection data, and
3. There wasn't time in the schedule" [SHI92]

While again these are not unique to HP, the first two suggest a poor Inspection process and the third that management did not plan well enough. The first two fall mostly to the Moderator, but both SQA and the Inspection Coordinator share a responsibility to help protect the organization.

Some organizations get skittish when they have old products in use but have limited knowledge about the product. When a defect is found in older or base product code during an Inspection for a change or enhancement, they may decide not to fix the defect out of fear that the fix may cause other problems. Their view is that if the users did not find the problem up to now, why run the risk of changing code that they do not sufficiently understand. While some quality experts may frown on this, it is a practical approach, but one that would fail in court. I would hope that knowledge about the newly discovered defect is put into the organization's defect database for aid in resolution, just in case a user discovers it.

11.18 Bureaucratic Data Collection

Not all people will see value in collecting data on Inspections. While we may want to win them over and classify them as late-adopters, we should make sure that the people who voice this issue are not the organization's technical leaders. If so, one could lose the game debating the wrong issue. Short-term victories with strong technical leaders will come back to haunt the Inspection initiative.

These people, while good technical personnel, may think that data gathering and analysis is "Mickey Mouse", as one once told me. In their view, if a defect is found, this is good, but then just fix it and get on with the work. Data and what they see as bureaucracy, makes them smile in a cultist way and they quote Dilbert cartoons as philosophic principles. Bear with them. They can change, but they need to see the value, and it can come to them. They are not against the right way, but they are dead set against what they think is bureaucratic. However, don't play into their concerns by asking them to classify defects into one of twenty types, when 6-8 is more than enough.

11.19 Inspections Are Too Formalized

I never really know how to react to this issue. Often it seems like an easy stone to throw, since Inspections by definition have some formality. I think what is really being said is "Inspections cramp my style." Welcome to the programmer's ego again?!

Now I'd be the first to argue that if Inspections or any process becomes so formal that it is onerous, something should be done. If it becomes downright inefficient or ineffective, the situation needs to be resolved. Formality, however, is not in itself a problem. Rather it is a question of whether the process repeatedly produces positive business results. If so, its formality is justified.

Rigor in engineering practices should be expected, and Inspections are an engineering practice. Inspections must adhere to some protocols to be effective and efficient. History has proven this. Inspections that are run according to the defined practices are more effective and efficient.

11.20 Inspections Waste Time

The repeated analysis of groups using Inspections shows the contrary. Projects save time rather than add time to the schedule when using Inspections. But some individuals cannot identify with the savings to the project; they are primarily concerned with their own time. It is especially hard on project team members when they are overloaded with schedules that are difficult to meet with or without Inspections.

The Inspection method described in this book focuses on both effectiveness and efficient use of time. These measures and controls are the responsibilities of the Moderator and the Project Lead. The measures must be monitored to ensure effective and efficient Inspections for Preparation, Inspection Meetings, resolution of identified defects, etc. Keep the feedback channels open with success stories and the issue will dissipate. Listen to the concerns and show you are actively listening by making necessary changes, but don't abandon the Inspection principles.

11.21 Redundancy with the Test Processes

In many cases I'd suggest the issue of redundancy with test comes about as another excuse to try to defeat Inspections. But analysis of this issue can add value. If testing duplicates what is done in Inspections then there is redundancy somewhere. Inspections are intended to remove defects as early as possible. They are a quality control mechanism. Testing is intended to 1) find the defects that leaked through the Inspection process and 2) revalidate that the delivered solution satisfies the needs of the customer. Testing is both a quality control and a quality assurance mechanism. Since it is both, there can be some redundancy. I'd like to see the day where it is solely an assurance mechanism of the product.

With analysis of data from the Inspection and Test results, both processes can be tuned to maximize efficiency and minimize redundancy, while maintaining effectiveness.

11.22 Arbitrary Style Viewpoints During Inspections

This issue can be a problem and can cause Inspections to become less effective and efficient. If the organization has not defined or agreed to an accepted style for specifications, design, code, or for other documents, then it is possible that Inspection participants may have different viewpoints. These viewpoints can lead to too much unnecessary discussion and disagreements which may be difficult, if not impossible, for the Moderator to control or resolve.

Style definitions as part of the work product form and format, process descriptions, or guidelines are a necessary precondition to effective and efficient Inspections.

11.23 Less Efficient than Debugging During Execution

This position arises from two reasons:

1. Some people believe that debugging within a test execution environment is faster and cheaper. The literature consistently has suggested otherwise. When the debate cannot be resolved, even with the evidence of other groups' experiences, I suggest that the organization try a "controlled study" to see which is more effective for them. So far, Inspections tend to pay off better. But let your study results be your guide. Of course, testing can be more exciting Inspections and this may be part of the reason this position is taken.
2. There may be languages where execution of the code during the Inspection would be more beneficial. For example, the visual type of languages (Visual Basic, PowerBuilder) may be best inspected in a permutation of the traditional Inspection using both the code and viewing the performance of the code by looking at the screens during the execution.

11.24 Design Knowledge Is Required To Do Code Inspections

Absolutely! However, the inspectors do not have to have full equivalence in domain knowledge as the Producer of the inspected materials. There are necessary preconditions nonetheless. For example, the inspectors should understand the code and design sufficiently to be able to find defects and the design materials should be made available to the code inspectors. These two preconditions will permit a resaonably effective Inspection. Of course, if the inspectors have more domain knowledge, the Inspections will improve in effectiveness. An Overview may sometimes be necessary, if the inspectors are too distant from the design.

If design documents are not available, for whatever reasons, then the next best alternatives should be provided; e.g., specifications, previous coded versions, etc. In lieu of any pre-code reference documents, the Producer should give a more detailed Overview. In all these cases, the code could still be inspected, but the effectiveness of the Inspection is clearly at risk. This risk would then have a bearing on the strategy for testing.

11.25 Only Superficial Errors Are Found

Predominantly people who seem to believe that they are the only ones who can understand their own work raise this issue. Strong egos again? If, in fact, only superficial defects are detected, especially during Inspection startup, then the Inspection process was most likely not well practiced. Minor defects can be culled out during the Preparation activity and gathered as a whole at the start of the Inspection Meeting. If these are the only defects found, the Moderator should look at the other Re-Inspection criteria before reaching a decision to re-inspect, but one signal is suggesting the Re-Inspection. See chapters 6 and 8 for further discussion on how to handle major and minor defects.

There is a relationship between effectiveness (volume of major defects found) and the domain knowledge of the inspectors. We would always prefer to have the best people for an Inspection, but this may not always be possible. We must do the best we can with who is available. Inspections can be fruitful even without experts. I sometimes think they may, in some situations, even be more fruitful, as these inspectors are more objective through independence. The important question that the Moderator and the Inspection team must ask at the conclusion of the Inspection Meeting is whether a Re-Inspection or change in test strategy is required. We should be looking at what the process signals suggest.

A precondition that the Moderator must verify is whether the inspectors are sufficiently qualified to participate. If they are not, then the issue must be taken up with the Project Lead. When the inspectors are not sufficiently qualified, an Inspection could still be performed, but then there is a risk, which should be re-evaluated during testing for the work product inspected.

No one should inspect an artifact that is "known" to be defect-free. It is a waste of time to inspect defect-free artifacts. The problem of knowing with proof or conviction is discussed in Chapter 14, where I discuss "What not to inspect." For now, let it be understood that not all artifacts or work products need to be inspected, provided there is sufficient evidence to show that not inspecting is a good business decision with minimal or no risks to the quality of the product.

Do not judge the Inspection process by any one instance. There will be variations in results across a sample or population of Inspections. You need to look to the data to determine what may be the cause of the variations and performances. If there are only minor defects being recorded, then look to revising or managing the process.

Finally, it is possible that there really are only minor defects to be found. If this is really true then it will also be reflected in the test activities and customer use. You should be so lucky. If test or the customers are finding defects that leaked through the Inspection process, then it needs to be improved and managed.

11.26 Inspecting Too Much

Yes you can. And models like the SW-CMM and ISO 9000 imply that you should inspect everything. With the SW-CMM, it can be argued that at Level 4 one has learned what not to inspect through Quantitative Process Management. However, these models do not provide sufficient guidance to learn how to select what to inspect or not. Perhaps they were written to be black and white because tailoring criteria are often used as an excuse to do fewer Inspections. This is equally the wrong decision, although it is probably a prevalent decision. I see few instances where organizations have well defined criteria for selecting what to inspect or not. They seem to default to the "or not" choice. Level 1 behavior?

11.27 Performance Characteristics Are Not Addressed

If this is true, it may be because performance is not included as a focus area for Inspections, or it does not appear on the checklists as a defect type to consider, or no one is assigned the role to focus on performance. It should be addressed in almost all software solutions. Therefore, if it is not included there is either evidence that suggests performance is not a factor of concern for the users or it was excluded in error. In this latter case, the process can be improved.

11.28 The "Not the way I would have done it" Attitude

This issue can manifest itself during an Inspection, and it must be controlled. The controls include: 1) proper and consistent training across the Inspection team members and 2) documented methods, styles, and notations to be used by the Producer in creating the artifact. The Producer maintains full freedom of choice within these defined constraints. The inspectors maintain full authority to call out a defect within the prescribed style, methods, or notations, but not "I would have done it differently." If methods, styles, and notation requirements have been defined then the Moderator must control behavior during the Inspection Meeting when discussion or defect identification begins to take an unproductive direction and especially regarding individual preferences of style, notation, or method.

The major interest in an Inspection is whether the work product is correct with respect to a previous referenced definition, not that someone would have done it differently.

11.29 Can We Do Less Rigorous Inspections?

My personal view is yes, but you must know when you are doing which type. I note a strong caution, however. Less rigor often seems to breed even less rigor until there is no rigor and chaos reigns again. If an informal approach is taken for any instance of an Inspection, it should:

1. Be done with forethought that this is a good business decision from an effectiveness perspective; i.e., there is a high likelihood of no defects in the artifact based on an analysis of data
2. The informal approach is noted as such and tracked as a potential risk
3. Review is made after test and customer use to learn if the decision was good

If the decision for less rigorous Inspection is proven to be a valid one, then you can reinforce the criteria for making these decisions. If the decision was in error, then the project team needs to learn from this experience and rethink the informal approach.

I vote for choice and tailoring, because I believe organizations can learn how to improve efficiency while remaining effective with Inspections. Some of this learning must be done through experimentation. The key is how the choice is taken. If it's based on data analysis, then fine. If it is because people do not like the defined Inspection practices, then training and education are in order. If choice is only taken to avoid the rigorous approach, then the organization loses.

ANECDOTE

THROWING DARTS

Imagine a project where they throw darts at printouts of coded units. Every time the dart is thrown and sticks on a line of code, it reveals a defective piece of code.

Clearly this is an absurd method of finding defects. But let's go further and say that after some succession of darts have been thrown and the dart thrower decides to quit, no defects remain, and that this fact is consistently proven in test and with users.

This apparently absurd method has proven to be very effective and we should accept this, not tamper with it. The point is that we are interested in the effectiveness of the method, not the method per se.

Now, I do not condone throwing darts to find defects, but I do support any method that is repeatedly effective. And if it's darts, so be it.

Anecdote 11.3

11.30 Customers Accept "Good Enough" Software Solutions

Yes, customers do often want the function early, but I've rarely met a customer who was pleased to encounter defects in function early or late. They may try to live with the defect or work around it, but they always pay a price. The price that they and your organization are willing to pay is a business choice. The premise is that you and your customers are willing to live with the problem when defects are manifested. If the customer is satisfied despite the defects, then timeliness must have been the primary driver.

If the customer is not happy, you and they will spend more time and money due to the defects. If you can afford to lose customers, then the risk may be worth taking. If you are in a business based on the "dice roll" of quickly getting function to the marketplace in the hopes that it will become the next hot software product, then you will probably take the risks. If, on the other hand, you have customers who have a dependency on the correctness of the function, then not only are you at risk but I would argue that you are liable when latent defects lead to problems. You can and should be held culpable for any damages caused to the customer.

ANECDOTE

WHAT DO LAWYERS KNOW?

We were requested by a law firm to be expert witnesses in litigation where party A was suing party B because the product was defective. The unbelievable defense of party B was that "defective software was the common practice in the software industry, and that party A was expecting more than was the standard." Sounds like a weak argument, doesn't it?

More significantly, some software suppliers believe that this defense may actually be acceptable. We did not engage as expert witnesses, so I don't know the outcome of the suit. But I can only hope that an absurd precedent was not set.

Anecdote 11.4

11.31 Many Successful Companies Do Not Use Inspections

This may be true, but this is not the point. Success can come for many reasons even dumb luck. Some questions that should be asked are:

- How much more successful could they have been?
- What was the cost of the success?
- What is the definition of success?

No, not all companies will go out of business if they don't use Inspections, but they could do a better job for themselves and their customers where quality is a business factor. I like PC software products for the function they give me, but I hate them when I run into one of the many defects the suppliers seem to know they have shipped in their code. Ever look at the length of some of the README files that are sent with PC software products? What beats me is that some of these companies announce the thousands of defects they ship. If I had a choice, I'd walk away from them, but they have me in a master-slave relationship or I put myself there.

If the customers can't change the attitude of the suppliers, then it falls to the management, and here I mean management that has the leadership ability to see a better way. Then they must support it and require it. I absolutely believe they will then get Inspections done well. If the practitioners feel no pain from customers, then the pain to change must come from within. The trouble is that management is often part of the problem in resisting change. So these types of organizations may never change and never use Inspections. We can only wish them well.

11.32 Modified Code Is Too Costly To Inspect

I often hear people ask, "Why should the whole module be inspected when only a few lines of code have been changed?" Why indeed? I am always confused as to how they came to the conclusion that they were required to inspect the whole module every time. Some even believe they must inspect the whole product. Let them have their views if it serves them, but they are wasting effort.

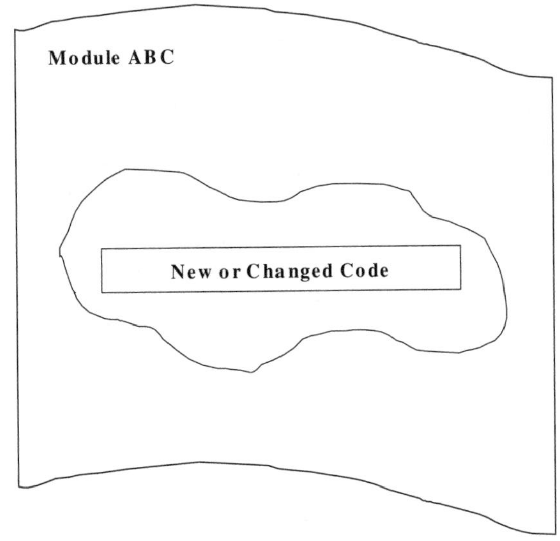

Surround Code and New/Changed Code
Figure 11.1

Simply stated, you do not need to inspect the entire module. If you choose to do so, it may be for some other reason such as re-engineering, training, or because you believe there are a high number of latent defects in the unchanged portion. It is your choice how much you inspect.

At a minimum I suggest that you will need to inspect the additions, deletions, and modifications plus some "surround code" to understand the context of the additions, deletions, and modifications. Surround code is code that surrounds the changes or additions. See Figure 11.1 for a graphic representation of "surround code". Here we see the new or changed code, by example, surrounded by code it may affect. It is almost impossible to add or change code without affecting some other existing code in the module; i.e., the surround code. Some surround code may be a distance away from the changes, additions, or deletions.

11.33 But It Seems Unreasonable To Inspect Deleted Code

If we recall that the artifact being inspected is inspected in the context of some previous state for that work product, then we need to ensure that we have not deleted too much or the wrong things. Inspection of deleted lines of code will obviously proceed faster. You do not need to read each deleted LOC instruction, just ensure the boundaries of what is being deleted, but they should be verified as being correctly deleted.

11.34 Some Inspectors Don't Contribute

This will happen and can be for a number of reasons. Since an objective is that all inspectors participate, the Moderator can try to draw out the silent inspectors by asking them if they have anything to add, or asking those who may be silent to contribute first, or to do round robins of defect identification.

11.35 We Tried Inspections and They Didn't Work

There is no one response to this issue, as there are so many possibilities and this experience is often given as a vote against trying Inspections again. Before responding, other questions must be asked; e.g.,

- What does the data show?
- Did they really use Inspections?
- What did management do to show commitment?
- Did management keep the data safe?
- Was the project not ready for Inspections?
- Were Inspections treated as a silver bullet in a chaotic environment?
- Were people trained?
- Was the process followed?

11.36 Deadly Sins of Inspections

- Superficial commitment from management
- Not enough time in the schedule
- Resources not allocated
- Insufficient preparation
- Wrong people assigned
- Not using the data
- Treating Inspections as a rubber stamp
- Using the checklist without thinking beyond it
- Not training the inspectors
- No entry/exit criteria
- Wrong pace
- Believing all review types are the same

End Quote:

"Learn from the mistakes of others-you can never live long enough to make them all yourself."
Anonymous

CHAPTER 12
WHAT TO INSPECT

**"It takes a lot of time to get experience,
and once you have it you ought to go on using it."
Benjamin M. Duggar**

12.1 Introduction

Throughout this book the emphasis was somewhat skewed toward code Inspections, though document Inspections are also addressed and certainly intended. However, Inspections can be applied on any work product that man has created. The checklists will obviously vary, but the process flow should be the same. The procedures should be tuned, but the principles should be constant.

Let's look at some other areas both in and outside software where Inspections can be applied.

12.2 Typical Software Work Products

Inspections can be applied to any type of software work product. The following software work products are typical for Inspections:

Production products:

- Requirements Specifications (RS)
- Architecture Definition (AR)
- High-level Design (HLD)
- Low-level Design (LLD)
- Code (CD)
- User Documentation (DOC)
- Data and Data Definitions (DD)
- Screen Designs (SD)
- Interface Descriptions (ID)

Test products:

- Unit Test Case (UTC)
- Function Integration Test Case (FTC)
- System Integration Test Case (STC)
- Use Cases (UC)

Changes:

Problem Reports (PR)
Change Request (CR)

Plans:

Software Project Plan (SPP)
Unit Test Plan (UTP)
Function Integration Test Plan (FTP)
System Integration Test Plan (STP)
Publications Plans (PP)

Basically any work product that people have created can be inspected. If we continue to accept the fact that people can make mistakes when creating a work product, then the Inspections can be used to help remove the resultant defects before they leak to other and more costly defect removal timeframes such as in test or in customer use.

Inspections are not limited to software work products. As noted in Chapter 2 (see Section 2.8), inspections have been widely used in other industries such as manufacturing long before there was software.

Fagan noted that "The purpose of the test plan inspection IT_1, ..., is to find voids in the functional variation coverage and other discrepancies in the tests plan. IT_2, inspection of the test cases, which are based on the test plan, finds errors in the test cases. The total effects of the IT_1 and IT_2 are to increase the integrity of testing and, hence, the quality of the completed product." [FAG76]

This makes sense when we understand that if an error occurs during test this could be due to defective test. These will eventually be proven out as test case defects during error analysis. While these types of defects waste time during test, the more critical type of defect attributable to test is the failure to test a function that should have been tested. Too often defects found by users can be traced back to insufficient testing.

While test Inspections have been defined since 1973, remarkably they are not widely practiced in the software community.

During architecture Inspections the focus is not just on the defined architecture, but should include views about the future directions for the product. These are the most difficult Inspections since a defect will be harder to identify when the architecture is new, as there may not be a sufficient basis for definition and comparison. If the architecture is an evolution, then prior baselines serve to compare for consistency. In both cases the subsystem structures, protocols, formats, boundaries and limitations, conceptual definitions, etc. should all be discussed during the Inspection.

During requirements specification Inspections it is not as helpful to just read the document. It will be more enjoyable for the participants if usage scenarios or function flows can be used to drive the Inspection to understand if the objectives and user needs are being met.

When the customer is invited to requirements specifications Inspections you will need to ensure that the customer representatives know what is expected of them and that they know the Inspection process, as they may have other agendas and these may conflict with the Inspection intent. You want the customers in attendance to ensure that their requirements are understood and that the specifications have transformed and elaborated these requirements correctly, not to tell you how to implement the solution, though these discussions may not be fully preventable.

**Customers could serve as Mappers primarily,
but you can also have them serve as inspectors,
if they sufficiently understand the role of the inspector.**

During High-level design Inspections it is also not as helpful to just read the document. Again, it will be more enjoyable for the participants if usage scenarios or function flows can be used to drive the Inspection to understand if the objectives and user needs are being met. The team should give sufficient attention and time to explore all interfaces and error conditions.

During Inspections of plans the key focus is to understand if the defined plan:

- Contains all necessary parts
- Addresses planning parameters; e.g., size, effort, cost, schedule
- Is achievable per the defined schedules, resources, and dependencies

User documents include all documents delivered to the users that they will use with the product. These include installation guides, product feature documentation, message manuals, references, debugging materials, etc.

During publications or user documentation Inspections there are also levels of documents to inspect, just as with the software; e.g., there should be an equivalent to the software design as a baseline and this is typically an outline for the document to be inspected, there may be drafts, and there is the final document.

The document outline is inspected to ensure:

- The organization of the document is sound
- Appropriate topics are covered
- Changes, if a revision, are identified

Drafts may be in stages of increasing detail, and in each stage of draft the Inspection must ensure the level of detail for that draft is complete, correct, consistent, and sufficient. The final draft is usually the one before going to press.

Message Inspections are more like User Documentation Inspections, except the defects with messages can be quite severe to a user. While the same process can be used, as for document Inspections, it is important the Message Inspections focus on:

- Are the messages complete; i.e., are all errors and helps addressed?

- Accurate; i.e., does the message address what is needed?
- Clear; i.e., can the user do something meaningful with the message?
- Usable; i.e., does the message lead to other information actions that may be needed by the user?
- Translatable; i.e., if the software is used in multiple languages, can this message be easily translated and keep the sense of the message?

Keep in mind that a defect and especially a major defect will have a different meaning for documents, as messages and documents will not often cause a system or product failure, but they can lead to incorrect user actions. Clearly some of these situations could be considered major. Therefore, I recommend that anything that requires repair in the document just be classified as a defect, without the major or minor differentiation. Is a typo major or minor? The answer may be yes or no. Who cares, just get it fixed in the document!

12.3 Systems Engineering

Today Systems Engineering is an area where more discipline is being applied since the inception of the SW-CMM. There are now equivalent models for Systems Engineering. These include the current CMMI, v1.02, which melds the SW-CMM v2.0 draft C, Electronics Industries Alliance/Interim Standard (EIA/IS) 731, and Integrated Product Development Capability Maturity Model (IPD-CMM) v0.98. [SEI00a] [SEI00b]

The CMMI includes Peer Reviews as one way to verify a work product as a part of the verification processes. While I believe the CMMI should have included a separate Process Area (PA) for Inspections as the SW-CMM (Peer Reviews) did, the modeling committee chose not to. Hopefully, this does not slow down the adoption of Inspections as a cost effective process within the Systems Engineering community. And more hopefully, it does not reduce the further adoption or application of Inspections in the software community.

The CMMI v1.02 has Peer Reviews as a Goal within the Verification PA. The Goal is stated as "Peer reviews are performed on selected work products." This is fine, but in the written elaboration that follows, the CMMI states, "The peer review is an important and effective method implemented via inspections, structured walkthroughs, or a number of other collegial review methods." While I do not care what one calls an Inspection to suggest that it can be "a number of other collegial review methods" opens the barn door a bit too much.

I think the CMMI steering committee missed a good chance to further the practice of a more rigorous "review method" as they call it.

The CMMI is aligned with the thinking that Inspections can be applied to any work product in software or systems, or as they state "key work products." This is actually an important point, as Inspections should only be applied where they will add clear business value. A soft spot, however, is that application with the CMMI is now more a matter of choice than a requirement as, for example, the SW-CMM stated, "Each code unit undergoes peer review and is unit tested before the unit is considered complete." [CMM93] There is no such statement in the CMMI.

Potentially organizations that do not see a need to perform Inspections will now have more of a hole to squeak through to "prove" their point that Inspections are not required. No model can prevent interpretation, and it is unfortunate that some miss the point of Inspections. I believe the SW-CMM did cause an increased focus on the Inspection process. I hope this focus is not lost due to how the CMMI is written, since it is applicable not only to systems but to software organizations.

ANECDOTE

LEVELS WITH ASSUMPTIONS

I once gave a tutorial at a conference and joked with the audience that erosion in interpretation seems to always happen with the best of models. I stated some examples of what I had been hearing about the application of the SW-CMM. I remarked that one organization said they were a "young level 3". The audience giggled, but I stated that this could be OK, since we all are young sometime during our maturing process.

Then I stated that I did have some concerns when an organization said they were a "level 3 with assumptions." My remark to them was why stop there, they should state they were a "level 5 with assumptions." The audience laughed as I thought they would.

After the tutorial when people will gather to ask questions one young lady stated she didn't understand why the audience laughed when I gave this story. I asked why she didn't understand. She replied, "Well we're a level 3, and we believe that Peer Reviews are not needed and that this was not the same as an assumption." Actually she was asking me. Fortunately I did not need to reply as the others around all proceeded to enlighten her.

Anecdote 12.1

12.4 Other Work Products

What other work products might we inspect if we believed it would add value? The following is a list by example:

- Microcode
- Training documents
- Data
- Process Improvement Plans
- Process Descriptions
- Procedures
- Life Cycle Descriptions
- Standards
- Messages, if they are in a separate file

- Screens
- On-line help
- Disaster Recovery Plans

Some user, internal or external to the organization, will use these work products, and any of these could contain a defect that would cause further errors to be made. Some of these types of work products are particularly important to be right the first time, since the defects they contain can ripple like a virus affecting all users.

Still other types of work products would include:

- Marketing materials
- Performance and tuning guides
- Maintenance guides
- Installation guides and instructions
- Anything else a user can read to learn or apply

Planning rates for the work products in this section tend to run between 4-12 pages per hour for documents. Messages if they are in a separate file may take longer than code, since there tends to be quite a bit of cross checking. For screens you can assume the rate for code as a start.

For some of these work products we may have participants who are not programmers; e.g., technical writers for some documents, marketing personnel, and even customers. The participants as always should have domain knowledge to be of maximum help.

I do not recommend that an organization start Inspection with all of these work products. For software, an organization should start with those that are noted in Section 12.1 above and I would further suggest starting only with the Production work products first. It will be easier to quickly show economic value with them. Prove that Inspections add value and then evolve their application to other work products that are key to your organization. And remember to track and analyze costs and returns regardless of which work products you select to inspect.

Classification of defects as major or minor will tend to be more difficult with these other work products.
In fact it may not even be necessary to make this classification.
Simply count all defects and, if accepted as defects, have them fixed.

The value, however, is somewhat subjective or in the case of microcode quite evident. While microcode has many of the same characteristics as soft code, it has a much greater need to be correct, since required fixes after delivery are far more costly. After the chips are manufactured it is not easy or likely that they will be recalled for a bug fix, unless absolutely necessary. The cost for a microcode bug can be quite dramatic as was demonstrated when Intel needed to finally declare that there was a bug on its Pentium chip. The result was almost a half billion dollars impact. The multiplier here far exceeds the 100:1 in software.

Inspections have also been applied to hardware development where the process requires some changes to help application, adoption, and success. For example, Glen Russell notes, "The major challenge was to devise an appropriate way to paraphrase circuit schematics. ... the team also includes a manufacturing test engineer to address testability." [RUS91]

Russell goes on to add that value was seen, "So far the technique has uncovered errors difficult to find in circuit simulation (the equivalent of software unit testing). Hardware inspections also appear to speed up and streamline simulation. The technique applies equally well to printed circuit packs and application-specific integrated circuits."

So once again we see that Inspections can find defects that traditional testing cannot find or, at least find them at a lower cost and proven productivity gain.

12.5 Checklists and Focus Areas

Inspections were designed to review a complete work product, or set of changes to existent work products. Defects can fall in a number of categories and checklists were designed to focus on various categories of interest to the organization. See the sample checklists in Appendix A and you will note that any checklist can be as short or as long as the organization may want.

Long lists tend not to be used as much as the writers of the lists believe. Short lists may leave out defect types that are important. A balanced list should be learned and improved over time and made relevant to the culture and performance of the organization.

Requirements documents tend to be the least specific, so focusing an Inspection on key quality attributes may prove to add value early in the project. These attributes commonly called the "ilities" include:

- Usability
- Reliability
- Serviceability or maintainability
- Traceability to the customer baseline
- Performance (performability? Yuk!)
- Stability
- Portability
- Understandability
- Modifiability

If defects no longer occur for items on a checklist, consider removing them from the checklist for another more important defect type. Requirements should be reviewed for these quality attributes prior to functional decomposition and defining the technical solution.

Usability Inspection is a complete field unto itself. I recommend the reader to Nielsen and Mack's book on Usability Inspection Methods. [NIE94] They state "Usability inspection is the generic name for a set of methods based on having evaluators inspect or examine usability-related aspects of a user interface." While they include use of Inspections in similar ways to those we discussed in this book, they do permit other methods for finding usability defects. I especially like their definition of defect as, "A characteristic of a product that makes it difficult or unpleasant for users to achieve their goals." Boy, would I like to be on a Usability Inspection for some software products I've had to use.

End Quote:

"Inspections are the worst form of defect removal technique except for all those others that have been tried from time to time."
Paraphrasing Winston Churchill

CHAPTER 13
OTHER APPROACHES

"There's more than one way to skin a cat."
Anonymous

13.1 Introduction

My answer to which Inspection method is best is directly a factor of the effectiveness of the method. Formalism is not the issue, though formal methods have proven highly effective. The name of the method is not the issue. Rigor leading to effectiveness is the issue. If you don't like the term *Inspection* and this stands in the way of you successfully using Inspections, then call them something else. I have seen organizations use what they called the Fagan method with less than 50 % effectiveness. I have seen organizations use what they called an informal approach that showed over 90 % effectiveness.

At the same time I have seen organizations say they were doing Inspections, when in fact they were doing something quite less. They seem to say they are using Inspections, maybe because this sounds more rigorous or it is the answer that is wanted when the question is asked. Others say they are doing a review, which is vastly overloaded a term in the software community. This is not to say that a "review" cannot be effective, but that we should calibrate what is meant when the term is used.

In this chapter I will briefly explore some other approaches to pre-test defect removal. Some of these have been reasonably effective, others much less so. We will explore them and learn that there are many names for almost the same thing as Inspections, many approaches that purport to be Inspections, and some approaches which are different from Inspections and which can be effective for their purpose.

Inspections, while effective for early removal of defects, have limitations in some environments. This is mainly because Inspections do not "execute" the work product. For example, code Inspections are generally limited to a static analysis wherein the work product is evaluated based on its form, content, intent, and documentation versus evaluating the code based on its behavior during execution. There is at least one exception to static analysis in code Inspections; e.g., visual-language Inspections where we can execute the code while reading the code that is executed. For documents, all Inspections are limited to a static analysis.

Figure 13.1 adapted and modified from Wheeler [WHE96] shows a schematic of the various approaches to defect removal based on the review approach. While I may not fully agree with this taxonomy, it is a good place to start to understand that there are many types of *reviews* available. The choice you take should be the one that offers the effectiveness you need in your business, but my vote will always be that of Inspections as discussed in this book, which I have added to this chart as shown by the rounded boxes. Evolved Inspections are the composition of choices as documented in this book. 1:1 Inspections and Solo:Inspections are also defined in this book.

Taxonomy of Review Approaches [WHE96]
Figure 13.1

Wheeler defines *unlimited reviews* as "those that have no limit on the number of personnel that participate in the review (and generally do not limit the amount of material reviewed)." Limited reviews are "those that permit a limited number of reviewers (and generally limit the amount of material reviewed)."

IEEE STD 1028-1997 defines 5 types of review:

- "Management Review: A systematic evaluation of a software acquisition, supply, development, operation, or maintenance process performed by or on behalf of management that monitors progress, determines the status of plans and schedules, confirms requirements and their system allocation, or evaluates the effectiveness of management approaches used to achieve fitness for purpose.
- Technical Review: A systematic evaluation of a software product by a team of qualified personnel that examines the suitability of the software product for its intended use and identifies discrepancies from specifications and standards. Technical reviews may also provide recommendations of alternatives and examination of various alternatives.
- Inspections: A visual examination of a software product to detect and identify software anomalies, including errors and deviations from standards and specifications. Inspections are peer examinations led by impartial facilitators who are trained in inspection techniques. Determination of remedial or investigative action for an anomaly is a mandatory element of a software inspection, although the solution should not be determined in the inspection meeting,
- Walkthrough: A static analysis technique in which a designer or programmer leads members of the development team and other interested parties through a software product, and the participants ask questions and make comments about possible errors, violation of development standards, and other problems.
- Audit: An independent examination of a software product, software process, or set of software processes to assess compliance with specifications, standards, contractual agreements, or other criteria." [IEE98]

IEEE in this version of the standard seems to not be endorsing any one review approach versus another. While IEEE shows five types of reviews, it is the limited reviews that I have been discussing in this book, and especially I have focused the relationship and differences between Inspections and walkthroughs as these two are most often confused as being the same. Indeed, the procedures for *IEEE 1028 Inspections and Walk-throughs* seem much the same. Thus the IEEE is adding to the confusion between the two approaches. By using the same procedural structure for the IEEE standards they have added a structure and definition to Walk-throughs that just was not originally there. They also do not address the wide disparity between how walkthroughs are defined and practiced in the software community. Maybe that's just the way it is going to be, but I would have hoped IEEE could have better sorted out the differences between Inspections and walkthroughs for the software community. Or maybe these two approaches are not really that different! After all, it is not so much what one calls the defect removal method, but how effective it is that really counts.

Jones has calculated that different defect removal methods provide different yields as seen in Figure 13.2. [JON86]

Method	Cost	Effectiveness
Self Check	Low	<20%
Peer Review	Low	<35%
Walkthrough	Medium	<50%
Inspection	Medium-High	>60%

Defect Yield by Method [JON86]
Figure 13.2

These numbers would suggest that Inspections are the more effective way to proceed.

All of these techniques have value in the sense that the IEEE has defined them. For example, Technical Reviews can provide a quick view by experts about the viability of a technical approach or alternative. But if the intent is for maximum or effective defect discovery at lowest costs, then Inspections must be your choice.

There are many other approaches for removing defects and it is not my intent to discuss them all. Those selected in this chapter are the most prevalent in use and the literature.

13.2 Reviews

IEEE differentiates between Management and Technical Reviews, and this is appropriate as they serve different purposes. I would suggest that both of these unlimited review types have a common characteristic that further differentiates them from the limited review types. Management and Technical Reviews lead to decisions on a course of action based on recommendations resulting from the review process. Inspections, walkthroughs, and audits, on the other hand, result in identified defects or non-conformances that require action for resolution.

The term *review* is so over-loaded in the software community that it can mean practically any approach where another set of eyes has looked at a work product. This may be unfortunate because it is misleading to suggest that a work product is completed when it has been "reviewed", without clear understanding of how well the review was performed and for which objective.

The spectrum of review types seems to go from another individual simply signing off on a document to full-fledged Inspections. IEEE 1028, ISO 9000, and the SW-CMM do not help when they further propagate various review types as part of their standards and guidelines.

I wish we could get rid of the term, but I think we are stuck with it in its many versions, approaches, and meanings. If a review of any type is used to find defects we should always be asking how effective was the review in addition to analyzing other data from the review to understand its costs.

Now let's briefly look at some review types of most interest for identifying defects in work products.

13.3 Walkthroughs

Walkthroughs, sometimes spelled as walk-thrus or walk-throughs, were defined before the Inspection approach to try to bring more discipline to defect removal before passing a work product into test. As with reviews there are many flavors of walkthroughs. One of the earliest public definitions comes from Weinberg in his book "*The Psychology of Computer Programming*" [WEI71], which predates the definition of Inspections in IBM.

While Weinberg gave a public definition that served to get the issue of early defect removal focused, there were many in-house definitions of walk-throughs in companies like IBM, Honeywell, and others.

Fagan made a comparison between Inspections and one type of walkthrough in his 1976 paper and pointed out that Inspections were not only more rigorous, but also more efficient and effective. [FAG76] This was discussed in Chapter 2: Inspections – An Introduction.

Comparing the methods, Fagan would argue that walk-throughs are a much lighter form of Inspection, typically missing:

- Formal moderator training
- Definite participant roles
- Use of checklists to help find defects
- Definition of defect types to look for
- Follow-up to reduce bad fixes
- Analysis of results

Wheeler gives a good description when stating, "Walk-throughs and informal peer reviews are frequently confused with inspections. Walk-throughs can easily be contrasted with inspections using the review process characteristics described where:

1. Walk-throughs are often used to present design and coding approaches and to inform coworkers and managers about work in progress. Although defects might be found, this is not always the principal focus of a walk-through. Inspections are narrowly focused on finding defects.
2. Walk-through audiences can include as many as 20 or more people. Inspections limit team size to five or six coworkers.
3. Walk-throughs require little or no preparation by attendees. Inspections require one to four hours of preparation by each team member.
4. The only roles that appear in typical walk-throughs are the author and the presenter, usually the same person. Inspections require a moderator and a recorder or scribe in addition to author and presenter. The author should not fill any of the other roles in an inspection.

5. Walk-throughs usually have no prescribed time limits. Inspection meetings are limited to a maximum of two hours.
6. Walk-throughs place little or no constraints on the amount of material that can be covered. Inspections limit the size of work products to 200 to 250 lines of code or a few pages of material.
7. Walk-throughs can cover work that has been completed for some time, work just completed, work in progress, and planned work. Inspections cover only work just completed." [WHE96]

There are too many definitions of walkthroughs and rarely are they consistent, which only confounds the issues of what they are and how they compare with Inspections. See [YOU79], [CIT84], [WEI84], [FRE90], [WHE96].

A report showing an effectiveness of 99.9% in removing defects before test and operational use of a 37,000 LOC release called the defect removal process used *walk-throughs.* [TAC99] But as one reads the report and the description, their walkthroughs satisfy, at least, the Duck Characteristics of Inspections. They attribute their success not to their walk-throughs but to what they call a State-Based-Process, which is more than what is used in other walk-throughs. Certainly, I believe their process contributed to their success, but we have always known that Inspections (or walk-throughs) will not work well in an environment that does not have a well defined process, and the process in this report is well defined for their environment.

The better the process used for production, the higher the effectiveness with Inspections. Does this have something to do with maturity?

Despite the different meanings of walkthrough, it is safe to say that walk-throughs are:

1. More variable than Inspections
2. Less effective in removing defects
3. Range from the very informal to what are almost *Inspections*

13.4 Producer Self-Checking, Self-Review, or Desk Check

This approach has been in practice in varying degrees probably since the first programmer wrote code. The Producer himself reviews the "completed" work products, looking for defects or inconsistencies. After the self-check is completed, the work product either proceeds to the next life cycle activity or is passed on to another individual for further work. Key to this review is that it is a personal examination. It may or may not have structure or use checklists.

There is no question that this approach should always be performed, since it permits the Producer to declare completion and to learn from defects discovered. This self-check is a primary aspect of the Personal Software Process (PSP) defined by Watts Humphrey. Humphrey calls the self-checks *personal reviews.* "As the PSP data will show, a little time spent carefully reviewing your code can save the much longer amount of time that would have been spent debugging and fixing the program during compile and test." [HUM95]

In a private correspondence Watts stated, "Many of our students get 100% yields before the first compile. My personal data was consistently at 80% before compile and most experienced engineers can reach that if they use defect data to update their check lists regularly."

In his book Humphrey notes "A PSP goal is to find and fix all defects before the first compile or test. By doing design and code reviews before you compile, you will find many defects that the compiler would have caught. You will also miss a lot. .... With care and practice, many students find they can catch 80 percent or more of their defects before their first compile. .... You may not ultimately set a personal goal of finding 100 percent of your defects before the first compile. However, that is the goal the PSP establishes." We see that Humphrey rightly sets the focus on the effectiveness of self-check and acknowledges that the personal review process is a learning process wherein the individual is focused to keep data, learn, and improve defect discovery until 100% effectiveness is consistently achieved.

Self-check, whether PSP or something less rigorous, requires a checklist that the individual uses during the self-check or personal review. The checklists are used as guides to ensure completeness of the self-check thought process. The code is compared to a predefined list of common types of defects made while coding. As the individual refers to the checklist, the thought process for facilitating defect discovery is made repeatable. Upon completion, which includes correcting all found defects and checking that the corrections are correct, the Producer declares the work product complete.

The checklist should evolve with the learning of the individual and in so doing will further enable achieving 100% effectiveness. The data kept for personal reviews will also enable the individual to focus future reviews on defects commonly made.

While there are methods like PSP that are helping to focus the discipline that engineers should follow to produce quality work products, good programmers have always practiced some type of self-check. What they tended to not do was to use this knowledge consistently to improve the organization's process of production.

By the way, the checklists used for Inspections should be the very same as used during a self-check. Whether one calls this self-check or PSP or desk check, the intent is to factor learning through Causal Analysis and Defect Prevention into checklists that the programmers can use before turning over the work product to an Inspection or test.

13.5 Two-Person Inspection

Bisant and Lyle in their paper, "*A Two-Person Inspection Method to Improve Programming Productivity*", discuss an experiment they executed in the use of two-person inspections. Their conclusion was that "The two-person inspection method appeared to improve novice programmer productivity." .... "The two-person inspection process probably imparted problem knowledge to the participants faster than those who did not use the inspections and this might account for some of the improvement." [BIS89] While the results are not very startling, they are supportive of the possibility of an alternative to the Fagan four plus

Inspection team. Clearly the efficiency of the Inspections improves when there are only two participants, since the effort costs decrease.

Work with some of our clients shows that two-person Inspections can and have been 100% effective in a number of instances, so we know the number of inspectors does not always have to be four or more. See 1:1 Inspections in Chapter 4.

Jalote defines the Infosys one-person review, where he means one inspector with the Producer, as "The process for one-person review is somewhat similar to the group review process. The author, in consultation with the project leader, identifies the reviewer. The review is scheduled, and the reviewer receives the review package in advance. The reviewer reviews the work product individually and comes prepared to the meeting with the author. The review meeting has only two participants—the author and the reviewer. During the meeting, the issues log and the defects log are generated. The reviewer informs the project leader when the review is finished. The project leader is responsible for tracking defects to closure." [JAL00]

While Jalote did not provide data on these one-person reviews we might assume he is comfortable that they are sufficiently equal in effectiveness, though he never provides a value for effectiveness. Infosys apparently uses control charts to determine if the review falls within defined limits and when not within the limits the review is considered not effective. In another portion of the book he provides data that suggests pre-testing effectiveness is about 75%.

13.6 *N*-Fold Inspections

Martin and Tsai, in their paper, "*N*-fold Inspection: A Requirements Analysis Technique", propose that if one Inspection is good, then multiple Inspections may be better. They call their approach *N*-fold where *N* is the number of independent teams performing an Inspection with the same material.

In this paper the work product was the user requirements document (URD). The Inspection activities are replicated using *N* independent teams. They conducted a pilot study to explore the usefulness of *N*-fold Inspection during requirements analysis.

Their comparison of *N*-fold Inspection with other development techniques convinced them that *N*-fold Inspection is a cost-effective method for finding faults in the URD and may be a valid technique in the development of mission-critical software systems. [MAR90]

The technique could be applied to other work products based on criticality, safety, or life sensitive solutions. There is no question that finding defects earlier is more cost effective than finding defects later This would be true for all early defect removal activities. However, the focus of this pilot study was not on improving the URD Inspection process to have a higher effectiveness, but to demonstrate that URD Inspections were not as effective when performed as a single Inspection versus *N*-fold Inspections of the same work product. So by performing *N*-fold Inspections, the overall effectiveness will increase above that of the singular URD Inspection. This has to be true, it is almost a given. But the cost will increase, also. Efficiency was not measured, though we can assume it decreases.

It would be better to evolve the URD Inspection process to a higher effectiveness when performed as a singular Inspection. This should be the objective. In the meantime, where cost is not an issue, then *N*-fold approach may offer value for some organization.

This approach works from the premise that if a pond has many fish, then casting a net again will probably yield even more fish. This will probably always be true, when the defect density is high.

13.7 Formal Technical Review

Freedman and Weinberg probably have the best seller in books about walkthroughs, Inspections, and technical reviews. In fact their book is entitled Handbook of Walkthroughs, Inspections, and Technical Reviews. [FRE90] While they use the term *Technical Reviews*, their approach differs from the classification of the IEEE. So again we must be careful when using terminology and assuming the meaning is the same for all. Freedman and Weinberg define their Formal Technical Reviews as a combination of:

1. "A *written* report on the status of the product reviewed—a report that is available to *everyone* involved in the project, including management;
2. Active and open participation of everyone in the review group, following some traditions, customs, and written rules as to how such a review is to be conducted;
3. Full responsibility of all participants for the *quality of the review*—that is, for the quality of the information in the written report."

This definition appears to be crafted to be open to interpretation by the reader. Later in the book they give more details, but they are clearly in favor of less formal reviews when they say "In our opinion, the best attitude to take about formal procedures is: Use them as little as possible, but use them when necessary." And later they point out "In other words, if you feel you can succeed with reviews without this much formality, by all means do so."

In spirit I agree that it is not the formality of the method that is the key, rather it is the effectiveness of the method. The authors never address the effectiveness of their approach. Indeed they do not publish any data reflecting the effectiveness or efficiency of Formal Technical Reviews as a stand-alone method or in comparison to other methods for early defect removal. The lack of data makes this method less compelling except to those who prefer informality.

Actually their approach has many similarities with Inspections as defined by Fagan and others. However, they have misinterpreted Inspections when they say:

- "Inspections are quite commonly used as part of a feasibility study."
- "An inspection is a method of rapidly evaluating material by *confining attention to a few selected aspects, one at a time*."
- "Only selected aspects of a selected sample of all the pieces of work were examined."
- "The distinguishing characteristic is the selection of aspects."

- "Although some installations do not practice it, we recommend some form of advance preparation."

Either they have not read and understood the vast Inspection literature, or they believe early defect removal with *formal technical reviews* is better. They provide only four pages for Inspections while giving six to Round-Robin Reviews and eight to Informal Reviews both of which are weaker methods than their Formal Technical Reviews.

13.8 Cleanroom

Cleanroom or Cleanroom Software Engineering maintains the principle of "Doing it right the first time" through use of mathematical verification and proof of correctness before coding begins. After coding the quality level is proven through sample testing based on a statistical approach.

Harlan Mills originally developed Cleanroom. [MIL87] [LIN94] [LIN96] [PRO99] The name "Cleanroom" was taken from the semiconductor industry, where a physical clean room is provided to prevent introduction of contaminants during hardware fabrication. Cleanroom in a software environment requires program proof of correctness, and then statistical testing certifies the software.

In Cleanroom projects, a program is expressed as a mathematical function. A design method called the Box Structure Method is used for specification and design, and verification is used to confirm that the design is a correct implementation of the specification. The design is an elaboration in detail of the specification. Verification of program correctness is performed through team reviews based on correctness questions. There is no execution of code prior to its submission for independent testing.

Software testing in Cleanroom projects is based on statistical principles. A "sample" of tests is used to draw conclusions about the "population" of the full project. If the sample tests and resultant defect level prove the desired quality level for the project, then testing is finished. If the quality level is not achieved, the code and design are returned to the project team for further work. The process is then repeated until the desired quality level has been statistically proven.

Cleanroom has been in limited practice since the 1980's. There are documented results demonstrating the high quality that is achieved with Cleanroom in new development or reengineering. [HAU94] [SHE96a] [SHE96b] Despite these excellent testimonies the practice seems to be limited to those programmers who are either inclined toward or are capable of mathematical proofs of correctness during development. Cleanroom also typically seems to have a limitation of 100 KLOC sized projects. However, the USAF Space Command and Control Architectural Infrastructure (SCAI) STARS 1 Demonstration Project at Peterson Air Force Base used Cleanroom. The size of their application was greater than 300 KLOC, partially due to reused code. [STA95]

13.9 Inspection Characteristics

So how does one know if they are performing an Inspection or another variety of pre-test defect removal? I provided my Duck Characteristics of Inspections in Chapter 3.

IEEE STD 1028-1997 gives a table of characteristics comparing Management Review, Technical Review, Inspection, Walk-through, and Audit. [IEE98] For Inspections they state the following characteristics:

1. **Objective:** Find anomalies; verify resolution; verify product quality
2. **Decision-making:** Review team chooses pre-defined product disposition; defects must be removed
3. **Change verification:** Leader verifies that action items are closed; change verification left to other protocols
4. **Recommended group size:** Three to six people
5. **Group attendance:** Peers meet with documented attendance
6. **Group leadership:** Trained facilitator
7. **Volume of material:** Relatively low
8. **Presenter:** A reader
9. **Data collection:** Strongly recommended
10. **Output:** Anomaly list, anomaly summary, inspection documentation
11. **Formal facilitator training:** Yes
12. **Defined participant roles:** Yes
13. **Use of checklists:** Yes
14. **Management participates:** No
15. **Customer or user representative participants:** Yes

This list defines the original method proposed by Fagan. I think you will now be able to see after the previous chapters that the Inspection process has indeed evolved and that more than half of these characteristics can and should be tailored to increase effectiveness and efficiency. They only characteristics I believe are inviolable are 1, 2, 3, 9,10, 11, and 13. This is meant to say, that if all 15 characteristics are in evidence there is an Inspection in practice per the IEEE.

But if one wants to have Inspections work optimally today for effectiveness and efficiency then some of these characteristics should be adjusted for improvement. My suggestions do not negate this list, but I ask that we interpret it for best purpose and that we evolve it for tomorrow's possibilities.

Both 1:1 Inspections discussed earlier and Solo:Inspections (see Chapter 14) are in alignment with the IEEE Inspection characteristics.

End Quote:

"None is so perfect that he does not need the advice of others."
Baltasar Gracián

CHAPTER 14

INSPECTIONS FUTURE

"Anything you can do, or dream you can, begin it.
Boldness has genius, power, and magic in it."
Goethe

14.1 Introduction

Let's start with the future.

I believe we will see a time when Inspections will be significantly reduced in use and need. They will no longer provide an advantage to as wide an audience as they do today or have in the past. Call me optimistic, but I think there are organizations that can get to a defect free status with work products and therefore reduce their dependency on Inspections to remove defects. The software community is evolving, even if yet slowly, to a stronger engineering discipline that enables building work products right the first time and building them faster at the same time.

This discipline may not be practiced or even desired by all, but it will be a reality for some, and they will have an advantage in their business sector. History shows us that if one person can learn a new practice or discipline, then more can do it too. And if more can do it, then many can do it. This progression is a natural evolution in the history of technology, and we are beginning to see it in software.

Software production cannot remain bound to labor-intensive and defect-prone development. This is too wasteful in an industry that has limited resources. We are fortunate that there is so much demand for software solutions. If history gives us a message it is that when there are limited resources and demand in excess of the resources, breakthroughs are made. Some practices that are in development today will change the present reality of defective software or at least the amount of defectiveness. Other practices are already yielding business advantage to some software organizations. The question we must explore is how to extend this reality to more organizations.

Inspections have served the software community well for over a quarter of a century, but, hopefully, sometime in the future we will not require Inspections in the same ways we do today. I believe this will come to pass, at least in some organizations, and not too far off in the future. The only question that remains is about the rate of change for when this future will become manifest.

The biggest criticism of Inspections is that they are labor-intensive. While it is a misdirected criticism, it is one that we must address. As noted many times throughout this book, effectiveness must be the first focus when using Inspections. When I speak of effectiveness I suggest that any organization that does not yet have the capability to remove 90% or more of the injected defects with Inspections is not yet getting sufficient value for their money or their customers.

After effectiveness has been achieved, then focus on improving the efficiency of Inspections.

I have walked this two-step value approach throughout the book. I will continue it here in the last chapter, and finally I will explore a future where Inspections may not be needed.

I will structure this chapter, therefore, to address:

- Work in progress that can change the effectiveness of Inspections
- Work in progress that can change the volume of injected defects through prevention practices
- Practices that improve efficiency to further reduce the costs of Inspections
- Lastly, I will explore the possibility of software development without Inspections

Let's now review some actions that may lead to these possibilities. Let's first look at some work in progress that will affect Inspections.

14.2 Improvements in Work Product Format/Presentation

One condition that limits both the effectiveness and efficiency of an Inspection is how the work product looks; i.e., the physical and visual representation of the solution. Certainly the required standards defined for a work product type will help consistency of representation and communication, and these are necessary for effective Inspections, but there are other restrictions, complexities, and difficulties in languages and representations despite the available standards.

Simply stated, software languages and representations are not simple enough and therefore the complexities they bring make it harder to use them and to inspect a work product developed with them. There is work in progress to address these complexities, but we have a way to go yet.

In one example of investigation, Gerrard has proposed that requirements can be stated using a behavioral model. [GER00] With this approach "A requirements document is intended to describe all the functions required to be performed in a system." Well no new news here, but he then suggests "The obligation of the behavioral model is to structure the requirements into a form that can be presented to the user for them to review directly."

He came to this conclusion after observing that there are repeatable problems with requirements documents and especially with the Inspection of these documents; e.g.,

- Delays in RAD projects were not acceptable to management, so they bypassed Inspections
- There usually is no source document to inspect a requirements document against
- It is difficult to get users to participate in Inspections, especially for large requirements documents
- Requirements documents tend to be too long and this therefore is an inhibitor to good Inspections

He is not arguing against Inspections, but that Inspections can be made more effective and efficient with this proposed behavioral model for requirements definitions.

I do not want to discuss the method here, and I introduce it simply to suggest that it and other approaches like it hold promise for simplifying requirements documents and therefore the Inspections of these documents.

The point Gerrard makes is valid; i.e., if the complexity of a work product via its representation can be made simpler, Inspections will be more effective and efficient.

Harel is addressing this problem from another perspective. He has demonstrated that "A development scheme for complex reactive system leads from a user friendly requirements capture method called play-in scenarios, to full behavioral descriptions of system parts, and from there to final implementation." [HAR01] He admits, "It is probably no great exaggeration to say that there is a lot more we don't know and can't achieve yet." But he and others will make the advance and when it is made, the nature of Inspections of requirements specifications and indeed the writing of requirements statements themselves should have been changed substantially.

The software community will define better languages and representations and these will make Inspections easier, but this is only one area where we should look for improvements. These advances will not remove the need for Inspections by themselves, but are one factor that will change the programmer's discipline in specification, reducing the volume of injected defects, and thus enabling more effective and efficient Inspections.

The opportunity to improve languages and representations to reduce defect injection exists across all work products from requirements specifications to designs to code. In the meantime we should all understand that some work products would be more difficult to inspect because of language type, method type, or representation type. I firmly believe that these differences are one contributor to the range we see in acceptance and success with Inspections across the community. Some languages are harder to inspect, so some practitioners may choose not to inspect!

14.3 Program Reading

Another approach to address the vagaries of requirements definitions is to improve how requirements specifications are inspected or read and understood. Shull et al. have defined a technique called Perspective-Based Reading (PBR) wherein inspectors stand in for specific stakeholders in the document to ensure that requirements are sufficient to support all the necessary later stages of software development. The intent is to focus on how to read the requirements document and what to look for. Guidelines are provided to each inspector to further enable detection of defects. Two questions that are focused for each inspector are "What information in these requirements should they check? How do they identify defects in that information?" [SHU00]

Three major uses of the requirements are addressed to determine if there is a defect:

- A description of the customer's needs
- A basis for the system design
- A point of comparison for system test

"A failure to satisfy any of these needs constitutes a *requirements defect* – a deficiency in the requirements quality that can hamper software development." The PBR technique then uses guided questions by perspective; e.g., the tester's perspective to answer questions about the work product. While no data is provided it is stated "Studies have shown that development teams that use PBR to inspect requirements documents tend to detect more defects than they do using other less-structured approaches." Review time and effort required should increase with PBR, but if the requirements are better stabilized and more defects found then this is a technique worthy of use.

While more data results would be appreciated about this technique, I believe it is moving in the right direction; i.e., more disciplined requirements Inspections. As more guidance and structure are added to requirements Inspections, the latter stages of the project will benefit and effectiveness for defect removal will be increased. If we can get the requirements right or at least more right, the design and code should proceed faster and with fewer defects.

In an earlier and related study, Porter et al. determined that:

1. "The fault detection rate when using Scenarios was superior to that obtained with Ad hoc or Checklist methods – an improvement of roughly 35%.
2. Scenarios helped reviewers focus on specific fault classes.
3. The Checklist method – the industry standard, was no more effective than the Ad Hoc detection method.
4. On the average, collection meetings contributed nothing to fault detection effectiveness." [POR95]

This latter point I've addressed before and I agree that when the effectiveness from Preparation is greater than 90% one might consider not holding the Inspection Meeting. The first three conclusions suggest that checklists are not enough. I agree, but they are necessary. The author suggests that, when guided scenarios are applied, effectiveness for requirements Inspections will increase. Again I agree. So a conclusion we can draw from this study is that focusing where and how to find defects can improve Inspections. This is an extension of what Causal Analysis and Defect Prevention can lead to when the cause is understood and then a possible preventive action is taken.

I previously discussed that you can only inspect what you could read. Well, to be more specific, you can only inspect what you understand. A native English speaker may actually be able to "read" a book in Old English, but they will not understand it unless they know the language. Defects could be looking them in the face and they just would not see them. This applies to software Inspections with the various languages and representations.

Advances have been made in program reading techniques and these offer value for the future in improving effectiveness across the software community. The PBR technique discussed in the previous section is an example of reading techniques for the requirements specification work product. However, all work product Inspections can benefit by reading and comprehension techniques.

Reading techniques such as PRB make use of guidelines to facilitate understanding while focusing on specific aspects of the work product and therefore increase the possibility of finding latent defects. See [SHU00] for an example of such a guideline for requirements specifications. The article provides pointers to other sources.

More can be done to facilitate comprehension and understanding of work product materials during Preparation, and this will allow an increase in the effectiveness of the Inspections. One caution we should keep in mind is that we must measure and see that effectiveness is actually increasing and as it does we should be evolving how the guidelines for reading are defined. My concern is that, as with checklists, these guidelines can become too bulky and less useful over time. Guidelines like checklists need pruning from time-to-time to keep them useful. Another area of research needed is how to define guidelines for different levels of experience and expertise in inspectors. Perhaps the PBR guidelines are best suited for novices, as the article by Shull suggests. Perhaps experts will not benefit as much from such guidelines.

Certainly one reason why defects are made is that there are mismatches of assumptions between readers and writers and between work product transformations. This starts with the customer, who sometimes does not really know what they want, but they pay for it and they'll know it when they see it. How can we address these situations? Being precise with poorly stated requirements will not help. This problem goes beyond formalisms that enable precise transformations. I think we know more about how to transform with precision than we know how to communicate with accuracy.

The software community does not seem to believe that any one language or engineering technique is good enough. The result is an inordinate proliferation of techniques, models, methods, and languages. For example, the list of known programming languages in use past and present was 2350 as of January 1995. [KIN95] And I am sure the number is larger today.

Do we need this many languages? Has the Babel syndrome bitten us to the nth degree? When does it stop? It seems we in software must always go one better with new languages appearing every year. According to The Cambridge Encyclopedia of Language, the number of known living natural languages is 6528. [CRY97] It took tens of thousands of years across billions of people for this many natural languages to evolve. Software is a bit more than 50 years old but we're closing that gap to Babel-dom.

Use of scenarios as in PBR is not limited to requirements specifications and designs. They can be applied to code; e.g., we could use test scenarios during a code Inspection to drive the reading of the code.

Scenarios have been applied to code even after it has seen some testing and too many defects were found or there was an opportunity to re-exercise the code before delivery. In these cases the scenarios flow through the modified and new modules in addition to any unchanged modules that may be necessary to "perform" functions in the product. The flow is static and symbolic versus dynamic since the code is not executed, but the paths of execution are followed (or flowed) based on inputs and variable assignments. This approach has been successfully used after code is completed; i.e., the combined set of interacting units have been inspected and tested, but are deemed not yet ready for delivery.

Russ used a similar approach in Guided Inspections wherein test cases are used to systematically examine a work product. The test cases are used but not executed. Rather they are used to guide the inspectors during the Inspection. The test cases include preconditions, an input scenario, and expected results from each test case used. Coverage metrics are taken for the portion of the work product exercised by the set of tests. The choice of coverage can come from customer priorities or specific defect types. [RUS00]

In a paper by Rifkin and Deimel, *Applying Program Comprehension Techniques to Improve Software Inspections*, they addressed the readability problem from another perspective in a case study where they designed Inspection training "to address the problem of understanding the artifact being reviewed." [RIF94]

Comprehension of the material inspected is quite necessary. This is why there is a tendency to state that only domain experts can perform well with inspected material. But as the authors note "Comprehension skills *can* be improved with training." However, comprehension skills can come from other sources besides training; e.g., experience, and as noted earlier in the book, the more domain knowledge (comprehension skill) an inspector has, the more they will contribute to finding defects.

What Rifkin and Deimel offer is that with training in comprehension skills even those who are not domain experts can improve in finding defects through a better understanding of what is inspected. This is an important contribution to more successful Inspections, and is required until software languages and representations are easier to read and understand.

14.4 Formal Methods

Work is continuing in formalisms and there have been more successes each year, so we might expect to see more use as the potential benefits become more available to others and as the methods become easier to apply. One example of an Avionic Control System study performed at GEC Marconi Avionics using rigorous methods for producing and analyzing requirements showed promise for more investigation, even though the authors gave no data or quantification of results. They concluded, "The case study experiment has confirmed the potential of formal methods for requirements analysis of safety critical systems. A formal specification provides clear advantages, such as clarity and precision; but the main benefit in our experiment was the feasibility of thorough analysis via proof. Formal verification can help uncover errors, misunderstandings, or subtle, unexpected properties which would easily escape other means of scrutiny such as review or animation." [DUT97]

Another formalism method is SPIN for use in the design and verification of asynchronous process systems. [HOL97] The author notes, "The design methodology that is supported by SPIN can be summarized as follows:

- A distinction is made between the behavior and requirements on behavior. The designer specifies the two aspects of the design in an unambiguous way by defining a verification prototype in the language PROMELA.
- The prototype is verified using the model checker SPIN. The requirements and behaviors are checked for both their internal and their mutual consistency.
- The design is revised until its critical correctness properties can successfully be proven. Only then does it make sense to refine the design decisions further toward a full systems implementation."

Voila! This is exactly the problem, situation, or opportunity we have with all software requirements and design statements; i.e., if they are clear and understandable we have a high probability of building it right the first time. Then if we gently wait until we know we have the right stuff, we can proceed to design. This is the approach that makes Inspections more effective also. I do not mean to suggest that SPIN is not useful. It clearly was. But the question now changes about where Inspections and where other approaches may be most useful. I believe that in some environments, such as asynchronous process systems or real-time safety critical systems, that formalisms may be a necessary choice and that selected Inspections may serve to further verify the correctness of these work products.

Despite the barriers that formalisms will have for many programmers, the work to address making requirements more understandable and hence complete, correct, and consistent must continue. There are many avenues under investigation, and we should expect that someone would break through this problem. At least let's hope so, since if we can get the requirements right enough, we can probably build the software more right.

It has been argued that proof of correctness techniques should be viewed as an alternative approach for defect removal, since "correctness proofs do expose defects". [DUN84]. There is no doubt that proof of correctness is a primary verification method. There are a number of approaches to proof of correctness. While proof of correctness methods currently are among the most labor thinking intensive of the verification methods, they offer a consistent and repeatable approach. Once the refined specification or design has been proven to be correct against the higher level specification or design, it is assumed to be correct and probably defect-free with respect to that baseline if the refinement has been done per defined rules. The argument that still must be addressed is whether the higher-level specification was the right statement of what is to be delivered as the solution. The assumption is that the high-level specification is, and that it has been "validated" as such. If it is, then proof of correctness can work well for transformations. If the higher level is not correct, the transformations can be precisely incorrect too.

While proof of correctness is compelling, one of its staunchest proponents, Dijkstra, stated, "One can never guarantee that a proof is correct. The best one can say 'I have never discovered any mistakes.' We sometimes flatter ourselves with the idea of giving watertight proofs, but in fact we do nothing but make the correctness of our conclusion plausible." [DIJ72] A cynic to the last, he basically argues that man makes mistakes and cannot find them all, or worse prove that he has found them all, when indeed he may very well have or have not.

So should we stop trying? Obviously not! But we may need to live with this ambiguity.

Cleanroom, as discussed in Chapter 13, is a defect removal method that has been in use almost as long as Inspections. It requires both a rigorous proof and a statistical approach to testing and has had a slower and less wide acceptance than Inspections. Perhaps this is due to the requirements that proof of correctness places on the average programmer. Where it has been used, "The findings were, in some cases, exciting. 91% of the errors were typically removed from the software product before the first test case was run. Computer time usage decreased by 70%-90%. Time spent fixing errors in rework was reduced by 95%. Productivity, at least in the first two studies, was improved by 70%." says Robert Glass. [GLA99a]

14.5 Tools

Let's look at some areas where tools may affect Inspections in the future, either in the way Inspections will be performed or even if they need to be performed.

DEBUGGERS AND STATIC ANALYZERS

A special issue of Communications of the ACM, April 1997, was entitled The Debugging Scandal and What To Do About It. Guest editor Lieberman concluded, "Debugging is still, as it was 30 years ago, largely a matter of trial and error." [LIE97] He ends his introduction article with a plea to the computer industry to fix this problem, and notes that "there are plenty of ideas with great potential for debugging this situation." While the problem has not been debugged or fixed, this issue is clear evidence of one factor that makes the cost of fixing user-found problems so expensive compared to Inspections, where the problem does not normally need to be debugged. As discussed, when an Inspection defect is discovered and agreed upon by the Producer the fix is normally apparent. In test, the time to just isolate where the bug really occurred can take much too long. We need better debugging tools, but until they come, we must do better with Inspection effectiveness.

The argument that it may be less costly to test than to inspect has been around since the earliest days of Inspections. This is simply and universally not true to date. Some development environments; e.g., large systems are just too expensive to use for defect removal during test. This is why the lower costs of Inspections became compelling in the 1970's. The costs to reboot large systems were visibly disruptive, which is why testing often occurred off-shift. If the system came down in the middle of the night, there was less noise from other impacted users.

Mainframe and mid-range systems are still with us and the numbers of large systems grow in use. All of these systems are dependent on software, but software that continues to work when something unexpected happens. Today the costs to find defects are still higher in test than with Inspections, but perhaps not as high as they were in mainframe and mid-range development environments or for large systems.

Static and dynamic analyzers have been around for a long time. They have advocates and seem to work well in some environments. There are numerous articles proclaiming success with their use. They should be used when they have proven value in finding defects that the programmer cannot easily find. However, an over-dependency on them may work against developing more discipline in the programmer for building it right the first time, which I will discuss in Section 14.14. However, when used, these tools can facilitate code Inspections, since they should remove a number of common defect types. If these tools are used with Inspections, the Inspection checklists should be modified to remove the defect types that these tools can find.

When we put these possibilities together, then in the not too distant future there may be environments where test could be cost competitive with Inspections.

Let's leave this as a thought more than a proposal at this time. I simply state it to ask that we keep ours minds open to the change around us and not hold to what was true in the past. Let the data speak. If the costs are less or comparable in test, then increased testing and reduced code Inspections may be the right way to go in some projects.

While tools cannot find all defects, they can find some, and with lower costs to execute, there is no reason not to use them where they are available, effective, and efficient. These include static analyzers, standards checkers, syntax checkers, compilers, etc. These tools should all be used, as appropriate and when available. They should be treated as preconditions to successful code Inspections.

Any tool that will aid the activities for Inspections should be considered.

Tools should be investigated to improve the following Inspection Activities:

- Overview
- Preparation
- Inspection Meeting
- Data Collection
- Data Analysis

CODE GENERATORS

I include this section, as we once had a client that was inspecting the code generated from a code generator they had recently put into use. When I asked why, they rightly said that they wanted to assure that the code generator was doing the job correctly. Good for them, I thought.

What they showed was that in their project (a safety critical project) quality was important to them and their client and that while they were willing to move to new technology, they were not willing to take an unmanaged risk. Good for their client, I thought.

They eventually eliminated inspecting the generated code after they had established that the code generator was working as required. They still will inspect sensitive units when they think it is warranted. Code Inspections have become a backup quality check for them.

This example shows that technology can reduce the need for some tasks; e.g., code Inspections. They had chosen a code generator because they could eliminate the coding activity and later the traditional code Inspection activity. We should see more of this in the future as code generators and 4th generation languages become more prevalent, in which case we should see less need for code Inspections.

VISUAL CODING TOOLS

How should one inspect the code for languages such as Visual Basic, Power Builder, JBuilder, and other visual based languages? The traditional approach says that we read the code and try to discover any existent defects prior to execution. We could do this with visual based languages, but there may be a better way.

We could look at both the code and the execution of the code concurrently, and we could make dynamic corrections to the code while we performed this type of Inspection. This is actually what is done with these languages in many projects. To do otherwise makes little practical sense. Coupling Inspections with code execution provides both flexibility and timely repair and should reduce costs. There are no studies proving this yet, but I believe it will be found to be true.

This then would change how we inspect, what our checklists look like for "code Inspections", and begs the question "Are we unit testing or inspecting?" Actually we are doing both. So the question of effectiveness now must be addressed in this combined Inspection/unit test. As with the code Inspections we've been discussing, our goal will still be high effectiveness, but the way we attain it is different than the traditional code-ready Inspection. Defects in many areas can be dynamically repaired. While this could be costly in the traditional Inspection with four inspectors, when using 1:1 Inspections, the costs are more reasonable. This is partially what pair programming is also advocating. [WIL00b]

In client environments where I have observed this approach, the costs for this combined Inspection/unit test appears at worst comparable to a separate Inspection or unit test. Sounds like a possible win for cost reduction. Hitting a command button and watching what happens should be faster than reading the code and trying to visualize what will happen. In either case, if there is a defect it should be evident, but more so when watching the execution of the code. This approach should not be random as often the unit tests are in projects. It should be structured to maximize effectiveness.

WEB-BASED INSPECTIONS

Traditionally Inspections are performed as a group at a meeting in a common room or area. This was the only way we could do it in the 1970's. Today we have the web and can inspect from a distance with participants all in different parts of the world. While web-based Inspections are less personal in that participants are not face-to-face with the each other, this could be a blessing and help keep the Inspection more objective.

Table 14.1 shows a list complied in 1998 by the Institute for Experimental Software Research in Germany.

"We considered the following inspection tools: (1) PAE (Program Assurance Environment) [Belli and Crisan, 1996] that can be seen as an extended debugger and represents an exception in the list of tools. (2) InspecQ [Knight and Myers, 1993] concentrates on the support of the Phased Inspection process model developed by Knight and Meyers (3) ICILE [Brothers et al., 1990] supports the defect detection phase as well as the defect collection phase in a face-to-face meeting. (4) Scrutiny [Gintell et al., 1995] and (5) CSI [Mashayekhi et al., 1993], support synchronous, distributed meetings to enable the inspection process for geographically separated development teams. (6) CSRS [Johnson and Tjahjono, 1997], (7) InspectA [Knight and Myers, 1993], (8) Hypercode [Perpich et al., 1997], and (9) ASIA [Perry et al., 1996] remove the conventional defect collection phase and replace it by a public discussion phase where participants vote on defect-annotations. (10) ASSIST [Macdonald and Miller, 1995] uses its own process modeling language and executes any desired inspection process model. All tools provide more or less comfortable document handling facilities for browsing documents on-line."

"To compare the various tools, we developed Table 3 (see Table 14.1) according to the various phases of the inspection process. We focused on whether a tool provides facilities to control and measure the inspection process, and the infrastructure on which the tool is running (a cross 'x' indicates support and a minus '-' no support).

Of course, for source code products various compilers are available that can perform type and syntactical checking. This may remove some burden from inspectors. Furthermore, support tools such as Lint that may help detect further classes of defects. However, the use of these tools is limited to particular development situations and may only lighten the inspection burden." [LAI98]

There are many tools too numerous to mention for performing analysis for code defects; e.g., pointer de-references, memory leaks, array boundary violations. For Inspections, in addition to those listed by SERN there are Reasoning, ReviewPro, CheckMate, Remote Inspection, and others. While some of these are still offered, none are resoundingly successful in the marketplace.

Tool	PAE	ICICLE	Scrutiny	CSRS	InspecQ	ASSIST	CSI/CAIS	InspectA	Hypercode	ASIA
Reference	[BEL96]	[BRO90]	[GIN95]	[JON93]	[KNI93]	[MAC97]	[MAS93]	[MUR97]	[PER97]	[STE97]
Planning support	-	-	-	X	X	X	-	X	X	-
Defect decision support	X	X	X	X	X	X	X	X	X	X
Automated defect detection	X	X	-	-	X	-	-	-	-	-
Document handling support	C-code	C-code	code	code/text	C-code (Ada)	code	code	code	code/text	code/text/ graph
Defect collection support	-	X	X	X	-	X	X	X	X	X
Defect correction support	-	-	-	-	-	-	-	(X)	(X)	X
Inspection process Control possible	-	-	-	X	X	X	-	X	X	X
Process Measurement support	-	X	X	X	-	X	X	X	X	X
Timestamp	-	-	-	X	-	-	X	-	-	X
Defect statistics	-	X	X	X	-	X	X	X	X	X
Infrastructure	UNIX	X-win	ConvB	Ergret	?	LAN	Suite	E-mail	Web	Web

Examples of Inspection Assistance Tools [LAI98]
Table 14.1

Refer to the ISERN survey article by Laitenberg [LAI98], which provides references for each of these tools. The article has an extensive bibliography of 4 ½ pages for Inspections and related topics.

14.6 Reusability

If we ever get to the point where reuse is more successful in practice, we should then find that the volume and cost of Inspections should be reduced on projects. We are not yet there and while reuse is always a compelling subject, there simply are not enough situations where it is well practiced nor has it paid off as hoped across the community. This does not mean we should stop trying to do reuse. I just wish we had a breakthrough that permitted wider adoption and practice.

Despite these quibbles, when reuse is in evidence, the Inspection process must be adjusted. We could do either of the following:

1. Not inspect the reused work products: this makes sense when we have evidence that the reuse components have a proven level of quality and we have not modified them for the current use in the project. This should be the goal in the future for all new component use.
2. Selectively include a subset of the reused components in some Inspections. This makes sense when there are interfaces that must be addressed during some Inspections.
3. Re-inspect some reused components. This might make sense in early reuse application, but should cease after we have established conviction that the reused components are of proven quality.
4. Focus on the "correctness" of the reused part to ensure it is a correct fit.

So as reuse increases in use, less effort should be required for Inspections on projects.

14.7 Verifying the Process of Building the Product

Inspections were put in place to verify the correctness of work products. As defects were found and fixed, the work product moved into the next life cycle stage with a presumed level of correctness. If effectiveness was high this presumption was reasonable for delivering a controlled quality product. The assumption was that if no other defects were found by an Inspection, then there probably were no more to be found. This would obviously be true if Inspections were 100% effective, but there is no way to prove the effectiveness during an Inspection.

The ultimate proof of zero remaining defects can only be substantiated after the work product ceases to be used. Any defects found in later project or product cycles are defects that leaked through the Inspection process. We could derive for any given Inspection the level of effectiveness in removing defects through dynamic calculations as discussed in Chapter 6.

Therefore with some minimal analysis we can begin to verify if the Inspection process is acceptably effective at the time of the Inspection by looking at patterns and comparing performance to expected boundaries of capability. For example, we saw earlier in Chapters 6 and 9 that there is a relationship between speed of the Inspection and defects detected in work products. Over time and with consistent practice, we find that there is an expected range in the rates of Inspections that will lead to the maximum defect density detection in the organization.

The analysis today is not precise, but it is a start. We do not need to be precise to find patterns that enable decisions to improve quality levels of software products. Analysis using techniques like control charts gives us increased confidence that we are employing engineering practices to advantage. It is possible that the analysis is creating a type of Hawthorne effect, but so what. If paying attention to the work that people do leads to better results, then let's pay more attention.

It is not Hawthorne effect, but good use of feedback into the system when data is analyzed and used to control and make further improvements.

We also need to look at other characteristics of the Inspection process to increase our confidence of best case Inspections to approach 100% effectiveness. These characteristics include using checklists for both the work product under Inspection and checklists for the Inspection process itself. When we use a product checklist during production we increase the probability that fewer defects go into the work product. When we use a process checklist during an Inspection we increase the probability that we have removed the maximum number of defects and bring ourselves closer to the 100% effectiveness possibility. The ETVX process structure in Chapter 3 contains the procedures and checklists to ensure best practice of the Inspection process for each Inspection activity.

We may not be able to have proof of 100% effectiveness at the time of the Inspection, but we can have a higher confidence of 100% effectiveness by paying attention to the process performance indicators. Our goal should always be to remove 100% of the defects inherent in any work product using Inspections. "Proof" will come with time wherein we consistently see zero (0) defects found after good Inspection processes are used. When we put Defect Prevention in place with Inspections we reduce the volume of defects coming into all defect removal activities. Then as we understand the relationships of management and technical task performance during a project, we can with increasing conviction state that we have a 100% effective Inspection defect removal process.

If 100% effectiveness cannot be achieved and/or it is not a requirement, we still need to know what our effectiveness is. Only then can we make an economic decision on how much more effective we should be, and the decision should be based on objective data.

An evolution to 100% effectiveness is possible for any task. If one wanted to learn how to solder pipes or fly a plane or perform surgery, there are steps to follow in a specific order with a set of actions to take at each step. As one started they might check against a list (written or mental) and then eventually these would be so ingrained that they wouldn't even think about the steps or actions. If our results are consistently 100% effective, then the process has been fully inculcated. We might not feel we need the checklists, but we should still keep them handy in case we need them.

14.8 Where Do Defects Come From?

I sometimes ask this question during SW-CMM or Inspection training, and once was surprised to hear from a participant, "The devil makes them!" Well, we all laughed, but if we extend this thought that the "devil is in the details," then maybe he was on to something. In tests and reviews we all do a good job of looking into the main function of a program. Yes, we find defects there, but after a while this settles down, but we keep inspecting and testing the same main function over and over. What we don't seem to do as well is test the error conditions or exception handling that are needed by the main function when something goes wrong. I believe this is true in Inspections also; i.e., not enough attention is given to inspecting error conditions.

In an issue of IEEE Transactions on Software Engineering, the guest editors state "The importance of exception handling is well-recognized by system designers and software engineers. Exception handling is very often the most important part of the system because it deals with abnormal situations. The goal of exception handling mechanisms is to make programs robust and reliable. However, for a variety of reasons, not the least among which is the fact that more than half of the code is often devoted to exception detection and handling, many failures are caused by incomplete or incorrect handing of these abnormal situations." [PER00]

For the purposes of this section, I am combining exception handling and error recovery. They are different, but in this discussion only in degrees. Error conditions are more concerned with processing return codes and status flags when instructions are executing in a running program. Exception handling is concerned with handling design or coding logic flaws, where the programs does not correctly or sufficiently address what might happen in a running environment when something goes wrong. For our purposes, both are the same; i.e., something has gone wrong and there is not a correct mechanism to address it in the program. I will lump the actions required to address both into the term "recovery."

Some reasons why exception handling and error recovery are not sufficiently handled in programs include:

- The design of the language used for code; i.e., it may be difficult to understand
- Performance tradeoffs made in executable code paths
- Readability and maintainability tradeoffs made due to too high a volume of recovery
- The network of possible errors can be huge
- The belief that it cannot be completely done in some programs

The answers to some of these reasons are:

- Know or learn the exception handling characteristics of the language and architecture being used

- Define the risks that are being taken for performance, readability, and maintainability; it is better to have comments in the code that acknowledge that recovery is not being addressed than to leave it as an unknown or as an assumption
- Address exception coverage and error recovery during the specifications and design stages using the techniques that are proven to offer repeatable value in reducing defects due to incorrect/insufficient recovery

Can this problem be solved completely? No, not completely. But this may be due to limitations of languages and software engineering techniques. I also believe it just is not a big enough issue for some projects. "Good enough" programming is becoming more a part of our times. Perhaps this is due to the time constraints to get something (anything) in the market or in the hands of the users. And then they pray. Deliver the function and hope nothing goes wrong; e.g., see the card reader anecdote (Anecdote 14.1).

Can Inspections help? Yes, there is no question about this. Have Inspections been used to the best advantage for error recovery? No! "For example, one experiment in software error data collection lists 53 different types of software errors, but does not list exception handling errors or errors of omission among them." [MAX00] But these cases are not the fault of Inspections per se. They are the fault of how Inspections, including checklists, have been used. In some sense we can say that any given Inspection is only as good as its checklist. This is not entirely true, but checklists are a necessary precondition to success. Good checklists are worth their weight in gold, at least.

An example of a complex program system was the IBM Space Shuttle project in Houston. A paper in the IBM Systems Journal described the processes used on this project; including Inspections and that they achieved zero defect discovery in flights during this program. [BIL94] I have to believe that during a space flight the number of possible error conditions is huge. This project used Inspections to the best advantage. So even in complex, safety critical programs zero defects are possible. Unfortunately, this does not seem to be a goal for many programs.

Those who choose to focus on exception handling and error recovery during Inspections will learn that much of the answer is in the evolution of their checklist. As we know, checklists should be tuned to the projects within an organization, so we should expect to see tailored checklists that lead to improved effectiveness.

Two issues of IEEE Transactions on Software Engineering focused on exception handling. [IEE00a] [IEE00b] Both of these issues have good bibliographies for further study. More needs to be researched in this area.

ANECDOTE

THOSE OTHER PATHS

When I joined IBM they had us apply the first six months of our career to training, some of which included projects that could become part of delivered customer products. My team was assigned a bootstrap loader for a core dump program on the first IBM time-sharing system, TSS.

We were cocky as many young programmers are, thank God. This energy is exciting in any industry. After looking at our design we gave ourselves the challenge of getting the entire bootstrap loader on one punched card of assembled code. This way there would only need to be one card in front of the core dump program. Why this was so important to us I am not entirely sure anymore, but at the time it seemed like a good programming trick if we could pull it off. And we did pull it off. This was our view of an elegant solution. We had to optimize the compiled code by hand punching the executable instructions, since the compiler was not efficient enough to allow us to get it all on one card. But with time, desire, and the clear challenge we gave ourselves, we actually did it.

What was interesting, and at the time we were convinced it was a reflection of our abilities, is that when we ran the card through the card reader the first time, it actually worked. It boot strapped into low memory and created a non-disruptive space in which to load the core dump program without losing any vital information from memory and then the dump routine went to work. We ran to our training supervisor to show him what we had done and that we were ahead of schedule.

That one-card, elegant program never worked any of the times we tried it in front of our supervisor. He thought we were joking with him, but we soon learned that the reason the one-card bootstrap loader did not work all the time was that we had no error recovery in the program. Nada. Zero. And if you have ever seen a card reader you know that there are many mechanical parts and fingers to position, process, and read the card. These all amount to potential errors when the card is not in the best shape or not positioned exactly right in the reader.

When we learned that we needed to account for the many error possibilities, all of which by the way were specified in the hardware manual for the card reader, we went back to the design and code of the full solution that was required. The program now amounted to 3 ½ cards of compiled code.

This lesson has stayed with me ever since, but the reality that most programs do not sufficiently account for error recovery also persists.

Anecdote 14.1

In summary for this section:

- Inspections can lead to zero defects in highly complex and safety critical programs
- Exception handling and error recovery are large sources of defects on most programs

Focusing on exception handling and error recovery during Inspections will lead to higher effectiveness for defect removal. These are only one source of defects, but defects due to exception handling and error recovery too often crash the software and systems.

14.9 100% Effectiveness

It took over 25 years before I saw repeatable 100% effectiveness with Inspections. While this level of effectiveness is still rare, it is increasing. This does not yet mean 100% effectiveness always or for every project, but the promise of more is within sight. Two questions that remain are:

1. Can all projects and all organizations see this possibility?
2. Which projects should try to achieve this goal?

Only time will tell, but the promise of the possibility has been fulfilled. There may be other instances in the software community, but few have been published or presented public information to date, so it is still not common enough. The only public presentation I am aware of to date was made at the 2001 Software Technology Conference and spoke about the successes seen at Tata Consultancy Services in India where multiple instances of 100% effectiveness were seen in one enhancement project. [RAD01]

There are a number of examples in the literature of 90%+ effectiveness having been seen, so we know these numbers are achievable. The challenge then is to see all software organizations achieve 90%+ and for some 100% effectiveness. We know it is doable, but why not within all organizations? This is partially a research topic and partially a requirement that customers need to bring to their suppliers. There will be advancement that will be increasingly demonstrated by testimonials. This I feel confident about. It is even possible that this behavior could be motivated and rewarded by contracts with enlightened customers.

McCann at Lockheed calculated that “If the code inspection process could be modified to 99 percent efficiency without increasing code inspection costs, then the savings would potentially exceed 107,000 labor hours/MSLOC.” [MCC01] Here “efficiency” means effectiveness and “MSLOC” are million source lines of code.

Of course, not all organizations or projects will feel the need for 90%+ effectiveness. Only their customers or competitors can tell them if this is a necessary business decision for them to take. I am sure we will continue to see projects that do not believe effectiveness is a necessary objective.

As discussed in Chapter 1, over the past twenty-eight years from the many experiences I have had with organizations practicing Inspections I have come to see the following effectiveness pattern in organizations using the SW-CMM.

SW-CMM	Effectiveness
Level 1	<50%
Level 2	50-65%
Level 3	65-75%
Level 4	75-90%
Level 5	90-100%

Inspection Effectiveness Increasing with Maturity Levels
Figure 14.1

Keep in mind that these numbers represent a pattern, and there may be some exceptions. The organization environment and characteristics need to be understood before judging the exceptions as outside the pattern. For example, in the initial IBM study in 1972, before there was a SW-CMM, the documented effectiveness of Inspections was approximately 65%.

In hindsight I could offer that the VTAM project would not have been rated a Level 2, primarily due to a lack in the Requirements Management process, but it would have been close to Level 2. The project was actually practicing various parts of all Level 3 Key Process Areas (KPAs). By the rules of assessments, however, they would have been a Level 1, but with an Inspection effectiveness typically seen in Level 3 organizations. Models are not perfect, but they can help give insights.

This Inspection Effectiveness pattern does repeat reasonably well across organizations that I have seen, worked with, or heard about. So part of the answer to achieving 100% effectiveness is to move up the SW-CMM maturity ladder, since the supporting process areas enable doing Inspections more effectively. As the SEI's data shows, there are an ever-increasing number of Level 4 and Level 5 organizations each year.

But do software organizations at Level 5 consistently achieve 90-100% effectiveness? The answer is an unfortunate "No." Partially this is due to variations in Level 5's and partially this is that some Level 5's may not have completely fulfilled the SW-CMM objectives as intended; i.e., they may not really be at Level 5 or have done so through liberal interpretations.

Should all Level 5's achieve 90% or greater effectiveness? Here my answer is a resounding Yes. But sadly it is not the same view for all, including some apparent Level 5 organizations. In a survey I conducted of documented Level 4 and 5 organizations, it was clear that there was wide variation in organization practice for the requirements defined for KPAs at Levels 4 and 5. [RAD00] Despite these exceptions there are Level 5 organizations with 90% or greater effectiveness experiences and it is these organizations that others should emulate.

As noted earlier, we must learn and prove by experience that an Inspection process is 100% effective. We cannot prove it beforehand, but we can ensure that all the processes are used that would enable it. Then we can reflect on the quality when the product is in use and we can improve again. Where the quality target is not zero defects or some other acceptable quantitative goal, we must learn how to continuously evolve and improve our processes so they can become effective to help achieve the goal.

There have been some articles proposing that the cost to remove the last defect is substantially higher and that the cost payoff may not be good business. This cost relationship for the last defect may be true in a test environment and is another reason why we should set the objective of reducing test costs. We should strive only to have a fixed cost in test and remove the variable costs driven by defects as discussed in Chapter 9. If all defects are found in Inspections, then, which was the last defect found? The answer is decidedly not the same during Inspections. When using Inspections we address the full area of opportunity for defects at one logical time for any work product. In test we do it in fits and starts. How can the cost for the "last" defect in an Inspection then be more than the cost for each of the others in Inspections? The normalized costs are the same for all defects in Inspections. The objective is to find them all in a fixed period of time. In test the time and cost are somewhat elastic even when bounded by the ship date.

14.10 Selective Inspections

A question that has been asked since the first Inspections is, "Do we need to inspect every work product?" A more interesting question is, "Would you inspect a work product that had no defects?" Well, the answer is probably that you would not. How can we know that there are no defects in a work product? Let me share some data from a project that I worked with, shown in Figure 14.2. The data reflects defects approximately one year after delivery, so it is probably a good enough approximation of defect distribution across the set of modules in the project.

This table requires some explanation. The first column is based on clusters of code partitioned into deciles based on defect density. Taking the code unit with the lowest defect density and putting it at the bottom of the stack starts to create the stack. The next lowest defect dense unit is then stacked on top of the previous. This is continued until the last code unit and consequently the highest in defect density is placed at the top of the stack.

Then approximate break points are made for the stacked units based on the total size of the product. For example, if we had 10,000 LOC, then each decile would be 1,000 LOC. But as nature will have it, code units rarely break so evenly, and we must make a placement based on the module that overlaps a break. If we had 5 units summing to 1150 LOC at the bottom of the stack, we would need to make a decision on where to include the unit that is overlapping. For example, should the overlapping unit go into 10th decile or the 9th? The rule we used was to put the unit into the decile that it most fits. This is not perfect, but for the analysis it is sufficient.

What we note after these unit allocations by decile for this example is:

- Pareto strikes again; about 80% of the defects occur in about 20% of the code; in this project: 74.3% of the defects occurred in 20% of the code

- About 75% of the code was below the average defect density
- 20% of the code has zero (0) defects
- Some units were very defective; e.g., the top 10%, and the defect density in the top-most unit was approximately one defect in every 4 LOC

Decile	Defects/KLOC
1st	114.1
2nd	41.6
3rd	27.0
4th	19.7
5th	15.7
6th	11.1
7th	7.9
8th	5.2
9th	0
10th	0
Average	24.4

Decile Ranking of Defective Code Modules
Figure 14.2

Thus if we could focus our Inspections, we would clearly focus on the top 20-30% of the code. If we knew ahead of time, we would not bother at all with the bottom 20% of the code. In this 20% of the code, there are no defects. Therefore, an Inspection cannot find defects, nor can test. There are no defects! We might even decide to not inspect the bottom 80% and give strict attention to the heavy hitter defective modules.

It is easy to know these characteristics after the fact as I've noted before. How can we know them before an Inspection? Data and pattern analysis is the answer. With data analysis we will learn; e.g., that some modules are more complex due to size or volatility or even who worked on it. With data analysis we can begin to define a set of characteristics that signal the probability of high defect dense units. We can then use these characteristics to make decisions on what to always inspect and where we are willing to take a risk and not inspect. This does not mean we will always be right in our decisions, so we must track after the Inspection to learn how good the decision was in fact. Then we can tune the selection characteristics based on the data.

As we do this we always maintain focus on effectiveness, but we have now introduced the management of Inspection efficiency. We do not want to impact the effectiveness. We want to sustain it at a lower cost. In Chapter 9: The Economics of Inspections, we learned that Inspections are a significant cost driver. In some organizations today Inspections can be 20% of the cost of the project.

Some might be willing to treat Inspection costs as a fixed cost of quality, but it is not fixed. The cost is a variable based on the amount of Inspection performed. The amount inspected is dependent on the risk we choose to take and the process maturity we have that enables us to know that we can manage the risk and sustain effectiveness. The amount to be inspected is directly related to how well the work product was built; i.e., how many defects entered the work product. With data analysis we can make decisions with less risk and we can affirm our level of process maturity and effectiveness. With a constantly improving and maturing process we can build confidence that we are building it right, not just once, but over and over again for many work products. This then is disciplined software engineering.

For every Inspection where we exclude work products that do not have defects and where we sufficiently believe that we cannot adversely affect our effectiveness, we gain in efficiency and reduce the Cost of Quality. This is a business decision that works to reduce costs, does not affect quality, and improves time for delivery. Is this a myth or miracle? Neither! It is process maturity working for us. It is organization discipline and institutionalization of capability.

We start by selecting some units not to inspect and we work our way incrementally to fewer and fewer necessary Inspections. In some projects we may be able to eliminate the need for Inspections entirely. We've already seen where test can be removed in some maintenance and enhancement projects. Next we must focus on reducing and maybe eliminating the need for Inspections in development projects. Today we are only capable of this in a few organizations that I know of. The others should not stop trying to reach that state.

14.11 Sampling

Sampling is used in manufacturing and process industries, but not frequently in software. In manufacturing there are large volumes of materials produced under a repetitive process and the sampling allows a low cost view to assure that the process is still performing within acceptable limits. In software we produce one work product at a time under varying conditions, but sampling can still be used with some limitations. We can use sampling as a guide or suggestion of actions to take, but not usually as a representation of the full product or even full work product to be inspected.

Also sampling in software tends to give more assurance about a negative situation than a positive one. For example, if by sampling we find a high volume of defects compared to what might be expected, this may suggest that there is a problem. If, however, a low density or zero defects were found, we must be careful to assure that we have a true representative sample before we conclude that the defect density is the same throughout the product. The same concern exists if too many defects were found and the sampling was not representative.

Unbiased sampling is more difficult in software since there is not the same volume of parts or artifacts as there would be in manufacturing, for example. It is easy to fall into a belief that the sample density may be representative; e.g., the same nominal process was used throughout the product, but I suggest one reconfirm that the sample is indeed representative. From what I've seen this is not done consistently in sampling practices in software.

We performed a version of sampling in the 1980's in a situation where we had already successfully demonstrated that the ship date and product quality for a project were both in serious jeopardy. We calculated the amount of code that should be re-inspected to flush out defects and help stabilize the product quality, but the management balked since the project was already well along its project cycle. We needed to demonstrate to them that our calculations were correct. We proposed running a sample with some accepted limits that would define the probable quality level. We assured them that the sample would be both random and representative.

Management accepted our sampling approach to decide if additional Re-Inspections were warranted. We took great pains to assure that the sample was not skewed; e.g., that we were not choosing the worst quality modules (highest defect dense) to re-inspect. As it turned out, the sample Re-Inspections more than proved our original predictions and the remainder of the code was either re-inspected or given additional testing. The sampling in this example helped to prove the latent defect density in the product at large.

Gilb recommends sampling to help determine the apparent quality level of the work product to be inspected. "Sampling selected portions of a document is an excellent practical alternative to complete checking. It can be used to estimate the issue density per page in the unchecked pages. Sampling can lead to exiting the document based on its sampled quality." [GIL93] He goes further to suggest that Inspections could even be skipped when a sampling justifies the risk. Thus sampling could be a technique to select which work product to inspect or not. "Use sampling to understand the quality level of a document. It is neither necessary nor desirable to check all pages of long documents. Representative samples will probably tell you whether a document is clean enough to exit." [GIL98]

Gilb advises its use and practice based on results; e.g., "I have seen half a day of Inspection (based on a random sample of 3 pages) show that there were 19 logic defects per page in 40,000 pages of an air traffic control logic design (1986, Sweden)." He also suggests "if while planning the Inspection, the team leader performs a 15 minute cursory check that shows up a few major defects on a single page, it is time for a word with the author in private." [GIL98] This will help flush out work products that are not ready for Inspection. This suggests that sampling should be an entry criterion for types of Inspections or that additional steps should be added to the Inspection process.

How might one do sampling for Inspections? Among other approaches, we might try the following:

1. Pick subsets of work products to inspect using a pre-defined selection criteria
2. Pick units from the full project set using pre-defined characteristics
3. Pick work products based on complexity
4. Pick work products based on who worked on the work product

Let's explore each of these possibilities.

1. **Pick subsets of work products to inspect using pre-defined selection criteria:** Here we would subset the project's work products into high probability areas for defects. We would use pre-defined defect density criteria for these subsets and if the defect density is exceeded during the Inspection, then decide to inspect more of

the work product. This is similar to the statistical selective testing in the Cleanroom method wherein a sample of tests are executed and the defect density compared to predetermined go/no-go criteria. This requires more sophistication in data analysis and the willingness to take risk, but it can reduce the Cost of Quality where we have a mature production process. The concept seems sound, and Gilb apparently used it successfully in the air traffic control logic design noted above.

2. **Pick units from the full project set using pre-defined characteristics:** This is similar to the selection process discussed in the previous section, but in this approach the focus is on the full product, not just the work products under Inspection. Then based on the results of selection and using pre-defined defect density criteria we might decide to inspect more of the full product than was originally planned. For example, we might have planned to inspect 20% of the code in a project, but results begin to suggest that the defect density in the full product is significantly higher than expected. In this case, we might select, for example, an additional 10% of the product's code to inspect and then monitor the results to ensure we achieve our quality objectives. In the previous section we were sampling within one work product; here we are sampling within the project or product set.

3. **Pick work products based on complexity:** Complexity can be measured in many different ways, but once a threshold for complexity is exceeded in a work product, it would become a candidate. This is similar to approach 1 above, but specifically is focused on the complexity characteristic.

4. **Pick work products based on who worked on the work product:** This is always a touchy area. As noted earlier we do not want to exclude work products and cause perception of being selective in an adverse manner. This is especially true for organizations starting with Inspections. In mature organizations where the people are focused on delivering high quality products at controlled costs we have more opportunity to use this approach. We could always require that Inspections be performed on work from new team members. We could come to understand that some individuals really can produce defect free code and choose to exclude their work.

Since these are sampling approaches, we must always analyze the data and results to learn if we are making the right decisions. If the analysis confirms our decisions, then we can move forward with confidence. If not, then we may need to take action to manage the risk. Yes, we are taking risks with sampling approaches, but there is nothing wrong with taking risk provided we are willing to live with the risk should it manifest itself. If we are not or cannot live with the risk, then think again about taking it. This is true in all of business and life, and in business the victory sometimes goes to those who are willing to take the risk. You decide.

To conclude, we could use sampling to:

- Prevent false starts; e.g., postpone highly defective work product Inspections
- Prove the quality level of the whole and reduce the amount of Inspection or testing

- Determine if remedial actions are necessary to improve the quality of the whole product

14.12 Reducing the Number of Inspectors

One example where reduced number of inspectors was effective includes AT&T's work as documented by Votta. [VOT93] In his paper he shows that across 13 studied Inspections "The average synergy rate is about 4%." Synergy being the contributing factor when a team of inspectors at the Inspection Meeting discusses defects found during Preparation and which in turn leads to additional defects being discovered at the meeting. Votta suggests, "Almost all inspection meetings requiring all reviewers to be present should be replaced with Depositions—3 person meetings (author, moderator, and one reviewer)." With this conclusion, he has reduced the number of inspectors to three.

Parnas and Weiss also suggested that the number of Inspectors should be reduced to a minimum set. They proposed active design reviews to help insure that all inspectors were actively engaged in finding defects and not just listening. They claimed that by keeping the team smaller it forced active participation. I agree. [PAR87]

In Chapter 4 I discussed 1:1 Inspections where there is only one inspector with the Producer for a team of only two people during the Inspection.

I strongly recommend 1:1 Inspections as a cost effective alternative to traditional Inspection. This is an especially efficient alternative when effectiveness is repeatedly high.

Now let's look at the possibility of reducing Inspections to only the inspector in attendance. Some readers may blanch at this and say, "But these are no longer Inspections." Well, they are no longer the traditional Inspection, but they are Inspections. Let's take a look at Solo:Inspections.

14.13 Solo:Inspections

Since project cost is related to the number of inspectors, we should want to minimize the number involved in any one Inspection. In the original method 4 inspectors were the norm and the IEEE standard suggests 3-6. If we can reduce to 3 from 4 we save 25% on traditional Inspections; reduce to 2 and we save 50%. If it is possible to perform an Inspection with only one inspector, we could save 75% of costs of Inspections.

How you might ask can we reduce to one inspector? Consider an Inspection where the Producer is only involved for an Overview, where warranted, delivery of the material, and resolution of defects. Let's explore how and whether this can be successfully applied.

We saw in Chapter 4 (see Table 4.2) that 1:1 Inspections follow the same activities in the traditional Inspections with some tailoring to ensure effective process performance with fewer participants. Needless to say when effectiveness is achieved, then efficiency will also be in evidence. Is the same effectiveness possible with Solo:Inspections as we are seeing with traditional Inspections? The answer as I have observed is Yes.

In the Solo:Inspections, the inspector logs on to his workstation and brings up the work product to be inspected. He has all required documents available through the organization's intranet for ancillary and reference documents he may need. He has access to the appropriate checklist, standards, and forms to record any defects found. He can open as many concurrent windows or views with required documents as he needs to perform the Inspection. His time is recorded based on log-on time. When he is done, he submits his Inspection documents to the Producer, Inspection Coordinator, and Project Lead. He is then available to the Producer if there should be any questions.

Another benefit is that the Inspection can be for longer than two hours, as the inspector can start and stop, chunking as he feels necessary. In Solo:Inspections the inspector makes a commitment to the Project Lead for a completion time or date and this is what he then can concurrently manage along with other work in his queue.

Organizations that are using Solo:Inspections move to them when their traditional Inspections have already proven high effectiveness. Since there is feedback and coaching to the inspectors about their effectiveness during this transition, the Solo:Inspection effectiveness remains high.

I do not recommend that organizations move to Solo:Inspections in one quick jump. But I do recommend that all organizations give it serious consideration. Recall that the first focus will always be on effectiveness. Solo:Inspections are an improvement in efficiency. After the effectiveness is proven, then the organization should look at efficiency improvements such as Solo:Inspections.

Table 14.2 shows how the assignment of responsibilities changes in Solo:Inspections. But observe that all the traditional Inspection activities are still performed. This set of activities is fully aligned with practice as defined by IEEE but a key difference is that the team is just one inspector.

Note that the Producer may still be involved, but only sometimes for the Overview, when an Overview is warranted. The Producer may also be involved in the Analysis Meeting and the Rework, when there are defects to analyze and discuss. It is also possible that the inspector may have questions for the Producer during the Solo:Inspection, but these and even the Analysis Meeting do not need to be face-to-face. It is also entirely possible that the Producer will not be involved in the Preparation or the Inspection Meeting, when the inspector has no questions. The Producer and inspector should agree on their protocol for asking and responding to questions during the Solo:Inspection.

Another advantage is that the Producer and inspector can be in two different locations. The inspectors I have observed seemed fully comfortable with this remote approach. One might wonder that given the starts and stops whether the inspector lost continuity of thinking and if this affected effectiveness. All I can say is apparently not, since effectiveness was consistently high. The programmers in these organizations were fully enabled to perform the best of Inspections, not to “just do an Inspection”. It was expected and tracked to learn that they would be within acceptable limits for time spent and for defects found.

Moderator Task	Required?	Who Performs
1. Inspection Scheduling	Yes	PL
1.1 Determine need for Overview	Yes	PL & I
1.2 Determine Inspection team	Yes	PL
1.3 Ensuring availability of materials	Yes	P
1.4 Assigning roles	NA	NA
1.5 Chunking materials	Yes	I
1.6 Defining activities schedule	Yes	PL & I
1.6.1 Overview	Yes	PL & I
1.6.2 Preparation effort	Yes	PL & I
1.6.3 Inspection Meeting duration	Yes	PL & I
1.6.4 Analysis Meeting	Optional	PL & P & I
1.6.5 Logistics	Yes	PL & I
2. Overview	Optional	P & I
3 Preparation	Yes	I
4. Inspection Meeting	Yes	I
5. Data Recording	Yes	I
6. Analysis Meeting	Optional	P & I
7. Rework	Yes	P
8. Follow-up	Yes	P & I

Solo:Inspection Activity Assignments
Table 14.2

Solo:Inspections, to date, have been best applied for code and Low-level design work products, but the concept could work for other work product types. Some work products, such as requirements specifications, may never be able to use Solo: Inspections, but most effort on Inspections is not in these work products anyway.

Lastly, we should recognize that Solo:Inspections would permit that we could use experts who are not part of our project, organization, or even company to perform Inspections for us on some work products.

A project could even subcontract Solo:Inspections to qualified domain experts.

14.14 The Professional Programmer

There are numerous articles, presentations, and committee meetings defining standards to judge or determine how programmers might become more professional including requirements for licensing exams to qualify the programmer and give them credentials as *software engineers*.

This path towards more discipline has happened in all professions, so we might eventually see licensing for software engineers. I would hope that the exams would test for understanding about the value of Inspections and how and when to practice them effectively and efficiently. So we might hope that the debate about the value of Inspections and when they should be performed will wither over time as more and more software engineers inculcate the practice as a normal and expected part of the job.

Humphrey has brought focus to increasing the discipline of software engineering in the very book by that title. [HUM95] While he addresses how an individual can come to learn about their capabilities and practices and then improve them, he only briefly addresses the contribution of Inspections within his Personal Software Process (PSP). He notes, "As you strive to achieve 100 percent process yield, you should consider incorporating inspections into your PSP process." Later he states "Whether you compile before the inspection is much more debatable. The issue concerns where you need help. While you are working to get your defects under control, it might be helpful to have some associates inspect your code before you compile." He puts emphasis on personal reviews to remove defects and I fully support this thrust. As the removal yield prior to Inspection increases, the need for Inspections decreases. PSP has been sufficiently demonstrated in many university environments, but has not yet achieved compelling industrial practice although it is growing in use. Nonetheless, the principles lead to consistently improved programmer discipline.

While there have been, are, and will be discussions on how software engineering is becoming more and more professional, we have a long way to go. The hope, I suspect, is that we will develop a worldwide cadre of programmers who will build defect-free products. I wouldn't bet on it. I do believe we will have a group of programmers who will learn how to build defect-free products at good productivity rates, but I think this still will be a limited group.

So what will the rest do? Make defects as they do today? If so, the issue will remain how best to remove the defects before they cause more impact than desired. The answer will be with Defect Prevention combined with Inspections as discussed in Chapter 7. The new professional programmer will be better than today's average programmer, but I believe we will always have to deal with defect removal pre-production and post-production on some projects.

As it should be, there are new challenges to the traditional ways of programming. Rather than challenges, I should say these are alternatives. At least there are propositions opening up new areas for consideration. One that has received recent coverage and some acceptance is the idea of pair programming as defined by Beck within his eXtreme Programming (XP) approach. [BEC99] The idea is simple, straightforward, and compelling, as it seems to blow off what some programmers have seen as a bureaucratic and heavy-handed approach with Inspections and software processes.

Beck in the preface to his book says, "If code reviews are good, we'll review all code all the time (pair programming)." However, Beck does not mean anything close to what we've been discussing as Inspections. Rather he means that, with two sets of eyes looking at the work while it is being designed, coded, and tested, a higher quality will be achieved faster. This would have value for developing products with a lower defect density. Pair programming puts two programmers working side by side with only one computer between the two. They work in a full collaborative manner on all aspects of the project; i.e., design, code, and test. "Anecdotal and statistical evidence indicates pair programming is highly beneficial." [WIL00a] While I suspect this is true, no industrial study data has yet been provided. Williams et al. in another article state, "In an online survey of professional pair programmers, 96% stated that they enjoyed their job more than when they programmed alone." [WIL00b] I am sure this is also true, since they have more freedom than in some process focused environments.

Nosek at Temple University found that two programmers working together on a 45 minute programming problem "outperformed the individual programmers, enjoyed the problem-solving process more, and had greater confidence in their solutions." [NOS98] The two programmer teams had a 30% higher rating on Readability and 30% on the Functionality of the solution, and they completed the solution in 29% less time than the control group of individual programmers. There are also suggestions that pair programming solutions have high quality; i.e., few bugs.

This is certainly an approach for programming that some groups should look into. However, as with all methods there are limitations. One is that pair programming and XP, which includes other practices, "is designed to work with projects that can be built by teams of two to ten programmers, that aren't sharply constrained by the existing computing environment, and where a reasonable job of executing tests can be done in a fraction of a day.' [BEC99] OK, so Beck puts some restrictions on where XP may work best, but he offers an alternative for certain types of projects.

XP and pair programming will grow in use, I have no doubt about this, but I also suggest that they are not appropriate for all projects. Nonetheless, it is too compelling as an extension of programmer freedom compared to methods like Inspections or use of models like SW-CMM and ISO 9000 or use of software engineering processes. How well it will succeed, only time will tell.

Aside from the apparent team size limitation, I suggest that pair programming will ultimately prove to work for some and fail for some. It is based on a consensual pairing environment. Mankind has not done so well with consensual pairing in marriages between men and women. I see no reasons why XP pairs will do so much better. They will have arguments, disagreements, and divorces also. Only the frequency and amount of these will determine how well XP pair programming will survive in commercial environments. I know I am sounding a bit negative, as I actually like the concept. However, I've seen too many good concepts fall into disuse in the last 35 years. In any event we need to take that next step as Williams et al. conclude, "Finally, we would like to see the same experiments applied in an industrial setting – perhaps with part of a larger development team. [WIL00b]

14.15 Defect Prevention

Inspections, as we've discussed, are not a Defect Prevention activity per se, but a defect detection (removal) activity. Inspections are part of Appraisal costs in Cost of Quality. Causal Analysis and Defect Prevention are part of Prevention costs in COQ.

Our goal should always be to reduce the costs of detection. One way to do this is to focus on prevention. Defect Prevention will result in changes to the environment; i.e., we might introduce or change our processes, tools, methods, procedures, training, etc. The changes are determined by the Causal Analysis and resultant likely root cause that should be addressed.

There is a relationship between the three categories in COQ. As Prevention and Appraisal costs increase, the Rework costs should decrease. As Prevention costs increase, the Appraisal costs should decrease. Given these relationships, we should invest in Prevention.

See Chapter 7 for a detailed discussion about the value added by Defect Prevention practices coupled with Software Inspections.

14.16 Will Inspections Become Obsolete?

Sometimes I hope so. I believe a clear possibility exists for Low-level design and code, but not for all work products. The highest cost for Inspections is in Low-level design, and code, so a reduction in these areas is a good contribution to reducing COQ. I suspect that for requirements and key design documents we will need Inspections for quite some time. For other artifacts such as plans, test cases, documents, I think we will see a reduction in a need for Inspections as we improve the disciplines of the activities for creating these work products through training, processes, and tools.

One focus we should take is that when an Inspection finds too many defects, this is a signal to management to do a better job of managing the software processes and people resources.

There is no reason why programmers should be put into positions of generating 100's of defects to be found by Inspections.

If we continue to inject high volumes of defects that are found in Inspections, then all we've done is shift the defect removal cost from test to Inspections. This will reduce costs; this is important, but it is not enough. We can do much better, by developing products with few defects that go into Inspections. We really can do it right the first time, if we try.

Deming in "*Out of the Crisis*" states "Cease dependence on inspection to achieve quality. Eliminate the need for inspection on a mass basis by building quality into the product in the first place." [DEM8] Can we meet this objective in software or will we always be plagued as Deming goes on to say about exceptions where "mistakes and duds are inevitable but intolerable." I am not sure I want to claim that the software engineering process is an exception and it certainly shouldn't lead to duds. We can be better than that. We can have excellence in programming on a broader scale than exists today.

Inspections should not be a requirement to achieve quality and they are not required for all work products.

14.17 Recommendations from an Advocate

Philip Johnson, who has done much to keep Inspections and related techniques focused across the software community, provided a list of seven recommendations for the future of what he prefers to call Formal Technical Reviews rather than Inspections, since his view is that "industry adoption of inspection appears to remain quite low" but he also uses FTR as "an umbrella term for review methods involving a structured encounter where a group of technical personnel analyzes an artifact in order to improve both the quality of the product and the review process." [JON98]

He suggested:

- Provide tighter integration between FTR and the development method
- Minimize meetings and maximize asynchronicity in FTR
- Shift the focus from defect removal to improved developer quality
- Build organizational knowledge bases on review
- Outsource review and insource review knowledge
- Investigate computer-mediated review technology
- Break the boundaries on review group size

These points are addressed in this book.

14.18 Is Software Becoming More Complex?

Well, we can suppose so, but this argument has been used since software first came about. I don't want to try to resolve what complexity may mean, since it is another of those terms that means different things to different people. So let's just live with a fuzzy notion of complexity for this discussion.

We certainly can make software more complex by doing it poorly and this starts with architectures and High-level designs usually. Or we can make it more complex by making it large. Whatever became of elegant programming? Or we can keep it "complex" by accepting the project when the requirements are fuzzy at best. It's hard to say "No." when a paycheck is involved. Regardless of what complexity may truly be, we have many opportunities to make software less complex.

Royce suggests that software is more and more complex and suggests that "other forms of assessment have a higher leverage at uncovering architectural issues, requirements, and design trade-offs.' [ROY00] If he is right, then Inspections will be less helpful versus "early demonstration, test, and automated analysis'" as he states. Well, I can salute his position provided there is evidence that these alternatives are more effective and efficient. We know there are alternatives, but are they more effective and efficient?

14.19 Aspects of a Best Case Inspection Process

Well, we've explored a lot of territory in these 14 chapters. This book has many ideas for an evolved and improved Inspection process, but here I conclude with some of my thoughts on the best Inspection process as I see it today.

1. **Defect Prevention:** Inspections can be displaced in the future by disciplines that show that building it right is possible. Unfortunately this won't be true in all software organizations. Nonetheless, we must actively move programmers into a "building it right" production environment, and this will be enabled by Defect Prevention techniques. Ensure that error conditions and exception handling defects are especially addressed.

   In the meantime practice Defect Prevention as a coupled activity with Inspections.

2. **Effectiveness:** Whatever you call the process; e.g., Inspections or FTRs it must always prove to be effective. If it is not, something must be changed. The results of effectiveness are the key to what is the best approach in any organization. But organizations should not delude themselves into believing any other approach such as the less rigorous reviews or walkthroughs are just as effective. The name we call the method is not the important issue, but the results are. Minimally 90% effectiveness should be in place. If an organization has that, then they can call the method anything they want.

   To know effectiveness we must start by setting it as a goal and then tracking it.

3. **Proven method:** There are obvious reasons why the original Inspection method needed tuning and improvement, but it is the baseline to build upon. Inventing something new for the sake of being new is not good engineering discipline. Keep what works and change what is needed, but prove it works effectively. Much has been gained using the original method, and now more can be gained by using an evolved Inspection method.

   Build upon the proven base.

4. **Evolve:** There is nothing sacrosanct about the original method. In fact, the method has naturally evolved to permit more repeatability and higher effectiveness. The Fagan Inspection method defined in 1972 is old news. There are better evolved ways today. Tailor Inspections to meet your organization's personality; e.g., if you're the type that needs to discuss solutions, then do it as long as effectiveness is achieved. Even for others, a discussion from time to time may be warranted. But as you tailor do not simply throw out the proven method defined by Fagan.

   If you have an idea to further evolve the Inspection process, try it, but measure it objectively.

5. **Metrics:** Keep them, use them to evaluate effectiveness, and share them. Always keep your eye on the effectiveness of Inspections until you evolve to high % effectiveness. Collect only what is necessary.

   Set aggressive but achievable goals, then manage to achieve them. Then set new goals.

6. **Keep the process simple:** No one wants extra work and Inspections can be made to cause extra work. Listen when the programmers offer suggestions to make it simpler, but don't lose the effectiveness by reacting to every suggestion or complaint.

   Implement the incremental changes that help. For example, use minor lists during Preparation, as there is little to be gained discussing minor defects at the Inspection Meeting. If your data shows that the Inspection Meeting is offering little above the effectiveness achieved during Preparation, then consider dropping it. But be sure you are high in effectiveness first.

7. **Sample:** There is no sense in inspecting a work product that has no defects. Learn how to select based on work product characteristics. Then use sampling to prove that your characteristics are sufficiently correct.

   Start use of sampling incrementally, then build upon your successes and tune your sampling criteria.

8. **Automate:** Use the web to store all documents to make them available to inspectors. Where necessary; e.g., with cross-location inspectors, use interactive web sessions to hold the Inspection Meeting. If Preparation is highly effective in finding defects, then the Inspection, without the Inspection Meeting, can be asynchronous. Use tools that can flush out types of defects before the Inspection. Make their use a precondition.

   But don't trade off dependence on tools for programmer professional development and building software right.

9. **Process Improvement:** The original method did not afford enough attention to improving the process, but we know that this can be a major benefit. Record process defects as well as product defects. Discuss these during the Analysis Meetings and Defect Prevention Meetings. Do not just focus on product defects.

   Process defects can be prevented and in turn have an amplifying affect on injecting fewer defects in future work products.

10. **Reading/comprehension techniques:** If you don't understand a document, you can't find defects. So ensure that all inspectors have been trained on or given guidance in reading and comprehension techniques. Begin to use scenarios and

Program-Based Reading techniques. These techniques will best serve novices, but even the experienced programmers need to have these techniques and skills. If they never have it they will always read; i.e., inspect, in less effective ways.

11. **Feedback:** The programmers and the organization must be in constant learning mode. Given the amount of change we see in the software industry people are learning anyway, but with data analysis we can channel their learning.

    Give all programmers feedback on what works and what is not yet working as well and focus on being effective first and then efficient.

12. **1:1 Inspections:** Move away from high numbers of inspectors toward 1:1 Inspections. Yes, some Inspections such as Requirements Specifications will need more inspectors, but for code and Low-level design, more than one inspector may be wasteful. Inspections are not a social event; they are a business quality control.

    As we've seen, Preparation could be highly effective in finding defects, wherein then the Inspection can become a combined Preparation and the Inspection Meeting. Of course, your effectiveness is the key to making this move.

13. **Integrate Inspections with development:** Cleanroom does this, as does Extreme Programming and pair programming. The Inspection process should not always be an add-on at the end of a work product production activity. This was originally done because the programmers were handing in defect-prone work. They did this because of time pressures, inadequate requirements, poor management, and lack of capability. We know some things better today, so we should be able to do better by adapting Inspections, rather than forcing a one size fits all approach.

    Tailoring makes sense, but not if we loss effectiveness. The key will be to measure the results during test. There should be no or very few defects found after the tailoring. If there are too many defects, then the tailored integrated process is not best for business, and an add-on Inspection process may still be needed. Ensure the management process is practiced and you will find the Inspection process will work very effectively. 1:1 Inspections is another approach to integrating the development process with Inspections.

14. **Solo:Inspections:** Once you have demonstrated high effectiveness with your Inspection approach, move to Solo:Inspections. You should be able to maintain the effectiveness you require as long as you monitor the results. Once you have demonstrated effectiveness with your gain in efficiency from Solo:Inspection, I suspect you will also make programmers feel much better about Inspections.

    Who knows, perhaps they will begin to see that Inspections can be fun.

The method documented in 1976 is no longer the most effective approach, as it was documented. We have learned where to evolve, extend, tweak, and discount some of the early ways. As Glass likewise concluded during his review of alternatives some people were recommending, "Since all of this is very different from the state of the inspection practice, and even from the state of the inspection art as described in the advocacy research literature, I think there are some important lessons to be learned here. I hope you agree." [GLA99b] Of course, why this is surprising is an example of how the software community has become stuck in the Inspection method definition as it was originally put forth. We have learned to do better, building upon the base that Inspections gave us, but we should no longer practice less than what is now available. Comparing to the traditional Inspection method defined twenty-eight years ago no longer makes sense. We have evolved, as has the Inspection method.

The next to last point then is to advise you to take action and to take it now. The final point is to ask you to enjoy the success you will definitely get with Inspections when you apply them fairly, consistently, and correctly.

No one should care what you call Inspections:
The test to apply is do they work; i.e., are they effective?
It they are effective, you are right.
If they are not, then you should revisit what you have chosen.

So let's finish where we started:

End Quotes:

"If you believe you can or if you believe you can't, you will be right."
Henry Ford
and
"If you don't understand now, you probably won't later."
Anonymous

APPENDIX A
CHECKLISTS

A.1 Introduction

Checklists are an integral part of successful Inspections. They provide the inspectors a focus that is derived from the organization's history of problems to avoid. They serve to educate when the inspectors are first using them. They should evolve as the organization learns about common defects that can be added to the checklists. They can change as true Defect Prevention is put into practice. Checklists serve to remind Producers and inspectors of some things the mind overlooks or forgets.

Some organizations such as the SEI have suggested a checklist of checklists [SEI89] to assure that each checklist is addressing common intents for:

- Completeness
- Correctness
- Style
- Rules of construction
- Multiple views or perspectives reflected in the product
- Metrics to be gathered
- Technology

This may be more than is necessary, but if it helps, fine. My view is that checklists need to be complete but as short as possible. I prefer one-page checklists, but in some situations two pages may be needed. Checklists that get too large do not get used and are not well thought out. This was a reason why the checklists in the VTAM study were not as successful as expected and one reason why there was regression in each of the next three VTAM releases. The programmers just put them aside. We thought we had done a good job of creating checklists that addressed all possible and meaningful defects, but we missed the point that checklists must be useful for them to be used.

They do not need to address every possible defect that can be made; this is what language manuals do. Checklists should be selective and focus on the key defect possibilities. But in safety critical software the checklists may be larger for specific legal and insurance reasons. Most software does not have the same constraints as safety critical software. The choice is yours, but keep the programmers involved in feedback on the usefulness of the checklists. Use the data to determine which items on the list could be dropped, what may be missing, and what should be added.

Checklists can be categorized into two types: Work Products and Quality Attributes. Each type can be classified into sub-types, for example:

Work Products
- Requirements specifications
- High-level design
- Low-level design
- Code
- Plans

Quality Attributes
- Usability
- Installability
- Performance
- Maintainability

Checklists vary throughout the public literature. It is not my intent to try to define a universal checklist. I am not sure one can be defined, and if it were, it would not be accepted by most users. Therefore, this appendix supplies checklists as samples only. The reader can use them as is, modify them, or build their own. I expect the checklists will be modified and improved. Over time, an organization will eventually have its own unique checklists.

A.2 Use of Checklists

Checklists serve best when they are product and domain specific. Checklists provide guidance for the types of defects that a software organization considers most prevalent and critical. The checklists vary by work product to be inspected. The checklists should be *tailored* based on project-specific knowledge by adding or deleting checklist items. Checklists are not a replacement for style guides, which are used to create the work products. However, Producers could use Inspection checklists when developing the work product.

The Moderator is responsible for distributing or ensuring that the inspectors have the current and appropriate checklists for Preparation and for ensuring the use of the checklists during the Inspection Meeting. An initial set of checklists should have been provided to each inspector during their Inspections training. The latest version should be made available on the web or master document library.

Inspectors are responsible for using the checklists during Preparation and the Inspection Meeting.

SQA can be responsible to ensure checklists are being used during Inspections and should review the appropriateness of the checklist contents when they are created and modified.

Checklists should be baselined in the Process Asset Library as part of the Organization Standard Software Processes and defined as a project-level process, when the checklist is tailored specifically for the project

How a checklist is used is an individual choice. Some inspectors read it before the Preparation to give them a focus for the Inspection. Some use it at the end to check that they have addressed all relevant checklist items. Some do both. As an inspector gains more practice with Inspections the dependency on the checklist will decrease, since much of what is on the checklist will have found its way into the inspector's memory and practice. Nonetheless, it is helpful to review the checklist from time to time.

It is suggested that the Moderator ask if the checklist was used during Preparation and then review the checklist items at the end of the Inspection Meeting to ensure it has been sufficiently addressed in the Inspection Meeting. This is most helpful when Inspections are first put into practice. It should not be unexpected that the Inspection team finds they need to go back to some part of the work product when reviewing the checklist items at the end of the Inspection. This case is optional, and is useful during start up. One of the purposes the checklist serves is coverage mapping.

Checklists are used:

1. During Preparation by inspectors to ensure that the material has been sufficiently examined for the Inspection Meeting.

2. At the conclusion of the Inspection Meeting by the Moderator to ensure the work product has been sufficiently inspected.

Data from Inspections should be reviewed periodically to update the checklists and make them more appropriate to the work product being inspected. This is a responsibility of the SEPG or Inspection Coordinator. A checklist that does not change cannot be as useful for improving effectiveness.

Checklists are typically intended to help an inspector find a defect, but other goals besides defect detection have been included. This is a choice, but then the Inspection process may be applied for other purposes than finding defects in the product or process.

Gilb provides a list of the characteristics of checklists, some of which I include below: [GIL93]

- "Checklists must ultimately be derived from the rules of the process which itself is being checked by Inspection;
- Checklists should be kept updated to reflect experience of frequent defects;
- A set of questions for one document type should never exceed one single page (about 25 items);
- The checklist does not need to contain every possible question;
- A checklist should concentrate on questions which will turn up major defects;
- Checklists are part of the on-the-job training of a checker."

Correspondingly there are items that checklists should avoid including: [BRY99]

- Checks that can be done with automated tools; e.g., Lint
- Outdated checklist items
- Items better suited as entry/exit criterion; e.g., "Is the compilation listing free of fault messages?"
- Items that are too general; e.g., is the code maintainable?

A.3 Checklist Examples

The following work product checklists are provided as examples only. The specific checklists to be used by any organization can be obtained initially from these lists and modified over time based on data from practiced Inspections.

These checklists are compiled from many sources, almost too numerous to quote. Most are available one way or the other in the public domain in books, articles, conference proceedings, web postings, etc. Many sources the reader may refer to are well documented in Brykczynski's survey of 117 checklists. [BRY99] Many of the references included in the bibliography of this book contain checklists of one type or another. These will all be noted with a **<CKL>** at the end of the reference.

These checklists should not be viewed as necessarily complete, but as examples of items found on checklists.

Checklists should not address code style. Style guides provide value for consistent form and format of presentation, and the Producer might use one to create a work product. Correctness is the focus of checklists. They must be used when required, but if they provide options, then the Producer has choice. Every newspaper and magazine has a style guide. Which is the best? Which is correct, if that is a question that even applies? We assume style guides are correct. Well, they at least can lead to consistency and in that they provide their primary service. Remember that style guides typically lead to minor defect identification unless stated otherwise.

Separate and specific checklists are used for each of the different types of Inspections:

- Requirements Specification (RS)
- Architecture (AR)
- High Level Design (HLD)
- Low Level Design (LLD)
- Code (CD)
- Unit Test Plan (UTP)
- Unit Test Case (UTC)
- Function Integration Test Plan (FTP)
- Function Integration Test Case (FTC)
- System Integration Test Plan (STP)

- System Integration Test Case (STC)
- User Documentation (DOC)
- Problem Reports (PR)
- Change Requests (CR)

Examples are included in this appendix for Requirements Specifications, Architecture, High-level design, Low-level design, and code.

REQUIREMENTS SPECIFICATION CHECKLIST

1. The format and structure of the requirements document maps to the organization's standard for requirements documents.
2. Any deviations to format and structure have proper approval and justification.
3. The requirements statements are not inconsistent.
4. The requirements are traceable to customer input or problem statements to be addressed by the project.
5. The requirements map to the needs analysis.
6. The requirements are stated clearly and cannot be misinterpreted.
7. All terms used, which can have more than one meaning, are qualified so that the desired meaning is readily apparent; e.g., review, area.
8. The customer profiles are clearly defined.
9. The hardware environment is completely defined, including engineering change levels and any constraints.
10. The pre-requisite and co-requisite software and firmware is identified, including release levels and any constraints.
11. The installation and migration requirements are completely defined.
12. The performance criteria are quantified such that they are testable.
13. All of the requirements can be verified during at least one test activity.
14. Error recovery and backup requirements are completely defined.
15. The requirements are expressed such that they can subsequently be modified or changed.
16. All materials required for the requirements Inspection have been received and are in the proper physical format.
17. The requirements document is complete; it defines the known customer needs.
18. The human interface meets project standards.
19. The infrastructure has been addressed, e.g., backup, recovery, checkpoints.
20. Reliability, serviceability, maintainability, and performance objectives have been identified.
21. Security considerations have been identified, if applicable.
22. The requirements are an adequate base for design.
23. Requirements are complete, correct, consistent, and unambiguous.
24. Quality attributes have been defined clearly.
25. Requirements are stated at the requirements level; i.e., they are not design solutions.

Some of the responses to these items can be gray; e.g., item 6 ("cannot be misinterpreted"). If an inspector says yes it can be, then the team needs to discuss to understand if this is generally true or limited to the one inspector. The team can come to a conclusion that this is a valid misunderstanding or is isolated to one inspector. This is a gray area where a defect may be in the eyes of some but not all.

ARCHITECTURE CHECKLIST

1. Materials required for an architecture inspection have been received and are in the proper physical format.
2. Architecture standards have been followed.
3. The architecture is complete; it allows for an implementation of all of the requirements.
4. Interfaces are clear and well defined.
5. Data passed at each interface is the minimal necessary.
6. The infrastructure has been specified; e.g., backup, recovery, checkpoints.
7. The architecture has been adequately decomposed.
8. Reliability, serviceability, maintainability, and performance requirements have been addressed.
9. Security considerations have been addressed.
10. The architecture considers existing constraints.
11. The architecture does not have unnecessary redundancy.
12. The architecture provides an adequate base for the High-level designs.
13. The architecture is complete, correct, and unambiguous.
14. The architecture is feasible.
15. Each architecture layer is clearly defined and distinctive from others for placement of function.

HIGH-LEVEL DESIGN CHECKLIST

1. The format and structure of the design document maps to the organization's standard for this type of design document.
2. Any deviations have proper approval and justification.
3. The design elements are traceable to requirements statements.
4. The external part of the design maps to the customer needs analysis and incorporates the customer profile information.
5. All error messages are defined for the level of design.
6. The design is stated clearly and cannot be misinterpreted; it is understandable.
7. All terms used, which can have more than one meaning, are qualified so that the desired meaning is readily apparent.
8. Any requirements constraints have been incorporated into the design.
9. All dependencies are clearly identified.
10. The installation and migration requirements have been incorporated into the design.
11. The performance, security, and reliability criteria, as specified in the requirements, have been refined and the design demonstrates that they will be met.
12. All of the design functions can be verified during at least one test activity.
13. Error recovery and backup requirements are incorporated into the design.
14. All error conditions are defined for this level of design.
15. The structure of the components and modules is clearly defined.
16. Materials required for a High-level design Inspection have been received and are in the proper physical format.
17. The High-level design is complete; it addresses all of the requirements.
18. Human interfaces follow organization standards.
19. Interfaces are clear and well defined.
20. Minimum data is passed at each interface.
21. Global data added or impacted by the design is kept minimized.
22. Data structures are clearly partitioned.
23. Data have been properly defined.
24. The infrastructure is addressed; e.g., backup, recovery, checkpoints.
25. The design has been adequately decomposed.
26. Error messages are unique and meaningful.
27. Error conditions are addressed and are reasonable and nondestructive.
28. The High-level design considers existing constraints.
29. The High-level design does not contain unnecessary redundancy.
30. The High-level design is an adequate base for the Low-level design.
31. Maintainability issues have been addressed.
32. The High-level design is complete, correct, and unambiguous.
33. The High-level design is feasible.
34. Assured functions from other sources; e.g., the operating system, function libraries, are clearly identified.

LOW-LEVEL DESIGN CHECKLIST

1. Standards for module and component naming conventions are adhered to.
2. Any algorithms in the design are stated clearly enough so that there can be no confusion when they are coded.
3. Any industry standard algorithms in the design accurately reflect the intended algorithm and any limitations of the algorithm still meet the requirements for the design.
4. All industrial requirements, including safety and security, are incorporated into the design.
5. All boundary conditions are clearly identified and the logic for the out of bounds conditions are clearly and completely defined and map to the requirements statements.
6. Each design element meets the organization's level of detail criteria, for example:

    - The number of processes or nodes per data flow diagram
    - The amount of text for a particular size function

7. Pseudo code, if used, adheres to pseudo code guidelines.
8. Structure charts accurately map to data flow diagrams.
9. Data hiding and encapsulation guidelines are being followed.
10. All data elements, including constants and variables, are defined and are consistent across all of the design elements.
11. All input parameters are validated.
12. There is no "extraneous" or "unnecessary" design.
13. Interfaces are clearly stated between design units (modules, sub-components, layers).
14. Interfaces to the user, where appropriate, are well specified and can be implemented.
15. Materials required for a detailed design inspection have been received and are in the proper physical format.
16. Low-level design standards have been followed.
17. The Low-level design is complete, i.e., it completely implements the High-level design.
18. For modifications to existing code, the Low-level design shows the code that needs to be changed and how it is to be changed.
19. Functions are clearly specified.
20. Functions are logically independent.
21. The calling protocol between modules follows project standards.
22. Error conditions are handled in a nondestructive manner.
23. Data have been properly defined and initialized.
24. All defined data is used later in the functional solution.
25. Maintainability has been addressed.
26. The Low-level design is testable.

CODE CHECKLIST

General:

1. The format and structure of the code adheres to the organization's standard for this type of code and language, examples:

    - Source module size
    - Content of header or prologue
    - Comments (number, placement, content)
    - Line tagging
    - Statements or constructs not to be used
    - Register usage

Data:

1. Data types map to design.
2. Ranges map to design.
3. Names map to design.
4. Data hiding and encapsulation guidelines are being followed.
5. Data elements are consistent across all of the code elements.
6. All constants are properly initialized.
7. Arrays are the right size and have the right indices.

Code:

1. There are no language keywords used incorrectly. The functions in the code are traceable to the design elements; there need not always be a one-to-one mapping.
2. The code accurately and completely reflects the design; including, but not limited to, boundary conditions, error messages, error handling, input parameter validation.
3. Any design constraints have been incorporated into the code; including hardware limitations such as memory size.
4. The performance criteria, as specified in the design, have been met and the organization's performance guidelines are adhered to.
5. All of the code can be verified during at least one test activity.
6. All error conditions have been properly coded and reflect the design.
7. The structure of the module maps to the design.
8. All input parameters are verified and the verification values reflect the design.
9. There is no "extraneous" or "unnecessary" code.
10. All input and output operations match the design:

    - File names
    - File types
    - Data types
    - All files are opened before use

- Opened with proper parameters; e.g., NEW, APPEND
- All files are explicitly closed

11. Any algorithms in the code accurately reflect the design.
12. All macro, subroutine, and procedure calls:

- Use the correct name
- Have the correct parameters, including correct data types and lengths
- Have the parameters in the correct position when required
- Are properly referred to if external to this source unit
- Return codes are all checked

13. All boundary conditions are clearly identified and the code for the out of bounds conditions is exactly what is specified in the design.
14. There are no incorrect references to similar labels.
15. All branches are properly "terminated" for all possible branch conditions.
16. All loops are properly coded:

- Initial value
- Increment
- Final value

17. The proper loop type structure is used; e.g., UNTIL, WHILE, FOR.
18. An ELSE clause exists everyplace it could be specified.
19. Any required initialization, such as saving register values, is complete and adheres to standards.
20. Any required termination, such as restoring register values, is complete and adheres to standards.
21. Storage has been allocated before using pointer variables.
22. The addressing is correct and sufficient.
23. Any instructions or data, such as indexing instructions and arrays, which can start with 0 instead of 1 are properly set up.
24. Boolean expressions are correct and the use of 0's and 1's is correct.
25. Any calculations where precedence is implicit in the order are coded in the correct order.
26. Any places where underflow or overflow conditions can occur have appropriate code to handle these and reflect the design.
27. There are no cases where the denominator in a division instruction can be zero.
28. No computations or comparisons have mixed data types unless explicitly intended.
29. There are no comparisons where the variables have different lengths.
30. There are no referenced variables whose value is unset or uninitialized.
31. For array references, subscript values are within the defined bounds of the corresponding dimensions.
32. For array references, subscripts have an integer value.
33. References through pointer variables have storage allocated.
34. Storage areas do not have alias names with different pointer variables.
35. Index of a string does not exceed its boundary.

36. All variables have been explicitly declared and initialized.
    - Variables are assigned the correct length, type, and storage class.
    - Variables do not have similar names; e.g., VOLT and VOLTS.
    - Computations using variables do not have inconsistent data types.

37. There are no mixed-mode (such as integer and floating-point) computations.
38. Any computations using variables have the same type and length.
39. Overflow or underflow exceptions are addressed during the computation of an expression.
40. Any comparisons between variables do not have incompatible data types.
41. Variables have meaningful names; e.g., not A or XYZ.

APPENDIX B
MATERIALS: FOR INSPECTIONS

B.1 Introduction

Inspections can be applied to any type of work product. The following work products are typical for Inspections:

Production products:

- ❑ Requirements Specification (RS)
- ❑ Architecture Definition (AR)
- ❑ High-level design (HLD)
- ❑ Low-level design (LLD)
- ❑ Code (CD)
- ❑ User documentation (DOC)

Test products:

- ❑ Unit Test Plans (UTP)
- ❑ Unit Test Cases (UTC)
- ❑ Function Test Plan (FTP)
- ❑ Function Test Cases (FTC)
- ❑ System Test Plan (STP)
- ❑ System Test Cases (STC)

Changes:

- ❑ Problem Reports (PR)
- ❑ Change Requests (CR)

Each of these work product Inspections has

1. A purpose:

    - To ensure that the inspected work product is in conformance with and represents the needs expressed in a previously stated reference source (see Table B.1)
    - To ensure that the work product to be inspected can be successfully transformed, implemented, or used
    - To ensure the work product transformation adds value to the delivered product
    - To detect missing, incorrect, and extraneous material

2. Relevant materials required for a successful Inspection
3. Entry criteria that must be fulfilled
4. Nominal Preparation and Inspection Meeting rates for effective and efficient Inspections
5. Participant lists
6. Procedures
7. Exit criteria
8. Checklists
9. Applicable defect types

Work Product To Be Inspected	Ensure Conformance With
Requirements Statement	Customer requirements
Architecture Definition	System requirements
High-level design	Architecture and Requirements Specification
Low-level design	High-level design
Code	Low-level design
Unit Test Plans	Code Coverage
Unit Test Cases	Unit Test Plan
Function Test Plans	Requirements Specification and Designs
Function Test Cases	Function Test Plan
System Test Plans	Customer Requirements
System Test Cases	System Test Plan
User Documentation	Customer Requirements
PRs and CRs	PR and CR Reports

Conformance of Work Products in Inspections
Table B.1

The Project Lead defines the work products to be inspected during the course of the project:

- A project plan exists which identifies work products to be inspected, including dates, timeframes, and resources.
- The Project Lead designates which work products will be inspected. The work products to be inspected should be identified in the project plan beginning with the initial version of the plan.
- All affected groups in the organization approve the project plan showing planned Inspections.
- A designated Moderator is notified of the need to perform an Inspection as the work product approaches readiness.

The Software Quality Assurance (SQA) function reviews with the Project Lead to ensure the work products selected are sufficient for the proposed project.

Table B.2 shows which roles are expected (X) when using teams of inspectors and which could offer extended value (A) based on the specific Inspection performed. Some roles are specific to the Inspection process (Moderator, Producer, Reader). Other roles are related to the product activities; e.g., customer, designer. Inspectors can have multiple roles.

	RS	AR	HLD	LLD	CD	UTP	UTC	FTP	FTC	STP	STC	DOC	PR/CR
Moderator	X	X	X	X	X	X	X	X	X	X	X	X	X
Producer	X	X	X	X	X	X	X	X	X	X	X	X	X
Reader	X	X	X	X	X	X	X	X	X	X	X	X	X
Recorder	X	X	X	X	X	X	X	X	X	X	X	X	X
Customer	A		A					A		A		A	
Analysts	A	A	A	A				A	A	A		A	
Designers	A	X	A	A	A			A	A	A	A	A	A
Coders			A	A	A	A	A	A	A				A
Testers	A		A	A	A	A	A	A	A	A	A	A	A
Maintainers					A	A	A	A	A			A	A
Architects	A	A	A							A			
Tech Writers	A	A	A									X	

Possible Inspection Roles
Table B.2

B.2 Types of Materials

Each work product has its own specific Inspection materials that should be distributed or made available to each of the inspectors. Additional reference material can be centrally located; examples are noted below. Reference materials are used to provide background that may not be directly included in the Inspection materials. Reference materials include the standards to be followed.

Ancillary materials may be available and should be considered for distribution, if it is decided they will enable a better Inspection. Ancillary materials are those that may be provided in the absence of some specific Inspection materials or which would enable a better understanding of the work product to be inspected. If sufficient specific materials are not made available, the Inspection is at risk and may require postponement until the material is available.

NOTE: Do not distribute Ancillary or Reference materials just to provide them. If they are judged to be essential for an effective and efficient Inspection, then do distribute them or make them available.

The following is provided as guidance only. There may be other or replacement materials that will be helpful.

1. Architecture Definition

Inspector materials:

- ❑ The architecture document itself
- ❑ Architecture checklist

- ❑ Any approved change requests not integrated into the architecture statement
- ❑ Known Open Issues coming into the Inspection

Reference materials:

- ❑ Product mission or vision statements
- ❑ Standards that may be required for regulatory or statutory purposes or for defining architectures
- ❑ Inspection process policy/procedures

Ancillary materials:

- ❑ Business cases for the product architecture
- ❑ Contracts
- ❑ Customer profiles
- ❑ Hardware requirements or restrictions

2. Requirements Specification

Inspector materials:

- ❑ The Total Requirements Specification itself
- ❑ Requirements specification checklist
- ❑ Any approved change requests not integrated into the requirements specification
- ❑ Known Open Issues coming into the Inspection
- ❑ Customer supplied specification or required definitions
- ❑ Usage scenarios

Reference materials:

- ❑ Product or project prospectuses
- ❑ Standards that may be required for regulatory or statutory purposes or for defining requirements
- ❑ Inspection process policy/procedures
- ❑ Documented decisions/justifications

Ancillary materials:

- ❑ Business cases/proposals for the product
- ❑ Customer/user profiles
- ❑ Architecture or technical strategy statements
- ❑ Hardware requirements or restrictions
- ❑ Verification information from previous releases
- ❑ Defect information from previous releases

3. High-level design inspections

Inspector materials:

- ❑ The High-level design itself
- ❑ High-level design checklist

- ❑ Requirements specification
- ❑ Architecture documents, if relevant
- ❑ Any approved change requests not integrated into the High-level design
- ❑ Known Open Issues coming into the Inspection
- ❑ Usage scenarios

Reference materials:

- ❑ Product or project prospectuses
- ❑ Standards that may be required for regulatory or statutory purposes or for defining High-level design
- ❑ Documented decisions/justifications
- ❑ Inspection process policy/procedures

Ancillary materials:

- ❑ Data models
- ❑ File structures
- ❑ Hardware and software configuration statements
- ❑ Test plans

4. Low-level design Inspections

Inspector materials:

- ❑ The detailed design itself
- ❑ Detailed design checklist
- ❑ High-level design documents
- ❑ Any approved change requests not integrated into the High-level design
- ❑ Known Open Issues coming into the Inspection

Reference materials:

- ❑ Product or project prospectuses
- ❑ Standards that may be required for regulatory or statutory purposes or for defining detailed design
- ❑ Architecture documents
- ❑ Requirements specifications
- ❑ Documented decisions/justifications regarding the design
- ❑ Inspection process policy/procedures

Ancillary materials:

- ❑ Data models
- ❑ File structures
- ❑ Hardware and software configuration statements
- ❑ Test plans

5. Code Inspections

Inspector materials:

- ❑ A clean compilation of the code itself
- ❑ Code checklist
- ❑ Detailed design documents
- ❑ Any approved change requests not integrated into the High-level design

Reference materials:

- ❑ High-level design
- ❑ Standards that may be required for regulatory or statutory purposes or for defining code
- ❑ Inspection process policy/procedures

Ancillary materials:

- ❑ Cross reference listings for data definitions
- ❑ Test plans

6. Unit Test Plan Inspections

Inspector materials:

- ❑ The unit test plan itself
- ❑ Unit test plan checklist
- ❑ Previous design level documents
- ❑ Any approved change requests not integrated into the code

Reference materials:

- ❑ Test environment definition
- ❑ Standards that may be required for defining unit test plans
- ❑ Inspection process policy/procedures

Ancillary materials:

- ❑ Cross reference listings for data definitions
- ❑ Known Open Issues coming into the Inspection

7. Unit Test Case Inspections

Inspector materials:

- ❑ The unit test cases themselves
- ❑ Unit test plan
- ❑ Unit test case checklist
- ❑ Detailed design documents
- ❑ Any approved change requests not integrated into the code

Reference materials:

- ❑ Test environment definition
- ❑ Related and available code
- ❑ Standards that may be required for defining unit test cases
- ❑ Inspection process policy/procedures

Ancillary materials:

- ❑ Cross reference listings for data definitions
- ❑ Test case generation tools, if available and used
- ❑ Traceability matrices
- ❑ Test plans

8. Function Test Plan Inspections

Inspector materials:

- ❑ The function test plan itself
- ❑ Function test plan checklist
- ❑ High-level and detailed design documents
- ❑ Any approved change requests not integrated into the code
- ❑ Traceability Matrix
- ❑ Usage scenarios

Reference materials:

- ❑ Requirements specification
- ❑ Architecture document
- ❑ Standards that may be required for defining function test plans
- ❑ Test environment definitions or requirements
- ❑ Inspection process policy/procedures

Ancillary materials:

- ❑ Unit test plan
- ❑ Known Open Issues coming into the Inspection

9. Function Test Case Inspections

Inspector materials:

- ❑ The function test cases
- ❑ Function test case checklist
- ❑ Function test plan
- ❑ Any approved change requests not integrated into the code

Reference materials:

- ❑ Requirements specification
- ❑ Architecture document
- ❑ High-level design

- ❑ Standards that may be required for defining function test cases
- ❑ Test environment definitions or requirements
- ❑ Test tools that may be used to generate tests
- ❑ Function Test coverage materials
- ❑ Inspection process policy/procedures

Ancillary materials:

- ❑ Unit test plan
- ❑ Results of unit testing
- ❑ Traceability matrix
- ❑ Test plans

10. System Test Plan Inspections

Inspector materials:

- ❑ The system test plan itself
- ❑ System test plan checklist
- ❑ Requirements specification
- ❑ Architecture document
- ❑ Any approved change requests not integrated into the code
- ❑ Usage scenarios

Reference materials:

- ❑ Standards that may be required for defining system test plans
- ❑ Test environment definitions or requirements
- ❑ Inspection process policy/procedures

Ancillary materials:

- ❑ Function test plan
- ❑ Known Open Issues coming into the Inspection
- ❑ Traceability matrix

11. System Test Case Inspections

Inspector materials:

- ❑ The system test cases
- ❑ Function test case checklist
- ❑ System test plan
- ❑ Any approved change requests not integrated into the code

Reference materials:

- ❑ Requirements specification
- ❑ Architecture document
- ❑ High-level design
- ❑ Standards that may be required for defining system test cases

- ❑ Test environment definitions or requirements
- ❑ Test tools that may be used to generate tests
- ❑ System Test coverage materials
- ❑ Inspection process policy/procedures

Ancillary materials:

- ❑ Function test plan
- ❑ Results of Function testing
- ❑ Traceability matrix
- ❑ Test plans

12. User Documents Inspections

Inspector materials:

- ❑ The user document itself
- ❑ User document checklist
- ❑ Requirements specification
- ❑ Architecture documents
- ❑ Any approved change requests not integrated into the code
- ❑ Content plans
- ❑ Design documents, if they were used to assist writing user documents
- ❑ Usage scenarios

Reference materials:

- ❑ Standards that may be required for regulatory or statutory purposes or for defining High-level design
- ❑ Inspection process policy/procedures

Ancillary materials:

- ❑ Data models
- ❑ Hardware and software configuration statements
- ❑ Business cases for the product
- ❑ Customer profiles
- ❑ Known Open Issues coming into the Inspection
- ❑ Test plans

13. Inspections for Problem Reports (internal or external) and Change Requests

Inspector materials:

- ❑ A clean compilation of the changed or fixed code itself
- ❑ Code checklist
- ❑ Related detailed design documents
- ❑ Any approved change requests not integrated into the code
- ❑ Unit Test Results
- ❑ Defect Reports

- ❑ Change Requests

Reference materials:

- ❑ High-level design
- ❑ Standards that may be required for regulatory or statutory purposes or for defining code
- ❑ Inspection process policy/procedures

Ancillary materials:

- ❑ Cross reference listings for data definitions
- ❑ Test plan

APPENDIX C
INSPECTION FORMS

C.1 Introduction

Included in this chapter are sample forms for:

1. Inspection Meeting Notice
2. Inspection Report

C.2 Inspection Meeting Notice

This notice is sent to all Inspection participants for a scheduled Inspection. The notice is to provide information for an upcoming Inspection and precedes the Overview, when there is one. It precedes the Preparation activity when there is no Overview, and may be sent with the Preparation materials. This notice should be sent to all inspectors as soon as it is known who will be involved. It may need to be reissued when further information is available, but the initial broadcast will give each inspector necessary information about a scheduled Inspection.

The form is shown as an example only. An organization may want to add specific information about other work product characteristics that are meaningful to them; e.g., Build Number, subsystem.

This form is used as one for confirmation to the participants, rather than as a first notice. It is expected that the Moderator would have made contact with participants to confirm that the planned dates are a fit for their schedules.

This notice can also optionally be sent to all who can benefit from the Overview. This includes the management and others who may be affected by the work product to be inspected.

This form should be simplified for 1:1 Inspections and Solo:Inspections

INSPECTION MEETING NOTICE

Work Product To Be Inspected: ________________ Project: ____________

Date of Inspection: ______________ Moderator: ______________

Meeting Type: ______________

Meeting Number (if there are more than one for the work product): ___________

Location: ____________ Start Time: _________ Expected Close: ________

Overview Date, if applicable: ______________ Re-Inspection. _______

Location: ____________ Start Time: ____________ Expected Close: _______

Inspection Type: RS, AR, HLD, LLD, CD, UTP, UTC, FTP, FTC, STP, STC, DOC, PR, CR, (circle one)

Date Materials to be Distributed: ________ Planned Preparation Time: ____________

Participant's Name	Role	Phone	Email address

Definitions of Notice Fields

Work Product To Be Inspected: the identifier for the material; e.g., document name, module name, test case name, plan name, including version number for the material

Project: the name of the project for which the Inspection will be held

Date of Inspection: the scheduled Inspection Meeting date

Moderator: the name of the Moderator

Meeting Type: Inspection, Re-Inspection, or Repair Inspection where:

> **Inspection** is the initial Inspection of the material added or changed
> **Re-Inspection** is a re-Inspection of material previously inspected
> **Repair Inspection** is for a small change or problem fix
>
> **Meeting Number:** the meeting session number for the full set of Inspection Meetings scheduled for the material under Inspection; e.g., 1 of 3, 1 of 1
>
> **Location:** where the Inspection Meeting will be held
>
> **Start Time:** the clock time for starting
>
> **Expected Close:** the clock time for ending

Overview Date: the date the Overview

> **Location:** where the Overview will be held
>
> **Start Time:** the clock time for starting
>
> **Expected Close:** the clock time for ending

Inspection Type: the type of work product inspected; pick from the following using the type code:

> Total Requirements Statement (RS)
> Architecture (AR)
> High Level Design (HLD)
> Low Level Design (LLD)
> Code (CD)
> Unit Test Plan (UTP)
> Unit Test Case (UTC)

Function Test Plan (FTP)
Function Test Case (FTC)
System Test Plan (STP)
System Test Case (STC)
User Documentation (DOC)
Problem Reports (PR)
Change Requests (CR)

Data Materials to be Distributed: this is the date by which Preparation materials will be available to the participants

Planned Preparation Time: this is the recommended time each inspector should allocate for Preparation

Participants Name: listed names of each participant

Role: the role assigned to each participant; if a participant is an observer at an Overview it should be so noted

Phone: contact phone number for each participant

Email address: email address for each participant

C.3 Inspection Report

This report is started prior to the Inspection Meeting during an Overview, if held,, mostly completed during or immediately after the Inspection Meeting and optional Analysis Meeting, and completed after rework has been reviewed during Follow-up. It is the full responsibility of the Moderator.

It is composed of three parts:

1. Inspection Data Sheet, used to gather general information about the Inspection gathered during the following activities:

    - Inspection Scheduling
    - Inspection Meeting
    - Follow-up

2. Detailed Data Sheet, used to capture data for each defect
3. Open Issue Log, used to capture data for each Open Issue

NOTE 1: Since defects can be identified in the Overview, Preparation, and Inspection Meeting, each defect Description entered should be prefaced with an O, P, I as applicable to the Inspection activity in which the defect was identified.

NOTE 2: Definitions of each field are included after the template. The definitions should be available, but not attached to paper copies.

NOTE 3: Open Issues, whether submitted by the Producer on entry to an Inspection or discovered at the Inspection Meeting, are tracked to resolution using the Open Issue Log.

INSPECTION DATA SHEET

1 of 3

Inspection Identification:

Date of Inspection: _______________ Meeting Type: ___________

Moderator: __________________Meeting Session Number: ________

Material Distributed: ______________ Type: _________________

Data About Material Inspected:

Work Product Identification: ______________________________

Project: ______________

Version: ______ Change Identifier: _______

Size: ______ Estimated New and Changed: _____ Estimated Base: ______

Size: ______ Actual New and Changed: ______ Actual Base: ______

Overview Data:

Date of Overview: ____________ Duration: _______________

Preparation Data:

Total Time: ___________ Number of Inspectors:___________________

Number of Unique Majors Found: ________

Number of Unique Minors Found: ________

INSPECTION DATA SHEET

2 of 3

Inspection Meeting Data:

Duration of Inspection Meeting: ________ Time Invested: ___________

Majors: ________Base Majors: _____

Minors: ________Re-Inspection Required: _______

Target Date for Re-Inspection: _________

Assigned to Verify Rework: ______________

Estimated Rework Effort: _________Estimated Rework Completion Date:__________

Inspectors:

____

____

____

____

____

____

____

____

INSPECTION DATA SHEET

3 of 3

Follow-up Data:

Actual Rework Effort: ______________Date Inspection Completed: ______________

Scheduled Date for Re-Inspection: ____________

Comments About This Inspection:

____

____

____

____

____

____

____

____

____

DETAILED DATA SHEET							
							Page __ of __
Inspection Identifier:							
Location	**Description**	**Where Found**	**Type**	**Severity**	**Class**	**Closed**	**Cause**

OPEN ISSUE LOG			
			Page __ of __
Inspection Identifier:			
Location	**Description**	**Where Found**	**Resolution**

Definitions of Report Fields

Inspection Identification

Date of Inspection: the actual Inspection Meeting date

Meeting Type: Inspection, Re-Inspection, Repair Inspection where:
- **Inspection** is the initial Inspection of the material added or changed
- **Re-Inspection** is a re-Inspection of material previously inspected
- **Repair Inspection** is for a small change or problem fix

Moderator: the name of the Moderator

Meeting Session Number: the meeting session number for the full set of Inspection Meetings scheduled for the material under Inspection; e.g., 1 of 3, 1 of 1

Material Distributed: the date the materials were given to the inspectors

Type: the type of work product inspected; pick from following using the type code:
- Total Requirements Statement (RS)
- Architecture (AR)
- High Level Design (HLD)
- Low Level Design (LLD)
- Code (CD)
- Unit Test Plan (UTP)
- Unit Test Case (UTC)
- Function Test Plan (FTP)
- Function Test Case (FTC)
- System Test Plan (STP)
- System Test Case (STC)
- User Documentation (DOC)
- Problem Reports (PR)
- Change Requests (CR)

Data About the Material

Work Product Identification: the identifier for the material; e.g., document name, module name, test case name, plan name

Project: the name of the project for which the Inspection will be held

Version: version number for the material

Change Identifier: the change request identifier for an approved change or the problem identifier for an accepted problem to be fixed

Size: the volume of the material to be inspected in the appropriate units of measure; e.g., lines of code, pages, and design elements

Estimated New and Changed: the size of material that is estimated to have been added or modified to the material

Estimated Base: the estimated size of the material that must be included during the Inspection to effectively inspect the new and changed volume

Actual New and Changed: the size of material that is counted to have been added or modified to the material at the end of the Inspection Meeting

Actual Base: the actual size of the material that was included during the Inspection to effectively inspect the new and changed volume

Overview Data

Date of Overview: if an overview were held, provide the date; if not held state NA

Duration: total clock time for the Overview

Preparation Data

Total Time: the sum of all the Preparation time by the inspectors

Number of Inspectors: the total number including the Moderator and the Producer

Number of Unique Majors Found: the unique set of major defects found by all inspectors during Preparation; this can only be determined during the Inspection Meeting

Number of Unique Minors Found: the unique set of minor defects found by all inspectors during Preparation; this can only be determined during the Inspection Meeting

Inspection Meeting Data

Duration: the total clock time used for this Meeting

Time Invested: the sum of the time that each participant was in attendance

Majors: the total of unique major defects identified during the Inspection Meeting and Preparation

Base Majors: the total of unique major defects attributed to the base upon which the new and changed material was added

Minors: the total of unique minors defects identified during the Meeting and Preparation

Inspectors: list of inspectors at the Inspection Meeting excluding the Moderator

Re-Inspection Required: state Yes or No; if the Re-Inspection is to be decided after the Rework and Follow-up activities, it should be noted

Target Date for Re-Inspection: enter a target date as understood at the Inspection Meeting

Assigned to Verify Rework: name of person to verify rework with the Producer

Estimated Rework Effort: the Producer's estimate of time needed

Estimated Rework Completion Date: the Producer's commitment for a completion date, if rework is needed

Inspectors: listed names of each participant

Follow-up Data

Actual Rework Effort: the actual total time the Producer used

Date Inspection Completed: the date the rework was verified as completed

Scheduled Date for Re-Inspection: the new target date set with the Producer during the Follow-up activity

Comments About This Inspection: any notes that would add understanding about this Inspection

Detailed Data

Location: an identifier of the defect's location in the material; e.g., line of code number, page and paragraph number

Description: a brief but complete description of the defect; this should be clear and helpful

Where Found: state the Inspection type and Inspection activity where the defect was identified; e.g., Requirements Overview, HLD Preparation

Type: one of the valid major defects sub-classified; the following are examples; pick the relevant types for your organization:

BA: the defect is not in the new or changed portion of the work product, but in a previous base or version of the work product

BL: baseline document was incorrect; e.g., the Low-level design when inspecting code

DA: data is improperly specified, declared, initialized, described, used, converted, or boundaries are violated

DC: documentation is incorrect, incomplete, missing, or inadequate; documentation is a physical description relevant to the material inspected; e.g., it could be the material itself, when a document is inspected, it could be the reference material, or it could be a comment in the code being inspected

EN: the operating environment is incorrectly, unclearly, or not accurately defined or is lacking in definition

ER: necessary error recovery is missing, incomplete, extraneous, or incorrect

FN: the specified function is incomplete, incorrect, imprecise, ambiguous, or extraneous; the required function is missing; the inspected material is not consistent with the reference material including the base to which the material is mapped

HF: the user interface or procedure is incorrect, incomplete, missing, or unnecessary; the user profile is not defined

IF: interfaces between product software components or modules are defective

IO: interfaces or communication with external devices (hardware) are defective

LO: the logic of performing a function is incorrect; e.g., sequence, selection, comparisons, termination, or iteration of operations

MN: maintainability of the subject material is at risk; e.g., it is not understandable, it is not structured

PF: performance in terms of speed, timing, throughput, or amount of memory does not meet specification

PR: process related

SN: incorrect use of design or code language syntax

ST: lack of conformance with a required standard

TC: the specified test case is incomplete, incorrect, or extraneous

TE: the defined test environment is incomplete, incorrect, or extraneous; the specified function is not testable

TP: the scope, plan, or strategy of the defined testing to be performed is incomplete, incorrect, or extraneous

OT: a defect not included in the defined types; a more detailed explanation should be provide any time OT is selected

Severity: Major, Minor, or Open Issue where

Major is a defect that requires repair due to a failure it could cause to occur and it could have been found in test or in customer use

Minor is a defect that would not cause a failure to occur; typically it is one of format or representation

Open Issue is a potential defect that could not be effectively resolved during the Inspection Meeting; these should only occur as an exception; if there are too many Opens, the Inspection Meeting process should be evaluated

Class: Missing, Wrong, or Extra where

Missing is not in the material inspected but should be

Wrong is incorrectly shown in the material inspected

Extra is in the material inspected but has no prior approved basis for being there

Closed: noted as closed by the person assigned to verify rework after verification demonstrates acceptance of the rework for the defect

Cause: select one of the valid cause codes within the organization; e.g., or develop your own set of causes:

ED: Education; where the Producer failed to understand something

CO: Communication; where there was a breakdown in communications between groups or team members

OV: Oversight; where something was not considered or handled

TR: Transcription; where the Producer knows what to do, but "for some reason simply makes a mistake"

PR: Process; where the process somehow misdirected your actions

Open Issue Data

Location: an identifier of the defect's location in the material; e.g., line of code number, page and paragraph number

Description: a brief but complete description of the defect; this should be clear and helpful

Where Found: state the Inspection type and Inspection activity where the defect was identified; e.g., Requirements Overview, HLD Preparation

Resolution: one of two types of resolution is to be noted:

- Closed as defect; the defect should be also be added to the Detailed Data Sheet
- Converted to Change Request; indicate CR number

BIBLIOGRAPHY

NOTE: Items with a **<CKL>** include checklists.

[ACK82] Ackerman, A. Frank, Amy S. Ackerman, and Robert G. Ebenau, *A Software Inspection Training Program*, Proceedings of COMPSAC82, IEEE Computer Society, 1982.

[ACK89] Ackerman, A. Frank, Lynne S. Buchwald, and Frank H. Lewski, *Software Inspections: an Effective Verification Process*, IEEE Software, Vol. 6, No. 3, May 1989.

[ARK89] Arksey, Cindy, *Fagan Method Pilot, Final Report*, Internal Technical Report, Boeing, Seattle, Washington, 1989. **<CKL>**

[ASC76] Ascoly, Joseph Michael J. Cafferty, Stephen J. Gruen, and O. Robert Kohli; *Code Inspection Specification*, IBM Technical Report TR21.630, Kingston, NY, May 1976. **<CKL>**

[BAR94] Barnard, Jack and Art Price, *Managing Code Inspection Information*, IEEE Software, Vol. 11, No. 2, March 1994.

[BAS84] Basili, V. R. and Perricone, B. T.; *Software errors and complexity: An empirical investigation*, Communications of the ACM, Vol. 27, No. 1, January 1984.

[BEA94] Beaulieu, Michael F., *How To Successfully Identify Defects During An Inspection*, 6th Annual Software Technology Conference, Salt Lake City, Utah, April 1994.

[BEC99] Beck, Kent, *eXtreme Programming eXplained*, Addison-Wesley, 2000.

[BIL94] Billings, C., J. Clifton, B. Kolkhorst, E. Lee, and W. B. Wingert, *Journey to a Mature Software Process*, IBM Systems Journal, Vol. 16, No. 1, 1994

[BIS89] Bisant, David B. and James R. Lyle, *A Two-Person Inspection Method to Improve Programming Productivity*, IEEE Transactions on Software Engineering, Vol. 15, No. 10, October 1989.

[BLA91] Blakely, Frank W. and Mark E. Boles, *A Case Study of Code Inspections, Hewlett-Packard Journal*, Vol. 42, No. 4, October 1991.

[BOE78] Boehm, Boehm, *Characteristics of Software Quality*, American Elsevier, New York, 1978.

[BOE81] Boehm, Barry W., *Software Engineering Economics*, Prentice-Hall, 1981.

[BOE01] Boehm, Barry and Victor R. Basili, *Software Defect Reduction Top 10 List*, IEEE Computer, January 2001.

[BOU97] Bourgeois, Karen V., *Advanced Software Inspection Metrics Tutorial*, Software Engineering Process Group Proceedings, SEPG97, San Jose, California, 1997.

[BRY99] Brykczynski, Bill, *A Survey of Software Inspection Checklists*, Software Engineering Notes, Volume 24, Number 1, January 1999.

[BUC81a] Buck, F. O., *Indicators of Quality Inspections*, IBM Technical Report TR21.802, September 1981.

[BUC81b] Buck, F. O., *Design Change Inspection Specification*, IBM Technical Report, TR21.821, December 1981.

[BUS90] Bush, Marilyn, *Improving Software Quality: The Use of Formal Inspections at the Jet Propulsion Laboratory*, Proceedings 12th International Conference on Software Engineering, IEEE CS Press, Los Alamitos, 1990.

[CHA68] Chase, Norman L., *The Programming Design Review*, IBM Technical Report, S-1166, July 1968.

[CHR90] Christel, Michael G., *A Digital Video Interactive Course on Code Inspections, Technology and Innovations in Training and Education*, March 1990, Colorado Spring, Colorado.

[CHR88] Christenson, Dennis A. and Steel T. Huang, *A Code Inspection Model for Software Quality Management and Prediction,* Proceedings IEEE Global Telecommunications Conference – 1988, Volume 1.

[CHR90] Christenson, Dennis A., Steel T. Huang, and Alfred J. Lamperez, *Statistical Quality Control Applied to Code Inspections*, IEEE Journal Selected Areas in Communications, Vol. 8, No. 2, February 1990.

[CIT84] Citron, Andrew, *A Software Review Method That Really* Works, Byte, January 1984.

[CON93] Constantine, Larry L., *Work Organization Paradigms For Project Management And Organization*, Communications of the ACM, October 1993.

[CON94] Constantine, Larry L. and Lucy A. D. Lockwood, *One Size Does Not Fit All: Fitting Practices to People*, American Programmer, December 1994.

[CMM93] Paulk, M.C., B. Curtis, M.B.Chrissis, and C.V.Weber, *Capability Maturity Model for Software, Version 1.1 (CMU/SEI-93-TR-024)*, Software Engineering Institute, Carnegie Mellon University, Pittsburgh, PA, February 1993. Also see ww.sei.cmu.edu.

[CRO79] Crosby, Philip B., *Quality Is Free*, McGraw-Hill Book Company, New York, 1979.

[CRY97] Crystal, David, *The Cambridge Encyclopedia of Language*, Cambridge University Press, 1997.

[DAV55] Davis, Harmer E., George Earl Troxell, and Clement T. Wiskoul, *The Testing and Inspection of Engineering Materials*, McGraw-Hill, New York, 1955.

[DEM82] Deming, W. Edwards, *Out of the Crisis*, Massachusetts Institute of Technology Center for Advanced Engineering Study, Cambridge, 1982.

[DIJ72] Dijkstra, E. W., *Programming Considered as a Human Activity,* in Structured Programming, O. J. Dahl, ed., Academic Press, 1972.

[DIO92] Dion, Raymond, *Process improvement and the corporate balance sheet*, IEEE Software, Vol. 10, No. 4, July 1992.

[DOB81] Dobbins, James H., *Software Quality in the 80's*, Proceedings – Trends and Application Symposium, 1981.

[DOO92] Doolan, E. P., *Experiences with Fagan's Inspection Method,* Software – Practice and Experience, Vol. 22, No. 2, Feb. 1992.

[DUN84] Dunn, Robert H., *Software Defect Removal*, McGraw-Hill Book Co., 1984.

[DUT97] Duterte, Bruno and Victoria Stavridou, *Formal Requirements Analysis of an Avionics Control System*, IEEE Transactions on Software Engineering, May 1997.

[EBE93] Ebenau, Robert G., and Susan H. Strauss, *Software Inspection Process*, McGraw-Hill, Inc, 1993. **<CKL>**

[EIC92] Eick, Stephen G., Clive R. Laoder, M. David Long, Lawrence G. Votta, and Scott Wiel, *Estimating Software Fault Content Before Coding*, Proceedings of the 14th International Conference on Software Engineering, 1992.

[EIS85] Eisele, R. C., and D. L. Rathburn, *What We Learned From Functional Testing of the DSD1 Generic*, Proceedings AT&T Software Quality Symposium: Achieving Productivity Through Quality, December 1985.

[FAG76] Fagan, Michael E., Design and Code *Inspections to Reduce Errors in Program Development*, IBM Systems Journal, Vol. 15, No. 3, 1976. **<CKL>**

[FAG77] Fagan, M. E., *Inspecting Software Design and Code*, Datamation, October 1977.

[FAG86] Fagan, Michael E., *Advances In Software Inspections*, IEEE Transactions on Software Engineering, Vol. 12, No. 7, July 1986.

[FLO99] Florac, William A. and Anita D. Carleton, *Measuring the Software Process*, Addison Wesley Longman, Inc. 1999.

[FLO00] Florac, William A., Anita D. Carlton, and Julie R. Barnard, *Statistical Process Control: Analyzing a Space Shuttle Onboard Software Process*, IEEE Software, July 2000

[FOR61] Forrester, Jay W., *Industrial Dynamics*, The M.I.T. Press, Cambridge, Massachusetts, 1961.

[FOW86] Fowler, Prisilla J., *In-Process Inspections of Workproducts at AT&T*, AT&T Technical Journal, Volume 65, Issue 2, March/April 1986.

[FRE90] Freedman, Daniel P. and Gerald M. Weinberg, *Handbook of Walkthroughs, Inspection, and Technical Reviews*, Dorset House Publishing, New York, 1990; NOTE: this book was available in previous versions as far back as 1977. **<CKL>**

[GAL90] Gale, J. L., J. R. Tirso and C. A. Burchfield, *Implementing the Defect Prevention Process in the MVS Interactive Programming Organization*, IBM Systems Journal, Volume 29, Number 1, 1990.

[GER00] Gerrard, Paul, *Testing Requirements*, The Journal of Software Testing Professionals, March 2000.

[GIL79] Gilb, Tom, *Some Recent Results of Fagan Inspection Method*, Computer Weekly, September 27, 1979.

[GIL93] Gilb, Tom and Dorothy Graham, *Software Inspection*, Addison-Wesley, 1993. **<CKL>**

[GIL98] Gilb, Tom, *Optimizing Software Inspections*, CrossTalk, March 1998.

[GIN93] Gintell, John W., *Scrutiny: A Collaborative Inspection and Review System,* Proceedings of Fourth European Software Engineering Conference (ESEC93), Springer Verlag.

[GLA99a] Glass, Robert L., *The Realities of Software Technology Payoffs*, Communications of the ACM, February 1999.

[GLA99b] Glass, Robert L., *Inspections – Some Surprising Findings*, Communications of the ACM, April 1999.

[GRA86] Graden, Robert B. and Palma S. Horsley, *The Effects of Software Inspections on a Major Telecommunications Project*, AT&T Tech Journal, Vol. 65, No.3, May/June 1986.

[GRA94] Grady, Robert B. and Tom Van Slack, *Key Lessons In Achieving Widespread Inspection Use*, IEEE Software, Vol. 11, No. 4, July 1994.

[GRA94] Grady, Robert, *Successfully Applying Software Metrics*, IEEE Computer, September 1994.

[GRA97] Grady, Robert B., *Successful Software Process Improvement*, Prentice-Hall, 1997.

[HAL95] Haley, Tom, Blake Ireland, Ed Wojtaszek, Dan Nash, and Ray Dion, *Raytheon Electronic Systems Experience in Software Process Improvement*, Technical Report CMU/SEI-95-TR-017, ESC-TR-95-017. See also http://www.sei.cmu/edu/products/publications/95.reports/95.tr.017.html.

[HAR98] Harding, John T., *Using Inspection Data to Forecast Test Defects*, CrossTalk, Volume 11, Number 5, May 1998.

[HAR01] Harel, David, *From Play-in Scenarios to Code: An Achievable Dream*, IEEE Computer, January 2001.

[HAU94] Hausler, P. A.; R. C. Linger, & C. J Trammel,. *Adopting Cleanroom Software Engineering with a Phased Approach.,* IBM Systems Journal 33, 1 (1994): 89-109.

[HOL97] Holzmann, Gerard J., *The Model Checker SPIN*, IEEE Transactions on Software Engineering, Volume 23, Number 5, May 1997.

[HUM89] Humphrey, Watts S., *Managing the Software Process*, Addison-Wesley Publishing Company, Inc., Reading, Massachusetts, 1989. **<CKL>**

[HUM95] Humphrey, Watts S., *A Discipline for Software Engineering*, Addison-Wesley Publishing Company, Inc., Reading, Massachusetts, 1995. **<CKL>**

[HUT92] Hutchings, Tony, *Formal Inspections & Continuous Improvement*, Electro/92 Conference, Boston, Massachusetts, May 12-14, 1992.

[IBM77] *Improved Programming Technologies - Management Overview*, GE19-5086-2, IBM, September 1977, Third Edition.

[IEE98] *IEEE Standards: Software Engineering*, Volume Two: Process Standards, The Institute of Electrical and Electronics Engineers, Inc., 1998.

[IEE00a] IEEE Transactions on Software Engineering, September 2000.

[IEE00b] IEEE Transactions on Software Engineering, October 2000.

[ISH68] Ishikawa, Kaoru, *Guide to Quality Control*, Asian Productivity Organization, Tokyo, Japan, 1982.

[JAL00] Jalote, Pankaj, *CMM in Practice*, Addison Wesley Longman, Inc., 2000.

[JOH98] Johnson, Philip M., *Reengineering Inspection*, Communications of the ACM, February 1998.

[JON73] Jones, T. C., *San Jose Design Review Procedures*, IBM, January 31, 1973

[JON75] Jones, Capers, IBM GUIDE 40, Miami, Florida, May 1975.

[JON85] Jones, C. L., *A Process-Integrated Approach to Defect Prevention,* IBM Systems Journal, Vol. 24, No. 2, 1985, pp.150-167.

[JON86] Jones, T. C., *Programming Productivity*, McGraw-Hill, New York, 1986.

[JON91] Jones, T. C., *Applied Software Measurements*, McGraw-Hill, New York, 1986.

[JUR88] Juran, Joseph, *Juran's Quality Control Handbook*, McGraw-Hill, 1988.

[KAN95] Kan, Stephen H., *Metrics and Models in Software Quality Engineering*, Addison-Wesley, 1995.

[KEL92] Kelly, John C., Joseph S. Sherif, and Jonathan Hops, *An Analysis of Defect Densities Found During Software Inspections*, Journal of Systems and Software, Vol. 17, No. 2, February 1992.

[KIN95] Kindersley, Bill, *The Language List – Version 2.4*, January 25, 1995. See also http://wuarchive/wustl.edu/doc/archive/misc/lan-list.txt.

[KIT83] Kitchenham, Barbara A., *The Use of Software Metrics to Assess Software Production Methods,* Proceedings FTCS - 13th Annual International Symposium on Fault-Tolerant Computing, Milan, 1983.

[KIT86] Kitchenham, B.A., A.P. Kitchenham, and J.P. Fellows, *The Effects of Inspections on Software Quality and Productivity,* ICL Tech. J., Vol. 5, No. 1, May 1986.

[KIZ84] Kizer, Les J, *Inspection Guidelines*, IBM Technical Report, TR 00.3321, Poughkeepsie, December 4, 1984.

[KOE94] Koester, Peter, *The Use of Metrics in Optimizing a Software Engineering Process*, CrossTalk, November 1994.

[KOH73] Kohli, O. Robert and Ronald A. Radice, *Design and Code Inspection Specifications*, IBM Technical Report TR21.525, Kingston, NY, June 1973. **<CKL>**

[KOH75] Kohli, O. Robert, *High Level Design Inspection Specification*, IBM Technical Report TR21.601, Kingston, NY, July 1975. **<CKL>**

[KOH76] Kohli, O. Robert and Ronald A Radice, *Low Level Design Inspection Specification*, IBM Technical Report TR21.629, Kingston, NY, July 1976. **<CKL>**

[KOL88] Kolkhorst, B. G. and A. J. Macina, *Developing Error-Free Software*, IEEE AES Magazine, November 1988.

[KOM74] Koman, Thomas E., *Human Error Detection in Developing Quality Software*, IBM Technical Report, TR 00.2583, December 1974.

[KOO86] Koontz, Warren L. G., *Experience with Software Inspections in The Development Of Firmware For A Digital Loop Carrier System*, Proceedings IEEE International Conference on Communications, 1986 Conference Record, IEEE Press, 1986.

[KNI93] Knight, John C. and E. Ann Myers, *An Improved Inspection Technique*, Communications of the ACM, Vol. 36., No.11, November 1993.

[KNO93] Knox, S.T., *Modeling the Cost of Software Quality,* Digital Technical Journal, Vol. 5, No. 4, 1993.

[KRA98] Krasner, Herb, *Using the Cost of Quality Approach for Software*, CrossTalk, November 1998.

[KRE75] Kremen, Thomas M., *Effects of Code Inspections and Testcase Walkthroughs on San Jose VS-1 3800 (Argonaut) Code Development*, IBM Technical Report, October 1975.

[LAI98] Laitenberger, Oliver and Jean-Marc DeBaud, *An Encompassing Life-Cycle Centric Survey of Software Inspection*, ISERN-98-32. http://www.iese.fhg.de/network/ISERN/pub/technical_reports/isern-98-32.pdf

[LAR74] Larson, Rodney. R, *Error Detection Model*, IBM Development Division, Kingston, N.Y., IBM Technical Report TR21.571, December 1974.

[LAR75] Larson, Rodney. R, *Test Plan and Test Case Inspection Specification*, IBM Development Division, Kingston, N.Y., IBM Technical Report TR21.586, April 1975. **<CKL>**

[LE85] Le, Ngoc-Mai T., Mark L. North and L. David Wyly, *Software Quality Analysis Using Quantified Parameters To Reduce Field Defects*, IBM Technical Report, IBM Technical report TR 29.0515, February 1985.

[LEE97] Lee, Earl, *Software Inspections: How to Diagnose Problems and Improve the Odds of Organizational Acceptance*, CrossTalk, August 1997.

[LEG98] Legoïc, Jean-Yves and Jean-Marc Morel, *Implementing the inspection technique: a profitable investment*, ICSSEA '98 Conference, Paris, France, December 1998.

[LIE97] Lieberman, Henry, *The Debugging Scandal and What To Do About It*, Communications of the ACM, April 1997.

[LIN91] Lindner, Rick, *Software Development at a Baldrige Winner, IBM Rochester*, Proceedings of the National Institute for Software Quality and Productivity Conference, November 1991.

[LIN79] Linger, R. C., H. D. Mills and B. I. Witt, *Structured Programming Theory and Practice*, Addison-Wesley, 1979.

[LIN94] Linger, Richard C., *Cleanroom Process Model,* Chapter 6 in Cleanroom Software Engineering: A Reader, Oxford, England, Blackwell Publishers, 1994.

[LIN96] Linger, Richard C. and Carmen J. Trammell, *Cleanroom Software Engineering, Reference Model, Version 1.0*, Technical report, CMU/SEI-96-TR-022, November 1996.

[MAH75] Mahoney, D. R., *Inspections As Used on The OS/VS1 VSPC Development Project*, IBM Technical Report, TR 03.008, December 1975.

[MAR90] Martin, Johnny and W. T. Tsai, *N-Fold Inspection: A Requirements Analysis Technique*, Communications of the ACM, February 1990.

[MAR97] Martin, Terry and Jim Kirk, *Software Inspections in a Commercial Setting*, Software Engineering Process Group Proceedings, SEPG97, San Jose, California, 1997.

[MAX00] Maxion, Roy A., and Robert T. Olszewski, *Eliminating Exception Handling Errors with Dependability Cases: A Comparative, Empirical Study,* IEEE Transactions on Software Engineering, Vol. 26, No. 9, September 2000.

[MAY90] Mays, R. G., C. L. Jones, G. J. Holloway and D. P. Studinski, *Experiences with Defect Prevention*, IBM Systems Journal, Volume 29, Number 1, 1990.

[MAY92] Mays, Robert, *Practical Aspects of Defect Prevention*, Total Quality Management for Software, Van Nostrand Reinhold, 1992.

[MCC75] McCloskey, Hugh A., *Programming Publications Inspection Procedures*, IBM Technical Report TR 21.612, December 8, 1975.

[MCC76] McCabe, Thomas J., *A Complexity Measure*, IEEE Transactions on Software Engineering, Vol. SE-2, No.4, December 1976.

[MCC81] McCormick, K.K., *The Results of Using a Structured Methodology, Software Inspections, and a New Hardware/Software Configuration on Application Systems*, Proceedings of the 2nd National EDP Quality Assurance, 1982.

[MCC01] McCann, Robert T., *How Much Code Inspection Is Enough?,* CrossTalk, Vol. 14, No. 7., July 2001.

[MIL73] Mills, Harlan D., *On the Development of Large Reliable Programs*, Proceedings IEEE Symposium on Computer Software Reliability, 1973.

[MIL87] Mills, Harlan D., Michael Dyer and Richard C. Linger, *Cleanroom Engineering*, IEEE Software, September 1987.

[MIL93] Miller, Ann, *Looking Ahead With Software Previews*, IEEE Software, September 1993.

[MYE78] Myers, Glenford, *A Controlled Experiment in Program Testing and Code Walkthroughs/Inspections*, CACM, 9, 1978.

[NEV98] Nevison, Jack, *Winning Project Management*, course material, page 27, Oak Associates, Inc., Maynard, Massachusetts, 1998.

[NIE94] Nielsen, Jakob and Mack, Robert L.; *Usability Inspection Methods*, John Wiley & Sons, New York, 1994. <CKL>

[NOR78] Norris, J. B., *An Analysis of the Value of Program Code Inspection in an Application Programming Environment*, IBM Technical Report, TR 00.2974, September 1978.

[NOS98] Nosek, John T., *The Case for Collaborative Programming*, Communications of the ACM, March 1998.

[OLS96] Olson Timothy G., *World Class Software Inspections*, 1996 SEPG Conference Proceedings, 1996

[ONE96] O'Neill, Don, *National Software Quality Experiment: Results 1992-1995*, Proceedings of the 8th Annual Software Technology Conference, Salt Lake City, Utah, April 1996.

[ONE97] O'Neill, Don, *Setting Up a Software Inspection Program*, CrossTalk, February 1997.

[PAR87] Parnas, David L. and David M. Weiss, *Active Design Reviews: Principles and Practices*, Journal of Systems and Software, No. 7, 1987.

[PEL82] Peele, R., *Code Inspections at First Union Corporation*, Proceedings of COMPSAC '82, November 1982.

[PER00] Perry, Dewayne E., Alexander Romanovsky and Anand Tripathi, *Current Trends in Exception Handling*, IEEE Transactions on Software Engineering, Vol. 26, No. 9, September 2000.

[POR95] Porter, Adam A., Lawrence G. Votta and Victor R. Basili, *Comparing Detection Methods for Software Requirements Inspections: A Replicated Experiment*, IEEE Transactions on Software Engineering and Methodology, June 1995.

[POR97] Porter, Adam and Lawrence Votta, *What Makes Inspections Work?*, IEEE Software, November/December 1997.

[POR98] Porter, Adam A., Harvey Siy, Audris Mockus, and Lawrence Votta, *Understanding the Sources of Variation in Software Inspections*, IEEE Transactions on Software Engineering and Methodology, January 1998.

[PRI72] Priven, L. D., *Managing the Programming Development Cycle*, IBM Technical Report, TR 21.463, Kingston.

[PRO99] Prowell, Stacy J., Carman J. Trammel, Richard C. Linger, and Jesse H. Poore, *Cleanroom Software Engineering: Technology and Process*, Addison Wesley Longman Company, Incorporated, 1999.

[RAD85a] Radice, R. A., N. K. Roth, A .C. O'Hara, Jr., and W. A. Ciarfella, *A Programming Process Architecture*, IBM Systems Journal, Vol. 24, No. 2 (1985).

[RAD85b] Radice, R. A., J. T. Harding, P. E. Munnis, and R. W. Phillips, *A Programming Process Study*, IBM Systems Journal, Vol. 24, No. 2 (1985).

[RAD90] Radice, Ronald A., *Process Control for Programming: A Case Study*, privately printed paper, September 1990. Also presented as *Software Inspections: A Case Study* at the Software Technology Conference, Salt Lake City, May 1, 1997.

[RAD97] Radice, Ronald A., *Getting to Level 4 in the CMM*, 1997 SEI Software Engineering Process Group Conference, San Jose, California.

[RAD00] Radice, Ronald A., *Statistical Process Control in Level 4 and Level 5 Software Organization Worldwide*, SEPG 2000 Conference, Seattle, Washington, March 2000.

[RAD01] Radice, Ron, Gargi Keeni, Radhika Sokhi, and P. Suresh, *One on One Inspections*, Software Technology Conference 2001, May 1, 2001. Also available on www.stt.com.

[RED85] Rdwine, S, and W. Riddle, *Software Technology Maturation*, IEEE 8th Conference on Software Engineering, August 1985.

[REV91] Reeve, J. T., *Applying the Fagan Inspection Technique*, Quality Forum, Vol. 17, No. 1, March 1991.

[RIF94] Rifkin, Stan and Lionel Deimel, *Applying Program Comprehension Techniques to Improve Software Inspections*, 19th Annual NASA Software Engineering Laboratory Workshop, Greenbelt Maryland, Nov. 30-Dec 1, 1994.

[ROG83] Rogers, E., *Diffusion of Innovation*, Macmillan Publishing, New York, 1983.

[ROY00] Royce, Walter, *Inspection Hype?,* IEEE Software, November/December 2000, pages 6-8.

[RUS91] Russell, Glen W., *Experience with Inspection in Ultralarge-Scale Developments*, IEEE Software, January 1991.

[RUS00] Russ, Melissa L, *Using Guided Inspections to Validate UML Models*, Software Technology Conference 2000.

[SAU00] Sauer, Chris, D. Ross Jeffrey, Lesley Land, and Phillip Yetton; *The Effectiveness of Software Development Technical Reviews: A Behaviorally Motivated Program of Research*, IEEE Transactions on Software Engineering, January 2000.

[SEI89] *Software Inspections Tutorial*, Don O'Neil and Albert L. Ingram, January 30, 1989.

[SEI00a] *CMMI^{SM} for Systems Engineering/Software/Integrated Product and Process Development, Version 1.02 (CMU/SEI-2000-TR-030), Staged Representation*, Software Engineering Institute, Carnegie Mello University, Pittsburgh, PA, November 2000. Also see ww.sei.cmu.edu.

[SEI00b] *CMMI^{SM} for Systems Engineering/Software/Integrated Product and Process Development, Version 1.02 (CMU/SEI-2000-TR-031), Continuous Representation*, Software Engineering Institute, Carnegie Mello University, Pittsburgh, PA, November 2000. Also see ww.sei.cmu.edu.

[SEI01] *Process Maturity Profile of the Software Community 2001 Mid-Year Update*, http://seir/sei.cmu.edu , Software Engineering Institute, August 2001.

[SHE85] Shen, Vincent Y., Tze-Jie Yu, Stephen M. Thebaut, and Lorri R. Paulsen, *Identifying Error-Prone Software — An Empirical Study*, IEEE Transactions on Software Engineering, Vol. SE-11, No. 4, April 1985.

[SHE96a] Sherer, S. W. *Cleanroom Software Engineering- the Picatinny Experience* [online]. Available WWW URL: http://software.pica.army.mil/cleanroom/cseweb.html> (1996).

[SHE96b] Sherer, S.W.; A. Kouchakdjian, & P.G. Arnold, *Experience Using Cleanroom Software Engineering,* IEEE Software, 1996.

[SHI92] Shirey, Glen C., *How Inspections Fail*, Proceedings of the 9th International Conference Testing Computer Software, 1992.

[SHU00] Shull, Forrest, Joana Rus and Victor Basli, *How Perspective-Based Reading Can Improve Requirements Inspections*, IEEE Computer, July 2000.

[SPE94] Spencer, Barbara, *Software Inspections at Applicon*, CrossTalk, October 1994.

[SLA98] Slaughter, Sandra A., Donald E. Harter, and Mayuram S. Krishnan, *Evaluating Cost of Software Quality*, Communications of the ACM, August 1998.

[STA95] Air Force/STARS Demonstration Project Home Page [online]. Also see http://www.asset.com/stars/afdemo/home.html>

[TAC99] Tackett, Buford D. and Van Doren, *Buddy; Process Control for Error-Free Software: A Software Success Story*, IEEE Software, May/June 1999.

[TRI91] Tripp, Leonard L., William F. Struck, and Bryan K. Pflug, *The Application of Multiple Team Inspections on a Safety-Critical Software Standard*, Proceedings 4th Software Engineering Standards Application Workshop, 1991.

[VOT93] Votta, Lawrence G. Jr., *Does Every Inspection Need a Meeting?,* Proceedings 1st ACM SIGSOFT Symposium Foundations of Software Engineering, 1993.

[WAL74] Waldstein, N. S., *The Walk-Thru – A Method of Specification Design and Review*, Technical Report TR 00.2536, IBM Corporation, Poughkeepsie, New York, June 1974.

[WEI71] Weinberg, Gerald M., *The Psychology of Computer Programming*, Van Norstrand Reinhold Company, New York, 1971.

[WEI84] Weinberg, Gerald M. and Daniel P. Freedman, *Reviews, Walk-throughs, and Inspections*, IEEE Transactions on Software Engineering, Vol. 12, No. 1, January 1984.

[WEI86] Weinberg, G., *IEEE Tutorial on Software Restructuring*, IEEE CS Press, Los Alamos, CA, 1986.

[WEL93] Weller, E. F., *Lessons from Three Years of Inspection Data*, IEEE Software, September 1993.

[WEL00] Weller, E. F., *Software Quality Management: Applying Quantitative Methods to Software Maintenance*, ASQ Software Quality Professional, Volume 3, Issue 1, December 2000.

[WEN85] Wenneson, G., *Quality Assurance software inspections at NASA Ames: metrics for feedback and modification*, Proceedings of the Tenth Annual Software Engineering Workshop, Goddard Space Flight Center, December 1985.

[WHE96] Wheller, David A., Bill Brykczynski, and Reginald N. Meeson, Jr., *Software Inspection An Industry Best Practice*, IEEE Computer Society Press, 1996.

[WIL82] Wilburn, N.P., *Guidelines for Technical Reviews of Software Products*, Hartford Engineering Development Laboratory, HEDL-TC-2132, March 1982.

[WIL00a] Williams, Laurie A. and Robert R. Kessler, *All I Really Need To Know About Pair Programming I Learned In Kindergarten*, Communications of the ACM, May 2000.

[WIL00b] Williams, Laurie A. Robert R. Kessler, Ward Cunningham, and Ron Jeffries, *Strengthening the Case for pair Programming*, IEEE Software, July/August 2000.

[YOR79] Yourdan, E., *Structured Walkthroughs*, Yourdan, Inc., New York, 1979.
<CKL>

INDEX

"Never memorize something that you can look up."
Albert Einstein